Comparing Welfare Capitalism

The current globalisation debate has revived interest in the viability of welfare states in competitive market economies. *Comparing Welfare Capitalism* challenges the popular theory of a downward convergence. It argues that there are at least two varieties of capitalism: Anglo-American free market economies, and Rhenish (Germanic or Japanese) coordinated economies; each variation in production systems is embedded in a national welfare regime.

The chapters range from historical case studies to cross-national analyses. Adopting an institutional perspective, they explore the various aspects of the relationship between welfare states, industrial relations, financial governance and production systems. *Comparing Welfare Capitalism* builds upon and combines two recent approaches: comparative studies of the varieties of capitalism and of the worlds of welfare stage regimes. The contributions cluster around three topics: the role of employers and unions in social policy, the interdependencies between financial markets and pension systems, and the current welfare reform processes.

Written by specialists from comparative political economy and welfare regime analysis, this book sheds new light on the tenuous relationship between social policies and market economies. Welfare states do not always institute 'politics against markets', as commonly assumed: social policies can also serve a productive function. Social policy does play a role in shaping economic structures such as financial governance, labour markets, and bargaining practices. *Comparing Welfare Capitalism* makes a strong case for the idea that particular welfare state regimes and certain political economies reinforce each other through 'institutional complementarities'. It will be of great interest to those involved in comparative politics – European/Asian/American politics – welfare state and social policy, and political economy.

Bernhard Ebbinghaus is Senior Researcher at the Max Planck Institute for the Study of Societies in Cologne. He was JF Kennedy Fellow at the Centre for European Studies, Harvard University (1999–2000) and has co-authored a comparative handbook, *Trade Unions in Western Europe since 1945*.

Philip Manow is Assistant Professor in the department of Politics and Management, University of Konstanz. He has written two books on German health policy and published widely on social policy.

Routledge/EUI Studies in the Political Economy of Welfare

Edited by Martin Rhodes and Maurizio Ferrera

The European University Institute, Florence, Italy

This series presents leading edge research on the recasting of European welfare states. The series is interdisciplinary, featuring contributions from experts in economics, political science and social policy. The books provide a comparative analysis of topical issues, including

- reforms of the major social programmes – pensions, health, social security
- the changing political cleavages in welfare politics
- policy convergence and social policy innovation
- the impact of globalisation

1 Immigration and Welfare
Challenging the borders of the welfare state
Michael Bommes and Andrew Geddes

2 Renegotiating the Welfare State
Gerhard Lehmbruch and Frans van Waarden

3 Comparing Welfare Capitalism
Social policy and political economy in Europe, Japan and the USA
Edited by Bernhard Ebbinghaus and Philip Manow

4 Controlling a New Migration World
Edited by Virginie Guiraudon and Christian Joppke

Comparing Welfare Capitalism

Social policy and political economy in Europe, Japan and the USA

Edited by
Bernhard Ebbinghaus and Philip Manow

London and New York

First published 2001
by Routledge
2 Park Square, Milton Park, Abingdon, Oxon, OX14 4RN

Simultaneously published in the USA and Canada
by Routledge
270 Madison Ave, New York NY 10016

Routledge is an imprint of the Taylor & Francis Group

Transferred to Digital Printing 2005

Typeset in 10/12 BaskervilleMT by
Newgen Imaging Systems (P) Ltd.

British Library Cataloguing in Publication Data
A catalogue record for this book is available
from the British Library

Library of Congress Cataloging in Publication Data
Comparing welfare capitalism : social policy and political economy in Europe, Japan, and the USA /
edited by Bernhard Ebbinghaus and Philip Manow.
p. cm. – (Routledge/EUI studies in the political economy of welfare; 3)
Includes bibliographical references and index.
1. Social policy – Economic aspects – Congresses. 2. Welfare state – Economic aspects – Congresses. 3. Europe – Social policy – Economic aspects – Congresses. 4. Japan – Social policy – Economic aspects – Congresses. 5. United States – Social policy – 1993 – Economic aspects – Congresses. I. Ebbinghaus, Bernhard. II. Manow, Philip. III. Series.

HN17.5 .C64 2001
361.6′1 – dc21 2001019478

ISBN 0–415–25571–6

Contents

PART II
Industrial relations and welfare state regimes

PART III
Pension regimes and financial systems

PART IV
The political economy of welfare state reform

PART V
Conclusions

Figures

Tables

Contributors

Hugh Compston, Lecturer, School of European Studies, University of Wales, Cardiff, UK. E-mail: Compston@Cardiff.ac.uk.

Colin Crouch, Professor, Department of Political and Social Sciences, European University Institute, Florence, Italy. E-mail: colin.crouch@iue.it.

Bernhard Ebbinghaus, Senior Researcher, Max Planck Institute for the Study of Societies, Cologne, Germany. E-mail: ebbinghaus@mpi-fg-koeln.mpg.de.

Margarita Estevez-Abe, Assistant Professor, Department of Government, Harvard University, Cambridge, MA, USA. E-mail: mestevez@cfia.harvard.edu.

Anke Hassel, Senior Researcher, Max Planck Institute for the Study of Societies, Cologne, Germany. E-mail: hassel@mpi-fg-koeln.mpg.de.

Anton Hemerijck, Associate Professor, Department of Public Administration, Leiden University, The Netherlands. E-mail: hemerijck@fsw.leidenuniv.nl.

Gregory Jackson, Researcher at Max Planck Institute for the Study of Societies, Cologne, Germany. E-mail: jackson@mpi-fg-koeln.mpg.de.

Philip Manow, Assistant Professor, Department of Politics and Management, University of Constance, Germany. E-mail: philip.manow@uni-konstanz.de.

Isabela Mares, Assistant Professor, Department of Political Science, Stanford University, Stanford, CA, USA. E-mail: isabela@leland.stanford.edu.

Fritz W. Scharpf, Professor and Director, Max Planck Institute for the Study of Societies, Cologne, Germany. E-mail: scharpf@mpi-fg-koeln.mpg.de.

Michael Shalev, Senior Lecturer and Chair, Sociology and Anthropology, Hebrew University, Jerusalem, Israel. E-mail: shalev@vms.huji.ac.il.

Wolfgang Streeck, Professor and Director, Max Planck Institute for the Study of Societies, Cologne, Germany. E-mail: streeck@mpi-fg-koeln.mpg.de.

Sigurt Vitols, Researcher, Social Science Research Centre (WZB), Berlin, Germany. E-mail: vitols@medea.wz-berlin.de.

Anne Wren, Assistant Professor, Department of Political Science, Stanford University, Stanford, CA, USA. E-mail: awren@stanford.edu.

Series editors' preface

One of the main impulses behind the launch of this series on 'The Political Economy of Welfare' was the desire to promote interdisciplinary research, especially that which bridges traditions and specialisations. The first volume in the series – *Immigration and Welfare*, edited by Michael Bommes and Andrew Geddes – combined research on welfare states and immigration in a new and innovative study of transnational social citizenship. In *Comparing Welfare Capitalism*, Bernhard Ebbinghaus and Philip Manow bring their own considerable expertise and that of their distinguished co-authors to bear on another pioneering enterprise – probing the links between welfare states and national capitalisms. In so doing they explore the scope for mutual learning between two literatures (comparative political economy and cross-national welfare state research) and several disciplines (sociology, political science and economics). In line with the editors' ambitions to understand 'institutional complementarities', most of the contributors consider how production regimes, industrial relations and social protection interact, and with what effect. Several authors also consider the welfare-finance nexus in analysing the links between financial markets and pensions.

The result is a rich collection of studies which is also ambitious in its reach. All of the contributions are comparative and between them span the west European and Scandinavian countries, as well as the US and Japan. Thematically, the book ranges across some of the most critical issues facing the advanced welfare states, from de-industrialisation and the challenges of unemployment to the search for appropriate new policy mixes – in early retirement and working time policies, for instance – and the problematic future of pensions funding and social concertation. The conciliation of literatures and disciplines produces a fascinating thread of reflection on connections between production systems and welfare and on 'path dependence' in innovation and reform. How did particular combinations of welfare and production emerge? How can we understand their development over time? What is that holds systems together in the face of external shocks; and why do some adjust more effectively and equitably than others? Of course, answering these questions requires new theoretical insights. In yet another innovation – the inclusion of a chapter by a guest critic – Michael Shalev assesses the various contributors in light of their own theories and assumptions and the broader conceptual aims of the editors.

The achievements of the book are threefold. First, the reader interested simply in contemporary developments will come away enriched, for all of the chapters are at the cutting-edge of welfare state research. Second, by spanning a series of approaches and arenas, it makes an important contribution to the study 'political economy' as such. For as Wolfgang Streeck puts it, the time has come for a new 'synthesis', bringing together the traditions of post-war social science 'that have often touched but never became systematically integrated'. Certainly an edited volume cannot achieve finds a synthesis by itself. But this book's interdisciplinary perspective has added to our knowledge of how welfare states are underpinned by a complex architecture of institutions (in the realms of production, finance and labour) and how the public and private elements of these systems interact. Its third innovation lies in the questions it raises for future research. The editors of *Comparing Welfare Capitalism* have managed to sustain a dialogue with themselves and their authors over the structural approach to political economy that is both influence and adversary for many in this book. Spurred on by Colin Crouch and Michael Shalev, the editors call for deeper reflection on the politics of change and innovation in apparently path-dependent regimes. Their stress on the role of political agency in shaping, sustaining and transforming welfare states is particularly apposite. Policy makers in Europe know all about the forces of inertia, since they grapple with them each day as they strive for reform. By illustrating how actors can shape their social, political and economic environments over time, we can also illuminate the path to future of greater efficiency *and* equity in how welfare systems perform.

Maurizio Ferrera
University of Paria

Martin Rhodes
European University Institute, Florence

Preface

Comparing Welfare Capitalism pulls together traditions in post-war social science that have often touched but never became systematically integrated. The first and perhaps most important of such traditions is epitomised in the work of authors like Reinhard Bendix, Seymour Martin Lipset and Stein Rokkan. Their attempt in the 1960s to uncover the social forces that drove nation building and state formation in Western societies placed *comparative politics* on a new foundation. Investigating in particular the origin of democratic government in its interaction with classes, parties and organised interests, they had to account for the differences and similarities between Western post-war democracies by combining political theory, history and comparative empirical macro-sociology. The work that resulted attained a level of sophistication and a historical depth unmatched since Max Weber wrote about a very different world more than half a century and two world wars away.

The seminal works of the comparative political sociology of the 1960s were written against the backdrop of an influential literature in *political economy* organised around core notions of cross-national convergence. Here the leading expectation was for modern societies to become increasingly similar as a result of identical pressures to find rational solutions to a set of identical functional problems posed by industrialisation. Sooner or later, according to authors like Clark Kerr and W. W. Rostow, even the countries of the then Soviet bloc would have no choice but converge on a regime of 'pluralist industrialism' governed by technocratic experts in pursuit of a politically neutral functionalist best practice. Nowhere was this theme more present than in the study of *industrial relations,* where it had entered through the foundational work of the institutional economist, John Dunlop. To Dunlop and his school, comparative industrial relations was basically a grand narrative of the international progress of collective bargaining, i.e. the backbone institution of labour relations reform under the American New Deal, and of the cross-national adoption of institutional arrangements that had so convincingly demonstrated their capacity to transform disruptive class conflict into peaceful class collaboration in pursuit of economic efficiency.

That narrative lost much of its credibility in the worldwide wave of worker militancy in the late 1960s. To many, the events of those years fundamentally invalidated the prospect of an American-led de-politicisation of politics, and of a peaceful settlement of conflicts of interest by sophisticated techniques of 'planning-programming-budgeting'. Instead what seemed to drive politics, in democratic societies as elsewhere, were 'irrational' struggles about power and identity, including elusive intangibles like collective dignity that very much seemed to follow historically conditioned national paths and patterns. That simultaneously the Great American Peace that had reigned since the Korean War, and the social and political stability of the Eisenhower years dissolved in the swamps of Vietnam and in the ghettos of the American cities further discredited the dream of American convergence theorists in the 1950s and 1960s of a world forever pacified by economic growth, Keynesian demand management and the 'logic of industrialism'. A new generation of social scientists that came of age in the 1970s thus began to study industrial relations, no longer as a recipe for de-politicised expert administration of an outdated class conflict, but rather as a central arena of struggle for economic and political power – a struggle on whose uncertain outcome hinged fundamental societal choices between alternative possibilities of organising work and life in modern society.

On the margins the new comparative industrial relations sometimes did make contact with comparative politics. But as it tended to carry with it traditional Marxist assumptions on the overriding importance of the class conflict for politics and society, authors like Lipset who considered other 'cleavages' as equally important were often perceived as too far to the Right to be relevant. As a result, the fact that their approach squarely contradicted the functionalist convergence view was rarely appreciated. Where the two traditions came closest was where comparative politics focused on the study of interest groups, and especially where it did so guided by the concept of *corporatism*, or neo-corporatism. It was above all through this concept that comparative industrial relations became connected with a more encompassing perspective on the political system and on social structure. More generally, the attention paid by comparative politics to organised interests and their social and political status – to what Rokkan had called the 'second tier of government' – provided a possibility to study the diversity of national industrial relations systems in an analytic framework that enabled the discipline of industrial relations to liberate itself from its narrowly pragmatic or even technocratic heritage.

In the 1970s in particular studies of comparative industrial relations drew on the concept of corporatism for a broader view of trade unionism and the collective action of social classes than offered by traditional industrial relations, where unions were essentially no more than agents of collective bargaining. Crucial for this development was the American political scientist, Philippe C. Schmitter. Precisely because his work appreciated the specificity of European, less-than-pluralist patterns of interest politics, he was able to serve as a conduit between the developing European-*cum*-New Left approach to industrial relations and authors such as Lipset and Bendix and other members of the highly influential Joint Committee on Political Social Sociology of the International Sociological Association and the International Political Science Association. As a result, comparative industrial relations, first in Europe but increasingly also in the United States, began to develop the conceptual tools that enabled it to view its subject as an element of a society's political system rather than, like Dunlop, merely as a subsystem of the economy confined to rule making on the employment relationship. In subsequent years, the study of what now was essentially *the politics of industrial relations* moved into the very centre of internationally comparative social science. Indeed given the wide variety of national industrial relations arrangements, as well as the traditional focus of the discipline on a limited range of empirical objects that had to be inventorised structurally and functionally in great detail, comparative industrial relations soon became a hotbed for the development of comparative methodology in the social sciences in general.

An important reason why comparative industrial relations was able to acquire such a strategic position in the formation of an institutionalist approach to *comparative political economy* was that the set of institutions on which it specialises are intimately linked, not just to the political, but also to the economic system of modern society. Indeed the 1980s saw a growing interest among industrial relations scholars in how the governance of the employment relationship might be linked to the governance of the economy as a whole, and in particular whether differences in industrial relations were associated with differences, not just in the relationship between state and society, but also in national *patterns of production.* Here concepts like flexible specialisation or diversified quality production were introduced, in an attempt to explore what seemed to be elective affinities or complementarities between national industrial relations regimes on the one hand and the orientation, or 'style', of economic activity on the other. Most of the respective literature mainly pointed out a number of apparent functional relations without exploring their origins or trying much to theorise about them. Even outside the French *régulation* school, however, there was a widespread notion that economic structures and strategies were not necessarily and always prior to a society's institutional structures, including those of industrial relations, and that in certain circumstances at least, the latter might in fact be the independent variable. The exciting prospect this raised was that production patterns, usually believed to be imposed by the market or, alternatively, independently chosen by management, might one day be treated as endogenous by a new *institutional economics* capable of accounting for diverse national versions of modern capitalism as an economic system.

Apart from sporadic connections in the work of seminal figures such as Walter Korpi, the comparative study of the *welfare state*, prominently represented in the 1980s and 1990s especially by Gøsta Esping-Andersen, seems to have developed largely unrelated to the debates in industrial relations. Korpi and Esping-Andersen seem to have felt closer to the new comparative politics tradition, in its American version as well as, in particular, in the work of Stein Rokkan. But like the industrial relations comparativists of the 1970s, they were not only unsympathetic to the Western-democratic triumphalism especially in the work of Lipset, but they were also inclined to regard classes as more than just one category of social actors among others. Indeed their class-theoretical assumptions, clearly rooted in the historical experience and self-perception of Scandinavian Social Democracy at the time, seem for some time to have made them largely unreceptive to the work of the neo-corporatist school, which for their taste may have appeared a bit too institutionalist – in the sense of the 'Oxford School' of industrial relations or even the Dunlop tradition – and certainly not 'political', i.e. class-theoretical enough. This ended only when in the early 1980s John Goldthorpe, to the surprise of many, redefined corporatism as a socially benevolent alternative to what he saw, under the impression of the first years of the Thatcher government, as an emerging new pattern of societal dualism. In 1984, then, the 'corporatists' and the theorists of the democratic class struggle and its most important achievement, the welfare state, including Korpi, joined forces under the leadership of Goldthorpe to produce the now famous volume titled *Order and Conflict in Contemporary Capitalism: Studies in the Political Economy of West European Nations.*

Nevertheless, for some time to come, the study of the welfare state and of industrial relations remained largely separate concerns. While Esping-Andersen developed his influential typologies and began to relate different versions of the welfare state to different employment systems, researchers in the comparative industrial relations tradition explored in ever greater detail the institutional implications of different production modes, produced increasingly elaborate taxonomies, not just of systems of collective bargaining or interest representation, but also of mechanisms of economic coordination, or 'governance', and related employment to innovation systems at national and company level. An important milestone on the way to a more encompassing comparative political economy was Scharpf's work on economic policy making during the European employment crisis of the 1980s, in which he explored the interaction between corporatist wage bargaining and monetary policy and the status of national central banks. Also, taking off again from the comparative study of industrial relations, 'historical institutionalism' became conscious of itself as a method, or as an approach, leading to more rigorous thinking about the relationship between history and theory, the limits of causal theorising, the notion of strategic action constrained and facilitated by institutional conditions, the merits of case studies and statistics, the significance of context, contingency, interdependence and path dependency, etc. In the 1990s, maturation of the various traditions of comparative politics, industrial relations, political economy and welfare state theory, and with only sporadic cross-fertilisation, generated a broad range of studies on the relations between politics and the economy, and on institutional change in advanced capitalist societies.

The present book indicates that the time for synthesis may now have come. Today the comparative study of politics, industrial relations, national systems of production and welfare regimes seems to be ready to converge under the auspices of a new perspective, that of the *varieties of capitalism.* That perspective began to suggest itself to the social sciences – to the extent that they had preserved their traditional interest in the macro-foundations of social life – with the disappearance of state socialism after 1989 and the accelerated internationalisation of the capitalist political economy in the subsequent decade. As a result of the latter in particular, the historically grown national variants of a capitalist market economy that had first been described in the 1960s by Andrew Shonfield now more than ever face each other in a global marketplace, quite unlike the post-war 'golden years' in which protective national and international institutions provided them with a carefully safeguarded measure of relative autonomy. At the end of the twentieth century, some of the functional sectors of national systems were found to combine across national borders into integrated sectors of a stateless international economy; the national demarcation lines between sectors and countries were increasingly straddled by multinational firms; and national sectors as well as firms became subject to international regulation threatening to pull them out of the ambit of national politics and policy. As always, the Owl of Minerva prefers to fly at dusk, and social scientists are now inquiring with growing intensity into what constitutes, and may perhaps preserve, the unity of the national systems of political economy out of which the global political economy is being built – trying to determine what has kept them together and made them distinctive in the past, in order to assess whether and to what extent it may continue to do so in the future.

The contributions to this volume suggest that there may be basically two mechanisms by which national systems of capitalism are held together, *functional interdependence* and the resulting efficiency benefits of institutional coherence on the one hand, and *politics* and the distribution of power between groups with different interests on the other. While the book does document the time-honoured division between the theoretical and research traditions associated with one or the other of the two mechanisms as their preferred causal domain, it also suggests that here, too, the time for synthesis may have arrived. Clearly national institutions may be shaped across sectors by a historically evolved distribution of power resources and may, as a result of this, form a coherent whole. But once an institution exists, and as this book shows this certainly applies to the welfare state, it constitutes a power resource in its own right and in this capacity may affect the very distribution of power on which it was originally based. Moreover, institutional arrangements once established give rise to and shape the collective identity of social groups, exercising a formative impact on the interests such groups perceive to be theirs. Similarly, while social groups are driven in their collective political action by their specific interests and identities, respecting the functional constraints inherent in their institutional environment may be rational for them as the efficiency price for solutions that do not observe extant imperatives of system integration may be high. In this way – through continuous interaction and mutual conditioning of political power and institutional interdependence, of interests and institutions, and of effective politics and good policy – stable and more or less coherent national configurations of institutional structures and collective identities may form that, in the absence of external shocks, will tend to evolve along distinctive although not necessarily linear paths. As especially the exchange at the end of this book between the editors and Michael Shalev documents, the central challenge for a future political economy – one that draws on the notion of national systems of capitalism to understand the effects of international regime interdependence and competition – may be to endogenise power in institutional and policy analyses while simultaneously embedding considerations of efficient 'problem solution' in traditional political analyses of interest and identity.

The editors and most of the authors of this book have in recent years been associated, in one way or other, with the *Max Planck Institute for the Study of Societies* (MPIfG) in Cologne. Some have worked there for years, others have spent time there as visitors, and yet others have attended workshops and conferences. During this period the focus of research at the MPIfG has evolved in a direction that can hardly be better illustrated than by the present book. Like the latter, most of the current research projects at the MPIfG explore the historical evolution of actors and institutions under conditions of an increasingly integrated international economy, with particular emphasis on that core post-war institution of democratic capitalism, the national welfare state, and its fate under growing international interdependence and declining functional completeness of national systems. The evolution of the research agenda at the MPIfG corresponds to a worldwide trend in the social sciences to redirect attention to subjects located, and long hidden, in the intersection between sociology, political science and economics. Given the lasting significance of national political systems as building blocs of the emerging global political economy, it is not surprising that the present surge of institutionalist theory and research in political economy is growing out of the rich and mature comparativist traditions of post-war social science. Their joining together in an effort to develop a theory of capitalist diversity may lay the foundations for a historical-institutional theory of an international market economy and its embeddedness in evolving national and supranational institutional arrangements.

WOLFGANG STREECK
Max Planck Institute for the Study of Societies, Cologne

Acknowledgements

In an effort to bring together scholars from welfare state research, industrial relations and political economy, the editors organised a conference on 'Varieties of Welfare Capitalism' at the *Max Planck Institute for the Study of Societies* (Cologne) in June 1998. For this edited volume, we have chosen the more comparative analyses, covering the different varieties of welfare capitalism: Anglo-Saxon 'free' market economies (UK, USA) vs 'coordinated' market economies (continental Europe, Scandinavia, Japan). We would like to thank the contributors for their collaboration and patience in rewriting their papers. We are also grateful for the insights and comments from other participants at the conference: Jochen Clasen, Susan Giaimo, Karl Hinrichs, Steve Jefferys, Kees van Kersbergen, Stephan Lessenich, Jim Mosher, Paul Pierson, Bo Rothstein, Akira Takenaka, Steven Teles, Christa van Wijnbergen and Jelle Visser.

The Max Planck Institute for the Study of Societies provided not only the venue and financial support for the conference, but also assisted in the production of the manuscript. The editors would like to thank the directors of the Max Planck Institute, Fritz W. Scharpf and Wolfgang Streeck, for their encouragement for this conference and book project. Our special thanks go to Cynthia Lehmann for coordinating the language editing by Dona Geyer, Susanne Harrison and John Booth, to Annette Vogel for meticulous copy-editing, and to Thomas Pott for reworking the complicated graphs. As visiting researchers at the Minda de Gunzburg Center for European Studies at Harvard University in 1999/2000, the editors profited from the stimulating intellectual environment. The intriguing discussions with Paul Pierson and Peter Hall surely left their mark on the book project. We are glad to be able to publish this edited volume in the new *Routledge/EUI Studies in the Political Economy of the Welfare State*, edited by Maurizio Ferrera and Martin Rhodes. We hope this volume will encourage further inquiries across the borders of disciplinary divides.

BERNHARD EBBINGHAUS
PHILIP MANOW

Abbreviations

A	Austria
AUS	Australia
B	Belgium
CDN	Canada
CH	Switzerland
D	Germany
DK	Denmark
E	Spain
F	France
GR	Greece
I	Italy
IRL	Ireland
FIN	Finland
JAP	Japan
LUX	Luxembourg
N	Norway
NL	The Netherlands
NZ	New Zealand
P	Portugal
S	Sweden
UK	United Kingdom
USA	United States

1 Introduction

Studying varieties of welfare capitalism

Bernhard Ebbinghaus and Philip Manow

Despite claims to convergence, modern capitalism still comes in a limited variety. While the neo-liberal doctrine gained in currency in the 1980s and led to deregulatory reforms advanced by the United States and the United Kingdom, many economic observers were struck by the resilience of 'Rhenish' (coordinated) capitalism in Continental Europe and Japan (Albert 1993). The same holds true for the area of social policy: Welfare retrenchment has been propagated with some success in Anglo-American liberal welfare states, yet the more generous and expensive social security systems of Continental and Northern Europe have proven to be more entrenched (Pierson 1996). Although there are pressures towards convergence due to economic internationalisation and socioeconomic changes, cross-national diversity both in economic and social policy still dominates the political landscape (Berger and Dore 1996; Crouch and Streeck 1997; Kitschelt *et al.* 1999).

Over the last decade, two strands of research have underlined the importance of institutional variations for economic activities and social policy. In comparative political economy, the *Varieties of Capitalism* approach (Hall and Soskice, forthcoming) claims that coordinated market economies operate differently from 'free market' economies.[1] And cross-national welfare-state research, most prominently Esping-Andersen's *Three Worlds of Welfare Capitalism* (1990), has detected different welfare regimes with significant variations in redistribution and market compatibility.[2] Both approaches focus on the cross-national institutional variations in their respective policy field, but the links between particular forms of social protection and specific economic systems have yet to be adequately examined. This volume begins to bridge the two fields of research and ventures to unravel some of these linkages on both the analytical and the empirical level.

Let us consider investment into skills as an example that may exemplify how the production system and the system of social protection can be interlinked. Assuming rational behaviour, we would expect industrial workers to be willing to acquire particular skills only if such investment pays off in the long run. If the skills are not firm-specific and if they are sought after on the labour market, workers can expect to find employment with another firm at the current pay level if they lose their current job. However, in the case of firm-specific skills, skilled workers would either need credible employer commitments for long-term employment or even better external reassurances. Thus, strong employment protection through labour law and collective agreements may convince them that they will remain employed even in hard times, and that their wages will keep in line with pay trends in other firms. And if they are laid off, they would expect to be compensated fairly and long enough to seek a similar job or be adequately retrained (Estevez-Abe *et al.* 1999).

This example indicates that there are certain 'institutional complementarities' between different production regimes, industrial relations practices and social protection systems. Moreover, we would expect these to vary systematically across production systems and protection regimes. For instance, American workers with general skills receive premium market wages when there is high demand for their skills, but have no statutory employment protection; Japanese workers are willing to obtain firm-specific skills since they trust the commitment of large firms to guarantee 'lifelong' employment and occupational benefits; German skilled workers expect to be compensated during unemployment and retrained if they have been laid off. In a comparative empirical study, Huber and Stephens 'contend that within a given country, different aspects of the welfare state "fit" together and "fit" with different aspects of the production regimes, in particular their labour market components' (Huber and Stephens 1999: 3). Yet they warn that 'this "fit"... is not a one-to-one correspondence between a whole configuration of welfare state and production regimes' (Huber and Stephens 1999: 3).

Thus far, as Peter Hall observes, 'we do not have a clear understanding of how... different kinds of welfare states interact with different models of the economy' (Hall 1997: 196). This volume is an attempt to overcome the prevailing research gap in exploring the multiple interfaces between capitalist production and social protection. We believe that for a better understanding of modern welfare states, we need to consider social protection provided by social security systems, collective bargaining practices and employment regimes. Our knowledge of modern welfare states, and especially the sources of their current crises, remains limited until we reconsider the economic foundation on which they stand. Moreover, the productive function of social protection has often been overlooked due to the focus on redistribution as the main goal of welfare state policies. Hence, we also believe that for a better understanding of modern capitalism we ought to take into account the important impact of the welfare state on employment, skill acquisition, wage setting and investment. For instance, an analysis of the current problems of the German welfare state would be incomplete without considering its economic base, as would an assessment of Germany's economic crisis without considering the consequences of the current welfare state (see Hemerijck and Manow, Chapter 10 in this volume). The German social insurance system supports an export-oriented, high-quality production model, but the contributions to social insurance have become so high that employment growth in services is thwarted. This low employment level in turn endangers social policy financing and increases payroll taxes, thus leading to a vicious circle of 'welfare without work' (Esping-Andersen 1996a,b; Scharpf, Chapter 12). Thus there are mutual interdependencies between social security and the production system which affect both economic performance and the vulnerability of a given welfare state.

That the production system–welfare regime nexus has gained little attention thus far is particularly surprising, given the similarities of the analytical approach between Hall and Soskice's *Varieties of Capitalism* approach and Esping-Andersen's *Three Worlds of Welfare Capitalism*. In this introduction, we will describe the approaches taken by comparative political economy and welfare state research. Then, we will briefly describe the different areas of mutual impact and interdependency between production and protection and present the contributions to this volume. Finally, we will discuss the importance of comparative and historical analysis for studying the welfare–economy linkages.

Varieties of capitalism

Proponents of the Varieties of Capitalism approach in comparative political economy study the 'social systems of production' (Hollingsworth and Boyer 1997b) which are at the basis of national capitalist economies. This approach builds on the work of Andrew Shonfield (1965) on post-war economic policy and the subsequent neo-corporatist studies of organised capitalism in the 1970s (Goldthorpe 1984; Lehmbruch and Schmitter 1982; Schmitter and Lehmbruch 1981), yet it also imports insights from institutional economics (Williamson 1975). Challenging the thesis of convergence, several comparative readers have looked at the resilience and specificity of national capitalist models, contrasting the uncoordinated Anglo-American market economies with the German, Japanese or Scandinavian coordinated market economies (Berger and Dore 1996; Crouch and Streeck 1997; Hollingsworth *et al.* 1994; Hollingsworth and Boyer 1997a; Kitschelt *et al.* 1999). In addition, several comparative studies include particular policy fields, such as the link between vocational training and production systems (Crouch *et al.* 1999; Culpepper and Finegold 1999) or the role of central banks on wage formation (Iversen *et al.* 2000). In our view, the Varieties of Capitalism approach is marked by three features (see Hall and Soskice 1999): (1) it is a *systemic account* of the functioning of the institutional components of economic systems, (2) it distinguishes *national models* of production and maps their comparative advantages, and (3) it seeks a *micro-foundation* of how institutions shape actors' behaviour and reinforce existing institutional infrastructures.

Systemic accounts of contemporary capitalism

One major feature of the Varieties of Capitalism approach is the assumption that economic activity is socially embedded and that 'institutions matter' (Granovetter 1985). While the approach acknowledges the role of actors, it seeks a 'systemic' account of the institutional architecture of contemporary market economies, focusing on the 'total cake of "institutions of governance" of the various ingredient institutions' (Dore 1997: 24). Its proponents assume that institutions coalesce in the social system of production, 'this occurs – in part – because institutions are embedded in a culture in which their logic is symbolically grounded, organisationally structured, technically and materially constrained, politically defended, and historically shaped by specific rules and norms' (Hollingsworth and Boyer 1997b: 266). The institutional landscape is relatively inert: It provides constraints on the behaviour of economic agents and offers them specific opportunities, limits their strategic alternatives for individual and collective action, and encourages them to employ certain strategies rather than others.

In this view, particular institutions seem to hang together in a systemic way. Social practices as diverse as the Japanese lifelong employment and cross-shareholding between firms within the same *keiretsu* (inter-firm groups) seem to be interrelated (Dore 1997). These linkages represent – in game-theoretic parlance – 'strategic complementarities' (Cooper 1999; Milgrom and Roberts 1994; Soskice 1999), that is, mutually reinforcing and enabling institutional configurations. Thus 'two institutions can be said to be complementary if the presence (or efficiency) of one increases the returns (or efficiency) available from the other' (Hall and Soskice 1999: 10). Although this perspective has the danger of assuming too much coherence and intentionality (Stinchcombe 1968), it is a useful heuristic for identifying particular institutional equilibria as they coexist and co-evolve in time and place. Since we cannot assume that institutions arose in the past for reasons of their current complementary functionality, we also need to explain how complementary practices have co-evolved historically and have reproduced and reinforced each other by positive feedback (Pierson 2000).

Therefore the new comparative political economy literature attempts to trace chains of causation that run through different institutional subsystems and tries to reconstruct how strategic complementarities have emerged over long historical periods. By looking at the social system of production, this approach adopts an interdisciplinary perspective, taking insights from organisational theory, industrial sociology and industrial relations. Indeed scholars have shifted their focus. Having once concentrated on industrial governance in the narrow sense, they now study systems of corporatist bargaining and specific production systems, which enables them to analyse a broader 'ensemble of institutions' and more general governance structures in contemporary capitalism. *Prima facie*, most of these institutions seem to be only loosely coupled to the production system: legal traditions, standard setting, vocational training, financial systems, national 'systems of innovation' and monetary regimes. Much of the new comparative political economy literature shows how particular strategic complementarities between these institutional features and the economy can provide national systems with beneficial constraints (Streeck 1997) that could prove to be competitive advantages (Soskice 1991, 1999). That particular systems of social protection also shape the character of a 'national system of production' and thus have to be analysed in the same light as institutions mentioned above is the main claim motivating the different investigations into the welfare–economy nexus in this edited volume.

National models of capitalism

The current debate over economic globalisation and the competitiveness of national market economies has revitalised the 'convergence or diversity' controversy

(Boyer 1996; Kitschelt *et al.* 1999; Rhodes and van Apeldoorn 1997). Studies in comparative political economy have shown that considerable diversity in national responses still prevails despite similar global and secular pressures on advanced industrialised countries and despite the diffusion of 'best practices' (Boyer 1996; Crouch 1996; Kastendiek 1990). National economies embody different mixes of social institutions, regulation and governance modes. 'Since the nation-state has been the unit providing the legal regulation on which many forms of coordination depend and within which the institutions supporting coordination have developed, systematic differences in forms of coordination and firm behaviour tend to be found across nations' (Hall 1997: 298).

'Institutional isomorphism' (DiMaggio and Powell 1983), the copying of institutional features for the sake of legitimation, provides one of many social mechanisms by which nationally distinct modes of economic activity become widespread. In the same vein, Ronald Dore claims that the behaviour of individuals in 'unstructured or weakly structured situations is determined by the behavioural dispositions they have acquired in the context of well-established institutions, and the way they behave determines the form that emerging or changing institutions take' (Dore 1997: 28). Given vested interests to maintain current comparative advantages, the established institutional landscape is largely entrenched. Modern capitalism shows a variety of governance forms between market and hierarchy, ranging from less to highly 'liquid' markets, and from less to highly 'negotiated' hierarchies (Crouch and Streeck 1997). Moreover, markets and hierarchies are complemented by and supplemented with varying degrees of additional coordination and governance, such as formal associations and informal networks, and they are subject to varying degrees of state regulation (Streeck and Schmitter 1985a; Powell 1990). Thus, different state traditions also account for the nationally different modes of market making and 'market breaking' and, consequentially, for the differences in economic performance from country to country. This line of argument has led to a renaissance of earlier insights from industrial sociology, on the distinctiveness of 'the' British vs 'the' Japanese firm (Dore 1973), for example.

Today's comparative political economy is marked by juxtapositions of two polar models of economic activities: Fordist vs specialised production (Piore and Sabel 1984); Anglo-Saxon vs Rhenish capitalism (Albert 1993); deregulated vs institutionalised political economies (Crouch and Streeck 1997); coordinated vs uncoordinated market economies (Soskice 1999). These converse concepts represent not only ideal-typical models of economic governance, they also serve as analytical devices to describe the dominant *national* models of economic governance in comparative empirical studies.[3] These authors claim that it is possible to distinguish particular national models of capitalism that differ in their institutional setup across the main subsystems. If there are distinct national models competing in a world economy, and if these models remain distinct despite trade liberalisation and the internationalisation of markets, then we can infer that a particular institutional configuration represents a 'viable' mix of comparative advantages and disadvantages.

Case studies of national economies, most importantly of the United States and the United Kingdom in comparison with Germany and Japan, have been used

Table 1.1 Two varieties of capitalism: Uncoordinated vs coordinated market economies

	Uncoordinated market economy	*Coordinated market economy*
Prime examples	USA, UK	Germany, Japan
Financial and economic governance	Short-term financial markets equity financing (shareholder value); limited business coordination, antitrust laws	Long-term patient capital debt financing (stakeholder value); strong business associations, inter-company networks
Production system	Low-skill production; mass products; numeric flexibilisation	High-skill production; high-quality products; flexible specialisation
Management–labour relations	Decentralised bargaining; contentious workplace relations	Coordinated bargaining; statutory worker representation
Training and employment	General education; short tenure, high turnover and inter-firm mobility	Vocational training; long tenure, low turnover and intra-firm mobility

Sources: Hollingsworth and Boyer (1997b); Soskice (1991, 1999); cf. Ebbinghaus (1999).

to show the contrast between coordinated and uncoordinated market economies (Soskice 1991, 1999; see Table 1.1). Empirically, some political economies seem to be hybrid cases that are situated between or even depart from the two conceptual poles of coordinated vs uncoordinated market economies. A national economy may be considered as a mixed case if there are subsystems, regions or economic sectors that divert from the dominant mode. For instance, the 'Third Italy' with its dense regional network and flexible specialisation diverts from the economy in northern and southern Italy. Moreover, economies with traditions of state intervention, like France (Schmidt 1996), cannot be easily accommodated within the coordinated–uncoordinated framework, as the editors of *Varieties of Capitalism* acknowledge (Hall and Soskice 1999). To juxtapose coordinated and uncoordinated market economies is not to deny that we find substantial variations between Continental European, Scandinavian and Asian coordinated economies, and it is certainly possible to discern subtle differences among Anglo-Saxon market economies.

Micro-logic

In contrast to earlier comparative studies of the macro-configurations conducive to economic growth and stability (e.g. Goldthorpe 1984), recent comparative case studies explain the micro-logic behind the variations in macroeconomic performance more systematically (see Hall 1997). As transaction-cost theory became an important part of modern economic analysis (Williamson 1981), economists became more receptive to the role of information, trust, institutions and histories of cooperation. As a consequence of the 'economic turn' in political science (Levi 2000), the comparative political economy literature now explains macroeconomic outcomes as being the result of individual choices by economic agents. This actor-centred institutional analysis (Mayntz and Scharpf 1995; Scharpf 1997) often uses game theory to explain equilibria under particular institutional configurations and actor constellations.

The Varieties of Capitalism approach is actor-centred in that it is 'firm-centred', putting 'special emphasis on companies as the fundamental unit in a capitalist economy adjusting to economic shocks' (Hall and Soskice 1999: 4). The relations between economic actors are crucial for their strategic capacity: does the institutional configuration and the actor constellation provide opportunities for coordination? A good example for this kind of analytical inquiry is the collective action problem involved in an employer's decision to provide the common good of non-firm-specific vocational training. This problem has attracted the attention of many political economists (Crouch *et al.* 1999; Culpepper and Finegold 1999). Recent studies on the role of employers in social policy development have also focused on the micro-level to explain national policy outcomes (Mares 1998; Martin 2000; Martin and Swank 1999; Swenson 1997). Depending on the firm structures, employer preferences vary as to the trade-off between social risk distribution and control over employees (Mares 1998). While employers' pre-strategic preference may be to fight against *any* social spending programme, there are instances when they are in favour of compulsory social insurance. Whether cross-class coalitions will form between employers and workers in order to take social risks out of competition depends on the associational capacities and the production regimes that are in place (Swenson 1997, 1999, 2000).

Worlds of welfare regimes

Esping-Andersen's *Three Worlds of Welfare Capitalism* (1990) has made a major impact on comparative welfare state analysis over the last decade. Adopting a political economy approach, his analysis has some striking similarities with the new Varieties of Capitalism approach. First of all, analysing social security systems in a wider, systemic perspective comes relatively close to the focus on national systems of production used by comparative political economists. Second, Esping-Andersen's regime analysis stresses cross-national differences across welfare states, which cluster, in fact, around at least three (if not more) 'worlds of welfare capitalism'. Here there are interesting parallels to the political economy perspective that claims that national models of production differ systematically.[4] Finally, following the political economy view, Esping-Andersen and others have started to explore the welfare–economy nexus, especially the linkages between welfare state policies and labour markets. Let us examine these three aspects of welfare regime analysis, see which parallels they have with *Varieties of Capitalism*, and look at how bridges between the two approaches can be built.

Welfare regime analysis

The concept of 'regimes' indicates that welfare states are not merely a heterogeneous ensemble of disjoint social programmes, but that they are interrelated. 'To talk of "a regime" is to denote the fact that in the relation between state and economy a complex of legal and organisational features are systematically interwoven' (Esping-Andersen 1990: 2). Much like the Varieties of Capitalism approach, such an analysis assumes and stresses the systemness which reflects distinct 'principles' of welfare provision: 'Welfare regimes bunch particular values together with particular programmes and policies' (Goodin *et al.* 1999: 5). The comparative welfare regime approach seeks to elicit the regime differences by using ideal-typical models, which, like typologies, have 'an obvious attraction in being able to characterise whole systems with the related implication that different systemic features "hang together"' (Lange and Meadwell 1991: 84). Analysing welfare regimes is, therefore, a persuasive heuristic in comparing welfare states.

Going beyond the quantitative approaches that measured welfare state expansion only by social expenditures, Esping-Andersen evaluates the different welfare regimes using three multifaceted dimensions: (1) the degree of de-commodification (the extension of social rights independent of market mechanisms); (2) the system of stratification (i.e. inequality in outcome); and (3) the state–market–family mix (i.e. the form and locus of social protection) (Esping-Andersen 1990: 21–3; see Kohl 1993: 69–70). Following T. H. Marshall (1950), Esping-Andersen stresses the redistributive function of social policy: do universal citizenship rights provide protection to every citizen? Drawing on Polanyi's view of a social movement for social protection against the vagaries of free markets (Polanyi 1944), Esping-Andersen's approach measures the welfare states by their degree of 'de-commodification' (Esping-Andersen 1990). To what extent are benefits and services provided without any consideration of market forces, and to what degree do citizens have social entitlements that make them independent from market forces? In addition, his consideration of stratification highlights important differences in solidarity or social risk pooling (de Swaan 1988). For example, if occupational groups are covered by separate insurance schemes, this reinforces status differences and intra-class cleavages (Baldwin 1990). Finally, an important dimension of welfare regime variations is the location of social provisions: is the state, the market, voluntary associations or the family the main provider of social support by transfers and services? In fact, welfare regime analysis does not presume that the welfare state is the main provider. Instead, it studies the public–private mix as the major differentiation across welfare societies (Kolberg 1992; Rein and Rainwater 1986).

Esping-Andersen's distinction between different ideal-typical welfare regimes focused on differences along the dimensions of de-commodification, social stratification and public–private mix (see Table 1.2). Esping-Andersen's 'worlds' of welfare capitalism build on Richard Titmuss' (Titmuss 1958, 1974) earlier distinction between three different welfare models: the residual model, the industrial-achievement or merit-oriented model, and the institutional welfare state model.

Table 1.2 Esping-Andersen's three worlds of welfare capitalism

Regimes	*'Liberal'*	*'Conservative'*	*'Social-democratic'*
Prime examples:	USA, UK	Germany	Sweden
De-commodification	Low	Medium	High
Social rights	Need based	Employment-related	Universal
Welfare provision	Mixed services	Transfer payments	Public services
Benefits	Flat benefits	Contribution-related	Redistributive

Sources: Esping-Andersen (1990); cf. Kohl (1993).

The residual welfare model limits the role of the state in intervening into the market to providing basic benefits and services to the needy. The industrial-achievement model applies the social insurance principle most extensively, making benefits dependent on employment and contributions. In the institutionalised model, the welfare state intervenes most vigorously into market allocation by implementing redistributive social policies, guaranteeing universal rights and providing public services to all citizens. While Titmuss only sketched these different models as possible organising principles of some social programmes, Esping-Andersen uses the three models to describe national welfare regimes and cross-national variations.

Real worlds of welfare

Esping-Andersen's three worlds of welfare capitalism do not only reflect different principles of social protection, they are also the outcome of unique legacies of state-building and specific socio-political forces (and ideologies) that have put their stamp on welfare states (Esping-Andersen 1990; see also earlier Flora 1986; Rokkan 1999). According to Esping-Andersen, the main differences reflect three political traditions: liberal conceptions of a residual welfare state that should not intervene into 'free' markets by limiting work incentives and individual choice; paternalist Conservative state traditions and Christian-democratic conceptions of 'subsidiarity' (van Kersbergen 1995); and, finally, social-democratic conceptions of a universalist and redistributive welfare state. The *Liberal* welfare state provides relatively low flat benefits to all citizens in order not to interfere with individual self-help and market incomes, its level of de-commodification is low. *Conservative* welfare states have a medium level of de-commodification. They provide various occupational or social groups with extensive social transfer payments which are largely based on employment and contributions. Finally, *social-democratic* labour movements (in alliance with other social groups, especially farmers) expanded the universalist de-commodifying Scandinavian welfare states to provide universal social benefits and extend public services to all citizens.

Although these ideal-typical models are partly abstractions from the historical traits of the Scandinavian, Germanic and Anglo-American welfare-state development, we should not reify them. They are primarily pragmatic conceptual devices for comparison (Kohl 1993: 75). While empirical accounts of cross-national variations in different social policy fields are often confusing, such a regime analysis provides a prism through which to shed light on salient aspects of welfare states and their interaction. Certainly, Esping-Andersen largely conceives the historical trajectories as the result of different distributions of power resources, thereby overemphasising the role of ideology and deliberate political strategy (Kohl 1993; Offe 1993). While some researchers have criticised the conflation of ideal and real type in Esping-Andersen's regime analysis (Rieger 1998), others refute the path-dependency argument, claiming that many welfare states have restructured and thus are not fixed in one particular regime (Borchert 1998; see also Crouch, Chapter 5). Only comparative historical analysis can show how particular regimes have emerged and whether they have changed over time. Yet, despite this criticism, it remains true that Esping-Andersen's analytical framework has proven extremely helpful for the comparative study of welfare states.

More recently, some comparative studies have challenged the limitation to three worlds of welfare capitalism, making strong cases for additional 'families of nations' (Castles and Mitchell 1993). As Castles (1995) and Ferrera (1996) point out, the southern European welfare states should not be subsumed under the heading of 'the' conservative regime, given the importance of family, clientelism and dualist labour markets. Some observers have claimed that the 'radical' antipodal welfare states of Australia and New Zealand (Castles and Mitchell 1993) are distinct from the Anglo-American liberal welfare-state regimes: since inequality is reduced by high wages, industrial relations play an important role in welfare outcomes. Finally, the classification of the Japanese case poses some problems: is it a unique case of Confucian welfare ideology or a hybrid mix of liberalism and conservative welfare regime ingredients (Esping-Andersen 1997; Goodman and Peng 1996; Gould 1993; Jacobs 1998; Leibfried 1994)? Interestingly, all these 'outliers' do not conform to narrowly conceived welfare-state boundaries, suggesting that there are important interactions between social policies and the political economy (or family structure).[5] Indeed, there might be functional equivalents between social protection with the help of welfare policies and other means that reallocate and redistribute resources with a welfare-enhancing goal. In the case of Italy, the impact of a shadow economy and family solidarity provides non-state support; in Australia, it is the successful bargaining for high wages and the juridical arbitration of labour conflicts; in Japan, the peculiar long-term company employment policies – just to give a few examples.

The political economy nexus

Esping-Andersen conceives welfare states as being 'fundamental forces in the organisation and stratification of modern economies' (Esping-Andersen 1990: 159). He views the welfare state as the 'principal institution in the construction of different models of post-war capitalism (Esping-Andersen 1990: 5)'. Yet, exactly how the welfare state covaries with other features of modern capitalism remains largely unexplained and underinvestigated. In his own research, Esping-Andersen focused on the labour market as part of the welfare state–economy nexus

(Kolberg and Esping-Andersen 1991; Esping-Andersen 1993, 1996a). Indeed, welfare states shape employment regimes, they have an impact on overall employment rates, the gender gap in participation rates, the average length of unemployment, the proportion of skilled to unskilled work, and the possible pathways into and out of work. These linkages are regime-specific. For instance, Continental 'welfare-without-work' societies responded to increasing unemployment with labour shedding strategies that fostered early retirement (Esping-Andersen 1996b; see Ebbinghaus, Chapter 4, and Hemerijck and Manow, Chapter 10). While Esping-Andersen has provided ample evidence that particular welfare-state regimes and employment regimes 'tend to coincide' (Esping-Andersen 1990: 159), the relationship and mutual influence between the spheres of capitalist production and social protection reach beyond the labour market and may be more fundamental than 'coincidental'.[6]

Despite claims of convergence due to globalisation, comparative studies still find an 'elective affinity between the types of production regime, patterns of socio-economic inequality and protection through welfare states, and the constitution of corporate political actors in parties and interest groups' (Kitschelt *et al.* 1999: 3). Nevertheless, the welfare–economy nexus is still almost completely absent from the analysis of the institutional features which influence economic performance and the organisation of production and exchange. The state of the debate is marked either by programmatic statements that call for a more thorough analysis of the work–welfare interplay (Hollingsworth and Boyer 1997a: 447–9; Hall 1997: 196) or by studies that identify patterns of systematic correlation between the spheres of production and social protection with the help of macroeconomic indicators (Huber and Stephens 1999). This lack of attention for the specific links between both spheres has been partly due to the fact that the function of the welfare state is often only seen as constraining the market (Hollingsworth and Boyer 1997a: 447–9). The welfare state is merely conceived as an 'institutionalised counter-principle of capitalism' (Lepsius) and social policy is predominantly perceived as 'politics against markets' (Esping-Andersen). Thus the importance of the welfare state for a nation's social system of production has been underestimated in the past.

While Esping-Andersen's work has begun a fruitful debate about the many interfaces between advanced welfare states and the organisation of contemporary capitalism, many additional linkages between both spheres – besides the labour–market nexus – remain to be explored. A comparison between welfare regimes and production systems reveals some elective affinities (Huber and Stephens 1999): Uncoordinated market economies go hand in hand with 'liberal' welfare states and low social expenditure (which is also true for the antipodes). Yet among coordinated market economies, we do find much more variation (Ebbinghaus 1999): Germanic social market economies and 'Christian-democratic' Continental welfare states go together as do Nordic neo-corporatist economies with 'social-democratic' universalist welfare regimes, and Latin state-led market economies and late-coming welfare states. Finally, Japan's coordinated market economy has a hybrid welfare regime that combines residual public and extensive private welfare arrangements. The obvious greater differentiation in welfare regimes may lead to a new reconsideration of the intra-regime variations among 'coordinated' market economies and to further study of the 'functional alternatives' and possible disfunctionality of different welfare regimes in coordinated market economies.

While there are unexplored institutional complementarities or elective affinities between the welfare state and the production regime, there is also a trade-off between equality and efficiency (Okun 1975; Esping-Andersen 1993). In the comparative political economy perspective, however, this trade-off is rather specific to a particular regime, and not a universal problem of all welfare states: a particular welfare-state regime can undermine the 'comparative institutional advantages' (see Hall 1997) of a given production regime, or the economic development can overstrain the buffering capacity of a given welfare-state regime. Some observers consider the impact of globalisation on welfare states to be far less important than endogenous challenges such as demographic shifts (Pierson 1998). Changes in the production systems due to the globalisation of financial markets and international economic competition may have dire consequences for welfare states, if there is indeed a complementarity between both realms. Related questions arise: Which kinds of political coalitions may emerge and develop vested interests in a given production and welfare-state regime (Manow 2000)? And what will happen in the future if one or both spheres come under pressure to change – will this undermine the remaining institutional 'complementarity'?

Studying welfare state–economy linkages

Following Esping-Andersen, we use the concept of 'regime' to denote the fact that 'a complex of legal and organisational features are systematically interwoven' (1990: 2). A neat separation of welfare-state regimes from other aspects of a national political economy, such as industrial relations, production systems, employment regimes and financial governance, is often difficult – the boundaries between these institutional complexes are often blurred both conceptually and empirically. Nevertheless, we need to delineate non-overlapping typologies in order to avoid a tautology when speaking of institutional complementarities between components of two conceptually differentiated spheres. Therefore we subsume the core programmes of social protection under the conception of the welfare regime: social insurance, social assistance, labour market policies and social services. Yet there are also social policies – 'private', occupational welfare benefits (Shalev 1996), for example, that are borderline cases between publicly mandated social policies and company-related benefits derived from a company's human resource policy. While we need to separate the different spheres conceptually, it is the possible linkages and interdependencies between these institutional complexes that are the main focus of this volume.

This book revolves around possible linkages between social protection and three areas of the political economy that are often specialised fields of research, though the 'Varieties of Capitalism' approach attempts to integrate all three in the analysis of capitalist systems. The first area is the system of industrial relations, comprising corporate actors, such as the state, labour and employers, and the laws and rules governing the conditions of employment relations, most importantly via collective bargaining. The second area entails the production system and employment regime, which involves the social organisation of the production process and the employment strategies of firms. Finally, the financial and corporate finance system is the third area, which defines the specificity of a capitalist system: the way financial markets are organised, companies are controlled and investments are financed. Let us briefly discuss some of the linkages between welfare states and these areas of the political economy and introduce examples from the following chapters.

Industrial relations

The 'social partners' – organised labour and capital – have not only played an important role in the expansion of modern welfare states, but they have also influenced the current reform processes (Esping-Andersen 1992; Pierson 1995; Swenson 1991, 1999). In addition, collective bargaining between employers and unions can have an important impact on welfare outcomes. But the reverse is also true: social policy can affect labour relations. Thus wage bargaining is conducted in the shadow of social wages and the non-wage labour costs set by social policy legislation (Hassel and Ebbinghaus 2000). Collectively negotiated wages, which affect the demand for labour and thus employment levels, are a major variable for employment-based and payroll-financed welfare states.

The policy stance of unions and employer associations was often assumed to be fixed: unions would promote universal welfare states, and employers would oppose each and every step leading to an expansion of social rights. Yet the preferences of unions and employers seem to vary with the social composition of their membership and the strategic interaction between collective actors. In Chapter 3 *Isabela Mares* uses a historical and game-theoretic analysis to reconstruct the strategic bargaining between unions, employers and the state over unemployment insurance in the interwar years in France and Germany. Although employers may be generally opposed to social insurance, the actual position of capital was a strategic response to the range of political options on the social policy agenda. *Mares* shows that compulsory unemployment insurance emerged in Germany thanks to a cross-class alliance with unions, while French employers remained opposed to anything but local unemployment assistance outside the control of unions.

Comparative studies have shown major cross-national differences in industrial relations from decentralised to centralised, voluntarist to corporatist and sectionalist to encompassing interest intermediation (Crouch 1993; Visser 1990). For countries with similar welfare regimes and social partnership models, we would expect common problems of economic coordination and adaptation. Several authors in this volume investigate the interplay between both realms and its impact on labour market performance. *Hugh Compston* (Chapter 6) compares the different degrees of state intervention in favour of working time reductions in Europe, discussing factors such as union density and union participation in economic policy making. *Anke Hassel* (Chapter 7) studies the impact of fragmented or encompassing associations and particularistic or solidaristic wage policies on the growth potential for low-wage–low-productivity sectors in Britain and Germany. *Bernhard Ebbinghaus* (Chapter 4) discusses the different forms of collusion between employers and organised labour in using early retirement as a labour shedding strategy in Europe, Japan and the USA. Whether organised labour and capital use labour shedding to ease the costs of economic adjustment while maintaining industrial peace depends not only on the available pathways to public pre-retirement programmes but also on the exigencies of national labour relations and production systems at the workplace.

These findings suggest intricate interdependencies between labour relations and labour market outcomes. In the German case, for instance, the system of collective bargaining is firmly entrenched and the social partners are powerful. The state, on the other hand, has limited capacity to intervene in industrial relations. Since strong unions and legal employment protection prevent German firms from being able to reduce wages or downsize their workforce, they can only achieve 'flexibility' by using such labour supply strategies as working time reduction or early retirement. But the causal link can also be reversed. Building on an argument developed by Peter Swenson, *Philip Manow* shows in Chapter 2 that employers in Germany and Japan were in favour of expanding welfare-state programmes. These policies promised to stabilise the sector-wide collective bargaining system and relieve it from the pressures stemming from the wage compression and wage stickiness resulting from coordinated wage bargaining.

Unions and employer organisations can derive organisational strength and influence outside the realm of collective bargaining if they have an institutionalised role in the self-administration of social insurance, as *Colin Crouch* argues in Chapter 5. However, he shows that there is no simple and fixed correspondence between particular types of industrial relations (contestative, pluralist or neo-corporatist) and specific welfare regimes. He warns about the dangers of overstraining path-dependency arguments and the analytical rigidities inherent in an approach that labels countries as having only one regime type. Analysis must allow for hybrid or 'mongrel' cases and for change over time. *Crouch* advocates an 'institutional probabilism' (Hirschman), stating that certain trajectories of change or continuity are more likely than others. The devolution of the British corporatism of the early 1970s into the market liberalism of the 1980s and 1990s is a case in point. Interpreting regimes as the 'diversified inheritance of action possibilities', *Crouch* emphasises that the development of an institutional setting can never be entirely explained by its legacy alone.

Production and employment regimes

Social policies are often seen as 'politics against markets', as the promotion of equity over efficiency (Esping-Andersen 1993). They are thought to have a de-commodifying, non-market related impact on the labour market and the labour contract. However, social policies also affect labour costs and alter work incentives. High labour costs due to social protection could represent a 'beneficial constraint' (Streeck 1997) for employers, forcing them to pursue a production strategy that emphasises high quality and flexible specialisation. But there are also negative effects, as *Anke Hassel*, *Anne Wren* and *Fritz Scharpf* demonstrate in their chapters. High non-wage labour costs hamper employment growth in the low-productivity service sector. While the encompassing Scandinavian welfare states provide many of the (social) services in the public sector and finance them largely through taxes, the Continental European welfare states with their strong emphasis on social contributions perform poorly when it comes to job growth in private and public services. How countries react to the structural change from an industrial economy to a service economy thus depends on the institutional architecture of their welfare states and their industrial relations systems. In contrast to the 1950s and 1960s, advanced capitalist societies face a trilemma. They can only achieve two of three macroeconomic goals – income equality, full employment and balanced budgets (see *Anne Wren*, Chapter 11). As *Fritz Scharpf* demonstrates in Chapter 12, the societal choices OECD countries made differed widely. Not fully determined by the given institutions in a country, these choices have ultimately been political ones, as *Anne Wren* argues in Chapter 11. Taking the three different ideological traditions, Social Democracy, neo-liberalism and Christian Democracy, *Anne Wren* describes the different distributive choices in France, the UK and the Netherlands, respectively.

Instead of contrasting the employment consequences of different welfare regimes, *Anton Hemerijck* and *Philip Manow* compare in Chapter 10 the responses of the more similar Dutch and German welfare state to the 'welfare-without-work' (Esping-Andersen 1992) dilemma. The successful labour market reforms in the Netherlands and the reform stalemate in Germany suggest that it is less the similar problem configuration than the nation-specific institutional and political capacities which explain the divergent reform trajectories. Small *intra*-regime differences between otherwise very similar industrial relations or social protection systems can lead to entirely different outcomes, thus calling for a much more fine-grained institutional analysis than *inter*-regime comparisons writ-large commonly imply.

Finally, one of the major burdens of today's welfare states is posed by structural unemployment which has increased the cost push on employment-related social spending and reduced the general tax and social wage base. On the other hand, welfare states may also serve an important function in stabilising, maintaining and enhancing production regimes by providing an educated and healthy labour force which is shielded from social risks. For example, we would expect a high degree of covariation between the transportability of welfare entitlements and of worker's skills, both of which play a large role in labour mobility. The more occupational benefits firms offer, the more likely workers will be to invest in firm-specific skills. Coordinated vs uncoordinated economies may differ from each other in the degree to which the welfare state provides economic actors opportunities for long-term engagements. As *Anke Hassel* points out in Chapter 7, only the interaction between the state, organised capital and labour can account for labour market outcomes. The effectiveness of a liberal or a Continental regime with respect to employment growth in the low-productivity sector also has important repercussions on welfare financing. If employers are free to hire and fire, this has profound impact on the willingness of workers to acquire firm-specific skills. A low-trust, low-productivity, low-skills, low-wage equilibrium is self-enforcing, while the opposite equilibrium can arise if organised labour and capital can use the welfare state to alleviate the costs of economic coordination. Moreover, the participation in social administration and institutionalised workplace participation make the long-term gains from cooperation superior to the short-term payoff from 'defection'. Therefore, the welfare state can provide external resources that support an infrastructure of cooperation between unions and business in general, and between workers and managers at the workplace level. The different industrial relations and welfare regime configurations affect not only the peaceful or confrontational nature of labour conflicts, but the feasibility of more skill intensive or more Fordist production systems as well, as *Bernhard Ebbinghaus* shows in Chapter 4.

Occupational welfare, financial systems and corporate governance

Several contributions to this volume focus on the public–private welfare mix, in particular the role of private occupational pensions. Although companies may provide occupational pensions merely for reasons of their human resource strategy (binding skilled workers to their company), these private pensions are part of a welfare state's social provision since they are at least partly regulated by the state and they interact with public pensions (see *Bernhard Ebbinghaus*, Chapter 4). Moreover, the public regulation of private pensions as financial instruments and the way they are taxed proves to be crucial (see *Margarita Estevez-Abe*, Chapter 9, and *Gregory Jackson* and *Sigurt Vitols*, Chapter 8). If we are to examine occupational welfare benefits, it is important to include Japan and the USA in our investigation, two prime cases of very different 'capitalisms' and welfare regimes. Their inclusion not only corrects for the Euro-centric bias of many comparative welfare-state studies, their peculiar private–public mixes show important commonalties and differences that are revealing for the intricate interaction between welfare regimes and production systems. Many scholars label the American and Japanese welfare states as liberal or residual, following Esping-Andersen (1990, 1997), but this squares oddly with the stark differences between the United States' 'free' market economy and Japan's coordinated market economy. Whereas in the American case, as *Ebbinghaus* shows, these occupational pensions remained part of a Fordist production and employment policy of 'hiring and firing', the Japanese companies provide occupational pensions and reemployment practices as a means to build long-term employment relationships. These differences in production and employment regimes are also linked to different forms of corporate governance: Japanese companies use their institutionalised links to firms within their group to find reemployment for their retired workers, while American hostile takeovers may lead to a 'raid' of pension funds, ending the previous employer commitment.

Moreover, *Estevez-Abe* and *Jackson and Vitols* map different types of interaction between occupational pensions and financial markets: Japanese pension funds and German book reserves reinforce 'patient' capital, whereas American and British pension funds amplified short-term financial market pressures. *Gregory Jackson* and *Sigurt Vitols* (Chapter 8) compare the two varieties of capitalism with two forms of pension systems: market-based pension regimes in Britain and the United States, and solidaristic pension regimes in Germany and Japan. Their research suggests that different pension systems do indeed have a differential impact on financial systems and corporate governance, reinforcing free market and coordinated capitalism, respectively. *Margarita Estevez-Abe* (Chapter 9) complements a comparative with a historical analysis of Japanese pension funds in order to uncover the forgotten link: the welfare–finance nexus. The design of Japanese pension funds and their state regulation helped to consolidate the bank-dominated financing system and stable stockholding systems upon which Japan's coordinated capitalism is based.

Analysing linkages through comparative-historical analysis

Although the contributions to this volume set out to identify the possible linkages between welfare regimes and political economies, they do not claim that there is a unidirectional or deterministic relationship. The linkages of the welfare state–political economy nexus are often rather indirect and conditional, depending on the type of regime in place. Therefore, a historical and comparative institutionalist analysis is needed to unravel the possible linkages. One of the principal aims of this book is thus to map several 'covariations' between the varieties of capitalism and the different worlds of welfare capitalism. Two methodologies may help us to explore the 'elective affinities' of production systems and welfare regimes. One approach applies 'process tracing' (Katzenstein) of the 'historically rooted trajectories of growth' (Zysman 1994). Yet unless path dependency is omnipresent, history may be less of a guide in judging the functional complementarities of today's structure and the challenges to its continuity. The other approach applies comparative analysis, which can help to reveal current institutional complementarities. In a comparative analysis, which tends to be more static, the coexistence and mutual support of 'equilibrium institutions' (see Shepsle 1986) can be delineated. However, without a historical analysis, there is the danger of the retrospective fallacy that sees today's institutional complementarity as the rational calculation of actors, disregarding that it might be merely the outcome of unintended consequences and unforeseen contingencies.

In order to understand the linkage of the welfare state and political economy, historical institutionalists have studied their origins and co-evolution over time. What are the origins and formation of welfare states and how did this legacy affect the development of labour relations, production and employment regimes, or the financial systems? While some have turned to history as a 'method' to check the validity of general theories (see Ragin 1987), most historical institutionalists are turning to history as a 'theory' (Immergut 1998: 19): 'They emphasise the irregularities rather than the regularities of history and demonstrate the limits of universal causal models'. The contingencies of history play an important role – the welfare state and its industrial economy were shaped under particular historical conditions, circumstances and coincidences. Thus the sequencing in the evolution of particular institutions has a long-term impact. For instance, the late formation of compulsory social insurance had an impact on the chances of voluntary insurance schemes or employers' occupational schemes of becoming entrenched. Path-dependent processes have been described by historical institutionalists. They point at the institutional inertia of processes that are often inefficient, unintended and accidental (Pierson 1997). There is hardly an 'efficiency of history'. Politics cannot easily change historically derived institutions, as functionalist or rational choice theorists imply (March and Olsen 1984). Instead, institutional change is a complex and a contingent process, and often an undetermined one.

Cross-national comparison, while often also historical in its approach, adds another methodology for unravelling the linkage between institutional arrangements. Instead of studying the institutionalisation processes over time, the comparative method makes it possible to analyse the coexistence of institutions in a snapshot manner (Ragin 1987). What kind of welfare state coincides with what kind of labour relations, production system, employment regimes or financial systems? Cross-national analysis drawing on typologies and statistical methods has been used to detect the overlap between particular welfare-state regimes and specific aspects of their political economy. Correlation statistics may not be very informative since they assume a functionalist logic and universal causality. Comparative institutionalists, on the other hand, argue quite convincingly that there are 'contextual logics of causality' (Immergut 1998). Hence, if there are linkages between the welfare state and political economy, we would expect them to take on particular forms in both realms. As Weber pointed out, there are 'elective affinities' between the two institutional complexes more or less 'tightly' coupled. When they are tightly coupled, we would expect changes over time in one realm to cause changes in the other realm, while this would be more open in the case of loosely coupled systems. However, we often face a small-*n* problem. We have more explanatory variables than cases, and more complex interaction effects than we can model in statistical analysis. If we want to go further than macro-configuration analysis, we may not only need historical accounts, but also assessment of the level of micro-processes.

Comparing Welfare Capitalism combines a plurality of approaches: Some authors have opted to trace historical processes, such as the co-evolution of production systems and protection regimes, some to compare at the macro-level the elective affinities between welfare regimes and economic variables and some to use game theory to reconstruct micro-level interest formation. By studying the linkages between welfare states and political economies, we hope that we can contribute not only in identifying institutional complementarities but also in suggesting causal mechanisms for their co-evolution and their mutual feedback. In the concluding Part V, Michael Shalev in his commentary (Chapter 13) calls for a reconsideration of the 'politics of elective affinities', i.e. how political forces have shaped the linkages between welfare state and political economy. Going a step further, the editors discuss several avenues for future research in their outlook (Chapter 14): exploring the feedback processes between politics and policy, combining new perspectives on gender and the life course, and investigating the role of social concertation in the adaptation of welfare states to the challenges of increased economic internationalisation. We hope that this volume is only one of many future collective endeavours to bridge the disciplinary divide and explore the indirect linkages between production and protection.

Notes

1 For a review of the recent literature on comparative political economy, see Hall (1997).
2 See the recent overview on comparative welfare-state research (Pierson 2000).
3 Originally, different forms of 'industrial order' and 'economic governance' were studied predominantly on the sector level (Hollingsworth *et al.* 1994; Streeck and Schmitter 1985b), while more recent contributions emphasise the importance of national models by providing studies on selected countries (Berger and Dore 1996; Crouch and Streeck 1997; Hall and Soskice, forthcoming; Hollingsworth and Boyer 1997a).
4 However, it should be emphasised that both approaches differ in an important theoretical/methodological respect: the comparative welfare-state research lacks the strict micro-foundation that we find in the Varieties of Capitalism literature. Instead, different welfare regimes are perceived to embody different (liberal, conservative, socialist) 'principles' of social protection (see Esping-Andersen 1990).
5 Responding to some of his critics, Esping-Andersen stresses now the family and household structures, including gender divisions of labour (Esping-Andersen 1999).
6 More recently, Esping-Andersen acknowledges the covariation with industrial relation systems (Esping-Andersen 1999), for a discussion of such covariations see the contribution by Crouch, this volume and Ebbinghaus (1999).

References

Albert, M. (1993). *Capitalism against Capitalism*. London: Whurr Publishers.

Baldwin, P. (1990). *The Politics of Social Solidarity. Class Bases of the European Welfare States 1875–1975*. Cambridge: Cambridge University Press.

Berger, S. and Dore, R. (eds) (1996). *National Diversity and Global Capitalism*. Ithaca, NY: Cornell University Press.

Borchert, J. (1998). 'Ausgetretene Pfade? Zur Statik und Dynamik wohlfahrtsstaatlicher Regime', in S. Lessenich and I. Ostner (eds), *Welten des Wohlfahrtskapitalismus. Der Sozialstaat in vergleichender Perspektive*. Frankfurt: Campus, 137–76.

Boyer, R. (1996). 'The convergence hypothesis revisited: Globalization but still the century of nations?', in S. Berger and R. Dore (eds), *National Diversity and Global Capitalism*. Ithaca, NY: Cornell University Press, 29–59.

Castles, F. G. (1995). 'Welfare state development in Southern Europe', *West European Politics* 18(2), 291–313.

Castles, F. G. and Mitchell, D. (1993). 'Worlds of welfare and families of nations', in F. G. Castles (ed.), *Families of Nations: Patterns of Public Policy in Western Democracies*. Aldershot: Dartmouth, 93–128.

Cooper, R. W. (1999). *Coordination Games. Complementarities and Macroeconomics*. New York: Cambridge University Press.

Crouch, C. (1993). *Industrial Relations and European State Traditions.* Oxford: Clarendon Press.

Crouch, C. (1996). 'Revised diversity: From the neo-liberal decade to beyond Maastricht', in J. Van Ruysseveldt and J. Visser (eds), *Industrial Relations in Europe. Traditions and Transitions.* London: Sage, 358–75.

Crouch, C., Finegold, D. and Sako, M. (1999). *Are Skills the Answer? The Political Economy of Skill Creation in Advanced Industrial Countries.* Oxford: Oxford University Press.

Crouch, C. and Streeck, W. (eds) (1997). *Political Economy of Modern Capitalism. Mapping Convergence and Diversity.* London: Sage.

Culpepper, P. and Finegold, D. (eds) (1999). *The German Skill Machine.* New York: Berghahn Books.

De Swaan, A. (1988). *In Care of the State. Health Care, Education and Welfare in Europe and the USA in the Modern Era.* Cambridge: Polity Press.

DiMaggio, P. J. and Powell, W. W. (1983). 'The iron cage revisited: Institutional isomorphism and collective rationality in organizational fields', *American Sociological Review* 48(2), 147–60.

Dore, R. (1973). *British Factory – Japanese Factory: The Origins of National Diversity in Industrial Relations.* London: Allen & Unwin.

Dore, R. (1997). 'The distinctiveness of Japan', in C. Crouch and W. Streeck (eds), *Political Economy of Modern Capitalism. Mapping Convergence and Diversity*, London: Sage, 19–32.

Ebbinghaus, B. (1999). 'Does a European social model exist and can it survive?', in G. Huemer, M. Mesch and F. Traxler (eds), *The Role of Employer Associations and Labour Unions in the EMU. Institutional Requirements for European Economic Policies.* Aldershot: Ashgate, 1–26.

Esping-Andersen, G. (1990). *Three Worlds of Welfare Capitalism.* Princeton, NJ: Princeton University Press.

Esping-Andersen, G. (1992). 'The emerging realignment between labour movements and welfare states', in M. Regini (ed.), *The Future of Labour Movements.* London: Sage, 133–59.

Esping-Andersen, G. (1993). 'Welfare states and the economy', in N. J. Smelser and R. Swedberg (eds), *The Handbook of Economic Sociology.* Princeton, NJ: Princeton University, 711–32.

Esping-Andersen, G. (ed.) (1996a). *Welfare States in Transition. National Adaptations in Global Economies.* London: Sage.

Esping-Andersen, G. (1996b). 'Welfare states without work: The impasse of labour shedding and familialism in Continental Europe', in G. Esping-Andersen (ed.), *Welfare States in Transition. National Adaptations in Global Economies.* London: Sage, 66–87.

Esping-Andersen, G. (1997). 'Hybrid or unique? The Japanese welfare state between Europe and America', *Journal of European Social Policy* 7(3), 179–89.

Esping-Andersen, G. (1999). *Social Foundations of Postindustrial Economies.* Oxford: Oxford University Press.

Esping-Andersen, G. and Korpi, W. (1984). 'Social policy as class politics in post-war capitalism: Scandinavia, Austria and Germany', in J. H. Goldthorpe (ed.), *Order and Conflict in Contemporary Capitalism.* Oxford: Clarendon Press, 179–208.

Estevez-Abe, M., Iversen, T. and Soskice, D. (1999). 'Social protection and the formation of skills: A reinterpretation of the welfare state', APSA Annual Meeting, Atlanta, GA, 1–5 September 1999.

Ferrera, M. (1996). 'The "Southern Model" of welfare in Social Europe', *Journal of European Social Policy* 6(1), 17–37.

Flora, P. (1986). 'Introduction', in P. Flora (ed.), *Growth to Limits. The Western European Welfare States Since World War II. Sweden, Norway, Finland, Denmark.* Berlin: de Gruyter, xii–xxxvi.

Goldthorpe, J. H. (ed.) (1984). *Order and Conflict in Contemporary Capitalism.* Oxford: Clarendon Press.

Goodin, R. E., Headey, B., Muffels, R. and Dirven, H.-J. (1999). *The Real Worlds of Welfare Capitalism.* Cambridge: Cambridge University Press.

Goodman, R. and Peng, I. (1996). 'The East Asian welfare states: Peripatetic learning, adaptive change, and nation-building', in G. Esping-Andersen (ed.), *Welfare States in Transition. National Adaptations in Global Economies.* London: Sage, 192–224.

Gould, A. (1993). *Capitalist Welfare Systems. A Comparison of Japan, Britain and Sweden.* London: Longman.

Granovetter, M. (1985). 'Economic action and social structures: The problem of embeddedness', *American Journal of Sociology* 91(3), 481–510.

Hall, P. A. (1986). *Governing the Economy.* Cambridge: Polity Press.

Hall, P. A. (1997). 'The role of interests, institutions, and ideas in the comparative political economy of the industrialized nations', in M. I. Lichbach and A. S. Zuckerman (eds), *Comparative Politics. Rationality, Culture, and Structure.* New York: Cambridge University Press, 174–207.

Hall, P. A. and Soskice, D. (1999). 'An introduction to varieties of capitalism', unpublished manuscript, Harvard University, Cambridge, MA/Social Science Research Center, Berlin.

Hall, P. A. and Soskice, D. (eds) (forthcoming). *Varieties of Capitalism. The Institutional Foundations of Comparative Advantage*, New York: Oxford University Press.

Hassel, A. and Ebbinghaus, B. (2000). 'From means to ends: Linking wage moderation and social policy reform', in G. Fajertag and P. Pochet (eds), *Social Pacts in Europe: New Dynamics.* Brussels: ETUI, 61–84.

Hollingsworth, J. R. and Boyer, R. (eds) (1997a). *Contemporary Capitalism. The Embeddedness of Institutions.* New York: Cambridge University Press.

Hollingsworth, J. R. and Boyer, R. (1997b). 'Coordination of economic actors and social systems of production', in J. R. Hollingsworth and R. Boyer (eds), *Contemporary Capitalism. The Embeddedness of Institutions.* New York: Cambridge University Press, 1–47.

Hollingsworth, J. R., Schmitter, P. C. and Streeck, W. (eds) (1994). *Governing Capitalist Economies. Performance and Control of Economic Sectors.* New York: Oxford University Press.

Huber, E. and Stephens, J. D. (1999). 'Welfare state and production regimes in the era of retrenchment', Occasional Papers, Institute for Advanced Studies, Princeton, NJ.

Immergut, E. M. (1998). 'The theoretical core of the New Institutionalism', *Politics and Society* 26(1), 5–34.

Iversen, T., Pontusson, J. and Soskice, D. (eds) (2000). *Unions, Employers, and Central Banks. Macroeconomic Coordination and Institutional Change in Social Market Economies.* New York: Cambridge University Press.

Jacobs, D. (1998). 'Social welfare systems in East Asia: A comparative analysis including private welfare', CASE paper CASE/10, Center for Analysis of Social Exclusion, London School of Economics.

Kastendiek, H. (1990). 'Convergence or a persistent diversity of national politics?', in C. Crouch and D. Marquard (eds), *The Politics of 1992. Beyond the Single European Market.* Oxford: B. Blackwell, 68–84.

Kitschelt, H., Lange, P., Marks, G. and Stephens, J. D. (1999). 'Convergence and divergence in advanced capitalist democracies', in H. Kitschelt, P. Lange, G. Marks and

J. D. Stephens (eds), *Continuity and Change in Contemporary Capitalism*. New York: Cambridge University Press, 427–60.

Kohl, J. (1993). 'Der Wohlfahrtsstaat in vergleichender Perspektive. Anmerkungen zu Esping-Andersen's "The Three Worlds of Welfare Capitalism"', *Zeitschrift für Sozialreform* 39(2), 67–82.

Kolberg, J. E. (ed.) (1992). *The Study of Welfare State Regimes*. Armonk, NY: M.E. Sharpe.

Kolberg, J. E. and Esping-Andersen, G. (1991). 'Welfare states and employment regimes', in J. E. Kolberg (ed.), *The Welfare State as Employer*. Armonk, NY: M.E. Sharpe, 3–35.

Lange, P. and Meadwell, H. (1991). 'Typologies of democratic systems: Form political inputs to political economy', in H. J. Wiarda (ed.), *New Directions in Comparative Politics*, revised edn. Boulder, CO: Westview, 82–117.

Lehmbruch, G. and Schmitter, P. C. (eds) (1982). *Patterns of Corporatist Policy-Making*. London: Sage.

Leibfried, S. (1994). 'Sozialstaat oder Wohlfahrtsgesellschaft. Thesen zu einem japanischen-deutschen Sozialpolitikvergleich', *Soziale Welt* 45(4), 389–410.

Levi, M. (2000). 'The economic turn in comparative politics', *Comparative Political Studies* 33(6/7), 822–44.

Locke, R. M. and Thelen, K. (1995). 'Apples and oranges revisited: Contextualized comparisons and the study of comparative labor politics', *Politics and Society* 23(3), 337–67.

Manow, P. (2000). 'Comparative institutional advantages of welfare state regimes and new coalitions in welfare state reforms', in P. Pierson (ed.), *The New Politics of Welfare*. Oxford: Oxford University Press, 146–64.

March, J. G. and Olsen, J. P. (1984). 'The New Institutionalism: Organizational factors in political life', *American Political Science Review* 78, 734–49.

Mares, I. (1998). 'Negotiated risks: Employers' role in social policy development', unpublished Ph.D. thesis. Cambridge, MA: Harvard University, Department of Government.

Marshall, T. H. (1950). *Citizenship and Social Class. The Marshall Lectures*. Cambridge: Cambridge University Press.

Martin, C. J. (2000). *Stuck in Neutral. Business and the Politics of Human Capital Investment Policy*. Princeton, NJ: Princeton University Press.

Martin, C. J. and Swank, D. (1999). 'Employers and the welfare state', APSA Annual Meeting, Atlanta, GA, 1–5 September 1999.

Mayntz, R. and Scharpf, F. W. (eds) (1995). *Gesellschaftliche Selbstregelung und politische Steuerung*. Frankfurt: Campus.

Milgrom, P. and Roberts, J. (1994). 'Complementarities and systems: Understanding Japanese economic organization', *Estudios Economicos* 9, 3–42.

Offe, C. (1993). 'Zur Typologie von sozialpolitischen "Regimes"', *Zeitschrift für Sozialreform* 39(2), 83–6.

Okun, A. M. (1975). *Equality and Efficiency: The Big Trade-Off*. Washington, DC: Brookings Institution.

Pierson, P. (1993). 'When effect becomes cause: Policy feedback and political change', *World Politics* 45, 595–628.

Pierson, P. (1995). 'The scope and nature of business power. Employers and the American welfare state, 1900–1935', Arbeitspapier 14, Bremen: Zentrum für Sozialpolitik, University of Bremen.

Pierson, P. (1996). 'The New Politics of the Welfare State', *World Politics* 48(2), 143–79.

Pierson, P. (1997). 'Increasing returns, path dependence and the study of politics', EUI Jean Monnet Chair Papers 44, Florence: European University Institute.

Pierson, P. (1998). 'Irresistible forces, immovable objects: Post-industrial welfare states confront permanent austerity', *Journal of European Public Policy* 5(4), 539–60.

Pierson, P. (2000). 'Three worlds of welfare state research', *Comparative Political Studies* 33(6/7), 791–821.

Piore, M. J. and Sabel, C. F. (1984). *The Second Industrial Divide. Possibilities for Prosperity*. New York: Basic Books.

Polanyi, K. (1944). *The Great Transformation. The Political and Economic Origins of Our Time*. Boston: Beacon Press.

Powell, W. W. (1990). 'Neither market nor hierarchy: Network forms of organization', *Research in Organizational Behaviour* 12, 295–336.

Ragin, C. C. (1987). *The Comparative Method. Moving Beyond Qualitative and Quantitative Strategies*. Berkeley, CA: University of California Press.

Rein, M. and Rainwater, L. (eds) (1986). *Public/Private Interplay in Social Protection. A Comparative Study*. Armonk, NY: M.E. Sharpe.

Rhodes, M. and van Apeldoorn, B. (1997). 'Capitalism versus capitalism in Western Europe', in M. Rhodes, P. Heywood and V. Wright (eds), *Developments in West European Politics*. London: Macmillan, 171–89.

Rieger, E. (1998). 'Soziologische Theorie und Sozialpolitik im entwickelten Wohlfahrtsstaat', in S. Lessenich and I. Ostner (eds), *Welten des Wohlfahrtskapitalismus. Der Sozialstaat in vergleichender Perspektive*. Frankfurt: Campus, 59–90.

Rokkan, S. (1999). In P. Flora, S. Kuhnle and D. Urwin (eds), *State Formation, Nation-Building and Mass Politics in Europe. The Theory of Stein Rokkan*. Oxford: Oxford University Press.

Scharpf, F. W. (1997). *Games Real Actors Play. Actor-Centered Institutionalism in Policy Research*. Boulder, CO: Westview Press.

Schmidt, V. A. (1996). *From State to Market? The Transformation of French Business and Government*. New York: Cambridge University.

Schmitter, P. C. and Lehmbruch, G. (eds) (1981). *Trends Toward Corporatist Intermediation*. Beverly Hills, CA: Sage.

Shalev, M. (ed.) (1996). *The Privatization of Social Policy? Occupational Welfare and the Welfare State in America, Scandinavia and Japan*. London: Macmillan.

Shepsle, K. A. (1986). 'Institutional equilibrium and equilibrium institutions', in H. F. Weisberg (ed.), *Political Science: The Science of Politics*. New York: Agathon Press, 51–81.

Shonfield, A. (1965). *Modern Capitalism. The Changing Balance of Public and Private Power*. Oxford: Oxford University Press.

Soskice, D. (1991). 'The institutional infrastructure for international competitiveness: A comparative analysis of the UK and Germany', in A. B. Atkinson and R. Brunetta (eds), *Economics for the New Europe*. London: Macmillan.

Soskice, D. (1999). 'Divergent production regimes: Coordinated and uncoordinated market economies in the 1980s and 1990s', in H. Kitschelt *et al.* (eds), *Continuity and Change in Contemporary Capitalism*. New York: Cambridge University Press, 101–34.

Stinchcombe, A. L. (1968). *Constructing Social Theories*. New York: Harcourt, Brace & World.

Streeck, W. (1997). 'Beneficial constraints: On the economic limits of rational voluntarism', in J. R. Hollingsworth and R. Boyer (eds), *Contemporary Capitalism. The Embeddedness of Institutions*. New York: Cambridge University Press, 197–219.

Streeck, W. and Schmitter, P. C. (1985a). 'Community, market, state – and associations? The prospective contribution of interest governance to social order', in W. Streeck and P. C. Schmitter (eds), *Private Interest Government. Beyond Market and State*. London: Sage, 1–29.

Streeck, W. and Schmitter, P. C. (eds) (1985b). *Private Interest Government. Beyond Market and State*. London: Sage.

Swenson, P. (1991). 'Labor and the limits of the welfare state: The politics of intraclass conflict and cross-class alliances in Sweden and West Germany', *Comparative Politics* 23, 379–99.

Swenson, P. (1997). 'Arranged alliance: Business interests in the New Deal', *Politics & Society* 25, 66–116.

Swenson, P. (1999). 'Varieties of capitalist interests and illusions of labor power: Employers in the making of the Swedish and American welfare states', Paper for the 'Conference on Distribution and Democracy', Yale University, Department of Political Science, 12–14 November 1999.

Swenson, P. (forthcoming). *Captitalism Against Markets: Employers in the Making of Labour Markets and Welfare States.* New York: Oxford University Press.

Titmuss, R. M. (1958). *Essays on the Welfare State.* London: Allen & Unwin.

Titmuss, R. M. (1974). *Social Policy. An Introduction.* London: Allen & Unwin.

Van Kersbergen, K. (1995). *Social Capitalism. A Study of Christian Democracy and the Welfare State.* London: Routledge.

Visser, J. (1990). *In Search of Inclusive Unionism.* Bulletin of Comparative Labour Relations 18, Deventer: Kluwer.

Williamson, O. E. (1975). *Markets and Hierarchies. Analysis and Antitrust Implications.* New York: Free Press.

Williamson, O. E. (1981). 'The economic of organization: The transaction cost approach', *American Journal of Sociology* 87(3), 548–77.

Zysman, J. (1994). 'How institutions create historically rooted trajectories of growth', *Industrial and Corporate Change* 3(1), 243–83.

Part I

The origins and development of welfare capitalism

2 Business coordination, wage bargaining and the welfare state

Germany and Japan in comparative historical perspective[1]

Philip Manow

The wage–welfare nexus

Academic interest in the role of employers in welfare state development has increased noticeably of late (see Gordon 1994; Jacoby 1999; Martin 2000; Mares 1996, 1997; Swenson 1991, 1997, 1999, 2000; Pierson 1995). This new literature provides us with many different ideas about why firms should have and actually do have an interest in (certain) social protection schemes, and why employers have historically not always taken an outright hostile stance in the social policy debates of the past. Take the following sample of explanations from the recent literature (Pierson 2000: 793–97): Employers or certain factions of them

1 have an interest in levelling the playing field with respect to national social protection standards for workers (Swenson 1991, 1999),
2 want to prevent worse things from happening and are therefore in favour of social policies that secure their influence on and control over social protection schemes (employers' strategic voting on social policy; see Mares 1996, 2000, and Mares, Chapter 3 in this volume),
3 value the important latent functions of welfare state intervention that contribute to social peace and help secure a high level of labour productivity,
4 'support social protection that facilitates [the acquisition of] the set of skills they need to be competitive in particular international product markets' (Estevez-Abe *et al.* 1999: 1; Martin 2000),
5 find extremely beneficial the possibility open to them by welfare state programmes to adjust flexibly their workforce to a volatile economic environment, and
6 appreciate the compensatory role of the welfare state within a liberal trade regime (Garrett 1998; Ruggie 1997; Rodrik 1997; Rieger and Leibfried 1998).

One of the most ambitious and theoretically sophisticated accounts of the positive role of business in the emergence of the modern welfare state has been provided recently by Peter Swenson (see especially Swenson 1999, 2000). In his comparison of the development of the Swedish and US-American welfare states between 1930 and 1960, Swenson emphasises that whether wage setting was centralised or decentralised had a great impact on the 'regulation of competition' among employers (Swenson 1999: 8), among big and small companies as well as among export-oriented and domestically oriented ones. In this context, Swenson stresses the important stabilising function of *different welfare regimes* for *different wage-setting regimes*. His argument, in condensed form, is as follows: the export sector in an economy has to fear that firms in the sheltered sector will give in too easily to workers' aggressive wage demands since these 'sheltered' firms can pass wage costs on to consumers via high prices. Firms competing on international markets have to fear both the negative impact of high factor prices on the prices of their products and the adverse effects on the national wage level exerted by aggressive unions in the sheltered sector. If, however, the exposed industries take the lead in wage setting within a centralised wage-bargaining regime, the distributive effects differ substantially. Now the most productive and bigger[2] firms pay 'below equilibrium' wages and thus enjoy a competitive advantage. For the economy as a whole, but not for each and every firm, wages are set below what would have been the outcome in a decentralised setting (Moene and Wallerstein 1995). Yet, low-productivity, labour-intensive firms have to pay above equilibrium wages.

If labour is generally underpriced, the demand for labour increases and labour becomes scarce. Under conditions of labour scarcity, larger and highly productive firms, able and willing to pay higher wages, are constantly tempted to overbid centrally set wages, thus producing wage drift. According to Swenson, the introduction of generous and industry-wide welfare programmes set up by the state can discipline employers and therefore help stabilise a centralised wage-bargaining system, which would otherwise erode given the evasion strategies of single employers. This is the reason why employers' associations, which usually are dominated by the very same companies that profit most from coordinated wage bargaining, often prove to be at least tacitly supportive of welfare state expansion. This is especially the case if entitlements benefit workers, blue- or white-collar, and are introduced in boom-periods when labour scarcity becomes a particularly pressing problem. The employers who benefit from centralised wage-bargaining 'acquire interests in policy designed to protect them against the results of disequilibrium' that wage centralisation itself creates (Swenson 1999: 10). Peter Swenson has provided ample empirical evidence that indeed this explanatory model can well account for the often tacitly and sometimes openly supportive position of Swedish employers in the debates over post-war social policy in the 1950s and 1960s – as well as their very aggressive anti-union, anti-welfare stance between 1900 and 1930.

However, the establishment of centralised wage bargaining presupposes the ability of employers to effectively cooperate among themselves, in particular to force unions into national wage negotiations with massive lockouts and to delegate bargaining responsibility from regional units to the national confederation.

Where these preconditions were not met, employers could not help but find individual, decentralised solutions for the management of their labour markets. According to Swenson, this explains the US-American trajectory of welfare capitalism and labour market segmentalism. Numerous impediments, legal and otherwise, to both within-sector and across-sector employer coordination have left business coordination on issues of wages and employment-based 'social' benefits out of reach for American companies. Within this decentralised, non-coordinated setting, firms with production technology that demands high workplace skills and thus low labour turnover pay 'above equilibrium' wages, making employment scarce. If employers voluntarily 'overprice' labour, they create excess labour supply. The labour market does not clear, and unemployment persists in equilibrium (for an overview of the large literature on efficiency wages, see Weiss 1990).

Part of employers' efforts to stabilise a core workforce is to offer better pay, more job security and more generous company-based social benefits than the average firm. They thus create internal labour markets and dualistic wage dispersion, and contribute to the emergence of a segmented industrial structure with a few large 'high-commitment' firms and many small 'low-commitment' firms. Efficiency wages and welfare capitalist benefit schemes, however, come under stress during recessions, when low wage–low benefit firms without any commitments to their workforce begin to challenge bigger firms with cut-throat price competition. In this situation it is often far too costly for big industry to revoke past commitments and to risk the destruction of the trust and loyalty that has slowly been built up over time and is so critical for the production technologies they use. Instead, employers often begin to support the extension of high social protection standards and generous social entitlements to the entire economy, thus forcing upon their less-committed competitors the same costly social protection standards. This, according to Swenson, can explain why the so-called 'corporate liberals' of large US-American companies turned out to be supportive of Roosevelt's New Deal legislation in the depression of the 1930s (Swenson 1997; Gordon 1994; Jacoby 1999), while Swedish employers came to back the Social Democrats' agenda for social policy reform not during times of economic slump, but during the high growth period of the 1950s and 1960s. Swedish employer *solidarism* and US-American employer *segmentalism* reveal the different business-cycle responsiveness of centralised and decentralised wage-setting regimes, which can account for the peculiar asynchronous development of welfare policies in these two countries. Once the long post-war growth period eased the competitive pressures on US big industry, the welfare capitalist trajectory became once again attractive for the major industrial enterprises.

Is this fascinating explanation of the US-American and Swedish welfare state trajectories applicable to other cases? How would it accommodate the German or Japanese cases, both countries which combine a relatively high degree of wage coordination and wage compression (see Fig. 2.1) with a welfare state so different from the Swedish model and, what is more, so different from each other? Japan's firm-based welfare schemes resemble in many respects the US model of large

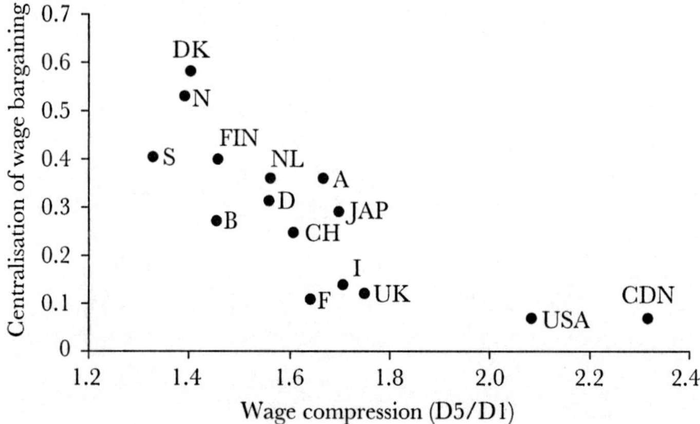

Figure 2.1 Wage compression and centralisation of wage bargaining, 1979–95.

Sources: Iversen (1998, 1999) and OECD Employment Outlook (various years).

Note: Wage compression is defined as the ratio between the median (D5) and the lowest (D1) income decile. Centralisation of wage bargaining according to Iversen (1998: 59): $\Sigma w_j p_{ij}^2$, where w_j is the weight accorded to each bargaining level j ($\Sigma w_j = 1$) and p_{ij} is the share of workers covered by union (or federation) i at level j.

employer welfare capitalism (Esping-Andersen 1997), whereas business coordination and wage compression are so prominent in the Japanese political economy that Japan, like Germany, is often treated as an outright counter-model to the market liberalism of the Anglo-Saxon variant (Albert 1991; Crouch and Streeck 1996; Streeck and Yamamura 2000; Soskice 1995). Hence, we may harbour doubts whether the neat fit between wage regimes and welfare regimes so convincingly described by Swenson for the US-American and Swedish cases indeed can be generalised to other cases.

In this chapter, I consider whether Peter Swenson's historical account of the Swedish and US-American welfare state development can tell us anything about what appear at a glance to be deviant country cases. In particular, the early establishment of collective wage bargaining in Germany between 1956 and 1963 is compared with the establishment of collective bargaining in post-war Japan. I highlight especially the parallel establishment of collective bargaining in the industrial sector with the reconstruction of the Bismarckian welfare state, and the correspondence between wage coordination S*hunto*-style (Takanashi *et al.* 1996) and the Japanese variant of company-based social protection. I argue that the parallel establishment of wage regimes and welfare regimes in Germany and Japan during a high growth period was not accidental, but backs Peter Swenson's claim that employers develop a positive interest in social policy if social policy promises to stabilise wage coordination and to lower employers' 'collective-action' costs in times of economic upswing. In the last section, I briefly summarise the argument and discuss some of its broader implications.

Why then? Full employment, domestic demand and wage moderation

In Germany, coordinated wage bargaining and the leadership role of the metal-workers' union (*IG Metall*) in the annual wage rounds is said to have been first established in 1956 with the so-called 'Bremen agreement'. Coordinated wage bargaining then ultimately was established in the wake of the 1963 conflict in the Baden-Württemberg metal industry (Noé 1970). We may ask with respect to the establishment of pattern wage bargaining in Germany: why then?

In 1955, the German *Wirtschaftswunder* reached its first post-war peak. GDP growth achieved a stunning 11.9 per cent. For the first time since 1945, the labour market was almost swept clean, with unemployment fluctuating around 3 per cent during the summer and autumn. In absolute numbers, Germany counted less than 500,000 unemployed in September 1955 as compared to more than 17 million in gainful employment. Due to the inflationary dangers of high growth under conditions of full employment, the German central bank for the first time embarked upon a restrictive monetary policy, even though in 1954 the inflation rate had still been very low, only about 2 per cent. Since Germany's current account remained relatively stable (but positive), the boom in the second half of the 1950s was now driven at least as much by domestic demand as by external demand (Giersch *et al.* 1992: 63–5). In the second half of the 1950s, Germany witnessed the onset of consumerism. Germans began to spend the incomes they earned during the Korea-boom on consumer goods. They started to buy cars, television sets, washing machines, etc. While the Korea-boom in first half of the 1950s allowed heavy manufacturing to prosper, the second half of the 1950s saw the rise of German consumer good industry.

Yet, in spite of de facto full employment and despite the union's official announcement to embark upon an expansionary wage policy (Victor Agartz's *expansive Lohnpolitik*), which was designed to redistribute wealth via wage demands above the level set by productivity growth plus inflation, real unit labour costs constantly fell throughout the 1950s, if less so in the second half of the decade (see Table 2.1).

Giersch *et al.* consider four different explanations for the decline of real unit labour costs throughout the 1950s: 'organisational weakness', 'political distraction', 'economic surprise', and 'social responsibility' (Giersch *et al.* 1992: 73–9; see also Flanagan *et al.* 1983: 216–75). They dismiss the weakness argument for very good reasons, but reject the political distraction argument for less convincing ones. This latter argument holds that the political struggle especially for co-determination in the early 1950s meant that unions stood 'still temporarily at the wage front so as not to endanger the far more daring prospect of a thoroughly syndicalist "industrial democracy"' (Giersch *et al.* 1992: 75). While it is true that the conflict over co-determination (*Mitbestimmung*) and over work councils (*Betriebsverfassungsgesetz* 1952) had ended by 1953 and thus cannot explain the unions' continuous wage moderation in the following years, Giersch *et al.* fail to see that the conflicts over weekly working time (1956), over sick pay (1956–7),

Table 2.1 The determinants of West German labour costs, 1950–60 (annual average rates of change in per cent)

	Earnings[a]	*Labour productivity*[b]	*Inflation*[c]	*Real unit labour costs*[d]
1950–1	15.8	7.0	11.8	−3.2
1951–2	8.3	6.9	4.7	−3.3
1952–3	5.9	6.0	−1.3	1.2
1953–4	5.0	4.7	−0.3	0.6
1954–5	8.1	7.8	2.1	−1.8
1955–6	8.0	4.6	2.7	0.6
1956–7	6.6	3.6	2.8	0.0
1957–8	6.9	3.5	2.9	0.4
1958–9	5.6	6.6	1.6	−2.5
1959–60	9.0	6.8	3.2	−1.0
1950–5	8.6	6.5	3.3	−1.3
1955–60	7.2	5.0	2.6	−0.5
1950–60	7.9	5.7	3.0	−0.9

Source: Giersch *et al.* (1992: 72).

Notes

a Gross annual earnings (including social insurance contributions of employers).

b Gross domestic product (at constant prices) divided by active labour force.

c Deflator of value added (i.e. gross domestic product).

d Earnings/(labour productivity × inflation).

and more generally over social reform and the reconstruction of the German welfare state (pensions in 1957 and – less so – health reform in 1959–61) had become the main issues in union campaigns in the second half of the 1950s and had replaced the emphasis on redistribution via generous wage hikes (Pirker 1979). These social policy issues were not only of general political relevance in the unions' manifestos, but especially the pension reform and the sick-pay law in 1957 had – in contrast to the conflict over co-determination – a direct impact on workers' (social) wages.

In this context it is also regularly overlooked that the Bremen agreement on reducing weekly working time from 48 hours to 45 hours was 'only part of a more encompassing social policy concept' of the IG Metall (Kalbitz 1978: 183) that carried over into the fierce fight for sick-pay reform in Schleswig-Holstein's metal industry in November 1956. I would argue that the social legislation in the second half of the 1950s helped unions to trade real wage increases for an expansion of welfare state entitlements, or to put it differently: especially the unions and the employers in vulnerable, export-oriented sectors were happy that the rise of the social wage due to the significant welfare state expansion in the second half of the 1950s reduced the wage push in times of de facto full employment. At the same time, the emphasis on social issues in the IG Metall campaigns almost 'naturally' established its leadership role within the unions' national confederation, the *Deutsche Gewerkschaftsbund* (DGB). A closer look at Table 2.1 reveals that the years 'in between' the struggle for co-determination and the fight for pension reform and sick pay, the years between 1953 and 1957, were the ones in which real unit labour costs showed an upward tendency.[3]

What was the pre-history of the 1956–7 conflict over working time reduction and sick pay? The IG Metall had entered the 1955 annual wage round by cancelling all collective contracts in the North Rhine-Westphalia district, by far the largest of all districts with 900,000 IG Metall members. Interestingly, the union sought to reach a different settlement for the iron and steel industry than it did for metalworking. The union wanted a moderate settlement in the more export-oriented, small-firm dominated metalworking industry and was quick to accept a moderate arbitration proposal. At the same time, the metalworkers' union hoped to achieve a higher wage hike in the iron and steel industry, where demand was more domestic in nature and where firms were much bigger (Pirker 1979: 174–5). This strategy backfired badly (Pirker 1979: 175–6). It failed in particular because the leading union representatives in the big firms of the iron and steel sector considered the IG Metall's wage demands to be out of proportion and did not back them. Especially the *Arbeitsdirektoren*, union members who belonged to the board of directors in the coal, iron, and steel industry thanks to the co-determination law (*Montanmitbestimmung*), opposed IG Metall's aggressive wage policy. The union thus was faced with a dilemma: It could not champion the cause for higher wages in sectors where firms were under strong competitive pressures from world markets. Yet the union also met with considerable resistance in those sectors where demand was more domestic in nature but where co-determination had infected union representatives with the virus of firm-level syndicalism or social partnership. All this coincided with workers' raised expectations concerning wage increases given the metalworker union's radical rhetoric (in times of very tight labour markets).

The IG Metall, under the leadership of Otto Brenner, who was part of the 'progressive wing' in the DGB, finally 'was condemned to act' (Kalbitz 1978: 184) if it did not want to lose out against the more moderate faction within the DGB. Aggressive mobilisation in support of significant welfare state expansion in the following years then became the solution to IG Metall's dilemma, as the Bremen agreement and in particular the Schleswig-Holstein metal worker strike in 1956–7 over sick-pay reform showed. It was to become soon clear that employers in the 'exposed sectors' of the economy favoured welfare state expansion as well because they hoped that this would weaken the upward pressure on wages in times of full employment. Insofar as the welfare state was going to become essential for the stability of medium-centralised collective bargaining and the ensuing *intra*-industrial wage compression, welfare state programmes were more and more perceived as being in the *general* interest of all employers, be they in exposed or sheltered sectors of the economy (see below).

What was the prime economic rationale behind pattern wage bargaining? The large firms in the Ruhr region knew that the unions had picked them in the 1955 wage round as their prime targets in the struggle for higher wages, even though the 'dual track' strategy of IG Metall had been a complete failure. While the big firms in the west clearly could afford to pay higher wages, they were not particularly eager to do so. Hence, the 'autarchic' firms in the Ruhr region (Herrigel 1996) would most benefit from collective bargaining for the entire industrial sector with the export industries setting the pace, since this would lead to wages significantly below what they would have to pay if unions negotiated firm contracts (Swenson 1999, 2000). If, in turn, wage moderation in the export-oriented firms would be achieved by an increase in workers' social wages (via welfare state expansion), those exposed firms and workers most vulnerable to external shocks would profit disproportionately *if* the welfare state would provide employers with instruments to flexibly and painlessly adjust employment to sudden shifts in demand, meaning with social programmes such as short-time allowance (*Kurzarbeitergeld*), early retirement programmes, and disability pensions. That was exactly what Adenauer's pension reform in 1957 delivered.[4] 'Wage redistribution' in favour of the large firms in the coal, iron and steel industries would be counterbalanced by 'welfare redistribution' in favour of those firms that used (contribution-financed) welfare state programmes to adjust their workforce to sudden shifts in demand or changes in market conditions.

Why there?

Shipbuilding, world markets and the intra-industry compromise

Both the Bremen agreement and the Schleswig-Holstein metalworkers' strike of 1956–7 were meant to lend credibility to IG Metall's claim to be the leading, pacesetting union among the sixteen DGB unions and to be also fully autonomous from directives of the unions' umbrella organisation. In Bremen and Schleswig-Holstein, the metal sector was dominated by shipbuilding. In the Schleswig-Holstein metal sector, 38.9 per cent of all workers were shipyard workers, by far the largest occupational group, but many more metalworkers were employed in the supply industry. A closer look at shipbuilding's economic situation can explain why so much union activity occurred here in the mid-1950s.

In the early 1950s, the demand for ships was largely domestic. The rebuilding of the German trade fleet, made possible by generous tax subsidies and by Marshall Plan funds (Wend 2000), kept employment and production levels up during the first half of the decade. Recovery had been slow for many reasons: the destruction caused by war (which was substantial in shipbuilding compared with other industries), the 'deconstruction' after the war, an insufficient supply of steel for the shipyards, and the military restrictions placed on production that were only slowly lifted in the wake of the Korea-boom. If the year 1936 is used as a yardstick, shipbuilding had only reached 72 per cent of its pre-war production capacity by 1951, while at that point coal mining was at 103 per cent, the car industry at 166 per cent and the textile industry at 132 per cent of their pre-war levels. Industry as a whole had reached 136 per cent of its 1936 capacity level (Albert 1998). With time, external demand became increasingly important for German shipyards. Already 48 per cent of all ships built between 1952 and 1955 had been exported, and this figure increased to 65 per cent between 1956 and

1961 (Albert 1998: 85). As early as 1955, German shipyards were the world's second most important producer of ships (Kuckuk 1998: 20), and shipbuilding had the highest export share among all German industries (Kuckuk 1998: 22), having reached 77.7 per cent by 1960 (Kuckuk 1998: 22). This sector thus was especially sensible to changes in the international terms of trade and in domestic wage costs, particularly since wage costs were comparatively high in shipbuilding (between 20 and 35 per cent of total production costs; Albert 1998: 107) and possibilities to substitute labour with capital were limited.

Shipbuilding was the seventh most important export sector if measured in terms of its contribution to the German trade surplus (1.368 billion DM in 1957 in absolute terms). Yet, terms of trade had eroded steadily since the mid-1950s and suddenly deteriorated rapidly in 1957. While the closing of the Suez canal had led to a sharp increase in the demand for ships and in freight rates, in early 1957, freight rates dropped significantly and literally overnight shipyards received no new ship orders. International competition turned extremely fierce, a development long foreseeable due to the advent of a new and competitive challenger: Japan. Japanese shipbuilders had increased their world market share significantly within only a short time period, from 11 per cent (1951–5) to 32 per cent (1956–60; see Albert 1998: 85). In 1958, German shipyards started to lay off workers.

Another important factor to take into consideration is that by the 1950s all of the major German shipyards had become vertically integrated into the 'autarchic' Ruhr region's iron and steel industrial complex (Leckebusch 1963). Since 1916, *Thyssen* held the majority of the stocks of the Bremen *Vulcan* shipyard. *Krupp* had holdings in the *Deutsche Schiff- und Maschinenbau AG*, a merger of *Vulcan Werke Hamburg* and *AG Weser*, the latter was acquired entirely in 1941 (Chandler 1990: 511). The *Germania* shipyard had been part of the *Krupp* concern since 1896. *Thyssen* bought *Blohm & Voss* in 1955. *Gutehoffnungs-Hütte* had acquired *Deutsche Werft* back in 1918 (Bankverein 1954). *Stinnes* owned *Nordseewerke Emden* and the *Stumm* conglomerate owned the *Frerichs* shipyards (Leckebusch 1963). Vertical integration was supposed to help balance the business cycles (Albert 1998: 124). And steel producers had foreseen the necessity to find new markets given the significant expansion of their production capacities during wartime (Strath 1994: 75). The vertical integration between the iron and steel industry and the ship construction industry, which was barely affected by the Allied deconcentration policy after Second World War (Diegmann 1993; Wend 2000), meant that managers and unions had to take into account the different economic situations of both of these industries *if* wages were to be set uniformly for the entire 'metal' sector. Furthermore, it is important to note that the extensive version of German co-determination was practised in the iron and steel industry (*Montanmitbestimmung*), but not in the shipyards.

Shipyards were highly unionised even by the standards of the time. In all of Schleswig-Holstein, union density in the metal sector was 71.9 per cent in 1956 (IG Metall 1978: 51), but at the shipyards, the best organised industry second only to the electrical industry, union density was even greater (Noé 1970: 340). Workers were also highly politicised, as was underlined by the fact that many shipyards had been occupied by workers immediately after the war, resembling the Japanese post-war experience of unions' 'production control' (Gordon 1985: 329–66). The communist movement enjoyed a relatively strong foothold. Work councils, on the contrary, had mostly pursued a policy of *Burgfrieden*, so called after the domestic 'armistice' between the state, the military, and the workers' movement during First World War. Given that *external factors*, namely the capital shortage and the Allied restrictions on production, were seen as the main obstacles towards the post-war recovery of the German shipbuilding industry, management, work councils, and local politicians formed broad coalitions and considered it to be in their common interest to put internal conflicts aside for the time being (Wend 2000). This was the shipbuilding industry's economic situation in the second half of the 1950s, when major wage increases triggered by a growing domestic demand were expected to endanger the industry's precarious international competitiveness, while a highly mobilised union membership did not want to wait any longer for its fair share of Germany's *Wirtschaftswunder*.

Cartels, coordinated capitalism and collective wage-bargaining: the metal-producing vs metalworking industry

Whereas the Bremen agreement and the metalworkers' strike in 1956–7 represented the first steps towards introducing pattern wage bargaining, coordinated wage setting finally became fully established in the south, in the industrial region of *Baden-Württemberg* where mechanical engineering, automobile firms and the electrotechnical industry dominated metalworking. Again we have to step a little back in time in order to explain the rationale of wage coordination for the metal industries.

A principal problem of Germany's dual industrial structure, namely the conflict of interests between large, domestic-oriented iron and steel producers and medium-sized and export-oriented steel consumers (Herrigel 1996) that in shipbuilding was solved in the 1920s via vertical integration, had historically found a different solution in the other metalworking industries, especially in mechanical engineering, the automobile and electrical industries. While quickly gaining in economic importance, the metalworking industry had been unable to acquire the corresponding political 'interest-group influence' until the end of 1924 because of seemingly insurmountable 'collective action' problems (Feldman and Nocken 1975).[5] The lack in lobbying power was due to the profound heterogeneity of interests within the metalworking sector. For one, economic concentration was far less developed than in the German heavy industries of coal, steel and iron (Chandler 1990: 550–61; Weisbrod 1978: 93–119). For another, the wide span of products ranging from automobiles and machine tools to cutlery and the corresponding heterogeneity of product markets long hindered effective interest aggregation and organisational unity.

When the metalworking firms finally managed to organise themselves into the *Arbeitsgemeinschaft Metallverarbeitende Industrie* (AVI) in 1924–5, the way was clear for settling the serious conflict with heavy industry via a complex contractual arrangement between the AVI and the Association of German Iron and Steel

Producers (*Reichsverband Eisen und Stahl*), the so-called AVI agreement (Nocken 1977; Weisbrod 1978; Feldman 1977; Hoffmann 1928). The core of the compromise was that, on the one hand, the metalworking firms would support heavy industry's campaign for protectionist tariffs on iron and steel once the Versailles treaty provision expired in 1925 that granted the victorious nations access to the German market on a most-favoured-nation basis; while on the other hand, heavy industry agreed to compensate the metalworking firms for the difference between the high German cartel prices and the world market iron and steel prices *for exported products* (and they supported efforts to obtain privileged access for these products especially to the French and Belgian markets). It would clearly go beyond the purpose of this chapter to describe in any detail the working of this sophisticated inter-sectoral arrangement (Hoffmann 1928; Schmid 1930; Tübben 1930; Preiss 1933; Blödner 1934). Suffice it to say that this form of conflict settlement via cartel price control and inter-sectoral price compensation clearly could not be revived after 1945, when the Allied *Entflechtungsverordnung* (deconcentration decree) was issued, nor later, in 1957, when the passage of the Cartel Law (*Gesetz gegen Wettbewerbsbeschränkungen*) forestalled the further use of these extreme practices of Germany's 'organised', 'guaranteed', 'riskless' capitalism so prominent in the interwar years (see Winkler 1974; Michels 1928; Liefmann 1938).

Moreover, the profound deconcentration measures imposed by the occupation forces on heavy industry (Herrigel 2000: 363–9) rendered the agreement on and enforcement of cartels a highly unlikely enterprise. Yet, the fact that the 1950s marked a sharp break with both the massive vertical integration of the early 1920s and with the cartel practices of the late 1920s is rarely emphasised enough in the literature. In particular, scholars infrequently discuss how the 'autarchic' firms in the west and the export industry in the south once again found a *modus vivendi* after the war. It is seldom asked what replaced the cartel agreements plus compensatory side-payments in post-war Germany (an exception, of course, is Herrigel 1996). Table 2.2 may give an initial, if insufficient

Table 2.2 Estimated numbers of cartels in Germany, 1880s–1960s

Years	*Number of cartels*
1880–90	50–60
1890–1910	400–500
1925–29	2,500[a]
1952–57	0
1957–62	111[b]

Sources: Chandler (1990: 423); Klump, quoted from Overy (1996: 27); Djelic (1998: 54–5, 63); Liefmann (1938); Michels (1928).

Notes
a In 1925.
b In 1962.

impression of how much the surge in cartel agreements in the second half of the 1920s had been brought to an abrupt end in post-war Germany.

Even if this data has to be interpreted with extreme caution, we know that the AVI agreement and the iron and steel cartel were quite efficient (Preiss 1933: 22–3; Weisbrod 1978: 101–2; Hoffmann 1928). Thus the turn against cartels in the 1950s did mark a substantial change in the practices governing the 'regulation of competition among business' for the metal industries (Swenson 1999: 8). A central claim of this chapter is that coordinated wage bargaining, as it came to be first established in this sector, proved to be a functional equivalent – at least in part – for inter-sectoral coordination via cartel agreements. And as Peter Swenson has argued convincingly, wage coordination, as a non-self-enforcing arrangement, needed reinforcement from an outside source. It was the welfare state that came to its aid when the costs of coordination threatened to undermine the solidarity among employers that was so essential for the functioning of the entire system.

Again we may ask with respect to shift in the location of industrial conflict from shipbuilding in the north (1955–7) to the automobile industry and mechanical engineering in the south (1960–3): Why there? A look at the structure of the metal industry in Baden-Württemberg shows that the sector was dominated by small to medium-sized firms in mechanical engineering and large automobile producers, both with a comparatively high export share (Noé 1970: 79–80). It was the employers who took the initiative and pressed the unions for the centralisation of wage bargaining in the early 1960s. The goal of the employers' association in the metal sector, *Gesamtmetall*, was to fully centralise wage bargaining on the national level. Gesamtmetall had already been granted full responsibility from its regional member associations to bargain on their behalf. In 1961, employers on a nationwide scale simultaneously cancelled all collective agreements with IG Metall in order to synchronise wage bargaining in the various districts (*Tarifdistrikte*). After this was achieved, employers entered the 1963 wage round with the 'offer' of a general wage stop in the metalworking industries, and later proposed to increase wages by 3.5 per cent, the expected rate of average productivity growth for all industrial sectors. Only in the district of Baden-Württemberg had the union prepared for a strike, and it was here that both parties finally decided to measure their strength in 1963. Taken by surprise by massive lockouts and unable to play large and small employers against each other, the union soon had to cave in to most of Gesamtmetall's demands. The agreement reached between the two parties brought about a wage hike of 5 per cent, which was roughly equal to the productivity growth in the metal industries or to the rate of the German economy's productivity growth plus the 'natural' rate of inflation of around 1.5–2 per cent (Noé 1970: 316). This settlement was then quickly extended to all other metal districts. While this settlement already represented a compromise between the medium and large employers within the Baden-Württemberg metal industry that particularly benefited the larger enterprises, the extension of the settlement to other districts again and a fortiori benefited those (especially large) firms that otherwise would have been forced to 'share their rents' with workers much more extensively.[6]

Thus wage coordination was not important for the metalworking sector alone. The employers of the iron, steel and coal industry (which is collectively referred to in German as the *Montanindustrie*) were not represented by Gesamtmetall because the special form of co-determination in this sector granted unions a seat on the executive board of these firms, so that unions would have been represented on both sides of the bargaining table. But there is ample evidence that the *Montan*-industry and the metalworking firms had made a concerted effort in the Baden-Württemberg conflict and had agreed upon a common strategy (Noé 1970: 120–1, 258–60). And although pattern bargaining, once established, did not make wages in the iron and steel industry simply identical to those set by IG Metall and Gesamtmetall in the metalworking sector, we can safely assume that the signalling function of wage agreements in metalworking effectively set the corridor for wage demands in the iron and steel sector *below* what otherwise, without 'the pattern', would have been the case. Especially IG Metall's dual track strategy of the mid-1950s would have been economically much more unfavourable for the large Ruhr firms.

As became obvious with the Baden-Württemberg conflict of 1961–3, the leadership role of the metalworker union tended to be exploited by employers. Once IG Metall had successfully established its pacesetting role within the DGB, especially by championing social policy issues in the late 1950s, the union could be tamed by employers with the help of coordinated, sector-wide lockouts. Just how widespread the use of sector-wide lockouts was as an instrument to discipline the metalworkers' union can be seen in Tables 2.3 and 2.4 showing the types of lockouts, number of lockouts, number of workers affected, and number of workers affected according to industrial sector.

Table 2.3 Lockouts in West Germany, 1949–68

	Number of lockouts	*Affected workers*	*Firm lockouts (in %)*	*Sector lockouts (in %)*
1949–58	7	5,543	57.7	42.3
1959–68	15	302,371	4.2	95.8

Source: Kalbitz (1979: 26, 42).

Table 2.4 Sector unions affected by lockouts, 1949–76

Union	*Number of lockouts*	*Affected workers*	*In %*	*Days lost*	*In %*
Metal industry	39	640,973	87.9	4,953,825	85.5
Textiles	12	8,317	1.1	161,129	2.8
Public services	7	17,166	2.4	469,887	8.2
Construction	5	1,650	0.2	39,276	0.6
Chemical industry	5	1,413	0.2	18,914	0.3

Source: Kalbitz (1979: 86).

Once confronted with sweeping union success in the fierce conflict over working time reduction and sick pay in the late 1950s, German metal employers now discovered the advantages of national wage coordination. They were obvious. Big industry came to benefit from wages that represented a middle road between the different 'abilities to pay' of medium-sized, export-oriented firms, on the one hand, and larger domestically oriented firms, on the other. With the establishment of pattern wage bargaining, company-based welfare schemes lost their role as a fundamental alternative to the collective, corporatist social policy as represented in the Bismarckian social insurance schemes. In particular, the Ruhr industrialists lost their interest in the old-style welfare capitalism so dominant in the Krupp, Stinnes and Thyssen conglomerates before the 1930s. Once heavy industry had lost its control over the market via cartel agreements, it developed an interest in better controlling wages. To this end, it needed coordination with the metalworking sector. Yet, effective wage coordination meant that the Ruhr iron and steel companies became less opposed to state social policies that covered the entire industry and threatened to critically restrict the impact of company-based benefit schemes. Large firms still offered higher employment security, more generous fringe benefits, additional company pensions and other social benefits. But 'wage drift' and 'benefit drift' now were mainly correctives for the rigidities that came with coordinated wage bargaining. Over time, this 'drift' became less important as a means to regulate the labour market and it was increasingly contained by the dynamic growth of public social programmes. The fundamental conflict of the 1920s over the relative importance of the public vs the private provision of social protection was over by the 1960s. Welfare corporatism and wage coordination became 'strategic complements' for each other (Milgrom and Roberts 1990, 1994; Cooper 1999): wage coordination reinforced employers' interests in collective/corporatistic social policy, while the quick expansion of public welfare programmes crowded out the forms of welfare capitalism and other 'efficiency schemes' that existed so prominently before 1945. Having been the fiercest opponents of the Bismarckian welfare state in the interwar years (Weisbrod 1978), employers in heavy industry slowly made their peace with the post-war compromise and even learnt to appreciate its particular advantages.

In the following section, I will briefly discuss the degree to which the parallel reconstruction of the Bismarckian welfare state had an impact on the political and economic equilibrium in industrial relations that became established in the late 1950s, early 1960s.

The reconstruction of the Bismarckian welfare state in the late 1950s

The Adenauer pension reform in 1957 brought a substantial expansionary step in welfare state spending. Expenses for pensions increased in real terms by some 27 per cent in 1957 alone. Mainly because of the pension reform, social spending as a share of total public spending jumped from 55 per cent in 1955 to 59 per cent in 1958 (Alber 1989: 84 and 78). Current pensions increased on average by

65 per cent (blue-collar worker pensions) or 72 per cent (white-collar worker pensions; Hockerts 1980: 422)! The contribution rate to the old-age insurance increased from 11 per cent of gross wages in 1956 to 14 per cent in 1957. Total pension expenditures doubled in only three years, from 6 billion DM in 1955 to 12 billion DM in 1958 (in current prices, but during a time of low inflation). Due to this significant expansionary step, Germany had the highest percentage of social spending as a share of GDP among all West European countries throughout the 1950s and until 1965 (see Table 2.5).

It was only later, in the second half of the 1960s, that first Austria, then the Netherlands and later Sweden surpassed Germany and became the leaders in social spending (Alber 1989: 41). Hence, the high growth period of the German economic miracle, its *Wirtschaftswunder*, was also a time of big (social) spending, and apparently the success of German industry on world markets remained largely unaffected by the above-average welfare costs. It is particularly interesting to note that in the reform debates of 1956 and 1957, few complaints were made about the sharp increase in social spending caused by Adenauer's pension reform (Hockerts 1980). The main concern was that the new 'dynamic' pension would endanger price stability, that it would set in motion a *scala mobile* between prices, wages and the 'dynamic' pensions. Inflation, not the immediate steep increase in social spending, was the most troubling question raised (Hockerts 1980; BDA 1956a,b). In response to the pension reform plans of the Adenauer government, the BDA recommended that firms should begin to 'exercise restraint' when deciding upon new voluntary company-based social programmes, given the significant expansion of the public commitments as introduced with the Adenauer reform (BDA 1956c: 4). Furthermore, employers called for a binding upper limit on the replacement level of private and public pensions combined and for the possibility to adjust past private commitments (downwards) to the new situation (BDA 1956c: 4). This clearly indicates how much the growth of public social programmes in the late 1950s began to crowd out the private schemes. Interestingly, this trend did not provoke much employer protest.

Table 2.5 Germany's rank in social spending among OECD countries, 1950–80 (in per cent of GDP)

	Germany (in %)	*Rank*	*OECD average (in %)*	*OECD maximum*		*OECD minimum*	
				(in %)	*Country*	*(in %)*	*Country*
1950	14.8	1	9.3	14.8	D	5.7	N
1955	14.2	1	10.2	14.2	D	6.8	CH
1960	15.4	1	11.4	15.4	D	7.5	CH
1965	16.6	2	13.4	17.8	A	8.5	CH
1970	17.0	5	15.8	20.0	NL	10.1	CH
1975	23.5	5	21.2	26.8	NL	15.1	CH
1980	23.8	6	22.8	32.0	S	13.8	CH

Source: Alber (1989: 40, table 4).

It is important to note that in Germany, as in Sweden, the most significant period in the post-war growth of the welfare state took place in times of high economic growth and de facto full employment, when strong wage pressures seemed to endanger international competitiveness. This sets Sweden and Germany clearly apart from the US, where the New Deal Keynesianism was primarily a response to the severe economic crisis of the 1930s (Swenson 2000). The political and economic logic of welfare state expansion and contraction thus seemed to have been diametrically opposed in these countries.

With the onset of the social reform debate in the second half of the 1950s, German unions shifted their emphasis from wage demands to demands for general 'social policy' issues like working time reduction, sick pay or early retirement (Pirker 1979). The 1956 Hamburg DGB conference was entirely devoted to the discussion of social policy issues. The new DGB chairman, Willi Richter, elected at the Hamburg conference, was a Social Democratic MP and an expert on social policy. With the 1956–7 Schleswig-Holstein strike, unions had visibly added 'social concerns to the predominantly economic issues which were considered "strike-worthy" by the labour movement' (Markovits 1986: 193). Apparently, the idea of substituting political demands involving the extension of welfare entitlements for wage demands pointed to a solution for the dilemma in which IG Metall found itself after 1955. Both the intense conflict over sick pay (in which the Schleswig-Holstein metalworkers' union staged in 1956–7 the longest strike (sixteen weeks) in the Federal Republic's history up to that point; see Markovits 1986: 190–5) and the significant extension of workers' pension benefits through the pension reform of 1957 have to be seen in this light.

The German post-war political economy came to be based on a quasi-corporatistic compromise among employers, unions and the government even though central corporatistic coordination, active macroeconomic management, a 'loose' monetary regime, Social-Democratic hegemony, and a commitment to full employment all remained alien to 'Modell Deutschland'. In particular, workers could expect to benefit from the 'industrial achievement–performance model' as established with the Bismarckian model. Initially, the welfare state helped balance unions' wage demands and the necessity to remain competitive in world markets. In giving social policy issues top priority, the IG Metall had almost 'naturally' established itself as a pacesetter, since no other union could afford not to fight for the extension of 'social achievements' like the 45-hour week, sick pay or increased employment protection. Employers, in turn, had a hard time justifying why workers should be treated differently across industries. What was at stake were questions of justice, fairness, workers' dignity and status, rather than the more mundane issues of productivity, business cycles and income distribution. It was only later, in 1963, when the metal employers had already learnt of the strength of the metalworkers' union through the Schleswig-Holstein strike, that a concerted and organised lockout in the Baden-Württemberg region established pattern *wage* bargaining (Kalbitz 1979; Noé 1970).

From the employers' standpoint, welfare expansion was viewed less critically as long as it helped moderate unions' wage demands. Employers valued the flexibility which the various welfare state programmes offered to them when coping with market volatility. This was especially true for the shipbuilding firms who were confronted with 'severe market fluctuations' (Strath 1994: 74) within a 'rapidly changing industry' (Strath 1994: 73). Furthermore, the generous and dynamically growing welfare state disciplined employers who were tempted to abandon employer 'solidarity' in wage setting and to pay wages above the level set by collective agreements (Swenson 2000). Generous welfare benefits, directly linked to wages, constrained 'wage drift' and 'welfare drift'. Also, by coupling the interests of the large firms in the Ruhr region with the economic interests of the small and medium-sized enterprises and the exposed firms, companies like Thyssen, Krupp, and other representatives of German heavy industry were integrated into the post-war order. The Ruhr magnates gave up their old paternalist *Herr-im-Hause* policy and slowly reduced their elaborate 'welfare capitalist' systems. Part of these firm-specific voluntary benefit packages had been comprised of continued wage payments in case of sickness exactly like those for which the IG Metall had called the Schleswig-Holstein strike. Again, it was obvious that big firms were only slightly affected negatively by the strike's outcome.

The next section will briefly discuss just how well the Japanese post-war settlement of industrial conflict may fit into the picture of the parallel and interdependent formation of wage and welfare regimes.

Japan's post-war compromise: the spring wage offensive, *keiretsu*, and the company-based welfare state

To 'regulate competition among employers' meant something quite different in Japan. Unlike the German and Swedish cases, Japanese employers neither had to worry much about the 'exposed' vs 'sheltered' divide, nor about a profound conflict of interest between large and small firms. The major industrial conglomerates, the *keiretsu*, organised both export-oriented and domestically oriented firms (horizontal *keiretsu*; Westney 1998; Nakatani 1998), and the large employers and small firms were often linked to each other via complex contractor–supplier relations (vertical *keiretsu*). Moreover and probably even more important, the Japanese state with a panoply of protectionist and regulative measures insulated the home market, encouraged the formation of cartels, and eased 'the great pressure on the smaller (firms) to modernise or to raise wages due to the "higher wages in the country's rapidly expanding larger firms" ' (Pempel 1998: 61). Thus, despite the fact that Japan's industrial structure was markedly segmentalized, competition between low- and high-commitment companies was less of a problem (Pempel 1998). Cartels and encompassing protectionism remained legitimate instruments of economic policy in post-war Japan. Compared with the Federal Republic, the deconcentration measures and the anti-cartel legislation initiated under US occupation had far less success in installing a liberal market economy (Pempel 1998: 93; Herrigel 2000).

More of a problem for Japanese industrialists was the regulation of the fierce oligopolistic competition among the major industrial groupings and the negative effect union militancy in the public sector was having on wage negotiations in the private sector. Whereas the latter problem was solved over time by the harsh anti-(public) union stance of the conservative LDP government that introduced compulsory arbitration for public enterprises and national corporations and finally revoked public workers' right to strike in 1973, the former problem, dubbed the problem of 'excessive competition', faded when *Shunto* finally established the coordination of wage setting. *Shunto*, the annual 'spring offensive' in which management and trade unions conduct wage negotiations throughout the country, came into being in the late 1950s (Hamada and Kasuya 1993: 177–8). As was to become apparent during this period, it was not only an instrument by which unions tried to achieve labour movement unity, it could also serve as a regulative device that promised to ease the competitive pressures among employers (Koshiro 1983: 212). *Shunto* improved the 'ability of the large companies to concert their wage policies and bargaining tactics both within and across industry boundaries' (Brown *et al.* 1997: 161), something of paramount interest to employers in times of high growth and labour scarcity. Moreover, because export industries had the leadership role in the spring offensive, the impact of public sector union radicalism could be effectively contained after 1965 (Koshiro 1983: 220–2).

From the unions' point of view, the spring wage offensive was an opportunity to make 'workers focus more strongly on their relative (interfirm) wages and thus to encounter the efforts of large scale firms to insulate their own labour markets' (Brown *et al.* 1997: 160). Seen from the employers' perspective, this attack on firm-specific 'insulated' labour markets finally provided the large industrial groups with a means to avoid the costly mutual overbidding under conditions of full employment. Yet, what was true in the German case was true in the Japanese case as well: it took employers some time to discover these beneficial side effects of coordinated wage bargaining. In 1956, in the initial *Shunto* wage round, unions managed for the first time to push through their coordinated wage demands against strong resistance from *Nikkeiren*, the national employers association (Takanashi *et al.* 1996: 2–3). As employers were to learn from this and coming wage rounds, unions also helped ease the competition among employers by levelling wage differentials between the major firms, and once the link between wage demands and productivity growth had been accepted, wage coordination Japanese style displayed most of the beneficial effects already pointed out above with regard to coordinated wage bargaining in the Swedish and German cases.

The most important of these advantages was that wages were set below equilibrium for the most productive firms, especially if 'major firms in the private *and open sectors of the economy*' took the lead in the annual wage rounds (Brown *et al.* 1997: 160; my emphasis). For large firms, it was essential that 'as long as wage negotiations and strikes were coordinated, management did not have to worry about losing its competitive position', while unions 'being ultimately organised along the company's line, also had a strong interest in not damaging the relative position of their own company' (Takanashi *et al.* 1996: 24). Again, Japanese employers, like their Swedish or German counterparts, also changed their attitude towards state social policy once wage coordination became entrenched. Japan's dual industrial structure had been replicated in the dual structure of the Japanese welfare state. Most large firms had chosen to opt out of the Employee Pension System (Kosei Nenkin Hoken, KNH/EPS), which had been founded in 1941 and rebuilt in the early 1950s, while workers in the many small- and medium-sized firms were usually members in the EPS, if not in the National Pension System (self-employed). Within this dual system, lower premiums, less co-payment, and higher benefits prevailed in the state-regulated company schemes and the contracted-out company schemes in health and pension insurance were even more generous (Employee Pension System, Employee Health Insurance and Employee Pension Funds), while residual provisions, lower benefits and longer qualifying periods were to be found in the public programmes (National Pension System (NPS, 1959) and National Health Insurance (NHI, 1938/58); see Estevez-Abe 1996; Estienne 1999). Yet, smaller firms in which the workers were in the 'lower' tax-financed, flat-rate social protection tier enjoyed a higher degree of public subsidies or enjoyed particular tax privileges for the pension plans that were tailored to their needs (Tax Qualified Pensions, introduced in 1962).

The contracting-out option had been given to business in 1966 in the form of Employee Pension Funds (Kosei Nenkin Kikin, KNK/EPF). A firm could contract out of the Employee Pension System if the company union consented and certain requirements were fulfilled (e.g. 30 per cent higher benefits than those paid by the EPS). The firm had to hand the income-related part of the EPS over to a life insurance company or trust bank (Estienne 1999: 53–4; Watanabe 1998). That is, firms were not allowed to run these schemes by themselves (for instance in the form of book reserves). This allayed union concerns about the potential misuse of company pensions as a paternalistic device to control and discipline workers, and it also coincided with the Ministry of Finance's (MOF) interest in supporting the domestic life insurance industry and the banking sector. What is more important in the context of our argument is that this stipulation subjected EPF pensions to tight state regulation that secured the pooling of funds, set a uniform revenue rate (5.5 per cent) for the pension funds of all firms (see Estevez-Abe, Chapter 9), and later secured the indexation of entitlements as well, strictly linking the 'private' EPF pensions to the development of the public EPS pensions (Estienne 1999: 94). While the Ministry of Finance mainly pursued a 'developmentalist' strategy in tightly regulating the investment strategies of trust banks and life insurance companies and in channelling pension capital assets into targeted industries, it also helped stabilise the industry-wide standardisation of wages and company-based social benefits. Moreover, the state regulation of the 'private' contracted-out schemes ensured that company welfare became more than a simple fringe benefit, more than voluntary commitments that could be revoked during an economic downturn. While companies could stabilise their workforce by offering more favourable provisions as compared to the public schemes, the state continued to tightly regulate company welfare, to force uniform standards upon the larger part of the industry, and to lend credibility to the private promises of business. The state played the role of a 'direct structurer and overseer of occupationally-linked pensions' (Shinkawa and

Pempel 1997: 170; Estienne 1999: 94). In this context it is important to distinguish between the *public provision* and the *public regulation* of social welfare, the latter often being highlighted as a distinctive feature of the East Asian model of the welfare state (Jacobs 1998; Goodman *et al.* 1998). The common assumption that the private provision of social benefits automatically is proof of the liberal, 'commodifying' character of a welfare state regime (for Japan see e.g. Esping-Andersen 1997: 183) ignores this important difference and substantially underestimates the degree to which 'private' welfare schemes can diverge from a pure market equilibrium. While they seem to resemble US-American welfare capitalism in many ways, Japan's 'private' company pension schemes actually differ quite profoundly, due to the tight state regulation and their character as 'defined benefit' schemes in contrast to 'defined contribution' schemes like, for instance, 401k pensions (Watanabe 1998: 9). Thus, in a detailed assessment of the Japanese pension funds, Jean-Francois Estienne concludes that 'contracting out' in Japan 'hardly resembles the Anglo-Saxon version since the mandatory state regime and the pension funds are organizationally linked and performance related' (Estienne 1999: 94; translation by the author). A closer look at the Japanese 'welfare production regime' (Estevez-Abe *et al.* 1999) reveals that the Japanese welfare state came to underpin business coordination much more than purely voluntary schemes would have been able to do.

Conclusion

In this chapter I have considered the extent to which Peter Swenson's historical account of Swedish and US-American welfare state development can shed light on the situation in other countries. Insofar as future research confirms the findings of this chapter, namely that the German and Japanese post-war experiences provide considerable evidence that welfare and wage regimes in these countries have developed in close correspondence with each other, the academic debate will have to focus on a new set of causal links between capitalist production and social protection. Peter Swenson's work and recent contributions in a similar vein by other scholars (e.g. Isabela Mares, Margarita Estevez-Abe and Cathie Jo Martin) call for a new political-economic view of the welfare state, a perspective that would have to take into account

1 the importance of industrial structure for the position of employers towards public social policy,
2 the impact of (different forms and degrees of) trade openness on employers' interest in business and wage coordination and, consequently, on employers' interest in social spending programmes, and
3 the ability of employers to coordinate within and across industrial sectors and the role that the welfare state plays for the 'regulation of competition' among employers.

Such a new perspective would also require a fresh look at the nexus between economic growth and the growth of social spending (Castles 2000), which could challenge the old claim made in industrialisation theory that the wealth created by economic growth was a precondition for subsequent welfare state expansion. The argument presented here implies an alternative explanation, namely that high growth periods in centralised/coordinated production regimes weakened employers' anti-welfare stance in the social reform debates of the times. Peter Swenson's contribution to the literature on comparative welfare regimes represents both a veritable challenge to what is held as conventional wisdom in this literature and a fruitful scientific programme for future research in this field.

Notes

1 I am grateful to Jim Mosher for fruitful discussions and to Peter Swenson, Michael Wallerstein, Kathy Thelen, Katharina Bluhm, Gary Herrigel and Sue Giaimo for their valuable comments. My thanks go to Dona Geyer and Cynthia Lehmann for their language editing.

2 Given that big firms within a decentralised setting would be forced by their workforce to engage in 'rent sharing' (see Katz and Summers 1989), in particular if union membership correlates positively with firm size. For more on the 'local pushfulness' of decentralised wage bargaining, see Soskice (1990) and Iversen (1999).

3 I will not discuss here at any length the two other explanations with which Giersch *et al.* (1992) try to explain the persistent gap between wages and productivity in the 1950s. 'Economic surprise', which they believe played a role, is largely incompatible with rational expectations, especially if we try to explain persistent differences over a time period of ten years. 'Social responsibility' presumably played a role, yet this explanation clearly overlaps with the one endorsed here, which holds that the IG Metall leadership tried to keep wages internationally competitive, but at the same time sought to increase workers' welfare and to avoid an increase in unemployment.

4 Besides the substantial increase in benefits, the Adenauer reform contained two elements that were quite significant for unions and workers: First, by strictly linking benefits to contributions, the reform put strong premiums on stable career paths, on high incomes and on the early acquisition of skills. It thus came to benefit in particular the core union clientele, the highly qualified core workforce (*Facharbeiter*). Second, by also entitling blue-collar workers to a pension at the age of 60 after a span of unemployment of more than twelve months, the Adenauer reform gave workers the assurance that they would not – under any circumstances – have to go through a longer period of unemployment toward the end of their career.

5 1.8 million were employed in the metalworking sector and 300,000 in the metal-producing industries in 1930 (Wrede 1933: 137).

6 The history of the establishment of German pattern bargaining highlights the importance of the employer's capability to act collectively for the functioning of corporatist labour–capital coordination (Soskice 1990) as compared to the factors usually emphasised in the corporatism literature, such as union centralisation and the monopoly of representation enjoyed by employer associations and union umbrella organisations (Schmitter 1979).

References

Alber, J. (1989). *Der Sozialstaat in der Bundesrepublik 1950–1983*. Frankfurt: Campus.

Albert, G. (1998). *Wettbewerbsfähigkeit und Krise der deutschen Schiffbauindustrie 1945–1990*. Frankfurt: Peter Lang.

Albert, M. (1991). *Capitalisme contre Capitalisme*. Paris: Seuil.

Bankverein (1954). *Wer gehört zu wem?* Frankfurt: Bankverein.

BDA (Bundesverband Deutscher Arbeitgeberverbände) (1956a). *Probleme der Sozialreform. Entwurf.* Cologne: mimeo.

BDA (1956b). *Stellungnahme und Vorschläge der Bundesvereinigung der Deutschen Arbeitgeberverbände zur Rentengestaltung.* Cologne: mimeo.

BDA (1956c). *Niederschrift über die Sitzung des Ausschusses für Sozialversicherung und betriebliche Sozialfürsorge am 30. Juli 1956 in Köln.* Cologne: mimeo.

Blödner, P. (1934). 'Preis- und Produktstabilisierung durch Kartelle. Eine Untersuchung ihrer Problematik am Beispiel der deutschen Großeisenindustrie', Dissertation, Martin Luther University Halle/Saale.

Brown, C., Nakata, Y., Reich, M. and Ulman, L. (1997). *Work and Pay in the United States and Japan.* New York: Oxford University Press.

Castles, F. (2000). 'The dog that didn't bark: Economic development and the postwar welfare state', *European Review* 8(3), 313–32.

Chandler, A. D. Jr (1990). *Scale and Scope. The Dynamics of Industrial Capitalism.* Cambridge, MA: Belknap Press.

Cooper, R. W. (1999). *Coordination Games. Complementarities and Macroeconomics.* New York: Cambridge University Press.

Crouch, C. and Streeck, W. (eds) (1996). *Modern Capitalisms.* London: Sage.

Diegmann, A. (1993). 'American deconcentration policy in the Ruhr coal industry', in J. M. Diefendorf, A. Frohn and H.-J. Rupieper (eds), *American Policy and the Reconstruction of West Germany, 1945–1955.* New York: Cambridge University Press, 197–215.

Djelic, M.-L. (1998). *Exporting the American Model. The Post-war Transformation of European Business.* Oxford: Oxford University Press.

Esping-Andersen, G. (1997). 'Hybrid or unique?: The Japanese welfare state between Europe and America', *Journal of European Social Policy* 7, 179–89.

Estevez-Abe, M. (1996). 'The welfare-growth nexus in the Japanese political economy', Paper for the 22nd Annual APSA Convention, San Francisco, CA.

Estevez-Abe, M., Iversen, T. and Soskice, D. (1999). 'Social protection and the formation of skills: A reinterpretation of the welfare state', Paper for the 95th American Political Science Association Meeting, Atlanta, GA.

Estienne, J.-F. (1999). *Réforme et Avenir des Retraites: Les Enseignements de l'Exemple Japonais.* Paris: La Bibliothèque d'Économie Financière.

Feldman, G. D. (1977). *Iron and Steel in the German Inflation 1916–1923.* Princeton, NJ: Princeton University Press.

Feldman, G. D. and Nocken, U. (1975). 'Trade associations and economic power: A comparison of interest group development in the German iron and steel and machine building industries 1900–1933', *Business History Review* 49, 413–45.

Flanagan, R. J., Soskice, D. W. and Ulman, L. (1983). *Unionism, Economic Stabilization, and Income Policies. European Experience.* Washington, DC: The Brookings Institute.

Garrett, G. (1998). 'Global markets and national politics: Collision course or virtuous circle?', unpublished manuscript, Yale University, New Haven, CT.

Giersch, H., Paqué, K.-H. and Schmieding, H. (1992). *The Fading Miracle. Four Decades of Market Economy in Germany.* New York: Cambridge University Press.

Gillingham, J. (1991). *Coal, Steel and the Rebirth of Europe, 1945–1955. The Germans and French from Ruhr Conflict to Economic Community.* New York: Cambridge University Press.

Goodman, R., White, G. and Kwon, H.-J. (1998). *In Search of an East Asian Welfare State.* London: Routledge.

Gordon, A. (1985). *The Evolution of Labor Relations in Japan. Heavy Industry, 1853–1955.* Cambridge, MA: Harvard University Press.

Gordon, C. (1994). *New Deals: Business, Labor and Politics in America, 1920–1935*. New York: Cambridge University Press.

Hall, P. A. and Franzese, R. J. (1998). 'Mixed signals: Central bank independence, coordinated wage bargaining, and European Monetary Union', *International Organization* 52, 505–35.

Hamada, K. and Kasuya, M. (1993). 'The reconstruction and stabilization of the postwar Japanese economy: Possible lessons for Eastern Europe?', in R. Dornbusch, W. Nölling and R. Layard (eds), *Postwar Economic Reconstruction and Lessons for the East Today*. Cambridge, MA: MIT Press, 155–87.

Herrigel, G. (1996). *Industrial Constructions: The Sources of German Industrial Power*. New York: Cambridge University Press.

Herrigel, G. (2000). 'American occupation, market order, and democracy: Reconfiguring the steel industry in Japan and Germany after the Second World War', in J. Zeitlin and G. Herrigel (eds), *Americanization and Its Limits. Reworking US Technology and Management in Post-war Europe and Japan*. Oxford: Oxford University Press, 340–99.

Hockerts, H. G. (1980). *Sozialpolitische Entscheidungen im Nachkriegsdeutschland. Alliierte und deutsche Sozialversicherungspolitik 1945 bis 1957*. Stuttgart: Klett-Cotta.

Hoffmann, E. (1928). 'Die Organisation der Verbindung der Eisen schaffenden und der Eisen verarbeitenden Industrie', Dissertation, University of Munich.

IG Metall (ed.) (1978). 'Streik der Metaller Schleswig-Holstein 1956/57', Dokumentation, Frankfurt.

Iversen, T. (1998). 'Wage bargaining, hard money and economic performance: Theory and evidence for organized market economies', *British Journal of Political Science* 28, 31–61.

Iversen, T. (1999). Contested Economic Institutions: The Politics of Macroeconomics and Wage Barganing in Advanced Democracies. New York: Cambridge University Press.

Jacobs, D. (1998). 'Social welfare systems in East Asia: A comparative analysis including private welfare', CASE paper CASE/10, Center for Analysis of Social Exclusion, London School of Economics.

Jacoby, S. M. (1999). *Modern Manors: Welfare Capitalism since the New Deal*. Princeton, NJ: Princeton University Press.

Kalbitz, R. (1978). 'Biographie über den Streik der IG Metall in Schleswig-Holstein 1956/57', in IG Metall (ed.), *Streik der Metaller Schleswig-Holstein 1956/57*. Frankfurt: Dokumentation, 181–217.

Kalbitz, R. (1979). *Aussperrung in der Bundesrepublik*. Cologne: EVA.

Katz, L. F. and Summers, L. H. (1989). 'Industry rents: Evidence and implications', *Brookings Papers on Economic Activity*, 209–75.

Koshiro, K. (1983). 'Development of collective bargaining in postwar Japan', Sh. Taishiro (ed.), *Contemporary Industrial Relations in Japan*. Madison, WI: University of Wisconsin Press, 205–58.

Kuckuk, P. (1998). 'Westdeutscher Schiffbau in der Nachkriegszeit. Ein Überblick', in P. Kuckuk (ed.), *Unterweserwerften in der Nachkriegszeit. Von der Stunde Null zum Wirtschaftswunder*. Bremen: Edition Temmen, 11–36.

Leckebusch, G. (1963). *Die Beziehungen der Deutschen Seeschiffswerften zur Eisenindustrie an der Ruhr in der Zeit von 1850 bis 1930*. Schriften zur Rheinisch-Westfälischen Wirtschaftsgeschichte. Cologne: Rheinisch-Westfälisches Wirtschaftsarchiv zu Köln.

Liefmann, R. (1938). *Cartels, Concerns and Trusts*. New York: Dutton.

Manow, P. and Seils, E. (2000). 'The unemployment crisis of the German welfare state', in M. Rhodes and M. Ferrera (eds), *West European Politics*, special issue on 'Restructuring European Welfare States', April 2000, 138–160.

Mares, I. (1996). 'Firms and the welfare state: The emergence of new forms of unemployment', Discussion Paper FS I 96-308. Berlin: Social Science Research Center.

Mares, I. (1997). 'Business (non) coordination and social policy development: The case of early retirement', Paper for the conference 'Varieties of Capitalism', Wissenschaftszentrum Berlin für Sozialforschung, Berlin, 6–8 June, 1997.

Mares, I. (2000). 'Strategic alliances and social policy reform: Unemployment insurance in comparative perspective', *Politics & Society* 28, 223–44.

Markovits, A. S. (1986). *The Politics of the West German Trade Unions. Strategies of Class and Interest Representation in Growth and Crisis*. New York: Cambridge University Press.

Martin, C. J. (2000). *Stuck in Neutral. Business and the Politics of Human Capital Investment Policy*. Princeton, NJ: Princeton University Press.

Michels, R. (1928). *Cartels, Combines and Trusts in Postwar Germany*. New York: Columbia University Press.

Milgrom, P. and Roberts, J. (1990). 'Rationalizability, learning and equilibrium in games with strategic complementarities', *Econometrica* 58, 1255–78.

Milgrom, P. and Roberts, J. (1994). 'Complementarities and systems: Understanding Japanese economic organization', *Estudios Economicos* 9, 3–42.

Moene, K. O. and Wallerstein, M. (1995). 'How social democracy worked: Labor-market institutions', *Politics & Society* 23, 185–211.

Nakatani, I. (1998). 'The economic role of financial corporate grouping', in P. Drysdale and L. Gower (eds), *The Japanese Economy, Part 1, Volume IV: The Nature of the Japanese Firm*. London: Routledge, 176–209.

Nocken, U. (1977). 'Inter-industrial conflicts and alliances as exemplified by the AVI-Agreement', in H. Mommsen, D. Petzina and B. Weisbrod (eds), *Industrielles System und politische Entwicklung in der Weimarer Republik*. Dusseldorf: Droste, 693–704.

Noé, C. (1970). *Gebändigter Klassenkampf. Tarifautonomie in der Bundesrepublik Deutschland. Der Konflikt zwischen Gesamtmetall und IG Metall vom Frühjahr 1963*. Berlin: Duncker & Humblot.

Overy, R. (1996). 'The economy of the Federal Republic since 1949', in K. Larres and P. Panayi (eds), *The Federal Republic of Germany since 1949. Politics, Society and Economy before and after Unification*. London: Longman.

Paqué, K.-H. (1996). 'Unemployment and the crisis of the German model: A long-term interpretation', in H. Giersch (ed.), *Fighting Europe's Unemployment in the 1990s*. New York: Springer, 123–55.

Paqué, K.-H. (1998). 'Zur Zumutbarkeit von Arbeitsplätzen: Bestandsaufnahme und Reformvorschlag', in E. Knappe and N. Berthold (eds), *Ökonomische Theorie der Sozialpolitik*. Heidelberg: Physica, 71–89.

Pempel, T. J. (1998). *Regime Shift. Comparative Dynamics of the Japanese Political Economy*. Ithaca, NY: Cornell University Press.

Pierson, P. (1995). *The Scope and Nature of Business Power: Employers and the American Welfare State, 1900–1935*, unpublished manuscript, Harvard University and Russell Sage Foundation, Cambridge, MA.

Pierson, P. (2000). 'Three Worlds of Welfare Research', *Comparative Political Studies* 33, 791–821.

Pirker, T. (1979). *Die blinde Macht. Die Gewerkschaftsbewegung in Westdeutschland, Teil 2: 1953–1960. Weg und Rolle der Gewerkschaften im neuen Kapitalismus*. Berlin: Olle & Wolter.

Preiss, K. (1933). 'Das System der Ausfuhrrückvergütungen in der deutschen Eisen- und Metallindustrie', Dissertation, University of Kiel.

Rieger, E. and Leibfried, S. (1998). 'Welfare state limits to globalization', *Politics & Society* 26, 363–90.

Rodrik, D. (1997). *Has Globalization Gone Too Far?* Washington, DC: Institute for International Economics.

Ruggie, J. G. (1997). 'Globalization and the embedded liberalism compromise: The end of an era?', MPIfG Working Paper 97/1. Cologne: Max Planck Institute for the Study of Societies.

Schmid, R. (1930). 'Das AVI-Abkommen als Mittel verbandsmäßiger Exportförderung', Dissertation, University of Cologne.

Schmitter, P. C. (1979). 'Still the century of corporatism?', in P. Schmitter and G. Lehmbruch (eds), *Trends towards Corporatist Intermediation*. London: Sage, 7–52.

Schneider, M. (1980). *Aussperrung. Ihr Geschichte und Funktion vom Kaiserreich bis heute*. Cologne: Bund Verlag.

Shinkawa, T. and Pempel, T. J. (1996). 'Occupational welfare and the Japanese experience', in M. Shalev (ed.), *The Privatization of Social Policy? Occupational Welfare and the Welfare State in America, Scandinavia and Japan*. London: Macmillan, 280–326.

Soskice, D. (1990). 'Wage determination: The changing role of institutions in advanced industrialized countries', *Oxford Review of Economic Policy* 6, 36–61.

Soskice, D. (1995). 'Finer varieties of advanced capitalism: Industry versus group-based coordination in Germany and Japan', manuscript, Wissenschaftszentrum Berlin für Sozialforschung, Berlin.

Strath, B. (1994). 'Modes of governance in the shipbuilding industry in Germany, Sweden, and Japan', in J. R. Hollingsworth, P. C. Schmitter and W. Streeck (eds), *Governing Capitalist Economies. Performance and Control of Economic Sectors*. New York: Oxford University Press, 72–96.

Streeck, W. and Yamamura, K. (eds). *The Political and Social Origins of Nationally-Organized Capitalism: Japan and Germany in Comparison* (forthcoming).

Swenson, P. (1991). 'Labor and the limits of the welfare state: The politics of intraclass conflict and cross-class alliances in Sweden and West Germany', *Comparative Politics* 23, 379–99.

Swenson, P. (1997). 'Arranged alliance: Business interests in the New Deal', *Politics & Society* 25, 66–116.

Swenson, P. (1999). 'Varieties of capitalist interests and illusions of labor power: Employers in the making of the Swedish and American welfare states', Paper for the 'Conference on Distribution and Democracy', Yale University, Department of Political Science, 12–14 November, 1999.

Swenson, P. (forthcoming). *Capitalism Against Markets: Employers in the Making of Labour Markets and Welfare States*. New York: Oxford University Press.

Takanashi, A. *et al.* (1996). *Shunto Wage Offensive*. Tokyo: The Japan Institute of Labor.

Tübben, W. (1930). 'Die nationale und internationale Verbandspolitik der Schwerindustrie vor und nach dem Kriege', Dissertation, University of Wurzburg.

Watabane, N. (1998). 'Occupational pension systems in Japan', *Japan Labour Bulletin* 38, 5–14.

Weisbrod, B. (1978). *Schwerindustrie in der Weimarer Republik. Interessenpolitik zwischen Stabilisierung und Krise*. Wuppertal: Peter Hammer.

Weiss, A. (1990). *Efficiency Wages. Models of Unemployment, Layoffs and Wage Dispersion*. Princeton, NJ: Princeton University Press.

Wend, H. B. (2001). *Recovery and Restoration: US Foreign Policy and the Politics of Reconstruction in the West German Ship Building Industry, 1945–1955*. New York: Praeger (forthcoming).

Westney, D. E. (1998). 'The Japanese business system: Key features and prospects for change', in P. Drysdale and L. Gower (eds), *The Japanese Economy, Part 1, Volume IV: The Nature of the Japanese Firm*. London: Routledge, 151–75.

Winkler, H. A. (ed.) (1974). *Organisierter Kapitalismus. Voraussetzungen und Anfänge*. Gottingen: Vandenhoeck & Ruprecht.

Wrede, J. M. (1933). 'Die internationale Verbandspolitik der nordwesteuropäischen Eisenindustrie in ihrer Bedeutung für die deutsche Eisenindustrie', Dissertation, University of Wurzburg.

3 Strategic bargaining and social policy development

Unemployment insurance in France and Germany[1]

Isabela Mares

Introduction

During the first decades of the twentieth century, a majority of European countries introduced national-level policies compensating against the effects of unemployment. However, the institutional features of these policies vary significantly. In some rare instances, governments have attempted to organise unemployment assistance as a means-tested system, in analogy to and as a continuation of pre-existing policies of poor relief; in other cases, they have chosen to subsidise unemployment insurance funds organised by trade unions; finally, a few countries have succeeded in introducing a system of compulsory unemployment insurance that is financed by contributions made by both employers and employees.

How can we explain the variation among these institutional outcomes? In what circumstances do governments choose one set of policies over another? What is the relative significance of unions, employers and the state in the choice of one system and the rejection of alternative solutions? In this chapter, I will address these questions by combining historical research and a game-theoretic analysis that models the strategic bargaining between employers, unions and the state during the policy deliberations about the choice of a system of unemployment assistance. Existing studies have explained the choice of a policy of unemployment compensation as the result negotiations between unions and the state (Rothstein 1992; Esping-Andersen and Korpi 1985) or of pre-existing policy legacies (Weir and Skocpol 1985). This study will build on the insights provided by these analyses and attempt to generalise them, by including an analysis of the role played by employers in these deliberations and by presenting a more formal analysis of the process of bargaining over the different institutional outcomes.

One of the goals of my approach is to contribute to the broad agenda of research advanced by this volume and to explore more systematically the political involvement of employers in the creation of social insurance. During recent years, a number of political economists have emphasised the important role employers play in the creation of corporatist institutions of centralised wage bargaining (Swenson 1991; Fulcher 1991), while other studies have analysed the role played by employers in the development of several social policies (Gordon 1991, 1994; Manow 1997; Mares 1997, 1998; Pierson 1995; Swenson 1991, 1997). Using the example of unemployment insurance, I will explore two related questions pertaining to the significance of employers in the development of the modern welfare state. The first is the question of employers' preferences for different social policy arrangements. When faced with different possible institutional solutions to the risk of unemployment, such as a means-tested policy of social assistance or contributory unemployment insurance, which alternative is preferable to employers and why? How can we explain inter-sectoral conflict among employers during the introduction of a new social policy? The second issue pertains to the influence of employers during the deliberations leading to the introduction of a new social policy. What factors increase the political influence of employers, allowing them to channel the policy-making process towards outcomes that are closer to their ideal policy point? What are the conditions leading to a *strategic* move by employers and to their support of their 'second-best' choice? By relying on game-theoretic analysis, I attempt to provide a more rigorous characterisation of the conditions that facilitate a strategic compromise between unions and employers and explore the social policy implications of various strategic cross-class alliances.

The remaining part of this chapter is organised as follows. The next section presents a brief overview of the different institutional alternatives addressing the risk of unemployment that were developed during the interwar period. I will then discuss the political experience of two European countries, France and Germany. While French policy makers succeeded in introducing a Ghent system of unemployment insurance as early as 1905, Germany did not establish contributory unemployment insurance until 1927. To explain these divergent social policy outcomes, I develop a game-theoretic analysis that models the choice of a social policy as a result of the strategic bargaining between unions, employers and the state. The last section summarises the implications of the model.

Institutional responses to the risk of unemployment: an overview

A recent wave of scholarship investigating the development of the idea of unemployment has analysed the radical transformation of collective representations that took place at the turn of the twentieth century in the majority of industrialising societies, concluding that the notion of unemployment underpinning the classificatory and redistributive practices of contemporary social policy institutions is a category of relatively recent origin (Salais *et al.* 1986; Piore 1987; Topalov 1994). In contrast to prior beliefs and practices that viewed unemployment as an individual risk resulting from idleness or unwillingness to work or from the moral shortcomings of the individual worker, the modern notion of unemployment stresses the social factors that determine this risk and the fact that unemployment is a natural, albeit regrettable, by-product of the particular way in which work is organised within modern enterprises. Broad changes in the organisation of work and, in particular, the emergence of stable employment relationships, the transformation of private and public institutions of poor relief, the dissolution of older forms of solidarity and the expropriation of independent producers contributed to this break and discontinuity in ideas and to the 'invention' of modern unemployment (Piore 1987).

However, as Christian Topalov has argued, 'the invention of unemployment did not necessarily imply the creation of the unemployed'[2] (Topalov 1994: 407). The latter – a recipient of unemployment compensation – should be distinguished from a person who happens to be 'out of work' and from the 'able-bodied pauper'. Topalov argues that the modern 'unemployed' is the product and outcome of a new set of policies and social practices that were institutionalised by the majority of governments during the first few decades of the twentieth century. As Table 3.1 shows, prior to the Second World War, all Western European societies had introduced one form of unemployment compensation. The frequent change of system in many countries and the intense experimentation with new policies suggests, however, that most of these institutions were the object of considerable political controversy. Germany, for instance, introduced a Ghent system on a limited scale prior to the First World War (Henning 1974), replacing it with a means-tested system of unemployment assistance in 1918, which, in turn, was replaced by contributory unemployment insurance in 1927. In 1905, France became the first country to establish a Ghent system of

Table 3.1 Legislation compensating the effects of unemployment in European countries

Country	*Ghent legislation*	*Contributory insurance*	*Unemployment assistance*
Austria		1920	1918, 1922, 1926
Belgium	1907, 1920	1944	
Denmark	1907		1921
Germany		1927	1918
Finland	1917		1960
France	1905	1967	1914, 1951
Ireland		1923	1933
Italy		1919	1917, 1946
Netherlands	1916	1949	1964
Norway	1906	1938	
Sweden	1934		1916, 1973
Switzerland	1924	1976	1917, 1924, 1942
United Kingdom		1911	1934

Source: Alber (1982: 171).

unemployment assistance at the national level. A means-tested system was temporarily introduced in 1914. Plans to introduce contributory unemployment insurance as part of the general social insurance legislation were defeated in 1928.

Two broad policy issues pertaining to the organisation of a system of unemployment compensation were the object of intense political debate between the social actors and the state. The first issue was the distribution of the costs of the new social program among unions, employers and the state. The second issue was control over the ability and willingness to work of the unemployed. The different systems of unemployment compensation institutionalised different compromises to these two problems. In the means-tested system of unemployment assistance, unemployment benefits were financed out of general taxation, yet decisions about the eligibility of the unemployed to receive unemployment benefits remained in the hands of bureaucrats and local government officials. This solution to the monitoring problem made the system vulnerable to multiple and contradictory complaints from unions and employers, who resented their lack of control over these decisions. The state, on the other hand, faced strong fiscal pressures to shift some of the costs to workers and firms. A brief cross-national comparison indicates that means-tested unemployment assistance was, in general, a very unstable solution, that was, in most countries, replaced either by a Ghent system or by contributory unemployment insurance. The Ghent system of unemployment assistance (named after the Belgian town where it originated) pioneered a system of financing unemployment benefits based on union unemployment funds, which were complemented by a subsidy from the state. In the Ghent system, unions continued to monitor the willingness of work of the unemployed. This outcome was desirable for state bureaucrats. It relieved them of the difficult task of withdrawing the means of subsistence from those who were no longer eligible for unemployment benefits. From the perspective of employers, this was a highly problematic institutional characteristic of the system. Employers feared both that this system might lead to an increase in the bargaining power of unions and that excessive generosity on the part of the unions in the distribution of unemployment benefits might undermine the minimum wage. Finally, contributory unemployment insurance was financed by contributions paid by workers and firms. Either labor exchanges or a commission in which employers and employees were represented monitored the willingness to work of the unemployed.

A brief look at the unemployment legislation introduced by European countries in the interwar period reveals several interesting patterns. The dominant outcomes are the Ghent system and contributory unemployment insurance, while the means-tested system appears to be a transitional solution which either coexists with a Ghent system or contributory insurance legislation or is replaced, at a later point in time, by one of the dominant solutions. Second, we observe that a Ghent system was introduced as national legislation compensating for the effects of unemployment in a first wave of reform prior to and during the First World War (in France, Belgium, Denmark, Norway, the Netherlands and

Finland) and that it remained a viable policy alternative during the period up to the Second World War (with Sweden and Switzerland introducing it during the early 1930s). Contributory insurance legislation emerged later and was preferred by countries who introduced unemployment legislation after the First World War (with Britain remaining an interesting exception). All the countries that did not introduce unemployment legislation for the first time until after the Second World War chose contributory unemployment insurance. An explanation of the choice of a system of unemployment compensation will have to (a) account for the predominance of the Ghent system and contributory insurance as policy outcomes; and (b) the transition between the different systems within the same country and (c) the different coalitional arrangements underlying these various institutional arrangements.

Comparative responses to the problem of unemployment: the French and German experience

The introduction of a Ghent system in France

The preoccupation of French policy makers with the question of institutional solutions to the risk of unemployment goes back to the second half of the nineteenth century (Journal Officiel 1879, 1884a,b). Nevertheless, a more sustained political effort that culminated in the introduction of a national system of unemployment assistance did not develop until the turn of the twentieth century. In 1895, the Labour Office (*Office du Travail*) initiated a series of inquiries about the possible institutional solutions to the problem of unemployment, devoting significant resources to the study of policy experiences in other countries and to the assessment of the depth of societal forms of support in case of unemployment (Office du Travail 1896). The permanent Commission of the Labour Office supported public intervention in the case of unemployment. Its goal was to standardise and generalise the isolated efforts of local governments, unions and the mutualities (mutual benefit insurance schemes) (Office du Travail 1896: 5–10).

The familiarity of policy makers with pre-existing societal institutions of support in the case of unemployment remained, however, limited. A survey conducted by the Labour Office exemplifies this incomplete knowledge of policy makers. Out of 2,178 unions that existed in France in July 1894, 487 proclaimed as one of their fundamental goals the support of their members in the event that they should become unemployed (Office du Travail 1896: 45–77). This remained, however, merely a proclamation of first principles, but did not necessarily reflect union practices. Out of the 246 unions that responded to a second survey initiated by the Labour Office, 159 unions had abandoned this initial goal, while eighty-seven unions continued to offer some form of unemployment assistance. Only one national federation, the Federation of Workers in the

Printing Industry (*Fédération des travailleurs du livre*), comprising 147 local unions (and 7,000 members), offered unemployment assistance.

The inconclusiveness of these statistical findings brought bureaucratic reformist efforts to a temporary stop in 1895 (Office du Travail 1897: 30). Being unable to formulate a clear policy recommendation, the Permanent Commission of the Labour Office called for a further study of this problem. However, the question of an institutional solution to the problem of unemployment resurfaced again, this time in the parliamentary arena. Alexandre Millerand, an important radical politician and, later, republican socialist, brought high political visibility to the question of unemployment and helped forge a public consensus around the necessity of public intervention (Topalov 1985). As Minister of Commerce in the cabinet of Waldeck-Rousseau, Millerand introduced a first draft bill of unemployment insurance legislation in 1902 and brought back to the political agenda of the Labour Office the question of reform of unemployment assistance.

In order to understand the political circumstances under which policy entrepreneurs were able to overcome the opposition of employers to a Ghent system of unemployment assistance, we need to turn to these debates that were held within the *Conseil Superieur du Travail* (Office du Travail 1903; Ministère du Commerce 1903). This institution, comprising representatives of unions, chambers of commerce and political parties, intended to act as a 'genuine economic parliament'.[3] A consensus concerning a Ghent system of unemployment assistance emerged only gradually, during a number of critical meetings in 1903. The analysis of these deliberations suggests that reform-minded policy entrepreneurs imposed a Ghent outcome on reluctant employers and union representatives.

Employers came to the policy deliberations of the *Conseil Supérieur du Travail* extolling the advantages of a private system of unemployment insurance, free of public intervention. They frequently invoked the traditional liberal values of self-reliance and individual savings as well as the virtues of the British experience, where support for the unemployed remained within the domain of voluntary associations (Ministère du Commerce 1903: 6; Fagnot 1905: 111). However, a large number of employers were ready to accept that unemployment was caused not only by 'the fault of the individual employee, but also [by] the fact that industrial production is still badly regulated' (Fagnot 1905: 112). If this was the case, employers concurred that 'it remained the duty of society as a whole to support the unemployed, in a way that safeguards their independence and dignity' (Fagnot 1905: 112). While the principle of public intervention became accepted by employers early on during the deliberations, their major concern remained the desire to limit the scope of this intervention (Fagnot 1905: 110–11). Additional circumstances, such as the recent electoral victory of leftist forces, grouped within the *Bloc des Gauches*, also help to explain the defensive attitude shown by employers throughout these policy deliberations. As Christian Topalov characterised this position of employers: 'While employers did not abandon their principles and made every effort to limit the reform, they did tacitly accept the final compromise' (Topalov 1985).

In contrast to the demands of employers, the demands of trade unions were imbued with policy radicalism. Some trade-union representatives fought for compulsory unemployment insurance to be extended to 'all human beings, with no exception' (Fagnot 1905: 122). Influential legal experts who participated in these meetings supported this view, arguing that the 'insurance will be compulsory or it will not exist' (Fagnot 1905: 122). The policy demands of unions were a unique mixture of a contributory form of insurance and a Ghent system that attempted to preserve institutional features of both systems. On the one hand, the system had to be financed by contributions from employees, employers and the state (similar to any other contributory insurance); on the other hand, unions demanded total control over the administration and distribution of unemployment benefits (a feature of the Ghent system; Ministère du Commerce 1903: 22). Any intermediate solutions that were not compulsory and that did not require any financial sacrifice from employers were viewed by unions as a provisional, transitional experiment, a 'palliative' (Fagnot 1905: 122–4).

For union representatives within the *Conseil Supérieur du Travail*, only the interaction between union control and compulsory insurance could ensure an increase in union membership (Fagnot 1905: 122). While compulsory insurance without union control over the distribution of unemployment benefits could bring about a very severe blow to unions (weakening any incentives for potential members to join unions), the juxtaposition of these two institutional characteristics of the system of unemployment insurance could, in a distant future, lead to *compulsory* union membership. For employers, the most threatening aspect of unions' plan has this vision of a fully unionised workforce, this 'pansyndicalisme' that was at the heart of the union project (Topalov 1985).

Other objections raised by employers to unions' proposals of a compulsory unemployment insurance solution centred around the potential costs of such a policy (Ministère du Commerce 1903: 26; Fagnot 1905: 123). These new social charges were both extremely unpredictable *and* potentially much higher than the contributions paid by employers to the existing accident insurance scheme (Fagnot 1905: 123; Ministère du Commerce 1903: 26). The higher costs were viewed by employers as the result of a pervasive impossibility to distinguish between real and simulated unemployment and to establish the true 'degree of unemployment' (Fagnot 1905: 123). Even reformist bureaucrats of the Labour Office shared employers' worries about the unpredictable financial costs entailed by this solution, invoking the example of the failure of a contributory form of insurance in the Swiss city of Saint Gall (Ministère du Commerce 1903: 26–8).

These arguments against contributory unemployment insurance formulated by cautious bureaucrats, the state and employers anticipated later debates that preceded the introduction of social insurance legislation in France. In 1928, the opposition of employers together with financial worries on the part of the state buried the legislative proposal to insure against the risk of unemployment

(Héreil 1932; Malivoire de Camas 1933; Mossé 1929). In 1903, as François Fagnot, a participant in these debates, recalled: 'Faced with the strong opposition of employers who were searching for a practical result, "something tangible", the workers finally abandoned their propositions favouring compulsory insurance' (Fagnot 1905: 127). Having compromised on the principle of public intervention, employers demanded a compromise of the same magnitude from unions. As an employer representing the cotton industry put it in the demands he made of the unions: 'If you would like to reach an agreement – and I am certainly ready to make a step in this direction – do not ask us to vote on first principles. If you demand a manifestation of our principles, we will be intransigent. We will be unable to commit ourselves to any specific obligations and to accept direct participation of the state' (Fagnot 1905: 124).

The third type of solution considered during these deliberations was the generalisation of the system introduced in the Belgian city of Ghent (Ministère du Commerce 1903: 23). Reformist political entrepreneurs, rather than union officials, were the actors championing this policy solution (Ministère du Commerce 1903: 23). The first and most immediate advantage of a Ghent system remained the fact that it relied 'on what already existed, furthering its development' (Ministère du Commerce 1903: 29). The second advantage was the fact that a Ghent system delegated to these associations an important role in controlling the willingness and ability to work of the unemployed, solving the most difficult policy problem of a system of unemployment assistance – the problem of control – 'in the most efficient way' (Fagnot 1905: 130).

At first, a policy consensus was reached to extend public subsidies (paid by the municipalities) to local associations distributing unemployment benefits (Office du Travail 1903: 987). However, a wide disagreement emerged on the question of the kind of associations that could receive these subsidies. To limit the influence of unions, employers demanded the extension of these subsidies to *any* association offering some form of assistance in the case of unemployment, not only to the union unemployment funds (Fagnot 1905: 131). The employers prevailed on this point. Philanthropic organisations, the *mutualités* and even unemployment funds organised by a local chamber of commerce became eligible for the subsidies paid by the municipalities. The most controversial issue during these deliberations, however, was whether associations offering unemployment benefits which were organised at the national level could also be eligible for these subsidies. After all, this was the point where France could depart from the Belgian model and transform the Ghent system from a local into a national policy.

Employers objected to the extension of these subsidies to union federations that offered unemployment benefits to their members (such as the Federation of Workers in the Printing Industry), fearing the increase in union organisation and membership that could result from this measure (Fagnot 1905: 140). They portrayed themselves as having gone far enough in accepting the principle of public intervention. According to employers, policies compensating for the effects of unemployment had to be developed at the local level: The Ghent system had to remain 'a communal system applied to local associations' (Fagnot 1905: 138).

Advocates of unemployment subsidies for the union federations (coming primarily from the ranks of unions and from the labour exchanges, the *Bourses du Travail*) argued that the goal of any system of unemployment insurance remained the job placement of the unemployed. From this perspective, union federations had greater resources to support the movement of workers from regions with high to regions with low unemployment and a better understanding of the conditions prevailing on the labour market (Ministère du Commerce 1905: 33–5; Fagnot 1905: 135–9). The abstention of the employers during this vote led to a narrow victory by the unions and social reformers.

These recommendations made by the *Conseil Supérieur du Travail* moved with great speed through the parliamentary arena, facilitated in part by the fact that Alexandre Millerand, the initiator of the policy effort, was now president of the Commission of Social Insurance (*Commission d'Assurance et de Prévoyance Sociale)* of the Chamber of Deputies (Office du Travail 1903: 985; Journal Officiel 1904b). It was Millerand who pleaded for the introduction of this policy before the Chamber (Journal Officiel 1904a). Encountering no opposition from the right-wing deputies, the unemployment insurance law was introduced as a supplementary measure in the budget of 1905 (Journal Officiel 1905a: 2577; 1905b: 5510–12). This law of 1905 remained the basis of the French system of unemployment assistance until the Second World War. A system of poor relief was temporarily introduced at the onset of the First World War and dismantled in 1918. After the political defeat of plans to introduce unemployment insurance as part of the *Assurances Sociales* of 1928, the Ghent system remained the only institutional arrangement that weathered the period of high unemployment in the 1930s.

Germany: the transition from unemployment assistance to unemployment insurance

In the case of policies compensating for the risk of unemployment, France pioneered welfare state developments, while Germany, surprisingly, remained the welfare state laggard. It was not until 1927 that a national-level policy became institutionalised. In contrast to the choice of a Ghent system by French policy makers, the policy deliberations in Germany culminated in the introduction of a system of unemployment insurance (Faust 1986; Führer 1992; Lewek 1992). Until 1927, Germany experimented with a system of unemployment assistance, the *Erwerbslosenfürsorge.* The effects of the Great Depression together with the general dissatisfaction with these policies – expressed by unions, employers and policy makers – facilitated the formation of a fragile consensus concerning the insurance solution in 1927. Given the failure of the existing system of unemployment assistance, the insurance solution became the preferred policy alternative both for unions and employers of large firms.

The Bismarckian social insurance legislation did not insure workers against the risk of unemployment. The absence of a national system of labour placement (due, among other things, to Germany's federalised state structure) and the strong and embittered opposition of employers directed against any policy compensating for the effects of unemployment were factors that blocked the efforts of policy makers to introduce policies of unemployment compensation during the period prior to the First World War (Faust 1986; Wermel and Urban 1949). The massive social dislocations caused by the conscription efforts of 1914 revealed the inadequacy of the labour market policies of the Wilhelminian era. A means-tested system of unemployment assistance – the *Kriegserwerbslosenfürsorge* – was introduced in 1914 and, due to the widespread fear of a social revolution, reorganised in 1918 (Wermel and Urban 1949; Lewek 1992: 37).

The policy introduced in 1918, the *Erwerbslosenfürsorge*, remained a highly improvised solution. This policy of unemployment assistance was financed out of general taxation – by the *Reich* (the central government), the *Länder* (the federal states) and the *Kommunen* (the local governments) – while the local governments remained responsible for the distribution of unemployment benefits. The benefits were means-tested. Local authorities were given wide discretionary powers to determine the need of the unemployed and to monitor the willingness of the unemployed to accept a job. The *Erwerbslosenfürsorge* was intended as a provisional solution that should not be in force for more than one year. However, the lengthy policy deliberations about a system that could replace it extended the life of this policy for nine years.

German trade unions (such as the ADGB)[4] deplored the means-tested nature of the unemployment benefits under the *Erwerbslosenfürsorge*, which opened up room for widespread discrimination in the day-to-day implementation of the system of unemployment assistance (Potthoff 1979: 194; ADGB 1921: 745). In order to remedy this situation, they proposed to increase union participation in the distribution of unemployment benefits. After 1918, a Ghent system was only a remote theoretical alternative, as the majority of the trade unions had abandoned their earlier demands for the introduction of a Ghent solution (ADGB 1920: 250; Potthoff 1979: 194). The desired policy alternative was now a system of contributory insurance, administered jointly (*paritätisch*) by unions and employers and financed by contributions of employers and unions and a subsidy of the state. According to the ADGB, contributions paid by employers to the unemployment insurance created a strong disincentive for them to lay off workers and were likely to increase their concern for job-creation measures (ADGB 1921: 746; Führer 1992: 195).

Contributory unemployment insurance gradually became the preferred policy alternative for employers in large firms as well. Throughout the Wilhelminian period, employers had dismissed all forms of compensation for the effects of unemployment as 'premiums for laziness' (Der Arbeitgeber 1914: 18). The introduction of the means-tested policy of unemployment assistance led them, however, to re-evaluate their position of undifferentiated opposition and to formulate more nuanced policy recommendations. A Ghent system was strongly resented and viewed as a way of subsidising union strike funds (Henning 1974; Der Arbeitgeber 1910; VDA 1927: 158–9). However, surprisingly, a means-tested system was less desirable for large firms than a contributory insurance solution, despite the potentially higher costs of an insurance solution.[5] Their dissatisfaction with the means-tested system of unemployment compensation resulted from the absence of employers' control over monitoring unemployed persons' willingness to work, over the definition of jobs the unemployed had to accept (*zumutbare Arbeit*), and over the relationship between unemployment benefits and the regional wage. Since all these policy decisions were in the hands of the local governments, one of the major motivations for this change in employers' preference was the desire to regain control over significant policy decisions.

The second cause of employers' dissatisfaction with the means-tested unemployment assistance was the flat-rate nature of unemployment benefits. According to employers who relied on skilled workers, unemployment benefits that were not tied to the workers' pre-existing skills and wages had two undesirable effects: they raised the relative income of low-skilled workers during periods of unemployment, but reduced the income of unemployed high-skilled workers, increasing the pressure on the latter to accept lower paying paid jobs that did not necessarily correspond to their skills and wage qualifications. Periods of unemployment could thus undermine the carefully elaborated wage hierarchies, the distinctions based on skills and the investment of employers in the skills of their employees. Large employers argued strongly for an insurance solution that linked benefits to the previous wages of the unemployed (VDA 1927: 164–5).

While large firms began to support contributory unemployment insurance as early as 1921 (VDA 1920), small firms never abandoned their opposition to the insurance solution to the risk of unemployment. The main political forum representing small firms, the Association of German Chambers of Industry and Commerce (*Deutscher Industrie- und Handelstag*, DIHT), loudly objected to the 'intolerably high social costs' that might result from the imposition of another contributory social insurance during a period when many small firms were already being forced out of business. Deliberations within individual chambers of commerce reflect a similar desire to keep the costs of social insurance low, although sometimes the preferred social policy outcome was different (some chambers of commerce expressed their support for a tax-financed, universalistic social policy; Handwerkskammer Kassel 1921). Small firms also opposed the introduction of a differentiated system of unemployment benefits based on wage categories – an outcome that was very much favoured by large firms – viewing it as another source of increase of their labour costs (DIHT 1920, 1926).

While the previous analysis has focused on a number of pre-strategic considerations that led to the endorsement of a contributory insurance solution by the Federation of German Employers (*Vereinigung der Deutschen Arbeitgeberverbände*), it is important as well to emphasise here that strategic considerations remained important. After 1918, the commitment of the state to *some* form of compensation for the effects of unemployment was very strong and stood in radical contrast to the policy immobilism of the earlier period. Employers' prior intransigence and veto of any form of unemployment compensation gave way to an attitude of cooperation with bureaucratic elites in the definition and articulation of the new institutions of unemployment insurance. Starting with 1922, we find employers in large firms cooperating with bureaucrats at the Employment Office of the German Reich (*Reichsarbeitsamt*) on all important questions pertaining to the future organisation of unemployment insurance. Among these, the most important policy decisions concerned the appropriate way to organise the risk pool within unemployment insurance.

Due to the persistence of wide regional and occupational differences in the level of unemployment, an important dilemma concerned the degree of redistribution of these differences within the insurance solution. With regard to the first issue – the question of how to organise the risk pool in order to counteract the wide regional disparities in the distribution of unemployment – employers preferred a wide administrative decentralisation that allowed a very low redistribution of these risks between regions with high and low unemployment (VDA 1927: 154–7). In contrast to employers, unions demanded a 'total equalisation of the risks' (*völliger Gefahrenausgleich*) between regions with different levels of unemployment (Gewerkschaftszeitung 1924: 342–3). During the policy deliberations, employers prevailed on this point (Führer 1992: 314). The final unemployment insurance bill institutionalised a three-tiered system that determined the level of insurance contributions, allowing for the possibility of regional differentiation in the level of insurance contributions.

The question of the redistribution of the occupational differences in the level of unemployment was solved by the creation of a single occupational risk pool. Throughout the policy deliberations, socialist trade unions, such as the ADGB, had supported the idea of a unitary risk pool and of unitary contributions across all occupations that should not depend on the level of unemployment in a particular industry (ADGB 1922: 520; Lindemann 1924; Spliedt 1924). Employers in industries exposed to high and unpredictable fluctuations in the level of unemployment (such as chemicals, electrical engineering and machine tools) supported the same institutional solution of a unitary risk pool, which had the advantage of spreading the risk across a large number of industries and of keeping the unemployment insurance contributions low (VDA 1920, 1924). During these political struggles, employers in large domestic firms, such as iron and steel companies, who had opposed the plans for equal unemployment insurance contributions paid by all industries, were defeated.

This brief overview of the policy-making process that culminated in the introduction of contributory unemployment insurance suggests that the different policies of unemployment insurance were supported by different political coalitions. While a Ghent system was introduced by reformist elites (against the opposition of employers and trade unions), a contributory insurance solution was based on a strategic alliance between large firms and trade unions. In the following section, I will develop a game-theoretic analysis that captures the different coalitional dynamics that preceded the introduction of a system of unemployment insurance.

A game-theoretic model for the choice of a system of unemployment compensation during the interwar period

The choice of a system of unemployment compensation will be modelled as the result of bargaining between employers in large firms (L), small producers (S), unions (U) and the government (G). The previous analysis indicates the presence of four possible outcomes to these strategic bargains. The first outcome, that of no provision for the unemployed or no attempts at the national level to institutionalise a particular system, will be denoted as 'None'. The second outcome – a means-tested system of unemployment assistance – will be referred to as 'Assistance'. The third alternative is the Ghent system of unemployment assistance ('Ghent'). Finally, unemployment compensation can be organised as a contributory insurance system ('Contributory'), which is financed by payroll taxes paid by unions and employers.

There are two stages in this game. In a first stage, large firms, small firms and unions (in this particular order) choose a move. The second stage attempts to model the response of the state to these moves. I will assume that the state observes the moves of the first three players and imposes the outcome of the game. This gives the state a privileged role. However, I will place one restriction on the state's choices: if two players form an alliance in support of a certain form of unemployment compensation in the first stage of the game, then the state will not intervene, but will choose the outcome favoured by the two players. This corresponds to the idea that it is generally too costly for states to veto the decision of a cross-class alliance or of a joint alliance between large and small firms. However, there will be an exception to this rule if, in the first part of the game, large and small firms form an alliance in support of 'no compensation at all' ('None'). Due to its interest in the introduction of a system of unemployment assistance, the government *might* in this case decide to ignore the preferences of the firms, despite the high costs produced by the structural veto of firms. If the first part of the game produces no alliance, the choice of the state will be considered to be unrestricted. This assumption incorporates two significant ideas developed by scholars on the welfare state. The first is that the state has partial autonomy from the social actors and that, in particular historical circumstances, social policy developments are the result of bureaucratic autonomy (Heclo 1974). This assumption also reflects important findings in the corporatist literature about the mediating capabilities of states where there are strong differences between the preferences of labour and capital.

Given the divergence in the preferences towards a policy of unemployment assistance among large producers and small firms – which are a consequence of wide differences in the production needs of their firms – large firms and small producers will be analysed separately from small producers. I will make the following assumptions about the preferences of large firms. A Ghent system is the least preferred outcome because it would increase the organisational resources and bargaining power of unions, but also because it would give employers no control over the definition of the conditions of re-employment or willingness to work of the unemployed, in short over the disciplinary functions of the system of unemployment compensation. Similar considerations apply to employers' preferences towards a means-tested system of unemployment assistance, which is ranked by large firms lower than a contributory insurance solution. Among the possible institutional solutions to the risk of unemployment, a contributory system of unemployment insurance is the preferred outcome for large firms. In exchange for contributions to social insurance, large firms gain both control over the definition of the conditions of re-employment and – by participating in the institutions distributing unemployment compensation – over the level of unemployment benefits. In addition, in a contributory system, unemployment benefits are often linked to the previous wages of the unemployed. For high-skilled workers, this provides an indirect guarantee that their skills will not be undermined during spells of unemployment. However, one of the major implications of the analysis presented in this chapter will be to show that strategically (i.e. in the presence of the other players), large firms might prefer to play 'Contributory'.

For small firms, I will make the following assumptions. Since the need to provide institutional guarantees for their skilled workers during periods of unemployment is lower than in large firms and because cost constraints are greater than in large firms, small firms rank contributory unemployment insurance lowest. They show no preference between a Ghent system and a means-tested system because, in contrast to large firms, their employees are often not unionised and they are thus less worried about the potential increase in worker militancy. Unambiguously, their preferred outcome is no system of unemployment compensation.

Unions oppose both 'None' and a means-tested system of unemployment assistance, which is viewed as stigmatising and discriminating. However, in accordance with the historical analysis presented in the previous two sections, I will make the counter-intuitive assumption that unions prefer a contributory insurance solution to a Ghent system. Although a Ghent system may seem to bolster the organisational and financial capabilities of unions and have a significant impact on union membership, a Ghent system has a significant disadvantage. Unions are in the delicate and unpopular position of administering unemployment benefits, which often amounts to withdrawing them, even from union members. Under a system of contributory unemployment insurance, on the other hand, benefits become a certain right, acquired through contributions to social insurance. In the appendix, I will present the solution to the unemployment compensation game under the assumption that unions prefer a Ghent system to contributory unemployment insurance.

I will assume that 'None' is the least preferred outcome for the government. This assumption incorporates the findings of the recent literature on the development of the modern unemployment insurance (Topalov 1985). During this period, state elites viewed unemployment as an insurable risk that necessitated one form or another of social intervention. The extension of suffrage to the working classes in the majority of these countries and the development of mass politics increased the pressures on state elites to develop an institutional solution to the risk of unemployment. A means-tested system was ranked by state elites as the least preferred solution among the possible institutional alternatives, given the strong fiscal problems associated with financing this system and given the increasing (political) unpopularity of the policies of *control* of the unemployed. I will assume that the state prefers to shift the burden of financing the system to firms and unions (under a contributory system) or (in part) to the unions (under a Ghent system) and that it also attempts to delegate the responsibility of monitoring the unemployed's willingness to work.

Given the relative advantages and disadvantages of both 'Ghent' and 'Contributory' – and given that there is no a priori reason to assume that the government will prefer one system to another – the preferences of the state for 'Ghent' and 'Contributory' will be modelled as incomplete information for the other players. I will assume that the state will play 'Ghent' with a probability q and 'Contributory' with a probability $1-q$. Table 3.2 summarises each of the preference orderings described above.

I will now analyse the outcome of the game by backwards induction. Figure 3.1 presents the extended form of the game.

Some comments about the extended-form representation of the game are now in order. For each of the players L, S and U, I have eliminated the worst move according to their preference ranking because this move is never optimal for any of them: L, S and U can only influence the outcome of the game if at least two of them make the same move (as explained before, in the case of pair-wise disagreement, it is the state which dictates the result of the game). It is therefore irrational for them to try to create an alliance based on their worst choice. Furthermore, when discussing the move of the state, we have to take into account the restriction mentioned above in situations in which two of the players form an alliance in favour of an outcome. If at least two of the players L, S and U choose 'Ghent', 'Contributory' or 'Assistance', then the state will accept their choice. If there is no alliance, the state chooses 'Ghent' or 'Contributory' (with probabilities q and $1-q$, respectively). If both large and small firms play 'None', then the state accepts this outcome with a probability $1-p$ and intervenes with a probability p – which means that it will impose a Ghent system with a probability pq and a contributory form of insurance with a probability $p(1-q)$.

To continue backwards induction, we have to find the optimal move of the unions, given the moves of L and S. The analysis is straightforward, and I will

Table 3.2 Summary of preference ordering

Player	*Ordering of preferences*
Large firms	None > Contributory > Assistance > Ghent
Small firms	None > (Assistance, Ghent) > Contributory
Unions	Contributory > Ghent > Assistance > None
Government	(Ghent, Contributory) > Assistance > None

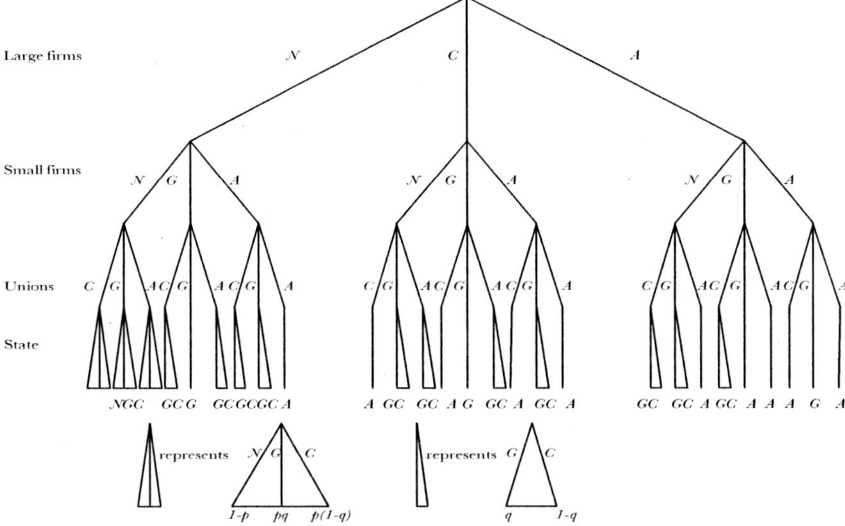

Figure 3.1 Extended form of the unemployment compensation game.

Notes
N: None; *C*: Contributory; *G*: Ghent; *A*: Assistance.

Table 3.3 The moves of unions

Player	*Moves*								
L	*N*	*N*	*N*	*C*	*C*	*C*	*A*	*A*	*A*
S	*N*	*G*	*A*	*N*	*G*	*A*	*N*	*G*	*A*
U	*GCA*	*AC*	*CG*	*C*	*C*	*C*	*GC*	*C*	*GCA*
Outcome	*NGC*	*G/C*	*G/C*	*C*	*C*	*C*	*G/C*	*G/C*	*A*

Notes
L: Large firms; *S*: Small producers; *U*: Unions; *N*: None; *G*: Ghent; *C*: contributory; *A*: Assistance.

only illustrate it by means of a few examples. The complete results are given in Table 3.3.

1 Both *L* and *S* play 'None'. As seen before, the outcome in this case is independent of the unions' decision to play 'Contributory', 'Ghent' or 'Assistance'.
2 *L* plays 'Contributory'. In this case, no matter what *S* does, *U* plays 'Contributory' (its preferred outcome), because its alliance with *L* is sufficient to guarantee that the outcome will be 'Contributory'.
3 *L* plays 'None', and *S* plays 'Ghent'. If *U* plays 'Ghent', then the state imposes 'Ghent' (due to the alliance between *S* and *U*). If *U* plays

'Assistance' or 'Contributory', there is no alliance, so that the outcome is 'Ghent'/'Contributory' (with probabilities q and $1-q$, respectively). Since U prefers 'Contributory' to 'Ghent', the optimal moves are 'Assistance' and 'Contributory'. If (L, S) play ('None', 'Assistance'), ('Assistance', 'None') or ('Assistance', 'Ghent'), the outcome is similar.

4 Both L and S play 'Assistance'. Their alliance forces the state to accept 'Assistance' as the outcome, no matter what U chooses. However, we will later see that it is not optimal for L to play 'Assistance', so this outcome is not in fact an equilibrium of the game.

We can now analyse the optimal moves of the small firms after the large firms have moved. The analysis is summarised in Table 3.4.

1 L plays 'None'. If S plays 'None', the outcome is 'None'/'Ghent'/ 'Contributory' (with probabilities $1-p$, pq, $p(1-q)$, respectively), whereas if S plays 'Ghent' or 'Assistance', the outcome is 'Ghent'/'Contributory' (with probabilities q and $1-q$, respectively). Denoting the utilities of the outcomes 'None', 'Ghent', and 'Contributory' for the player S as N_S, G_S and C_S, we need to compare the expected payoffs which are

$$(1-p)N_S+pqG_S+p(1-q)C_S$$

for 'None'/'Ghent'/ 'Contributory' and

$$qG_S+(1-q)C_S$$

for 'Ghent'/'Contributory'.
Since $N_S>G_S>C_S$, it is easy to see that

$$(1-p)N_S+pqG_S+p(1-q)C_S>qG_S+(1-q)C_S,$$

which proves that the best move for small firms is 'None'.

2 L plays 'Contributory'. As explained in the previous step, U will form an alliance with L, no matter what S does, hence the entry 'None'/ 'Ghent'/'Assistance' in Table 3.4.

3 L plays 'Assistance'. In this case, S can either form an alliance with L (with the outcome 'Assistance') or play 'None '/'Ghent', in the latter case the

Table 3.4 The moves of small firms

Players		*Moves*	
L	*N*	*C*	*A*
S	*N*	*N/G/A*	*A*
Outcome	*N/G/C*	*C*	*A*

Notes:
L: Large firms; S: Small producers; *U*: Unions;
N: None; *G*: Ghent; *C*: Contributory; *A*: Assistance.

outcome being 'Ghent'/'Contributory'. Since S is indifferent between 'Ghent' and 'Assistance' but prefers both these outcomes to 'Contributory', the optimal move is 'Assistance'.

Finally, we need to discuss the best move for the large firms. From the preceding analysis (and based on our assumptions about the rationality of the players), we find that the L's move leads to the following outcomes: 'None'/'Ghent'/'Contributory' with probabilities $1-p$, pq, $p(1-q)$, respectively, if L plays 'None', 'Contributory' if L plays 'Contributory', and 'Assistance' if L plays 'Assistance'. Since the utilities of L are such that $C_L > A_L$, L will always prefer to play 'Contributory' rather than 'Assistance', so we are only left with the comparison between the expected payoffs from playing 'None' and 'Contributory'. These payoffs are

$$(1-p)N_L + pqG_L + p(1-q)C_L,$$

and C_L, respectively, so the optimal move of L is 'None' if

$$(1-p)N_L + pqG_L + p(1-q)C_L > C_L,$$

and 'Contributory' if the inequality sign is reversed.

Let us now try to understand the significance of the above condition in the limit cases $p=0$ and $p=1$. If $p=0$, the left-hand side reduces to N_L, and we know that $N_L > C_L$, so L will therefore play 'None'. Intuitively, $p=0$ corresponds to the case when the government does not veto the coalition between large and small firms on no compensation – a strong incentive for L to play 'None'. If $p=1$, the left-hand side of the inequality is

$$qG_L + (1-q)C_L,$$

a weighted average of G_L and C_L. Since $G_L < C_L$, the inequality sign is now reversed, so the optimal move is 'Contributory'. This is also intuitively clear. Since it is certain that the state will intervene in the case of a 'None–None' alliance between large and small firms, large firms prefer to ensure the outcome 'Contributory' rather than face the risk of a 'Ghent' system. We can rephrase the previous analysis in terms of the critical probability p_0 given by

$$p_0 = \frac{(N_L - C_L)}{[N_L - qG_L - (1-q)C_L]}.$$

If $p < p_0$, then large firms will prefer to play 'None', whereas if p increases beyond p_0, the optimal decision is to play 'Contributory'.

This game-theoretic analysis makes a few interesting and counter-intuitive predictions about the political coalitions supporting the different types of policies of compensation for unemployment. As the previous analysis showed, there are two equilibria of the game, with outcomes 'None'/'Ghent'/'Contributory' and 'Contributory'. It is interesting to note that the outcome is never 'Assistance', since the large firms have the ability to impose an outcome which is more favourable for them ('Contributory').

Although pre-strategically, large firms rank 'None' higher than 'Contributory', strategically, there are situations in which large firms prefer to play 'Contributory'. Since unions prefer 'Contributory' to 'Ghent', large firms know that their support of a contributory system will lead to an alliance with the unions which will prevent the more unfavourable outcome 'Ghent' from occurring. A contributory insurance solution rests on a cross-class alliance between large firms and unions – and cannot be imposed by the unions alone.

It is also important to point out that a Ghent system (G) can occur as an equilibrium of the game, but it is *never* the result of a cross-class alliance, nor can it be imposed by unions alone. This result holds even under the assumption that unions prefer 'Ghent' to 'Contributory', as can be seen in the appendix. A Ghent solution can be imposed by the state in situations in which no alliance between the other players is formed.

Conclusions

Most studies of the development of modern social policies do not take into account the role played by employers during the policy deliberations leading to the choice of a particular social policy outcome. This chapter has attempted to take some of the insights developed within the existing literature on modern social policies as its starting point and to refine and challenge them by presenting a more complex picture of the bargaining process that includes not only unions and reformist bureaucrats or policy entrepreneurs, but also employers. Since these numerous political negotiations involve, to a significant degree, *strategic* interaction between these actors, this chapter has used the tools provided by game theory to explore the circumstances that lead to a strategic change in the preferences of different players and to specify more rigorously the different political coalitions supporting each social policy outcome.

By neglecting the role played by employers within the policy deliberations, existing analyses of social policy development can mischaracterise the underlying political dynamics leading to a particular policy. On the one hand, the political coalition supporting a particular social policy can be misspecified: policies that are, in reality, the result of cross-class alliances have sometimes been analysed as the result of union strength or of cooperation between unions and the state. Many studies have often overlooked important political conflicts among different sectors of the business community. These conflicts can often channel the policy deliberations away from outcomes desired by the unions or the state.

By omitting the 'policy input' of employers, most studies have mis-specified the political leading to the introduction of unemployment insurance. Existing analyses have attempted to explain the differences in policy outcomes as being either the result of variation in union influence or of differences in 'policy legacies' available to reformist statist elites. Both explanations mischaracterize the important policy conflicts and fail to explain the differences between the French and German experience. Both the game-theoretic analysis and the historical evidence have shown that the Ghent system was not the victory of trade unions by the result of the imaginative political efforts of policy entrepreneurs.[6] In contrast to a Ghent system, a contributory insurance solution rests on a very fragile cross-class alliance between unions and large firms. Contributory unemployment insurance is not only the political victory of strong and well-organised unions, but also the silent political victory of employers.

Appendix

Unions prefer a Ghent system to contributory unemployment insurance

It can be argued that unions in which low-skilled workers predominate will prefer 'Ghent' to 'Contributory' (this being the only way for them to increase membership, for instance). The game-theoretic analysis under this different assumption is very similar to the above analysis. We will therefore only present the most important steps of the backwards induction reasoning.

If large firms play 'Contributory' or 'Assistance', the optimal move of small firms is to play 'Ghent'. Since the unions now favour 'Ghent', they will form an alliance with the small firms, and the state will be forced to accept 'Ghent' as the outcome. If small firms played 'None', the state might impose the outcome 'Contributory', which is worse for the small firms – this is why they prefer to play 'Ghent'.

If large firms play 'None', the outcome depends on the move made by the small firms as follows:

1. if S plays 'None', the outcome is 'None'/'Ghent'/'Contributory' with the probabilities $(1-p)$, pq and $p(1-q)$, respectively, no matter what U plays;
2. if S plays 'Ghent', the outcome is 'Ghent' because the unions form an alliance with the small firms; and
3. If S plays 'Assistance', no alliance is possible, so the outcome is dictated by the state: 'Ghent'/'Contributory' with probabilities q and $(1-q)$, respectively; compared with the previous case, we find that 'Ghent' is a better move for the small unions than 'Assistance'.

In terms of utilities, the optimal move for S is either 'None' or 'Ghent', depending on whether

$$(1-p)N_S+pqG_S+p(1-q)C_S$$

is greater (or smaller) than G_S. As was noted in the explanation of Table 3.4, N_S, G_S, C_S denotes the utilities small firms associate with the outcomes 'None', 'Ghent' and 'Contributory'.

Since 'Ghent' ranks worst among the large firms' preferences, L prefers the outcome 'None'/'Ghent'/'Contributory' (with the probabilities given above) to 'Ghent'. Large firms will therefore play 'None', as this is the only way in which they can prevent the outcome from being 'Ghent'. This actually only happens if

$$(1-p)N_S + pqG_S + p(1-q)C_S > G_S,$$

otherwise small firms will play 'Ghent'. Notice that 'None' is the best move for L.

The main implications of this model are as follows:

1 If unions prefer 'Ghent' to 'Contributory', large firms are no longer interested in supporting a contributory system.[7] Hence large firms will play 'None', i.e. they will oppose any system of unemployment compensation, in the hope that similar action by the small firms will force the state to accept the outcome 'None'.
2 As soon as small firms prefer a Ghent system to the uncertain outcome 'None'/'Ghent'/'Contributory', a cross-class alliance between them and the unions is formed, leading to the acceptance of a Ghent system by the state.
3 It is interesting to notice how the balance of power is shifted in this case. In our main analysis, in which it is assumed that unions prefer 'Contributory' to 'Ghent', the move made by the large firms is decisive – it completely determines the outcome of the game. Here, by contrast, the move of small firms will determine the final outcome.
4 Under the new assumption about the preferences of the unions, 'Ghent' can be the outcome of a cross-class alliance, but this time the alliance is formed between unions and small firms – in contrast to the alliance described in the main analysis.

Notes

1 This paper emerged from a series of conversations with David Soskice and Torben Iversen, and I would like to acknowledge their very insightful comments, suggestions and criticisms. I am also grateful to Peter Hall, Robert Hancké, Paul Pierson and the participants of the 'Varieties of Capitalism' conference at the Max Planck Institute for the Study of Societies, Cologne, for comments on a preliminary draft. I would like to acknowledge the research support of the Center for European Studies, Harvard University, the Harvard School of Business Administration and the Center for German and European Studies, Georgetown University.
2 This and all subsequent translations from the French are by the author. Original text: 'L'invention du chômage n'est pas encore la naissance du chômeur'.
3 During these crucial meetings, the *Conseil Supérieur du Travail* had the following composition: eight members of Parliament, nineteen representatives of the Chambers of Commerce, nineteen union representatives, eight employers' representatives, eight representatives of the *Conseils des prudhommes* (industrial conciliation boards), one representative of the Chamber of Commerce in Paris, one delegate of the *Associations de Production*, two law professors (see Fagnot 1905: 110; Office du Travail 1903: 985).
4 That is *Allgemeiner Deutscher Gewerkschaftsbund* (German Federation of Trade Unions).

5 Given the lack of statistical knowledge about the extent of unemployment and of the relative costs of one system versus the other, there was wide uncertainty among employers as to whether contributory insurance would impose higher costs than the existing *Erwerbslosenfürsorge*. On arguments that contributory insurance would be more costly for employers (mainly because of the elimination of the means test), see VDA (1923), Reichsarbeitsblatt (1924) and Tänzler (1928); on arguments that an insurance system would actually impose lower costs on employers, see Böhm (1924).

6 A second proposition generated by the game-theoretic analysis which has not yet been tested is that, if unions prefer a Ghent system to contributory insurance, they can only impose a Ghent system by forming a coalition with small firms.

7 If they try to support it, small firms and unions form an alliance in favour of 'Ghent' – the worst outcome for large firms.

References

ADGB (Allgemeiner Deutscher Gewerkschaftsbund) (1920). 'Ein Gesetzentwurf über Arbeitslosenversicherung', *Correspondenzblatt des Allgemeinen Deutschen Gewerkschaftsbundes* 30(20), 249–51.

ADGB (1921). 'Zur Arbeitslosenversicherung', *Correspondenzblatt des Allgemeinen Deutschen Gewerkschaftsbundes* 31(53), 745–6.

ADGB (1922). 'Zum Entwurf einer Arbeitslosenversicherung II', *Correspondenzblatt der Generalkommission der Gewerkschaften Deutschlands* 32(36), 520–3.

Alber, J. (1982). *Vom Armenhaus zum Wohlfahrtsstaat.* Frankfurt: Campus.

Böhm, G. (1924). 'Bedeutet die Ersetzung der Erwerbslosenfürsorge durch die Arbeitslosenversicherung eine Mehrbelastung der Wirtschaft?', *Reichsarbeitsblatt* 24(8), 591–3.

Der Arbeitgeber (1910). 'Das Problem der Arbeitslosenversicherung', *Der Arbeitgeber* 1(1), 3–5.

Der Arbeitgeber (1914). 'Zur Frage der Arbeitslosigkeit', *Der Arbeitgeber* 5(2), 18.

DIHT (Deutscher Industrie- und Handelstag) (1920). *Erklärung des DIHT an das Reichsarbeitsministerium. 25. November 1920.* Potsdam: Zentrales Staatsarchiv Potsdam, RAM 4311/197–198.

DIHT (1926). *Denkschrift des DIHT an das Reichsarbeitsministerium. 16. April 1926.* Potsdam: Zentrales Staatsarchiv Potsdam, RAM 4311.

Esping-Andersen, G. and Korpi, W. (1985). 'From poor relief towards institutional welfare states: The development of Scandinavian social policy', in R. E. Eriksson (ed.), *The Scandinavian Model: Welfare States and Welfare Research.* New York: M.E. Sharpe, 39–74.

Fagnot, F. (1905). *Le Chômage.* Paris: Société nouvelle de librairie et d'édition.

Faust, A. (1986). *Arbeitsmarktpolitik im deutschen Kaiserreich: Arbeitsvermittlung, Arbeitsbeschaffung und Arbeitslosenunterstützung 1890–1918.* Stuttgart: Franz Steiner.

Führer, K. C. (1992). *Arbeitslosigkeit und die Entstehung der Arbeitslosenversicherung in Deutschland 1902–1927.* Berlin: Colloquium.

Fulcher, J. (1991). *Labour Movements, Employers and the State: Conflict and Co-Operation in Britain and Sweden.* Oxford: Clarendon Press.

Gewerkschaftszeitung (1924). 'Die preußische Gefahrengemeinschaft für die Erwerbslosenfürsorge', *Die Gewerkschaftszeitung* 34(37), 342–3.

Gordon, C. (1991). 'New Deal, old deck: Business and the origins of social security 1920–1935', *Politics and Society* 19(2), 165–207.

Gordon, C. (1994). *New Deals: Business, Labor and Politics in America 1920–1935.* Cambridge: Cambridge University Press.

Handwerkskammer Kassel (1921). *Bericht über die Vollversammlung am 28. November 1921.* Potsdam: Zentrales Staatsarchiv Potsdam, RWM 2071/150.

Heclo, H. (1974). *Modern Social Policies in Britain and Sweden. From Relief to Income Maintenance.* New Haven, CT: Yale University Press.

Henning, H.-J. (1974). 'Arbeitslosenversicherung vor 1914: Das Genter System und seine Übernahme in Deutschland', in H. Kellenbenz (ed.), *Wirtschaftspolitik und Arbeitsmarkt.* Munich: Oldenbourg, 271–88.

Héreil, G. (1932). *Le Chômage en France, étude de legislation sociale.* Paris: Librairie du Recueil Sirey.

Journal Officiel (1879). 'Secours aux ouvriers sans travail de Flers, de Condé-sur Noireau et de leur rayon. Texte de la proposition de MM. Delafosse et de Mackau, tendant à ouvrir à cet effet un crédit extraordinaire de 200 000 F', *Journal Officiel, C. D.*, No. 1323.

Journal Officiel (1884a). 'Exposé des motifs et texte d'une proposition de loi présentée par M. Marius Poulet et autres deputés, ayant pour objet de venir en aide à la population ouvrière atteinte par la crise industrielle', *Journal Officiel, C. D.*, No. 2578.

Journal Officiel (1884b). 'Exposé des motifs et texte de la proposition de loi, presentée par M. Laroche-Joubert, ayant pour objet d'atténuer le chômage qui subissent les travailleurs français', *Journal Officiel, C. D.*, No. 2815.

Journal Officiel (1904a). 'Budget 1905. Titre I. Budget général. État A. Commerce et Industrie. Discussion de l'interpellation de M. Vaillant sur la nécessité d'une enquête parlamentaire et de mesures immédiates relatives au chômage', *Journal Officiel,* 30 novembre 1904.

Journal Officiel (1904b). 'Exposé des motifs et texte de la proposition de loi, présentée par MM. F. Dubief et Millerand, tendant à allouer des subventions aux Caisses de secours contre le chômage involontaire', *Journal Officiel, C. D.* , No. 1698.

Journal Officiel (1905a). 'Loi portant fixation du budget des dépenses et des recettes de l'exercise 1905', *Journal Officiel,* 23 april 1905: 2577–9.

Journal Officiel (1905b). 'Ministère du commerce, de l'industrie, des postes et des télégraphes. Rapport au Président de la République Française', *Journal Officiel,* 13 septembre 1905: 5510–12.

Lewek, P. (1992). *Arbeitslosigkeit und Arbeitslosenversicherung in der Weimarer Republik 1918–1927.* Stuttgart: Franz Steiner.

Lindemann, H. (1924). 'Gewerbedifferenzierte Arbeitslosenfürsorge', *Die Arbeit* 1(4), 201–13.

Malivoire de Camas, J. (1933). *La France et le chômage. Étude de législation (moyens mis en œuvre par l' État et les collectivités pour venir en aide aux chômeurs involontaires par manque de travail).* Paris: Librairie du Recueil Sirey.

Manow, P. (1997). *Social Insurance and the German Political Economy*, MPIfG Discussion Paper 97/2. Cologne: Max Planck Institute for the Study of Societies.

Mares, I. (1997). 'Is unemployment insurable? Employers and the introduction of unemployment insurance', *Journal of Public Policy* 17(3), 299–327.

Mares, I. (1998). 'Negotiated risks: Employers' role in social policy development', Ph.D. dissertation, Department of Government, Harvard University.

Ministère du Commerce (ed.) (1903). *Conseil Supérieur du Travail. Commission Permanente. Extraits des Procès-Verbaux.* Paris: Imprimerie Nationale.

Mossé, R. (1929). 'L'assurance obligatoire contre le chômage au point de vue social. Étude de législation comparée et d'économie sociale', Paris: Thèse Droit.

Office du Travail (ed.) (1896). *Documents sur la question du chômage.* Paris: Imprimerie Nationale.

Office du Travail (1897). 'Rapport du Conseil Supérieur du Travail', *Bulletin de l'Office du Travail* 1897, 30–3.

Office du Travail (1903). 'Conseil Supérieur du Travail. Séance de Novembre 1903', *Bulletin de l'Office du Travail* 1903, 985–8.

Pierson, P. (1995). *The Scope and Nature of Business Power: Employers and the American Welfare State 1900–1935*, ZeS-Arbeitspapier 14/95. Bremen: Center for Social Policy Research.

Piore, M. J. (1987). 'Historical perspectives and the interpretation of unemployment', *Journal of Economic Literature* 25(4), 1934–50.

Potthoff, H. (1979). *Gewerkschaften und Politik zwischen Revolution und Inflation.* Dusseldorf: Droste.

Reichsarbeitsblatt (1924). 'Die Soziale Belastung der Deutschen Wirtschaft', *Reichsarbeitsblatt: Nichtamtlicher Teil* 24 (8 November 1924).

Rothstein, B. (1992). 'Labor market institutions and working class strength', in S. Steinmo, K. Thelen and F. Longstreth (eds), *Structuring Politics: Historical Institutionalism in Comparative Analysis.* Cambridge: Cambridge University Press, 33–56.

Salais, R., Bavarez, N. and Reynaud, B. (eds) (1986). *L'invention du chômage.* Paris: PUF.

Spliedt, F. (1924). 'Einheitliche Gefahrengemeinschaft in der Arbeitslosenfürsorge', *Die Arbeit* 1924, 257–66.

Swenson, P. (1991). 'Bringing capital back in, or social democracy reconsidered: Employer power, cross-class alliances and centralization of industrial relations in Denmark and Sweden', *World Politics* 43(4), 513–44.

Swenson, P. (1997). 'Arranged alliance: Business interests in the New Deal', *Politics and Society* 25(1), 66–116.

Tänzler, F. (1928). 'Die Soziale Belastung der Deutschen Wirtschaft', *Reichsarbeitsblatt* 28, 608–12.

Topalov, C. (1985). *Aux origines de l'assurance chômage. L'État et les secours de chômage syndicaux en France, Grande-Bretagne et Etats-Unis.* Paris: Centre de Sociologie Urbaine.

Topalov, C. (1994). *Naissance du chômeur.* Paris: Albin Michel.

VDA (Vereinigung der Deutschen Arbeitgeberverbände) (1920). *Denkschrift der Vereinigung der Deutschen Arbeitgeberverbände.* Potsdam: Zentrales Staatsarchiv Potsdam. Reichsarbeitsamt 4310/470–476.

VDA (1923). *Mitteilungen der Vereinigung der Deutschen Arbeitgeberverbände.* Berlin: VDA.

VDA (1924). *Geschäftsbericht der Vereinigung der Deutschen Arbeitgeberverbände 1923.* Berlin: VDA.

VDA (1927). *Geschäftsbericht der Vereinigung der Deutschen Arbeitgeberverbände 1925–1926.* Berlin: VDA.

Weir, M. and Skocpol, T. (1985). 'State structures and the possibilities for "Keynesian" responses to the Great Depression in Sweden, Britain and the United States', in P. Evans, D. Rueschemeyer and T. Skocpol (eds), *Bringing the State Back In.* New York: Cambridge University Press, 107–63.

Wermel, M. and Urban, R. (1949). 'Arbeitslosenfürsorge und Arbeitslosenversicherung', *Neue Soziale Praxis* 6, 1–3.

4 When labour and capital collude

The political economy of early retirement in Europe, Japan and the USA[1]

Bernhard Ebbinghaus

The institutionalisation of old-age retirement as full exit from work has become a universal feature of post-war industrial economies (Myles and Quadagno 1991) and the largest income programme of modern welfare states (Esping-Andersen 1990). Since the rise of mass unemployment following the first oil shock, early exit from work before the normal pension age (around 65) has become a social trend that goes beyond the political expansion of social rights, but resulted from unintended policies and collective responses to the new socioeconomic pressures. Early retirement seemed to be a panacea for certain pervasive labour practices, including shedding workers to restructure in response to the changing economy, buying worker consent to downsizing by offering 'soft landings' and the efforts of government and unions to reduce labour supply. However, with increased early retirement, the negative economic and financial consequences have become more worrisome to governments, employers and union leaders alike: rising non-wage labour costs harm competitiveness; unemployment persists despite early exit; current social expenditure and future liabilities have risen substantially; the entry age into retirement is becoming increasingly early; and continued training and re-skilling of older workers is lacking. The multiple pathways of welfare policies and the complex web of industrial actors thus brought about a trend that was partly unintended and has proved difficult to reverse. In fact, early exit has become institutionalised as an acquired social right and an integral part of contemporary political economies.

Early exit from work is embedded within institutional incentives and constraints that shape the push and pull of early retirement. Labour-shedding policies are an interesting case for exploring the linkages between welfare regimes (Esping-Andersen 1990; see also Huber and Stephens 1999), production regimes (Hall 1997; Hollingsworth and Boyer 1997; Soskice 1999) and industrial relations practices (Crouch 1993; Ebbinghaus and Visser 1997). Given the complexities of early retirement policies, I can only chart some of the broader cross-national differences in the linkages between welfare regimes, production systems and labour relations.

Exit from work

Early exit from work for older people has become a popular route in all industrial societies, especially since the onset of mass unemployment following the first oil shock in 1973. Older male workers (55–64 years old) in all countries experienced a decline in employment rates (excluding the unemployed and non-actives), though Japan was least affected (see Fig. 4.1). Among Continental European welfare states, employment rates dropped very dramatically from four-fifths of older men (aged 55–64) in the 1970s to only one in three Frenchmen and only 40 per cent of Dutch and German men of the same age group in the 1990s. In the second group of countries – with medium declines – were the Anglo-American welfare states: the UK and the USA. The UK went through a significant reduction from a high employment rate above 90 per cent in the early 1970s to below 60 per cent in the 1990s, while the USA experienced a more gradual decline, levelling off at above 60 per cent since the 1980s. Until the crisis of the 1990s, when employment rates dropped to American levels, Sweden's decline was slow and a level around 70 per cent was maintained, partly due to part-time work and gradual retirement. Finally, Japan stands out in that it has

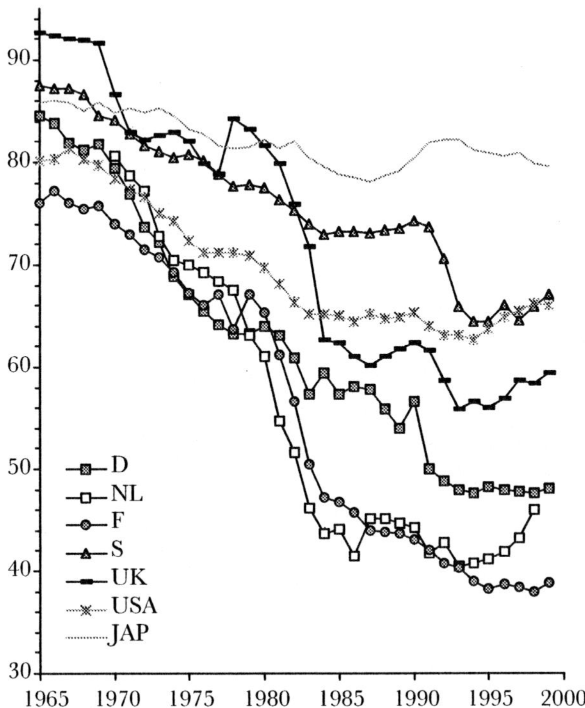

Figure 4.1 Male employment rates, ages 55–64 (in per cent).

Sources: OECD Labour Force Statistics (various years). Calculations by author.

maintained the highest level of employment: four out of five older Japanese men (aged 55–64) remain employed, although not necessarily in the same job. Note that employment among senior citizens (aged 65+) has declined to below 20 per cent everywhere, except in Japan, where nearly 40 per cent of men are still working when they draw their basic pension.

Early retirement among female workers is more difficult to trace in the development of employment rates (see Fig. 4.2), since two processes tend to counteract each other. On the one hand, each cohort of women tends to have a higher participation rate, as more and more women stay in or return to employment during or after a period of raising children. On the other hand, women are often allowed to draw retirement pensions earlier than men. Thus a rising female participation rate across cohorts and an increase in early retirement over time may cancel each other out and might not lead to an overall change in employment rates for the 55- to 64-year-old age group. Indeed, Sweden, with its early expansion of female participation, shows a long-term increase in employment among older women, while the US rate has slightly increased, the Japanese rate stagnated and the British rate oscillated around a medium level. However, Germany

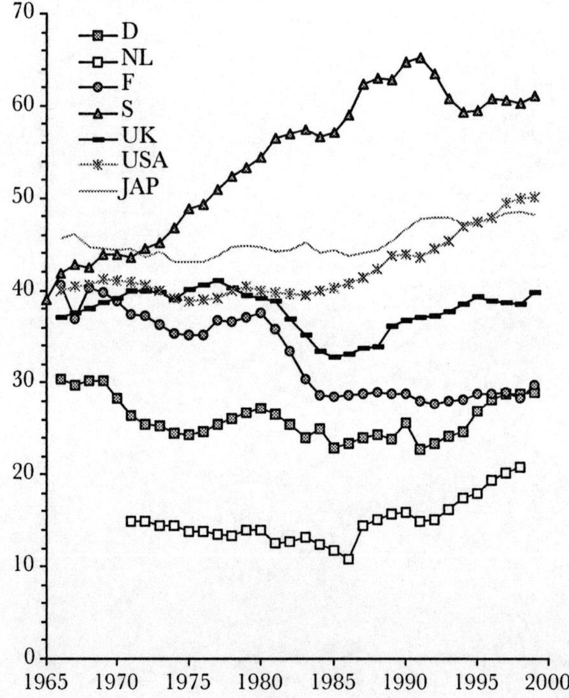

Figure 4.2 Female employment rates, ages 55–64 (in per cent).

Sources: OECD Labour Force Statistics (various years). Calculations by author.

and France show real declines, and the Netherlands traditionally has a very low employment level among older women.

Notably, early retirement and full exit from work do not always coincide (Guillemard 1991b). For instance, Swedish men receiving a partial pension work part-time between the ages of 60 and 64 (accounting for about 25 per cent of Swedish employment in this age group). Their German colleagues may draw a five-year partial pension and get five years of part-time pay but actually work the first 2.5 years full time and then retire completely from the company. Moreover, in the past, it was common for companies in Germany (Jacobs *et al.* 1991a) and Sweden (Wadensjö 1991) to dismiss their workers at an age when they could receive long-term unemployment insurance until they were entitled to early retirement or disability pensions for older unemployed workers; thus the unemployed at age 59 were not seeking employment but had in fact retired. On the other hand, Japanese workers are often forced to retire from their company and thus become self-employed in a small shop or on a farm, work at a smaller supplier firm or the company re-employs them on less favourable conditions (Kimura *et al.* 1994). 'Early' retirement has a very different meaning not only from society to society, but also depending on the perspective, whether seen from the angle of the worker, the firm or the social security system. With the secular trend towards early exit, the normal pension age as a transition from work to retirement has lost its clear-cut defining edge. Public policies which foster gradual or flexible pensions have further blurred the demarcation between work and retirement (Guillemard and Rein 1993).

Grouping the countries in respect to their 'early exit' pattern shows systematic differences across countries. The Continental European welfare states have relied most heavily on the labour-shedding strategy: in both France and Germany, only one in five older men (aged 60–64) *and* only half of the men in the younger age group (aged 55–59) work. The Anglo-American liberal welfare states have seen a decline in employment rates for older workers due to economic forces, roughly following the business cycle. Half of older American or British men (aged 60–64) are not working, while this figure is around one-quarter in the younger age group (aged 55–59). The Scandinavian welfare state shows high employment performance even during old age, partly by fostering part-time work (one-third of Swedish male workers aged 60–64). However, in recent years, unemployment has risen to unprecedented levels, also affecting older workers. Japan has maintained a high level of activity in older age, yet workers have often been forced to quit jobs in large companies and seek re-employment or self-employment in much less favourable jobs.

Welfare state regimes

In order to explain the differences across countries, however, we need to understand the different welfare state policies that provide a 'pull' factor towards early retirement. In all countries, old-age insurance was initially developed merely to supplement income loss due to lower productivity (Myles 1989). Yet with the post-war extension of old-age benefits above subsistence levels, full exit from work at 'normal' retirement age became institutionalised as a major stage in the life course (Guillemard and Rein 1993; Kohli and Rein 1991). In several countries, paternalist social policy considerations motivated an earlier retirement age for women on the grounds that they could receive pensions at the same time as their husbands, who were 3–5 years older on average. Similarly, earlier retirement was granted for groups with particular health impairments, taking into account the difficulty in finding jobs in older age. During the 1960s and early 1970s, when particular provisions for the older unemployed were granted by legislation, court rulings or administrative practice in several countries, these were justified by older workers' difficulties in finding re-employment. Whether initially intended by policy makers or not, these early retirement options have become major pathways to early exit.

In addition, some governments introduced early retirement options to help older workers in the transition from work to retirement. In 1976, Sweden lowered its high normal retirement age from 67 to 65 and introduced an initially successful partial pension for those wishing to work part-time before 65, though later governments changed the conditions several times (Wadensjö 1996). France (since 1985) and Germany (since 1989) have experimented with partial pensions, but these were less attractive schemes (Reday-Mulvey 1996; Schmähl *et al.* 1996). Some countries allowed early drawing of benefits ('flexible' pensions); thus, under US social security, actuarially reduced benefits could be drawn from the age of 62 onwards, though combination with income from part-time work led to severe benefit cuts (Chen 1996). Since 1973, German male workers with long working lives profited from a 'flexible' seniority pension at 63 (and thirty-five contribution years), again requiring full exit from work, but it was phased out by the 1992 reform (Jacobs *et al.* 1991a).

Special early retirement programmes were also initiated by governments in order to reduce labour supply and ease economic restructuring. As early as 1963, the French government provided several early retirement programmes for companies in need of restructuring. In 1983, the new French socialist government granted normal pensions at 60 (after 37.5 years of contributions), partly to shift costs to the less generous pension scheme, but this led to new bridging arrangements allowing even earlier pre-retirement via unemployment benefits (Guillemard 1991a). In Britain, the Labour government introduced a Job Release Scheme (JRS) for men (women already profited from earlier normal pensions at the age of 60) in 1977, which existed for twelve years with many stop-and-go changes until it was closed by the Conservatives in 1989 (Laczko and Phillipson 1991). The German centre–right government introduced a special early retirement scheme in 1984, partly to counteract the unions' demand for shorter working weeks, but closed it within four years (Jacobs *et al.* 1991a).

In addition, unemployment benefits or disability pensions provided a common but not always intended 'bridging pension' until normal retirement age. In Germany and Sweden, long-term unemployment benefits covered more than a year before early retirement (or disability) pensions at 60 (later up to three years in Germany, twenty-one months in Sweden), while they lasted for several years until normal retirement in the Netherlands (ages 57.5–65) and France (ages 60–65 before 1982). In the Netherlands, the disability insurance, which had introduced favourable labour market considerations for older unemployed workers in 1973, became the major exit pathway, at least for women. This has led the government to deplore the 'Dutch disease' and to cut back on disability rules since the late 1980s (Aarts and de Jong 1996). Sweden completely closed its old-age disability pathway in 1992, as it had become too popular and costly during the sudden unemployment surge since 1989 (Wadensjö and Palmer 1996). In Germany, nearly half of all men and women received a disability pension until the early 1970s (for women lasting until the early 1980s), and since then about one in five new pensions has been based on disability grounds, including a new additional pension for the 'severely disabled' at age 61, later already at age 60 (Frick and Sadowski 1996).

There is some evidence for the 'pull' thesis: the Dutch and Swedish disability pensions were the most generous (70 per cent replacement in 1995), followed by Germany and the USA (around 45 per cent), and the least generous were France, the UK and Japan (25 per cent); thus the Netherlands and Sweden had the highest take-up rates among older workers, followed by Germany, while the other countries had much lower rates (Ebbinghaus 2000: table 2). The more favourable benefits are and the less continued employment pays off, the stronger the incentives are for older workers to quit work early (Gruber and Wise 1999). This does not imply that the 'pull' completely determines the overall level of exit, but that generosity and accessibility play a role in the choice of pathways. The labour market consideration of disability pensions in the Netherlands, Germany and Sweden made these schemes accessible, while this was less the case in the other countries, which considered only medical criteria. Yet even in the UK and the USA, disability benefits strictly under medical indication remain the main pathway to early retirement for lack of other publicly provided means. Rates of new entry have followed economic cycles by forcing more workers to file a demand and doctors to become increasingly willing to grant them during economic downturns (Berkowitz and Burkhauser 1996; Lonsdale and Aylward 1996). Thus 'pull' (welfare eligibility) and 'push' (economic pressure) are often interrelated.

From a comparative perspective, each national system of social protection differs in the availability of alternative pathways and in their generosity, eligibility and selectivity (Kohli *et al.* 1991). There are systematic differences across welfare regimes (Esping-Andersen 1990, 1996). The most generous pension system (Sweden) still maintains a high employment level, followed by the more sturdy US social security, while the Continental pension states with medium-level de-commodification seem to have the highest level of early retirement. Thus much depends on the way in which a particular welfare regime interacts with the exit from work decision. On the one hand, the liberal (or residual) welfare regimes do not have much 'pull' on early exit, since they provide insufficient or no early retirement pensions, long-term unemployment benefits and labour market-oriented disability insurance. The Japanese government allows male workers to draw on their earnings-related pension at 60, but this is only a supplement to other partially state-subsidised income (Takayama 1996). US social security allows flexible retirement at 63, but with substantial actuarial reduction, and thus disability pension remains the only other alternative. The British early retirement programme was short-lived, while British male workers have to wait until 65 to receive their flat-rate basic pension. All three countries lack long-term and sufficient unemployment insurance for older workers, and thus there was no bridging via unemployment available.

On the other hand, the Continental European and Scandinavian welfare states have provided multiple pathways to early exit via the pension, unemployment and disability insurance systems. The most important difference between these systems, however, was the successful use of partial and flexible pensions in Sweden, which allows combination with part-time work and led to a gradual transition and prolongation of exit from work (Wadensjö 1996). While Dutch, Swedish and, to a lesser degree, German workers profited from more widespread use of disability insurance, French workers could withdraw earlier due to unemployment bridging pensions. At times, the French and German government intervened directly by setting up special early retirement schemes, with subsidies for re-employment of young workers, though these did not bring the expected labour market improvement and proved relatively expensive (Guillemard 1991a; Jacobs *et al.* 1991a).

Since the late 1980s, government officials, social policy experts and employers – worried about rising public expenditures and payroll taxes – demanded a reversal of early retirement policies. Yet, as several ineffectual reform efforts have shown, closing down or cutting benefits in one scheme may only lead to the substitution of alternative, second-best pathways and thus merely shifts costs from one insurance to another without reducing overall early exit (Casey 1989). Moreover, retrenchment of these popular policies seemed to meet the resistance of a large clientele and significant vested interests. Undertaking major reforms in difficult times, both the Dutch and the Swedish government were able to cut back on pension and disability expenditure in the 1990s (Aarts *et al.* 1996), while reforms have met with more resistance in Germany and France (Ebbinghaus and Hassel 2000). There is also a general shift from public to private, from pay-as-you go to funded, from defined-benefit to defined-contribution schemes, though the obstacles for a radical shift of institutionalised pension systems are also formidable (Myles and Pierson 2000). Nevertheless, private occupational pensions already play a substantial role in some cases and will gain in importance in the future.

Private occupational pensions

Public policy is not the only 'pull' factor, since private occupational pensions provided by employers or social partners also play an important role in workers' retirement decisions. In fact, as governments seek to close down early retirement programmes or make public benefits less attractive, private occupational welfare efforts may gain in importance, as they may counteract welfare cuts by filling replacement gaps. Given the more limited public pensions in liberal and residual welfare states, employer-provided occupational pensions may have had more space to develop in Britain, in the USA and also in Japan. To the degree that universalistic or corporative European welfare states have well-developed basic pensions and/or earnings-related social insurance, occupational pensions assumed a less important role in the post-war period.

The administration of occupational pension funds differs considerably cross-nationally and sometimes across sectors. In the UK, the USA and Japan, occupational pensions are employer-sponsored plans (only exceptionally do workers contribute to them, often for tax reasons). In the German private sector, the plans are mainly employer sponsored, and workplace representatives have a secondary role. On the other hand, the mandatory French, the Swedish negotiated, the Dutch collective and the German public-sector supplementary schemes were set up jointly by unions and employer associations, and companies therefore do not have much discretion. Coverage rates are lower where plans remained voluntary employer decisions (Gern 1998; Turner and Watanabe 1995), as in Britain, the USA, Japan and also in the German private sector, compared to collectively negotiated plans, not to mention the French mandatory plans. Universal coverage and portability of pension rights from job to job in collective schemes, although desirable from a public-policy view, undermine the selective benefits of occupational pensions to employers who seek to attract and bind (especially skilled) workers to a firm (Casey 1997; Steinmeyer 1996) and reward their investment in firm-specific skills (Estevez-Abe *et al.* 1999). Competition for better benefits between status groups or sectors may emerge in less centralised collective bargaining systems. Thus the (increasingly) decentralised labour relations (and lack of state intervention) in Britain, the USA and Japan have prevented an evolution towards sector- or nation-wide schemes as in France, the Netherlands or Sweden. These variations in overall coverage and control by employers of occupational pensions have important repercussions for early retirement in addition to the 'pull' by public policies.

Occupational pensions have often provided an additional pathway or supplementary inducement to early exit from work (Ebbinghaus 2000). Most important is whether companies can promote early retirement through occupational pension plans. Under defined-benefit plans, employers as sponsors may be able to offer early retirement pensions that are more favourable than normal actuarial deduction would dictate, while this would not be possible in the more and more popular defined-contribution plans, especially in individual savings plans. Most larger British occupational pension schemes allow earlier drawing than the state pensions (65 for men and 60 for women), thus providing a major pathway to early retirement, especially for men. In addition, British employers have relied on 'voluntary redundancy' for downsizing, i.e. the payment of lump-sum compensation based on years of service, and in fact older workers and young workers are more likely to become redundant (Casey and Wood 1994: 367).

In the USA, occupational pensions provided a means to induce workers to retire, especially after Congress raised the mandatory retirement age that a firm could impose from 65 to 70 in 1978 and finally abolished it in 1986. Some employers had already provided favourable early retirement options before flexible social security (at 62 instead of 65) was introduced in 1961, and they later used the defined-benefit plans to provide low or no actuarial deductions (Hutchens 1994). The Employee Retirement Income Security Act (ERISA) of 1974 introduced important regulations on private-sector pensions, requiring vesting of occupational pensions when an employee leaves a company, forbidding benefit cuts after raises in social security benefits and introducing collective protection against bankruptcy. Favourable tax rules apply as long as a company does not discriminate; it can design (or negotiate with the unions) particular plans for subgroups, but it cannot restrict benefits only to higher management. In addition, employers use early retirement incentive plans (ERIPs) or 'window' plans to foster voluntary retirement at particular times. During the 1980s, when high interests and stock market profits increased pension funds, employers could use excess funds that would otherwise be taxed to finance early retirement options (Hutchens 1994). In recent years, with falling unemployment, employers are now worried about retaining workers and cut back on early retirement incentives, again confirming the cyclical nature of employment policies. Moreover, there has been a long-term shift away from defined-benefit plans, thus reducing the financial incentives for early retirement (apRoberts and Turner 1997).

The Japanese occupational pensions are often defined-benefit plans that allow early retirement at age 60, i.e. at the time of mandatory retirement from larger companies. Further deregulation to boost contracting out and public pension reform to increase the retirement age and lower benefits in the 1990s (Kimura 1997) will make occupational pensions more important for retirement, but the current recession also highlighted the danger of bankruptcy and brought a lower rate of returns. In addition, Japanese employers provide lump-sum severance pay and also use re-employment practices to enforce mandatory retirement from 'lifelong' jobs.

An even greater variety of schemes exists for German private employers; they can choose between different financing methods with different tax and financial security regulations (see Chapter 8 by Jackson and Vitols in this volume). Larger companies tend to have book reserves (or, less frequently, support or pension funds), while more than half of smaller firms have direct insurance contracts. Book reserves and support funds function as deferred wages that are reinvested into the company (but reinsured against bankruptcy). Pension rights are only guaranteed after five years of service, and former employees' pensions have only statutory accrual. Accrued occupational pensions are an important incentive to stay with a current employer, thus cutting labour turnover. Most occupational pensions of larger private-sector companies (above 1,000 workers) are earnings-related benefits and thus show the commitment of employers to safeguard the standard of living, especially for higher income groups (Schmähl 1997: 120). An occupational pension is thus enjoyed more frequently by white-collar than blue-collar workers, among more qualified than lower-ranking employees and among men than women (data from 1990, table 4.4 in Schmähl 1997: 123).

Nevertheless, German companies, especially larger firms, have relied mainly on public schemes to allow early exit for their older workers, and occupational pensions have only been used as a top-up.

The second-tier Dutch private pensions are required to be funded (since 1956), and rights are already vested after one year of employment (after age 25). Portability across firms even outside sectoral schemes has become common since the 1980s (legally required since 1994). Besides the civil servant scheme (covering more than 20 per cent of all employees), which was recently privatised, there are around eighty sectoral plans (60 per cent) and over 1,000 company plans (less than 20 per cent; Blomsma and Jansweijer 1997: 240). Since 1976, an increasing number of collective agreements have established early retirement plans (VUT) financed by employer and employee contributions (pay-as-you-go) and requiring at least ten years of contributions (Blomsma and Jansweijer 1997). Private pensions and early retirement plans can already increase replacement rates to 90 per cent at age 59, compared to 60 per cent at age 65 for those dependent on a public pension only (Kapteyn and de Vos 1999: 284–5, table 7.1).

The mandatory French occupational pension scheme, as the general public scheme, provided no early retirement options before the government lowered the normal retirement age to 60 in 1982. It only followed suit when the government was willing to continue subsidising a transitional fund (ASF) for lowering the pension age by five years. The ASF fund was initially set up by the social partners to finance 'bridging pensions' within the unemployment insurance (UNEDIC), which is also run by the social partners following a collective agreement signed in 1958. A joint agreement within UNEDIC in 1972 introduced an unemployment allowance for older dismissed workers (aged 60–64), guaranteeing 80 per cent of net wages (and later full public pensions) and since 1977 for the voluntarily unemployed as well (Guillemard 1991a: 136–7), but it continued to function as an early retirement option even after the pension reform in 1982 (a new job replacement scheme was introduced in 1995 for workers aged 58 with forty years of contributions).

All four Swedish occupational schemes provide full pension supplements after thirty contribution years, based on last peak years of wage or salary, and allow for earlier withdrawal with some actuarial reduction. Until the change of normal pensions in 1976, the white-collar occupational scheme granted earlier pensions than under the public pension (age 65 instead of 67). Given the high organisation rate of Swedish unions and employers, nearly all dependent employees are covered by these collective schemes, with the exception of employees working less than 16 hours per week. The occupational pensions not only supplement old age but also disability pensions and for three out of four schemes also provide partial pensions. When the public disability pension for the older unemployed was abolished in 1991, the blue-collar unions and private employers negotiated an occupational scheme in 1993, though it was abolished three years later (Wadensjö 1997: 300). Recent changes away from pay-as-you-go and towards larger funding and defined contributions will further reduce the already small impact on early retirement.

In contrast to the common view in the public debate, it is not only the public welfare state but also private occupational pension arrangements, largely determined by employers, that add to the 'pull' towards early exit. Occupational welfare policy thus provided a supplementary measure closing the replacement gap of public benefits or an alternative pathway if public schemes were less accessible or generous. In the Netherlands and France, special early retirement schemes negotiated by the social partners played an important role in addition to supplementary pensions, reinforcing the pervasive trend of early exit and externalisation of costs at the sectoral or national level. In Germany and Sweden, occupational pensions were mainly supplementary pensions, not changing the course of early retirement very much, since employers and workplace representatives externalised early exit costs to public schemes. In Japan, the USA and the UK, on the other hand, occupational pensions provided by employers played a more crucial role for early retirement in the absence of generous and widely available public schemes. The Anglo-American early exit pathways, in particular, were thus subject to economic rationales and cyclical trends to a greater extent and entailed a larger internalisation of labour-shedding costs by employers and individuals.

Employment protection and mandatory retirement

We will now turn from the perspective of 'pull' factors, public or private welfare policies, to the flip side: 'push' factors that lead to a decline in labour demand for older workers. Early retirement is commonly seen as a response to mass unemployment following the two oil shocks in 1970s; in Continental European welfare states, in particular, governments, employers and unions colluded to shed labour at the expense of the welfare state (Esping-Andersen 1996). Both Japan and Sweden had a low record of unemployment, at least until 1989, and showed a low tendency for early retirement, while in the case of the Continental European welfare states high unemployment and high levels of exit from work seem to go together, supporting the labour-shedding thesis. However, employment regulation and human resource management strategy also play a role in limiting or promoting early retirement.

Employment protection and anti-age discrimination regulations by legislation and collective agreements have an impact on old-age employment by constraining the hiring and firing of older workers (Buechtemann 1993). Commonly, employment protection laws not only make dismissal contingent on procedural rules and substantial grounds, but they often also provide for severance pay based on age or years of employment. These seniority rules protect older workers or those with long service to the firm. While protecting the 'insiders' by age-specific employment protection rules, they may have the opposite effect for 'outsiders'. Employers will be more reluctant to hire older workers given the lower flexibility in firing older workers under seniority rules. Employment protection based on the length of service would be such a deterrent. Thus smaller firms that are often exempted from seniority employment protection would be more likely to hire older workers. For example, small Japanese firms provide employment opportunities (at lower wages and with less protection) to older workers who have been forced to retire from larger companies.

The length of notice of dismissal is age-specific in Sweden (two months under 30, rising to six months for those aged 45 and older) and in the Netherlands (workers over the age 45 have two weeks of notice, instead of one, per year of service, up to twenty-six weeks), while the other European countries stipulate dismissal conditions only by length of service and thus only indirectly protect older workers (Ehrenberg and Jakubson 1993: 203–5, table 7.1). Germany used to have more favourable rules for white-collar employees (six months after twenty years), but the government under Chancellor Kohl harmonised these rules on a medium level in a rare case of employment flexibilisation, thereby improving the situation for blue-collar workers, who used to have only three months after twenty years. Of the European countries, the shortest period is stipulated in France (two months after two years) and the UK (about three months after twelve years). American employers are free to hire and fire, and there are no age- or service-related rules at the federal level, though the 1988 WARN Act introduced a two-month notice in the case of plant closure (Ehrenberg and Jakubson 1993). Despite the lack of statutory protection in Japan, courts have enforced the obligation of employers to prove just cause in the case of both redundancy and individual dismissal.

More important for older workers' retirement decision are the disincentives of combining work and pensions as well as the regulation of mandatory retirement enforced by employers. In some systems, in order not to forego full pension benefits, workers may be forced to quit working when drawing public pensions. Most early retirement schemes and full disability pensions require withdrawal from work or at least have earnings caps, but even some normal public pensions impose such rules (French pensions and, until the 1994 reform, Swedish pensions). Public pensions' earnings rules that cut benefits according to other income 'can be considered a form of mandatory retirement "through the backdoor" ' (Casey 1997: 17), since they are a disincentive to continue working beyond the statutory retirement age. The earnings rule was removed from the British flat-rate public pension in 1989, the USA lowered the reduction factor (finally abolished in 2000), and Japan has increased the earnings cap. To prevent abuse, disability insurance, early flexible retirement and gradual (part-time) pensions have elaborate rules on reducing benefits according to income. The Anglo-American and Japanese disability schemes require strict standards, recognising only full disability and thus full withdrawal from work (only recently did the USA allow the transitional combination of benefits with work).

In the absence of enough 'pull' from public benefits, American and Japanese companies relied on 'push' forces, i.e. mandatory retirement. However, the US Congress legislated the Anti-Discrimination in Employment Act in 1967, initially raising the mandatory retirement age to 65, and increasing it to 70 under the Carter administration in 1978, but finally abolishing such rules altogether under the Reagan administration in 1983 (Sheppard 1991: 278). In Japan, after several efforts to increase old-age employment by subsidies and after a failed bill by the opposition in 1979, the government announced its plan to raise the mandatory retirement age to 60 by 1985 and legislated the 1986 Employment Act and reformed pensions (Kimura *et al.* 1994). These policies to lift or abolish mandatory retirement, however, were less motivated by anti-discrimination concerns than by an effort to increase the retirement age and thus improve the public pension schemes. Here, employment protection seems to simply be welfare retrenchment by other means.

The Japanese mandatory retirement ('teinen') has to be seen in the context of a company's human resources strategy and responsibility to provide income opportunities after retirement (Kimura *et al.* 1994). Larger Japanese companies rely on 'teinen' in response to their long-term employment guarantee, age-related career trajectories and seniority pay structure, all of which make older workers more expensive. Japanese employers terminate seniority pay increases around the age of 50 and enforce mandatory retirement from the job at 60. In return for lifelong loyalty, large companies provide considerable lump-sum severance pay and occupational pensions, or they may re-employ workers within their company network. Some retirees find re-employment in small firms or on farms, in some cases becoming self-employed using their lump-sum severance pay as a business investment. As a result, older workers are over-proportionally employed in smaller firms (Kimura *et al.* 1994: 250). This early retirement practice relies on a web of social customs and public policies which allows larger companies to maintain their employment tenure system. However, the financial and economic crisis and long-term ageing has put pressure on the government to raise the pension and mandatory retirement age and threatens to undermine these re-employment practices, which are closely tied with Japan's production system.

Varieties of production systems

Early retirement not only provides a means to overcome seniority rules, but also to restructure and downsize in a socially acceptable way; it thus interacts with the existing production system. The first explicit early retirement policies began when Fordist mass production industries came under major restructuring pressures, particularly mines, heavy steel mills and shipyards. In fact, the first French early retirement programmes date back as far as 1963 and were part of state subsidies to ailing industries (Guillemard 1991a), but early retirement also occurred in other countries before the mid-1970s. The economic crisis following the oil shock of 1973 intensified the trend towards de-industrialisation and the shift towards a service economy. As a consequence of the differential demographics of the old versus new sectors, de-industrialisation particularly affected older male blue-collar workers, while new labour market entrants (increasingly women) profited from white-collar and part-time employment opportunities in the growing new sectors. Older sectors tend to have an older age structure, reflecting the entry of young workers into these industries during earlier times of expansion, while new sectors attract more younger workers and have not yet aged (Stinchcombe 1965). With increasing early retirement, both firms and public authorities have been reluctant to invest in continuing training and education of older workers, since they expect them to leave relatively soon, which in turn makes them less productive and thus reinforces often ungrounded beliefs about their lower productivity (Casey 1997). As older workers are particularly affected by the downsizing of older industries and have less re-employment chances, early retirement seems a reasonable alternative.

Economic restructuring accounts for some of the functionality of retirement and the secular trend towards early exit in modern economies, yet it does not explain the variation across countries. The USA and the UK have moved rapidly from a largely industrial to a dominantly service-oriented economy, but only have a medium level of early exit. France and Germany still have a larger share of industrial employment but rely heavily on labour shedding, while the Netherlands has changed towards a service economy with the help of early retirement. Finally, Sweden and Japan, at least until the late 1980s, maintained industrial employment without such extensive labour shedding. A comparative study of early exit at the level of economic branches comes to the conclusion 'that countries do indeed have quite different industrial mixes and industry-specific age structures; yet these differences do not correspond strictly to differences in the rates of early exit' (Jacobs *et al.* 1991b: 93). Moreover, the shift-share analysis of German, Dutch and Swedish older workers during the 1970s shows 'that a decrease in employment shares of older men within all the industries, rather than changes in industry distribution, is the main factor underlying the overall changes in the old-age share of male employment' (Jacobs *et al.* 1991b: 83). However, these inconclusive inter-industry analyses do not take into account intra-industry differences such as the dualism between early exit for the core workforce in large companies and low exit for workers in small and medium-sized firms. Within the same industry, larger firms are usually more capable of using public policies and additional private means to finance early exit than smaller or medium-sized firms (Naschold and de Vroom 1994).

Economies not only differ in their industry mix, but also in their national production systems, which are embedded in supporting social institutions (Hollingsworth and Boyer 1997; Soskice 1999). In order to look at the interaction between production systems and early exit patterns more closely, comparative cases studies of early retirement policies at the firm level are more revealing than macroeconomic analysis (Naschold *et al.* 1994a). The question here is whether firms with different production systems vary in their human resources management and early retirement policies. In traditional, 'Fordist' mass production factories, workers have low or general skills, and turnover is relatively high, with employers not committed to employment tenure. Thus a sudden decline in market shares and long-term technological changes may cause these firms to shed the less productive and inadequately skilled older workers first. This production model has been prevalent in the 'unorganised' market economies of the USA and the UK (Soskice 1999), and in fact we have seen that US and British companies have used occupational pension and window plans to 'downsize' in a market-driven, cyclical and *ad hoc* fashion.

On the other hand, firms with a quality production strategy (Streeck 1992) rely on internal labour markets with a skilled workforce and low turnover. If sudden market changes occur, they tend to hoard labour by cutting back on overtime and working time, instead of resorting to mass dismissal. They also respond to technological change by retraining workers in new production methods. In fact, promises of lifelong employment provide an incentive for workers to invest in firm-specific skills and cooperative employment relations (Estevez-Abe *et al.* 1999; Soskice 1999). Germany is a prime example of the quality production system, but Sweden, the Netherlands and partly France have also shared some of these features.

Externalisation of early retirement costs has been used by both Fordist companies that came under pressure to restructure and by diversified quality production firms that used these pathways to maintain seniority pay and career paths for their highly skilled workforce (Naschold *et al.* 1994b). Similarly, larger Dutch companies in both the industry and service sectors have used externalisation strategies to restructure their male workforce, relying on their own or collectively negotiated occupational pension plans, while small firms and female workers tended to use (on an individual basis) the public disability and unemployment pathways (Trommel and de Vroom 1994). In France during the 1970s, private and (semi-)public employers were able to dismiss older workers and restructure with the help of the early retirement unemployment allowances administered by the social partners. Employers have come under more pressure since the 1980s, as the state intervened by lowering the retirement age, negotiating re-employment conditions in 'solidarity contracts' and intervening in the social partners' unemployment funds (Guillemard 1991a).

Although some Swedish companies have used early retirement options to shed older workers with the consent of workplace unions, the larger emphasis on retraining, reassignment and part-time work led to a much lower level of early retirement and internalisation of costs (Olofsson and Petersson 1994). Production methods that used job rotation and active labour market policies that sought to relocate workers have further helped to maintain higher employment levels among older workers. This internalisation tendency is even more pronounced in Japan. In order to gain flexibility, Japanese firms rely on workers to train and perform multiple tasks on lower-paid temporary contracts at the same firm or lend them to subsidiaries or smaller firms within the 'keiretsu' (group of companies with cross-shareholdings, see Estevez-Abe, Chapter 9). They can rely on large internal labour markets, sending some white- and blue-collar workers on secondment ('shukko') to subsidiaries and suppliers within the company group, especially after mandatory retirement (Kimura *et al.* 1994), which helps to improve information flow between the main company and suppliers (Dore 1997).

Although this sketch of production systems describes the dominant national regimes, there are exceptions to the rule in some sectors and for some firms. Fordist firms with low skill profiles use early retirement to achieve numerical flexibility and increase productivity, while relying on 'buying' general skills on the external market and at the cost of high turnover. Quality production firms with skilled workforces use early retirement not primarily as a mean to downsize or restructure in difficult times, but in order to maintain lifelong employment, seniority pay and career trajectories irrespective of the business cycle. The institutionalisation of multiple public and private pathways to early retirement, particularly when firms have control over who can exit early, are an institutional complement to the tenure employment system.

The paradox of the skill-intensive production regime is that the more employers have to rely on seniority wages and employment tenure, the more they are interested in shedding older workers when seniority pay, career trajectories and employment protection reach their limits. The Swedish and Japanese firms are under similar pressures, yet because of active employment policies in the former and for lack of multiple pathways in the latter, they have resorted to relying on early exit from work in order to solve the structural ageing problem of their production system. The Swedish part-time pension and Japanese re-employment strategies allow a gradual transition from work to retirement, a longer retention or sharing of experience within or among firms and lower expenditure on early retirement programmes. Whether the gradual pension policy of Sweden and the Japanese re-employment practice could be adapted to the economies of Continental Europe in order to reduce early retirement while maintaining the current production system remains an open question.

The institutional differences in corporate and financial governance between coordinated and uncoordinated market economies (see Jackson and Vitols, Chapter 8) also have repercussions on human resources management and employment strategies. Anglo-American liberal market economies rely on capital markets that impose short-term horizons and on anti-trust policies that foster competitive inter-company relations (Soskice 1999). Publicly listed companies are thus under more pressure to respond to a sudden decline in demand or profitability by downsizing employment, flattening corporate hierarchies and selling off unprofitable units. Moreover, companies seek 'hostile' takeovers to boost profits, partly by economies of scale through merger and by selling off assets after a takeover. The new parent company may choose not to honour the long-term employment and future pension commitments of the acquired company. On the other hand, in 'coordinated' market economies, particularly stable ties between companies and banks have also reinforced the long-term commitment to employment stability and corporate welfare benefits. Nevertheless, the potential risks of book reserve schemes have become partially regulated, and German book reserve schemes have had to be reinsured since 1976, for example. Further shifts towards defined-benefit and funded pensions as a result of the demographic challenge might in the long run undermine the institutionalised systems, and changes in financial and corporate governance might reinforce the decline in employer commitments towards their lifelong employees. The long-term commitment of employee and employer enshrined in this production system is becoming increasingly undermined.

Industrial relations

There is an important linkage between retirement policy and industrial relations. Commonly, trade unions were seen as a major force, together with social democratic parties, in expanding welfare states (Esping-Andersen 1992). Over the last quarter of a century, union power has not only decreased in most post-industrial societies due to membership decline, but also due to an increased heterogeneity of interests, decentralisation of collective bargaining and enfeebled party–union ties (Ebbinghaus and Visser 2000). British, American and Japanese unionism is fragmented and workplace oriented, and it also suffers from declining, low union density: only one in three British, one in four Japanese and one in six American workers are unionised (Golden *et al.* 1999). Since the state and employers had first taken on the unions in the industrial relations realm, the British and American unions have been not very effective in lobbying against retrenchment efforts by the Reagan or Thatcher governments. The well-organised Swedish unions were much better placed to lobby for welfare state expansion and later against welfare retrenchment, but also the weaker and partly politically divided Continental European unions had some power to block retrenchment, as the strikes against the Berlusconi government in Italy in 1994 and the Juppé government in France in 1995 demonstrated (Ebbinghaus and Hassel 2000). Moreover, together with the employers, these unions play an institutionalised role as 'social partners' in the self-administration of social insurance and labour exchanges (see Crouch, Chapter 5).

Although unions historically developed mutual old-age funds in some instances, they learned that public pension schemes and supplementary occupational pensions would provide better coverage and benefits. In Germany, worker representatives supported by the unions have played a role in the self-administration of public social insurance since its beginnings in 1889 and provided many union activists with their first institutionalised role in the German welfare state (Manow 1997). However, this role was rather decentralised and limited and remained restricted to the Continental European welfare states.

More direct union influence came to the fore when negotiating occupational pension plans with employers, most notably in the USA. Following the New Deal, US unions such as Teamsters and the UAW fought for the right to negotiate pension plans to supplement the meagre old-age benefits of social security and urged employers to press Congress for a rise in benefits in the 1950s and 1960s. Yet the role of unions was undermined due to underfunding of union plans in declining industries and due to union membership loss, particularly in the 1980s. While in 1979 half of all privately insured workers were covered by a union-negotiated plan and one in four workers was still organised (three-quarters with a pension plan), a decade later less than 15 per cent were organised and only one-third of privately insured workers have a union card (Sass 1997: 229–30). Even though union-negotiated old-age plans seemed to provide a selective incentive for members, they also intensified the union/non-union gap in labour cost (wages and fringe benefits), thus providing an incentive for employers to 'go non-union' (Freeman and Medoff 1984). In the growing non-unionised sectors and where employers voluntarily provided occupational pensions, unions played no role in corporate welfare.

In Britain, where occupational pensions were set up unilaterally by employers as independent trusts, unions hardly had any say, and workers rarely had representation on the board (Davies 1996). In Germany, too, private employers could set up and run pension funds without any union role. In the public sector, however, the collective pension scheme was negotiated for those public employees with social insurance coverage. In Sweden, blue-collar and public-sector unions sought to negotiate similar occupational pension plans as existed for white-collar employees in the 1960s, leading to four major collective plans (for private blue-collar, private white-collar, central and local government employees) in addition to the public basic and earnings-related pensions (Wadensjö 1997). The Swedish unions were able to use the funded part of the funds for their investment policy (the blue-collar plan was pay-as-you-go until 1996). In Japan, company unions play a role in occupational pension schemes: an employer is required by law to obtain their consent to opt out of the earnings-related public pension scheme.

The union role in occupational pensions thus depends not only on union attitudes towards private schemes, but also on their ability to bargain such fringe benefits. More decentralised and fragmented unions at the workplace have played a lesser role than those with bargaining power in industry as long as they thought it crucial to supplement public schemes. On the other hand, unions opted against a direct role when they were not strong enough to force employers in their sector to set up a multi-employer scheme. In Sweden, France, the Netherlands and in the German public sector, and traditionally in the USA, unions in well-organised sectors had the clout to bargain such schemes, when they initially sought to negotiate additional benefits for their members as compared to other sectors. Since these negotiated multi-employer plans allowed portability of benefits within an industry and set a playing field at least within a unionised sector, the incentives for employers to offer fringe benefits in order to lure and bind employees to their firms were largely lost. In addition, when negotiated occupational benefits became extended *ergo omnes* for a whole industry as in the Netherlands or mandatory as in France, the unions lost a 'selective incentive' (Olson 1965), though gaining at the same time an institutionalised role as a social partner in welfare provision. Moreover, the collective occupational schemes were no longer voluntary fringe benefits, but became part of the wage-bargaining parcel negotiated between employers and unions. Particularly where high income taxation exists and employer contributions have tax relief, as in Sweden, such negotiated benefits become a form of deferred wage. In recent years, occupational pension benefits came to be part of the political exchange between unions and employers on wage moderation, as are concessions by governments on welfare reforms (Ebbinghaus and Hassel 2000).

The more direct impact of organised labour on early retirement practice results from its position in dismissal procedures. Unions have a long tradition of enforcing seniority rules in mass redundancy ('last in–first out') that protect those with longer service and/or older workers, following the interests of their members (unionisation increases with seniority) and even protecting their own union or workplace representatives (Golden 1997). Most prominently, American unions have enforced seniority rules through collective bargaining. In Japan, it is the employers' commitment to lifelong employment that provides an equivalent (some US companies such as IBM also had similar voluntary policies, but broke with them after the oil shock). Employment protection legislation in the 1960s and 1970s provided additional support for seniority rules in Germany and Sweden, and the works council legislation in Germany in 1972 and collective agreements in Sweden included workplace representatives in the notice of dismissal and 'social plan' negotiation process.

Employment protection legislation and union seniority rules, however, reinforced early retirement practices, instead of retaining older workers. When mass redundancy was necessary and early retirement plans were available, employers could seek the consent of unions and worker representatives to dismiss those older workers who would be able to retire early. Thus the German unions in the coal and steel sector were the first to agree to employer dismissal of those workers at 59 who could rely on the combined pathways of long-term unemployment benefits for one year and a early retirement pension for old-age unemployed at 60 (Jacobs *et al.* 1991a). During the 1996 Alliance for Jobs talks, promoted by the centre–right government, which eventually failed, the unions and employers were nevertheless able to come to an agreement on gradual retirement in response to retrenchment by the government (Bispinck 1997). Swedish workplace unions also negotiated for the dismissal of workers aged 57 years and 3 months, who could draw on long-term unemployment and subsequently disability or gradual pension (Wadensjö 1991). In the USA, unions pressed employers for early retirement options for workers with long tenure ('30 and out'; Sass 1997: 231).

Conclusion

Although early exit from work has become a general trend in all advanced industrial societies, there are remarkable differences in the use of public and private pathways to early retirement and the forces behind them (see Table 4.1). We have been able to detect at least four groups of countries with particular early exit patterns: the Continental European 'welfare without work' societies where labour shedding was widespread, the Anglo-American market economies where downsizing led to cyclical redundancies, the Swedish 'work society' which allowed for gradual transition to retirement, and Japanese social traditions that helped re-employ older workers after mandatory retirement from larger firms. A comparison limited to the first two groups of countries would suggest that the multiple (public and private) pathways of the continental European welfare societies are responsible for the 'pull' on all older working people, while the more limited pathways in the Anglo-American market economies only lead to early exit following the economically induced 'push'. However, if we include Sweden, we see that extensive social protection does not necessarily lead to massive labour shedding. Active employment and integration policies for older workers have been successful in mitigating these pressures, though the sudden unemployment shock in the early 1990s posed a major challenge. Finally, the Japanese case is instructive in showing that even in 'residual' welfare states (with similarities to

Table 4.1 Typology of exit patterns and regime linkages

Country: Exit-rate	*Welfare state regime*	*Occupational welfare*	*Employment system*	*Production system*	*Financial governance*	*Industrial relations*
France: High	'Welfare without work' multiple pathways	Mandatory collective schemes	Employment regulation, long-term employment	Mixed: nationalised/ private	'Coordinated': nationalised banks	Weak social partners: decentralised bargaining
Netherlands: Medium-high	'Welfare without work' multiple pathways	Negotiated collective (pre)retirement schemes	Employment regulation, long-term employment	'Organised': quality production	'Coordinated', but also multinationals	'Social partnership': corporatist bargaining
Germany: Medium-high	'Welfare without work' multiple pathways	Voluntary occupational pension	Employment regulation, long-term employment	'Organised': quality production	'Coordinated', long-term patient capital	'Social partnership': works councils, sector bargaining
UK: Medium	Liberal welfare state: limited pathways	Voluntary employer or private pension (opt-out of state pension)	Low employment regulation, high turnover	'Unorganised': mass production	'Uncoordinated', short-termism	'Voluntarism': decentralised bargaining
USA: Medium	Liberal welfare state: limited pathways	Voluntary/negotiated pension plans	Low employment regulation, high turnover	'Unorganised': mass production	'Uncoordinated', short-termism	'Voluntarism': decentralised bargaining
Sweden: Medium-low	Universal welfare state: gradual pathways	Negotiated supplementary pension	Employment regulation, reintegration policies	'Organised' quality production	'Coordinated': public investment, long-term ownership	'Neo-corporatist': centralised and workplace bargaining
Japan: Low	Residual welfare state: limited pathways	Employer pension plan (opt-out)	Employment tenure, 'shukko' practice	'Organised': flexible production	'Coordinated': large groups	Peaceful: company unionism

American and British occupational pensions), the economic 'push' to force older workers to retire can be accommodated by social practices of re-employment and self-employment, partially supported by the state.

Indeed, the analysis of the interaction of human resources policies and financial governance, i.e. the impact of particular 'production regimes', turns out differently in early exit from work policies. All competitive firms experience the need to restructure their workforces in order to adapt to technological change. They have also come under pressure to downsize in order to meet falls in demand and profitability slacks. However, the need for adaptation seems to be more widespread in diversified quality production systems with highly skilled workforces, while the downsizing pressures are stronger in uncoordinated market economies. We therefore expect the 'push' to shed older workers to be cyclical in liberal market economies, and more long-term and structural in coordinated market economies. This is indeed the case: German, Japanese and Swedish companies have sought to shed labour as means to allow skill enhancement and plant restructuring, while not undermining their pledge to tenured employment and a seniority wage system. While German and other Continental European firms used early retirement as a means to offer an early exit, Swedish and Japanese firms used alternative means: re-employment, job rotation and part-time work. Under uncoordinated financial governance, American and British firms are hard pressed to downsize for higher dividends required by the stock market and after (unfriendly) mergers. Ironically, the workers' pension funds, as institutional investors, have reinforced such financial market pressures. Initially, Anglo-American firms were willing to pay for occupational pensions in order to attract and retain skilled blue-collar workers and white-collar employees; they later applied these schemes to use early retirement for restructuring and downsizing, and they are now seeking to relieve themselves of the burden of defined-benefit plans and instead offer portable cash plans as mere fringe benefits to a mobile and flexible workforce.

The third institutional variable, and the 'missing link' between the welfare state and production regimes, is the industrial relation system: the institutionalised rules and interaction of capital and labour in collective bargaining and the role the 'social partners' play in social policy making and implementation. In the case of American and British firms, downsizing became the overriding concern. Only when unions strongly enforced seniority rules and when management was committed to maintaining employment tenure were *ad hoc* offers for topping up public social security granted. The common early retirement practice by Continental European firms relies heavily on consensual externalisation by the social partners, while Japanese and Swedish firms partially internalise the costs of keeping older workers employed (Naschold *et al.* 1994a). In Continental Europe, employers and unions have been willing to 'collude' to foster early retirement for the sake of upholding employment protection and seniority pay. Management was interested in maintaining good relations at the workplace by allowing older workers to retire on favourable conditions. Employer associations and unions at a national or sectoral level were willing to bargain over collective early retirement schemes that would complement, if not supplement, public pathways. However, as early retirement increasingly became an acquired social right, defended by unions, and less and less controlled by management, employers grew increasingly critical. Moreover, the externalisation of costs by management–worker collusion has pushed up social expenditure for both public and private schemes, which in turn will increase payroll and general taxes that have a negative impact on competitiveness and subsequently labour demand.

Facing this 'continental dilemma' (see Scharpf, Chapter 12) of rising labour costs through increased inactivity, and the demographic 'time bomb', governments and employer associations are now calling for policy reversal. However, a reform of early retirement has proven very difficult for various reasons (Ebbinghaus 2000): multiple pathways allow instrument substitution (as one pathway becomes reduced, the second-best alternative is used); the configuration of multiple actors leads to mere cost shifting (the government cuts public benefits, and the social partners finance the reduced benefit gap); multi-level governance leads to implementation problems (higher-level actors agree on reform, but lower levels, e.g. workplace management and labour, counteract this by externalising costs to the public); the institutional interdependencies make reform efforts complex (reforms of various institutional arrangements such as employment and social security law have to be coordinated). My main argument here is that there are intricate 'institutional complementarities' between the particular welfare states, production regimes and industrial relation systems that structure the incentives under which actors make decisions on work and retirement.

These institutional complementarities that shape the 'collusion' between capital, labour and the state are formidable obstacles to reform. While institutional theory does not rule out change, it highlights the fact that discontinuous institutional change will only happen at critical junctures and that otherwise change is largely path dependent, structuring the available alternatives given 'sunk costs', positive feedback, vested interests and network externalities (Pierson 2000). The current reform efforts are thus more dispersed (Ebbinghaus 2000): the closing down of temporary early exit programmes, a gradual increase in the retirement age, stepwise reforms of the eligibility criteria of public programmes, cost shifting from public to private actors, training and reintegration of older workers, active employment policies and more flexible employment regulations. In order to overcome the political opposition and implementation problem, social concertation between government, employer associations and trade unions has also been sought in countries with social partnership traditions (Ebbinghaus and Hassel 2000). For these societies, a unilateral policy reversal by the government is unlikely to be successful, given the veto powers of labour and the welfare constituency. A sudden shift of costs from public pay-as-you-go to privately funded schemes would lead to severe double-payer problems (Myles and Pierson 2000). Moreover, a fundamental change in early retirement policies threatens to undermine the social consensus that has prevailed thus far, with unpredictable consequences for social welfare, peaceful labour relations, long-term human resources policies and coordinated financial governance. Thus reform efforts should seek to renegotiate the underlying social pact and to adapt the historically derived institutional complementarities to the new challenges in a coordinated way.

Note

1 This chapter is an abridged version of the working paper PSGE 00/4, Center for European Studies, Harvard University, July 2000.

References

Aarts, L. J. M., Burkhauser, R. V. and de Jong, P. R. (1996). 'Introduction and overview', in L. J. M. Aarts, R. V. Burkhauser and P. R. de Jong (eds), *Curing the Dutch Disease.* Aldershot: Avebury, 1–19.

Aarts, L. J. M. and de Jong, P. R. (1996). 'The Dutch disability program and how it grew', in L. J. M. Aarts, R. V. Burkhauser and P. R. de Jong (eds), *Curing the Dutch Disease* Aldershot: Avebury, 21–46.

ap Roberts, L. and Turner, J. (1997). 'Enterprise and the state: Interactions in the provision of employees' retirement income in the United States', in M. Rein and E. Wadensjö (eds), *Enterprise and the Welfare State.* Cheltenham: Edward Elgar, 352–79.

Berkowitz, E. D. and Burkhauser, R. V. (1996). 'A United States perspective on disability programs', in L. J. M. Aarts, R. V. Burkhauser and P. R. de Jong (eds), *Curing the Dutch Disease.* Aldershot: Avebury, 71–91.

Bispinck, R. (1997). 'The chequered history of the Alliance for Jobs', in G. Fajertag and P. Pochet (eds), *Social Pacts in Europe.* Brussels: ETUI, 63–78.

Blomsma, M. and Jansweijer, R. (1997). 'The Netherlands: Growing importance of private sector arrangements', in M. Rein and E. Wadensjö (eds), *Enterprise and the Welfare State.* Cheltenham: Edward Elgar, 220–65.

Buechtemann, C. F. (1993). 'Introduction: Employment security and labor market behavior', in C. F. Buechtemann (ed.), *Employment Security and Labor Market Behavior.* Ithaca, NY: ILR Press, 1–66.

Casey, B. (1989). 'Early retirement: The problem of "instrument substitution" and "cost shifting" and their implications for restructuring the process of retirement', in W. Schmähl (ed.), *Redefining the Process of Retirement.* Berlin: Springer, 133–50.

Casey, B. (1997). 'Incentives and disincentives to early and late retirement', *ILO Conference*, Geneva, September 1997.

Casey, B. and Wood, S. (1994). 'Great Britain: Firm policy, state policy and the employment and unemployment of older workers', in F. Naschold and B. de Vroom (eds), *Regulating Employment and Welfare.* Berlin: de Gruyter, 363–94.

Chen, Y.-P. (1996). 'Gradual retirement in the United States: Macro issues and policies', in L. Delsen and G. Reday-Mulvey (eds), *Gradual Retirement in the OECD Countries.* Aldershot: Dartmouth, 164–85.

Crouch, C. (1993). *Industrial Relations and European State Traditions.* Oxford: Clarendon Press.

Davies, B. (1996). 'Trade union involvement in supplementary pensions', in E. Reynaud *et al.* (eds), *International Perspectives on Supplementary Pensions.* Westport, CT: Quorum, 49–61.

Dore, R. (1997). 'The distinctiveness of Japan', in C. Crouch and W. Streeck (eds), *Political Economy of Modern Capitalism.* London: Sage, 19–32.

Ebbinghaus, B. (2000). 'Any way out of "exit from work"? Reversing the entrenched pathways of early retirement', in F. W. Scharpf and V. Schmidt (eds), *Welfare and Work in the Open Economy. Vol. II.* Oxford: Oxford University Press, 511–53.

Ebbinghaus, B. and Hassel, A. (2000). 'Striking deals: Concertation in the reform of Continental European welfare states', *Journal of European Public Policy* 7(1), 44–62.

Ebbinghaus, B. and Visser, J. (1997). 'Der Wandel der Arbeitsbeziehungen im westeuropäischen Vergleich', in S. Hradil and S. Immerfall (eds), *Die westeuropäischen Gesellschaften im Vergleich.* Opladen: Leske + Budrich, 333–75.

Ebbinghaus, B. and Visser, J. (2000). *Trade Unions in Western Europe since 1945 (Handbook and CD-ROM).* London: Macmillan.

Ehrenberg, R. G. and Jakubson, G. H. (1993). 'Introduction: Employment security and labor market behavior', in C. F. Buechtemann (ed.), *Employment Security and Labor Market Behavior.* Ithaca, NY: ILR Press, 200–14.

Esping-Andersen, G. (1990). *Three Worlds of Welfare Capitalism.* Princeton, NJ: Princeton University Press.

Esping-Andersen, G. (1992). 'The emerging realignment between labour movements and welfare states', in M. Regini (ed.), *The Future of Labour Movements.* London: Sage, 133–59.

Esping-Andersen, G. (1996). 'Welfare states without work: The impasse of labour shedding and familialism in Continental Europe', in G. Esping-Andersen (ed.), *Welfare States in Transition.* London: Sage, 66–87.

Estevez-Abe, M., Iversen, T. and Soskice, D. (1999). 'Social protection and the formation of skills: A reinterpretation of the welfare state', *APSA, Altanta, 2–5 September 1999.*

Freeman, R. B. and Medoff, J. L. (1984). *What do unions do?* New York: Basic Books.

Frick, B. and Sadowski, D. (1996). 'A German perspective on disability policy', in L. J. M. Aarts, R. V. Burkhauser and P. R. de Jong (eds), *Curing the Dutch Disease.* Aldershot: Avebury, 117–31.

Gern, K.-J. (1998). 'Recent developments in old-age pension systems: An international overview', *Kiel Working Paper* (863).

Golden, M. A. (1997). *Heroic Defeats. The Politics of Job Loss.* New York: Cambridge University Press.

Golden, M. A., Wallerstein, M. and Lange, P. (1999). 'Postwar trade-union organization and industrial relations in twelve countries', in H. Kitschelt *et al.* (eds), *Continuity and Change in Contemporary Capitalism.* New York: Cambridge University Press, 194–230.

Gruber, J. and Wise, D. A. (1999). 'Introduction and summary', in J. Gruber and D. A. Wise (eds), *Social Security and Retirement around the World.* Chicago: University of Chicago Press, 1–35.

Guillemard, A.-M. (1991a). 'France: Massive exit through unemployment', in M. Kohli *et al.* (eds), *Time for Retirement.* New York: Cambridge University Press, 127–80.

Guillemard, A.-M. (1991b). 'Pathways and their prospects: A comparative interpretation of the meaning of early exit', in M. Kohli *et al.* (eds), *Time for Retirement.* New York: Cambridge University Press, 362–87.

Guillemard, A.-M. and Rein, M. (1993). 'Comparative patterns of retirement. Recent trends in developed societies', *Annual Review of Sociology* 19, 469–503.

Hall, P. A. (1997). 'The role of interests, institutions and ideas in the comparative political economy of the industrialized nations', in M. I. Lichbach and A. S. Zuckerman (eds), *Comparative Politics. Rationality, Culture and Structure.* New York: Cambridge University Press, 174–207.

Hollingsworth, J. R. and Boyer, R. (1997). 'Coordination of economic actors and social systems of production', in J. R. Hollingsworth and R. Boyer (eds), *Contemporary Capitalism. The Embeddedness of Institutions.* New York: Cambridge University Press, 1–47.

Huber, E. and Stephens, J. D. (1999). 'Welfare state and production regimes in the era of retrenchment, Occasional Papers, Princeton, NJ: Institute for Advanced Studies.

Hutchens, R. (1994). 'The United States: Employer policies for discouraging work by older people', in F. Naschold and B. de Vroom (eds), *Regulating Employment and Welfare.* Berlin: de Gruyter, 395–431.

Jacobs, K., Kohli, M. and Rein, M. (1991a). 'Germany: The diversity of pathways', in M. Kohli *et al.* (eds), *Time for Retirement.* New York: Cambridge University Press, 181–221.

Jacobs, K., Kohli, M. and Rein, M. (1991b). 'Testing the industry-mix hypothesis of early exit', in M. Kohli *et al.* (eds), *Time for Retirement.* New York: Cambridge University Press, 67–96.

Kapteyn, A. and de Vos, K. (1999). 'Social security and retirement in the Netherlands', in J. Gruber and D. A. Wise (eds), *Social Security and Retirement around the World.* Chicago: University of Chicago Press, 269–303.

Kimura, Y. (1997). 'The role of the Japanese company in compensating income loss after retirement', in M. Rein and E. Wadensjö (eds), *Enterprise and the Welfare State.* Cheltenham: Edward Elgar, 195–219.

Kimura, T. *et al.* (1994). 'Japan: Shukko, teinen and re-employment', in F. Naschold and B. de Vroom (eds). *Regulating Employment and Welfare.* Berlin: de Gruyter, 247–307.

Kohli, M. and Rein, M. (1991). 'The changing balance of work and retirement', in M. Kohli *et al.* (eds), *Time for Retirement.* New York: Cambridge University Press, 1–35.

Kohli, M. *et al.* (eds) (1991). *Time for Retirement. Comparative Studies on Early Exit from the Labor Force.* New York: Cambridge University Press.

Laczko, F. and Phillipson, C. (1991). 'Great Britain: The contradictions of early exit', in M. Kohli *et al.* (eds), *Time for Retirement.* New York: Cambridge University Press, 222–51.

Lonsdale, S. and Aylward, M. (1996). 'A United Kingdom perspective on disability policy', in L. J. M. Aarts, R. V. Burkhauser and P. R. de Jong (eds), *Curing the Dutch Disease.* Aldershot: Avebury, 93–115.

Lynes, T. (1997). 'The British case', in M. Rein and E. Wadensjö (eds), *Enterprise and the Welfare State.* Cheltenham: Edward Elgar, 309–51.

Manow, P. (1997). 'Social insurance and the German political economy', *MPIfG Discussion Paper* 97/2, Cologne: Max Planck Institute for the Study of Societies.

Myles, J. (1989). *Old Age in the Welfare State. The Political Economy of Public Pensions,* 2nd edn. Lawrence, KS: University Press of Kansas.

Myles, J. and Pierson, P. (2000). 'The comparative political economy of pension reform', in P. Pierson (ed.), *The New Politics of the Welfare State.* Oxford: Oxford University Press 305–33.

Myles, J. and Quadagno, J. (eds) (1991). *States, Labor Markets and the Future of Old-Age Policy.* Philadelphia, PA: Temple University Press.

Naschold, F. and de Vroom, B. (eds) (1994). *Regulating Employment and Welfare. Company and National Policies of Labour Force Participation at the End of Worklife in Industrial Countries.* Berlin: de Gruyter.

Naschold, F., de Vroom, B. and Casey, B. (1994a). 'Regulating employment and welfare: An international comparison between firms and countries', in F. Naschold and B. de Vroom (eds), *Regulating Employment and Welfare.* Berlin: de Gruyter, 433–89.

Naschold, F. *et al.* (1994b). 'Germany: The concerted transition from work to welfare', in F. Naschold and B. de Vroom (eds), *Regulating Employment and Welfare.* Berlin: de Gruyter, 117–82.

OECD (Organisation for Economic Co-Operation and Development) (various years). *Labour Force Statistics.* Paris: OECD.

Olofsson, G. and Petersson, J. (1994). 'Sweden: Policy dilemmas of the changing age structure in a "work society"', in F. Naschold and B. de Vroom (eds), *Regulating Employment and Welfare.* Berlin: de Gruyter, 183–245.

Olson, M. (1965). *The Logic of Collective Action. Public Goods and the Theory of Groups*, 2nd edn. Cambridge, MA: Harvard University Press.

Pierson, P. (2000). 'Increasing returns, path dependence and the study of politics', *American Political Science Review* 94(2), 251–67.

Reday-Mulvey, G. (1996). 'Gradual retirement in France', in L. Delsen and G. Reday-Mulvey (eds), *Gradual Retirement in the OECD Countries*. Aldershot: Dartmouth, 45–68.

Sass, S. A. (1997). *The Promise of Private Pensions. The First Hundred Years*. Cambridge, MA: Harvard University Press.

Schmähl, W. (1997). 'The public–private mix in pension provision in Germany: The role of employer-based pension arrangements and the influence of public activities', in M. Rein and E. Wadensjö (eds), *Enterprise and the Welfare State*. Cheltenham: Edward Elgar, 99–148.

Schmähl, W., George, R. and Oswald, C. (1996). 'Gradual retirement in Germany', in L. Delsen and G. Reday-Mulvey (eds), *Gradual Retirement in the OECD Countries*. Aldershot: Dartmouth, 69–93.

Sheppard, H. L. (1991). 'The United States: The privatization of exit', in M. Kohli *et al.* (eds), *Time for Retirement*. New York: Cambridge University Press, 252–83.

Soskice, D. (1999). 'Divergent production regimes: Coordinated and uncoordinated market economies in the 1980s and 1990s', in H. Kitschelt *et al.* (eds), *Continuity and Change in Contemporary Capitalism*. New York: Cambridge University Press, 101–34.

Steinmeyer, H.-D. (1996). 'Labor mobility and supplementary pensions', in E. Reynaud *et al.* (eds), *International Perspectives on Supplementary Pensions*, Westport, CT: Quorum, 185–90.

Stinchcombe, A. L. (1965). 'Social structure and organizations', in J. G. March (ed.), *Handbook of Organizations*. Chicago: Rand McNally, 142–93.

Streeck, W. (1992). *Social Institutions and Economic Performance. Studies of Industrial Relations in Advanced Capitalist Economies*. London: Sage.

Takayama, N. (1996). 'Gradual retirement in Japan: Macro issues and policies', in L. Delsen and G. Reday-Mulvey (eds), *Gradual Retirement in the OECD Countries*. Aldershot: Dartmouth, 135–63.

Trommel, W. and de Vroom, B. (1994). 'The Netherlands: The Loreley-effect of early exit', in F. Naschold and B. de Vroom (eds), *Regulating Employment and Welfare*. Berlin: de Gruyter, 51–115.

Turner, J. A. and Watanabe, N. (1995). *Private Pension Policies in Industrialized Countries. A Compartive Analysis*. Kalamazoo, MI: W.E. Upjohn Institute for Employment Research.

Wadensjö, E. (1991). 'Sweden: Partial exit', in M. Kohli *et al.* (eds), *Time for Retirement*. New York: Cambridge University Press, 284–323.

Wadensjö, E. (1996). 'Gradual retirement in Sweden', in L. Delsen and G. Reday-Mulvey (eds), *Gradual Retirement in the OECD Countries*. Aldershot: Dartmouth, 25–44.

Wadensjö, E. (1997). 'The Welfare Mix in Pension Provisions in Sweden', in M. Rein and E. Wadensjö (eds), *Enterprise and the Welfare State*. Cheltenham: Edward Elgar, 266–308.

Wadensjö, E. and Palmer, E. E. (1996). 'Curing the Dutch disease from a Swedish perspective', in L. J. M. Aarts, R. V. Burkhauser and P. R. de Jong (eds), *Curing the Dutch Disease*. Aldershot: Avebury, 133–55.

Part II

Industrial relations and welfare state regimes

5 Welfare state regimes and industrial relations systems

The questionable role of path dependency theory

Colin Crouch

Introduction

There is an ostensibly clear but curiously fugitive link between recent attempts at classifying industrial relations systems and welfare states. Let us forget for the moment the problem of whether empirical cases neatly fit the types presented in a classificatory scheme, and look simply at typologies.

Theories of comparative industrial relations systems have identified contestative, pluralist and neo-corporatist types (Crouch 1993).[1] The first comprise situations in which at least one of the group comprising the state, employers and their organisations, and trade unions refuse to accept the legitimacy of at least one of the others. Under the second there is mutual acceptance, and this takes the form of a diversity of essentially competing organisations, each seeking its own advantage in a defective analogy of the free market.[2] Under the last there is also mutual recognition, but among hegemonic organisations constrained by virtue of their centrality to the system to pursue certain collective or possibly even public goods, and to have concern for externalities. Further sub-divisions are possible, but only one interests us here, as it helps make the link with the analysis of welfare states. That concerns a certain difference between those neocorporatist systems based on particularly powerful labour movements, and those with relatively weaker labour organisations but where employers and the state are for various reasons required to incorporate them within the general task of economic management.

Comparative analyses of welfare states have identified liberal, social democratic and corporatist forms (Esping-Andersen 1990). Under liberal regimes priority is given to the maintenance of the market economy. Welfare therefore tends to be residual and concerned with ensuring that labour is not de-commodified and does not lose the market incentives that require it to participate. Social democratic regimes move to the opposite pole and prioritise the maintenance of workers' earnings when they are outside the labour market. Corporatist systems are also less concerned with retaining labour as commodified, but do this through non-redistributive welfare organised by occupational category.[3] There has again been considerable discussion of potential sub-types, one of which has proved to be particularly important, especially in western Europe. That is the separation from the corporatist camp of certain welfare states where the family rather than the occupational group has the prime responsibility.

If we try to pair the four types from each pattern, we have the following *Wahlverwandschaften* (elective affinities):[4]

The pluralist and liberal models belong together as those in which social policy most clearly follows either markets or market analogies, there being a concern among whichever interests might have shaped such systems to stay as close as possible to the idea of market forces allocating resources and income distributions.

The neo-corporatist form of industrial relations with strong labour parallels the social democratic welfare form. In both cases there is departure from a pure market economy determined by the power of movements of organised labour.

The neo-corporatist form of industrial relations with relatively stronger organised employers can, perhaps less obviously, be related to the corporatist welfare state. In both cases labour organisations are not powerful enough to enforce a strongly redistributive agenda, but for various reasons employers and the state are constrained to incorporate them in organisational form rather than through the operation of more or less pure markets.

This leaves the least obvious potential pairing: contestative industrial relations and familial welfare states. Again here the link is power relations in an empirically observable institutional context. Labour is too weak either to secure recognition in industrial relations or to secure a welfare state geared primarily to labour concerns. This might be expected to produce an extreme form of the market-liberal model. That it does not do so suggests the presence of additional interests apart from the simple conflict between capital labour. Something of this kind clearly also lies behind the third pair, since the organisation of interests and systems based on occupational positions results from something other than the use by labour of organisation, as is assumed in most theories of the role of organisations in the economy, from Max Weber onwards. We must remember here that in Esping-Andersen's original formulation no distinction was made between these two sub-forms of welfare states.

Elsewhere (Crouch 1999: chapter 13) I have suggested that both the link between them and the error of combining them can be related to the same point: the role of 'tradition' in these structures. By tradition I mean essentially pre-industrial structures which resist and are distinct from both market forces and working-class interests. This trinity of forces is embedded in the conflict among conservatism, liberalism and socialism which, translated into real organisational form through any number of complexities, lay at the base of nearly all twentieth century politics. The general idea of traditional conservatism gives us the essential unity of Esping-Andersen's neo-corporatist form. The need to discriminate within it derives from the diversity of forms of tradition, which is nothing like so clear and simple in its meaning as market capitalism or the organised working class. Potentially it might be very diverse indeed. In practice it relates to two specific forms. Most clearly and simply we can identify tradition, as inherited in nineteenth century Europe, as embodied in the churches and the favourite institution of their protection, the family. Theoretically the familial welfare state is that in which the church retained considerable influence during the process of industrialisation. An alternative version of traditionalism in the course of modernisation was the use of pre-industrial craft forms as the model for industrialism. This gives tradition as an essentially guild-form, as opposed to *sui generis* free-market, organisation of industrialism; hence an essentially organised kind of capitalism and occupationally based welfare regime.

There is a remaining incoherence in this. Why should strength of the church and family be associated with contestative industrial relations? There is certainly no reason to associate these exclusively, as we shall see. However, we can identify a link, even though it is disappointingly untheoretical. Where the church, particularly the Catholic church, was strong, it was able to produce its own labour organisations. This weakened labour unity and therefore made contestative structures more feasible even after a period in which the organisation of workers as such could not be prevented. There is another, even more empirical link: Where the Catholic church was cultural hegemonic the more likely was opposition to traditional authority to take a totalising, counter-cultural form. This because historical Catholicism itself was totalising and cultural – hegemonic in the sense originally intended by Gramsci. In the history of European working-class organisations, counter-cultural counter-hegemony usually required organisation by the Communist party, which was more likely than pragmatic social democracy to regard itself and its potential constituency as an isolated, alienated bloc within existing society both requiring and being capable of a counter-cultural form of opposition. In turn, the stronger such currents within the working class, the more likely were both labour and capital to pursue contestative policies.

We could display these differences along two orthogonal variables. One clearly relates to the relative strength of organised labour and capital. The other is a continuum between traditionalism and industrialism, with guild forms of traditionalism occupying a kind of mid-point, urban guilds having been the least traditional component of pre-modern European societies.

Such a model is of use only if individual systems, which for simplicity's sake we shall treat here as national systems, can be analysed in terms of it, and we ought to find, at least at an initial view, some correlation between countries' positions in the two policy areas.

Some cases seem to fit such an approach quite well. Models of industrial relations systems usually allocate the Scandinavian countries, including in more recent decades Finland, as straightforward examples of neo-corporatism with strong labour. Esping-Andersen's social democratic welfare state category is indeed sometimes known as Scandinavian. The United Kingdom, along with the USA outside Europe, is usually seen as having a predominantly pluralist industrial relations system, and welfare state analyses often treat the liberal bloc as an Anglophone one. Germany and Switzerland are prime examples of neo-corporatism with strongly organised employers and of the corporatist welfare state based on occupational categories. Italy and Spain often occupy the contestation box in industrial relations models, and are the leading examples of the familial welfare state.

Quod erat demonstrandum. However, on a closer view matters are not so simple. Where are Austria, France and the Netherlands? Also, where the welfare state is concerned, the UK is more of a compromise between liberalism and social democracy, particularly if health care rather than retirement pensions are the focus of analysis.[5] Meanwhile and complicating the situation even further, that country's institutions in general are often seen as embodying very strong doses of traditionalism.

But empirical cases never fit models perfectly. Provided we can explain a case *in terms of* the model, it is not relevant whether it fits snugly into a specific box. If, to cite a prominent example, the Netherlands shares attributes of both corporatist and social democratic welfare state forms, to analyse it in this way is to demonstrate the power of the model, not to refute it. The model has a problem here only if there are empirical components which cannot be related to any of its terms. This is possibly the case where France is concerned. Republican political forces in that country, particularly during the nineteenth century, seem at times to correspond to economic liberalism; but the state is too autonomous; or they seem to correspond to social democracy, but the working class is too weak. A need to incorporate *étatisme* does require some more radical reshaping than just adding another box to the model or point on one or other of the continua.

Setting this last problem aside, while allocating cases across theoretical boxes is not a problem for the theory, it does create difficulties for particular kinds of empirical and in particular policy-oriented research. This wants to know, for example, whether neo-corporatist industrial relations systems deliver better inflation control than pluralist ones, or whether there is more female employment under social democratic than corporatist welfare regimes. Given the small number of available cases, such research can only proceed in terms of a quantitative methodology by taking cases as proxies for types. The fact that this is commonly done should not blind us to the dubious scientific procedure of the process. The problem cannot be solved by forcibly shovelling a case into one box or the other in order to increase the *n* of a particular box. The only solution is to follow procedures which are more true to genuine scientific method, even if they offend the crude application of statistical techniques which often passes for such procedures in applied economic and social research.

The role of path dependency theory

There is a second question. This theoretical approach is heavily rooted in assumptions of path dependency; it derives its predictive power from the assumption that successive generations of political and social actors have difficulty in departing from patterns set by their predecessors. The popularity of path dependency theory originates in Douglas North's highly successful use of the concept in his study of the history of capitalist institutional development (1990). This has encouraged the search for 'lock in', when social actors pursue a path which, initially offering advantages, eventually becomes a trap. This approach then links up with the comparative research methodology of allocating cases to theoretical boxes, and the behaviour of the inhabitants of the boxes then statistically compared.

One problem with this is that countries have demonstrably not always occupied the same niche in the model. What are we to make of the ferociously contestative periods in the Nordic countries in the interwar years; in Austria and Germany during both the late nineteenth century and the Nazi period; in the UK during the mid-nineteenth century and late twentieth; and in the USA for much of the twentieth century with the exception of a prolonged interlude from around 1935 to 1980? Italy, Portugal and Spain on the other hand can no longer be defined as contestative, though they were for long periods and are usually identified as such in models of comparative industrial relations. There is a way round this. It can be shown (e.g. Crouch 1993, part III) that particular institutional configurations are likely to produce extreme conflict under one set of power relations, but quite different ones under another. For example, very strongly and centralised organised actors are likely to produce severely contestative and conflictual relations if they refuse mutual recognition; but neo-corporatist understandings if they accept each other's right to exist.

But that is not the end of the matter. It only makes it more difficult for social scientists to play the predictive part that they are expected to perform when they work in policy-related areas. This might leave them still able to deal with examples of varying relations between historical trajectory (institutional patterns) and changing power relations, but the ideas of mixed institutional legacy that cut across boxes creates further problems. If an institutional system has a very mixed parentage, its path dependency may be uncertain. Temporarily forgetting 'paths', let us examine further the different analogy suggested by 'parentage'. It is well known among animal breeders that 'mongrels', individuals with a very mixed parentage, are likely to be more robust and adaptable than pedigree specimens, who embody extreme concentrations of characteristics reproduced without admixture over generations. It is far easier to predict the typical congenital weaknesses of a pedigree animal than a mongrel. Something similar may well be true of social structures. A system which embodies a diversity of inherited characteristics is able to shift to an alternative strand if one aspect of its inheritance no longer serves to resolve its problems.

For example, it was common in the 1970s to predict that the heavily pluralist structure of British industrial relations, with very little capacity for neo-corporatist coordination, would be able to do nothing but fall deeper into crisis, ungovernability and decline (Beer 1982). Observers did not notice the important but temporarily sidelined strand of market liberalism embedded in British institutions, particularly in the financial sector, which happened to be undergoing a crisis of role and purpose during the 1970s. A combination of political change and the transformed role of the financial sector during the 1980s and 1990s led to outcomes in British industrial relations which no one predicted in the 1970s. But it lay there latent all the time.

To express the point this way is temporarily to assume a very functionalist model; of course, there will be conflicts of interests over whose identification of problems and acceptable solutions prevails, and this will be at least as much a matter of power relations as of objective perception of hypothetical system 'needs'. This is a point to which we shall return. All we need to take from the analogy is the idea of a diversified inheritance of action possibilities.

The point has a number of implications. First, for social scientists there is clearly a problem. If they can assume path dependency, they can make confident predictions. To return to the path analogy, they are in the happy position of someone trying to predict at which platform an approaching train will arrive, having already seen on which track it is running. If we add the possibility of diversified institutional legacies we are asking our trainspotter to repeat his predictions when there is a confusing mass of points between the approaching train and the potential platforms of arrival. There is a possible answer to this. Accounts of path dependency need to search for latent and potential institutional resources. This involves treading a difficult path between simple extrapolations of existing dominant patterns (the usual practice with path dependency theory) and disappearing into the totally *ad hoc* empiricism of British historiography.

A second question raised is that nation states (or other institutional networks which might be the object of analyses of this kind) may well differ in the extent of their institutional diversity. Is it perhaps the case that societies which are difficult to allocate to boxes in the classificatory scheme have a more diverse potential repertoire than those which are more straightforward? For example, are France, the Netherlands and the UK adaptable mongrels, where Sweden, Germany and Spain are unhealthy interbred specimens? Or is it more likely to be the case that anything as complex as an advanced industrial nation state is likely to have potential alternative resources? This is an intriguing question, suggesting that we should consider, not so much the substantive characteristics of a system, but the formal fact of the possible diversity and indeed its internal incoherence. For example, what is more important, the fact that Sweden is the most complete empirical example of social democracy yet produced, or the fact that it is also the country which has the highest relative proportion of multinational enterprises among its domestic capital, and one of the most tightly integrated family networks of capitalist inheritance? Similarly, Germany, with its extraordinary combination of religious confessions, powerful industrial capitalism, powerful trade unions, strong but federal state, and extreme diversity of twentieth century political regimes can never be regarded as a simple vase with a limited repertoire of path dependencies. Finally Spain, during its relatively brief period of democratic history, has already demonstrated in its regional differences as much social structural diversity as almost the rest of western Europe combined.

From this point in the argument it is, as noted, easy to slip into the methodology of British empirical historiography and argue that history is just a series of events, connected maybe by the integration of individual human biography, but little else. Prediction is impossible; explanation is a matter of the reconstruction of the motivations of significant individuals. Such an extreme conclusion is however not necessary. The train approaching the platform will encounter a finite and in principle knowable set of points, not an infinity of possibilities. The particular inheritances of specific institutional systems are similarly not infinite, and it is the task of social science to lay bare the extent and limits in individual cases. To take an extreme example: Faced with a problem of gender competition, the resources available to the governments of Afghanistan and Sweden are not identical and are heavily context-dependent. Both however do have some scope for manoeuvre around their relative fixed points. Policy regimes are neither caged beasts nor wild ones. They are tethered, with ropes of varying lengths. That said, there is considerable scope for creativity in how the potential policy mixes are pulled together.

Social scientists will always be at a disadvantage in such situations. Real-world social actors acting under sometimes intolerable pressures will find solutions, often perhaps unconsciously, that would never have been predicted by a think-tank or academic study group removed from the nerve-wracking pressure of events. Just as economic theory is very poor at dealing with innovation and entrepreneurship, even though these activities seem to be at the base of its reasoning,[6] so sociology and political science are poor at anticipating policy innovation. Rather than either produce doom-laden predictions of path dependency or construct abstract but unrealisable policy models, the best service which academic social science can probably render the policy-making process is to explore the obscure and forgotten byways of past repertoires suited to individual cases. What we can and should do is to build scope for innovation by policy actors into our models, by at least trying to anticipate the moments at which it is most likely to happen. There are two possibilities here. First there are situations where an existing actor (be it the state or a particular social partner) has power to act, but cannot achieve any goals by continuing to pursue existing paths. To some extent examples here would be the French and Swedish governments trying to continue with Keynesian policies in the early 1980s, in a context where newly powerful financial markets were not prepared to tolerate such action. These governments had reached a kind of 'end of the road', but they continued to have capacity for action and could change policy direction, however painful this was for them. A similar example would be the approach of the Italian centre-left late-1990s governments and the trade unions facing the contradiction between their desire that Italy should enter the European single currency and the problems which membership posed to their policy preferences. In the event they took decisive and painful action, because no viable course of action promised no pain at all.

A second possibility is virtually the opposite of that one, and this is when a government or other social actor has considerable power for action, and faces a context that imposes very few constraints on how it uses that power. This leaves it free, if it so chooses, to break free from the constraints of past compromises to pursue courses of its own choosing. The approach to industrial relations of the Thatcher government in the UK after the defeat of the coal miners' strike in 1985 would be an example.

In both types of cases we can gain clues from knowledge of the surrounding situation as to what action is likely to be taken. In the case of an actor retaining capacity to act but finding it very difficult to pursue familiar preferred paths (as in the French, Italian and Swedish cases), we predict a new compromise between existing preferred preferences and the exogenously imposed constraints – though the precise policy mix that ensues will depend on policy makers' capacity for innovation under the pressure of constraint. While the second case is in principle less free of constraint and therefore in principle more free to range wherever it likes, in practice it is likely to move close to existing policy preferences, which are usually knowable. There will therefore be some continuity of path dependency, but innovation within its terms because of the liberation from prior context.

North (1990) derived the idea of path dependency from studies of scientific and technological methodology, where researchers following a particular design paradigm would become unable to cope with challenges that were not anticipated by the logic of that paradigm. But transferred to something as incoherent as a social institution this analogy can be only partial and eventually deceptive. It leaves out of account the mixed character of real as opposed to ideal typical institutional legacies, and the importance of different weighting of calculations of action induced by exogeneity.

To a considerable extent the utility of the concept of path dependency depends on what we understand by the analogy of path. It is likely that, in the late twentieth or early twenty-first century, we envisage a clear, well made and signposted track that leads from A to B. This however assumes a path maker with strong central power, able to design the path and enforce its construction. This is not a very useful analogy for complex societies without clear directing centres and with uncertain knowledge of their futures. More useful is the medieval concept of a route. Pilgrims and other long-distance travellers asking 'the way' to a particular destination did not expect to find a clearly marked road, but a series of alternative possibilities, the use of which required considerable trial and error. One route between A and somewhere on the way to B might be flooded, or beset by wild beasts, or subject to avalanche. In that case there were alternative possibilities that could be inquired about and tentatively followed. The path was a series of possible alternatives. The number was certainly not unlimited, and it would be possible to know the full range of such alternatives at certain points, though there would be some doubt whether particular travellers might traverse any particular path or indeed invent a new one.

Viewed in this version of the analogy, the analysis of welfare state and industrial relations regimes regains its role. It becomes a question of indicating what seem to be the range of possibilities, and possibly where innovation might be expressed. A combination of, say, a powerful labour movement and a non-traditional capitalist elite does not necessarily imply a social democratic and neo-corporatist compromise. Either side in that combination might well try a contestative struggle, using its considerable resources for a fight to the finish. This is indeed what occurred in Scandinavian industrial relations in the 1920s and early 1930s, until that particular path seemed blocked, the parties returned to base and sought out a neo-corporatist alternative instead. It could have worked out differently. Given a different power balance, there might have been a complete victory for liberal capitalism and a breaking of the labour movement, as occurred in the UK in the 1980s and as some Swedish employers would like to try today. Alternatively, the neo-corporatist compromise might have encountered political and legal obstacles turning it in a pluralistic direction, as occurred in the USA despite a starting point in the mid-1930s similar to the Swedish case. Perhaps more in industrial relations than in welfare regimes, we are made aware of such possibilities for change all the time.

Social insurance systems

We can examine the implications of these arguments in more detail if we consider a point where industrial relations systems and welfare state regimes come together, at least in most western European societies: co-determinative social insurance systems. For a long time these institutions were not called upon to perform any strategic tasks of note and became among the most boring routinised institutions of modern society. Recently they have suddenly been faced with some urgent new challenges: to reform their rules and procedures in order to facilitate labour market changes in a post-Keynesian economy. In so doing, these institutions are rediscovering their connections to industrial relations, with which they have always been linked but which often developed in different ways. This is happening during a period of quite diverse changes, embodying often very different logic: globalisation, the decline of manufacturing, the feminisation of the labour force, European integration, the dominance of neo-liberalism. We should not expect to be able to make hand-me-down predictions of how whole classes of cases will react without precise observation of the forces at work in individual instances.

An initial point of interest is British exceptionalism on this issue. This is something which developed over the years. British unions originally doubled as industrial relations actors and as the organisers of rudimentary providers of contributory, occupation-related social insurance schemes. When government began to establish a state system, in the National Insurance Act 1911, trade union and other voluntary schemes were given a role alongside the new state provision, and unions could participate in the administration and distribution of benefits even if they had not previously organised their own voluntary scheme. Had this been maintained, this aspect of the British welfare state, like several others, would have resembled those of Scandinavia.

However, the unions' own schemes took a severe beating as they tried to cope with the extraordinary increase in unemployment of the late 1920s. Gradually the unions reached the conclusion that this was not an area where they wanted to be directly involved. They continued to lobby for the strengthening of welfare benefits and took up policy stances on issues like the means test, but by the time of the major advance in British welfare policy thinking in the mid-1940s, they had decided to shed their involvement in administration in favour of a pure state-run scheme (Finlayson 1994: 264–70).

This proved very useful in the construction of the particular British form of the post-war compromise and welfare state enlargement. Lazy thoughtways lead to anything specifically British within the European context being dubbed 'liberal', with reference to both the nineteenth century legacy of English liberalism and the increasing tendency of the British during the 1980s and 1990s to remodel their institutions on a version of US economic liberalism. Not only is the latter rather anachronistic for an account of the 1940s, but it omits a fundamental compromise, or more accurately a convergence, between two forces in the Britain of that time. One of these was social democracy, or socialism. Following the experience of how the country had been organised during the Second World War, this was full of a new confidence in the planning and steering capacities of the central state. The other was the 'mandarin' tradition of the civil service: Elitist, always self-confident, imbued with a genuine concept of public service, and reinforced in its sense of the capacity of the central state by both the war and the colonial experience, especially the government of India. In the wake of the war these two forces, coming though they did from very different, often opposed, classes within the society, had much in common: a belief in the capacity of the state to do public good, but also of its almost Jacobin lack of a need to consult with or embed itself within the wider population.

This latter might appear to be the price the Labour Party had to pay to win the former, but it must have seemed a cheap price at the time. The Labour Party was inclined to feel that it itself constituted the voice of the relevant part of the wider population and therefore required no wide consultation. ('Socialism is what the Labour Government does', as Herbert Morrison famously remarked.) And the unions had demonstrated clearly that they did not want to be involved in running the welfare state, just as they had renounced any ambitions for worker participation in managing either nationalised industries or private firms. This might reveal to us a subtle *Wahlverwandschaft* between market liberalism and statism. This is in fact a possibility which is not to be excluded, even though it seems to contradict one of the most fundamental organising principles of contemporary political antagonism; but it certainly requires a very subtle form of path dependency analysis.

Meanwhile, in most of continental western Europe unions had become firmly installed in the governing bodies of national or specific occupational social insurance and similar systems, with a particular moment of consolidation coming in the reconstruction years immediately following the Second World War. For many years after that the diverse national developments which had created these systems seemed to be of minimal interest outside those concerned with the minutiae of administrative arrangements. In Austria, Belgium, Germany, the Netherlands and above all in Switzerland, union participation in running social insurance seemed all of a piece with the neo-corporatist and co-determinative models of the industrial relations system, but a very uninteresting part of it. These institutions were rarely if ever engaged in any interesting issues of coordination or inflation avoidance. They possibly just added some of the cement that held together a structure, the main business of which was steering collective bargaining outcomes and changes in working conditions. Things seemed more interesting in Scandinavia, where such participation seemed even more fully part of the tripartite character of the state. Sometimes, especially in Sweden, these had important macroeconomic effects, when government, advised by social partners, used to steer pension fund accumulations into industrial investment. This forms a coherent part of the social democratic power resource explanation of Scandinavian welfare state and industrial relations regimes.

In France and Italy formal union involvement in the management of pension and social security schemes seemed totally at odds with the prevailing industrial relations context. This involvement had developed fitfully from the late nineteenth century onwards, and had been consolidated in the participatory consensus institutions with which those countries had equipped themselves in the solidaristic atmosphere of 1944–7. Then had followed the Cold War, the exclusion of the majority Communist wings of the labour movement from national respectability, and the marginalisation of the weakly representative and internally divided non-Communist minority. Industrial relations became, as it had been in the 1920s and 1930s, a non-existent arena, or one of uncompromis-ing conflict, with co-determinative and tripartite institutions of the immediate post-war years being reduced to residual status. The continuation of union involvement in the management of social insurance schemes seemed just an aspect of the last of these alternatives, its very survival in such an otherwise hostile environment serving as a testimony to its lack of seriousness.

Today matters look very different. Given a widespread belief that welfare states, and especially their social insurance components, must be reformed, union participation in the reform process has become fundamental in all systems where unions and employer organisations have a formal role of the kind we are discussing. Unless governments are willing to risk the conflict that would ensue from expelling unions from social insurance management, they have to win union agreement jointly to make the reforms. As we shall see below, the Dutch and Italian cases show that this can be achieved. The French and German ones suggest that it can be very difficult (Ebbinghaus and Hassel 1999). From this flows a number of rather diverse consequences.

First, no matter how weak they might become in terms of the main indicators of union strength (membership, resources, engagement in collective bargaining), unions with this kind of institutionalised role in an arena high on the policy agenda at the present time cannot be easily marginalised or excluded from national respectability. This can be seen from a comparison between the UK and France. Unions in the former country retain a considerably higher membership and material resource base than their French colleagues, and they are engaged more effectively in serious collective bargaining. They have however been effectively excluded from serious participation in national events. Following the poor experiences of the 1970s, no major political party is interested in their cooperation in the management of wage inflation. During the 1980s Conservative governments either expelled union representatives from national consultative bodies or closed down the bodies themselves. The Labour government elected in May 1997 made important improvements in union workplace rights, but showed no inclination to treat them as serious participants in national economic or social policy. Although this exclusion can be partly explained by the specific policies of governments in the 1980s, the prior, earlier unnoticed, specificity of British unions' earlier voluntary exclusion from administration of the welfare state has contributed further to their weakness in these years when elsewhere the national political role of unions is being intensified.

Although French unions now have barely 7 per cent of the private-sector workforce in membership, and only 12 per cent of the public sector, and though they are too divided among themselves to engage in any concerted action, successive governments seek to cultivate their participation in national policymaking. One reason is that the French unions retain an extraordinary capacity for social disruption irrespective of their formal strength. Another however is the government's realisation that no reforms can be achieved in the welfare arena without their support and preferably their active cooperation.

The British case

From a governmental point of view, the UK demonstrates the advantages of the British elitist model of welfare state development, of not having to bother with consultation with groups in the population affected by a policy area: the British social insurance system has presented far fewer barriers to employment flexibility than those in most of the rest of western Europe, and reform of the system is fairly easily achieved. This is a judgement which will not necessarily be shared by British workers and pensioners. And it is certainly not how the British system appeared in the late 1970s. Meanwhile the reform capacity of systems embodying greater employee rights has in fact varied quite considerably.

In the first instance it might be assumed that the involvement of social partners in management of the systems inhibits reform. If they are primarily concerned with protecting the interests of those within the system, they will not be concerned with expanding opportunities for those outside, and may even see such an expansion as threatening those for whom they are concerned. Surely, if the social partners are not involved, there is nothing to prevent governments – who in theory are responsible to insiders and outsiders alike – from reallocating costs and expenditures in order to produce the benign effects that it is possible to achieve.

The British case presents both the demonstration of this point and its limitations. After the initial world-leading character of its post-war reforms, the elite-led character of the British welfare state seemed to make it rather proof against subsequent democratic demands for expanding generosity. The idea of income replacement hardly developed at all; instead a subsistence model of benefits remained dominant, and by the 1990s the income replacement rate of British unemployment benefits was the lowest in western Europe apart from Greece and Italy (OECD 1994, 1997). When an element of earnings-relatedness was introduced in the 1960s, it was rather minor; a compromise between the egalitarianism of the socialists and the desire of the private pensions industry to have a public system that left a lot of scope for private provision and occupational schemes.

True to its status as a social insurance system without social partner participation, the British system became one of weak universal (as opposed to occupational) citizenship. It was however a citizenship model rather than a residual one, because all except the wealthiest expected to make some use of it. This had ambiguous consequences. While it produced one of the meanest benefit systems in western Europe, it did produce a far less gender-differentiated system than many others. Further, benefits not being tied closely to occupational contributions, it did not discourage part-time work or periods of temporary participation in the labour force – two further factors which considerably assisted female employment. Because the level of benefits and therefore contributions has been low, the latter do not constitute a severe barrier to the employment of low-productivity labour, enabling the lower end of the labour market in private services to grow, by the mid-1990s off-setting the decline in manufacturing employment.

The British social insurance system and general welfare state are currently undergoing a reform wave, just as elsewhere in Europe. Part of the agenda is the same as elsewhere: trying to use the benefit system to re-equip people for employment rather than simply support their absence from it. As everywhere else, this is a stick-and-carrot policy: criteria of eligibility for benefit become tougher and rougher; opportunities for retraining and for assistance with obstacles to taking on work become more creative and helpful. What however seems distinctive about the current British debate over pensions reform is that there is virtually no public debate at all. The whole issue is dealt with in private discussions between government representatives and the handful of pensions firms which dominate the private sector. There is no involvement by the generality of employers, by the unions or by representatives of pensioners themselves. This is a distinctiveness that stems clearly from the absence of any representative component in the management of British social insurance institutions.

If these are the mixed consequences of the absence of a social partnership model, the presence of social partnership should give us the opposite characteristics: generous benefits related to income replacement; based on occupational citizenship and therefore tied to male breadwinner interests, discouraging part-time or non-continuous labour-force participation (Hemerijck and Manow, this volume; Esping-Andersen 1996); associated with weak development of low-productivity employment; difficult, blocked, but open and public debate over reform.

France and Germany

This stereotype does seem to characterise the German and French social insurance reform debates. As noted above, both countries have strong models of co-determination in the welfare system – running with the grain of general industrial relations in the German case, rather incongruous with it in the French. There are differences in the outcomes of the two cases. France does not so much exhibit the low female labour-force participation anticipated by the model, though French women do share the dislike of working part-time that one would expect from a social insurance system based on the accumulation of time served in the work force. Quite separate aspects of social policy have somewhat eased the position of working mothers in France. For many years French policy makers were obsessed with the country's low birth rate; since republican rather than Catholic groups dominated policy making, the result was a series of natalist policies which did not at the same time try to keep women in a home-making role.

The German manufacturing model remains extremely strong, so that country has less need than many others to move into new service sectors in order to protect its economic performance. It is also not a system which protects existing workers at the expense of the young. As a result of the vocational education system, the Germany economy remains almost alone in the advanced world in having youth employment levels below those of the adult population. However, partly for these very reasons, the German case does show even more clearly than the French the way in which a social insurance system moulded to the interests of full-time males in manufacturing and governed by co-determination mechanisms is slow to adapt to the encouragement of female and part-time working and services sector development. Until now, representatives of workers in the core sectors have had little incentive to reform their system, because their members are doing very well. Their numbers are being reduced as productivity in the export sectors continues to rise, and this must soon have an effect in threatening opportunities for their sons. They have however little reason to accept changes which might threaten the security of their own anticipated benefits in order to get their wives and daughters into part-time jobs. The German *collective bargaining* system still functions more or less as 'responsibly' as it did in the 1970s and 1980s; it was probably always the dominant role of the price-sensitive export sector and the stern stance of the Bundesbank rather than 'encompassingness' as such which ensured non-inflationary wage behaviour. Within *social insurance* however the system has had fewer disincentives to protect its insiders at the expense of those outside (Hemerijck and Manow, this volume).

In fairness to these insiders one must also point out the major issue that all German institutions have had to face following unification in 1990: no other advanced society has faced a comparable task to that of absorbing 16 million people who had experienced a far lower standard of living and completely different working patterns, but who had strong expectations of rapidly moving to the life style of their new fellow citizens. Ensuring that the whole existing work force of the eastern *Länder* did not become a mass of outsiders was in itself a major institutional challenge. It has been achieved with some success, but has probably absorbed and even exhausted much of the capacity of the system for strategic action and change.

However, this very point reminds us that it can be factors and institutions outside the strict terms of a system itself which can affect its behaviour. While one can demonstrate that the internal conditions of co-determinative occupational insurance systems make them resistant to reform, exogenous or partly exogenous elements might provide incentives for change, to which the system can respond. Indeed, the fact that these systems do have a clear representative arrangement for their governance means that they are capable of responding strategically when the incentive for change is sufficiently strong. Two cases which can be set against the French and German are the Dutch and Italian.

The Dutch reforms

As is now well known, largely thanks to the detailed study by Jelle Visser and Anton Hemerijck (1997), the Dutch collective bargaining and welfare state system has been subject to an extraordinary reform wave during the 1990s, which considerably increased the country's employment participation rate, especially among women where it had previously been exceptionally low. The case is discussed in detail elsewhere in this volume (Hemerijck and Manow). For our current purposes the main question is how this system, which shared the characteristics of a model which enable us accurately to predict lack of change in the French and German cases, eventually demonstrated a capacity for reform.

One answer is that the government took decisive action, clearly threatening a major dismantling of the co-determination structure of the social insurance system if the social partners did not respond (Ebbinghaus and Hassel 1999). One can also add two further factors. First, the Dutch unions had been becoming progressively weaker, with dramatic and continuing membership losses. Related to this, and in contrast with Germany, the Dutch economy was not a strong industrial power. Rather like the British economy, the Dutch has long had major commercial and financial services sectors which reduced the priority of manufacturing industry in both public policy and the approaches of the social partners. There was therefore little to compare with such German unions as IG *Metall* and IG *Chemie* in fostering and protecting the manufacturing model. The Dutch industrial relations system was therefore vulnerable to very serious threat of collapse; the position of its insiders was not therefore necessarily much stronger than that of the outsiders. This served as a disincentive to rent-seeking behaviour and an incentive among employer and employee representatives alike to listen seriously to plans for reform.

By themselves, however, vulnerability and fear of collapse do not induce action to reform; they can simply cause collapse. The second important characteristic here was that the relevant Dutch organisations had not lost their institutional position and therefore potential strategic capacity (Ebbinghaus and Hassel 1999; Hemerijck 1992; Hemerijck and Kloostermans 1995; Visser and Hemerijck 1997). In the 1980s their combination of formal institutional security and drastic membership loss was making Dutch labour-market organisations seem like a group of abandoned and broken-down vehicles blocking up a roadway while being incapable of any movement. The combination of government threat, looming existential crisis, but continued potential steering capacity, seemed to be enough to bring drivers and passengers back to the vehicles, to repair them, and to start them moving, often in a decisive way.

In comparison with the Germans, Dutch labour market institutions have had to face both the determination of government and the weakness of the manufacturing sector: vulnerabilities which provided paradoxical advantages. Although observers usually place more stress on the former (Ebbinghaus and Hassel 1999), I suspect the latter was not only important in its own right but a factor determining government behaviour. While it is true that German federal governments are subject to a number of constitutional limitations, its coalitions are usually considerably more focused than the multi-party groupings of the Netherlands; it cannot be taken for granted that Dutch governments would be more decisive than German ones.

The French would seem to share the Dutch vulnerabilities, such as a manufacturing sector that has not been functioning anything like as well as the German one and trade unions with problems of declining membership. Indeed, the private sector is in a considerably worse situation than in the Netherlands. Also, while electoral calculations and subsequent cohabitation had blunted the usually confidence and autonomy of the French state, the centre-right government did go so far as to change the constitution of the governing bodies of the social insurance system, reducing the role of the unions (Ebbinghaus and Hassel 1999). Also, there must always be a strong expectation that at some point the French state will act in a tough manner. I believe that the fundamental factor preventing French imitation of the Dutch lies not so much in state capacity as in the lack of strategic capacity among the social partners, especially the unions. As noted, the co-determination of the social insurance system is very much at odds with the dominant traditions of French industrial relations, which remain deeply conflictual. There is therefore little support for action in the social insurance sector from the wider industrial relations system. One aspect of this, which also stems directly from the low membership level, is the lack of resources at the disposal of the unions. This makes it very difficult for them to develop the expertise that something like social insurance reform requires, and inclines them to take up general ideological stances instead.

Perhaps more important for lack of strategic capacity, the French labour movement remains deeply divided. The religious differences among Dutch unions had long ago been submerged in an overall commitment to cooperation, and in any case today the two main wings (socialist and Catholic) have merged into a common organisation. The main French union confederation, the communist *Confédération Générale de Travail* (CGT), remains opposed to reaching agreements with employers or governments, and this defiance seems to increase as the organisation's relative position within the labour movement declines. The other four or five organisations are all willing to participate in collective agreements and co-determination, but since they are rivals they are likely to try to outsmart each other in any major bargaining event. Therefore, any union going down the road of cooperation with government plans for reform, or even broaching its own proposals for change, will immediately be accused by the CGT of betrayal of workers' interests, and will probably not be able to construct a coalition with other unions either. The crucial characteristic here is not so much the ideological colour of one or another union, but the complete lack of strategic capacity which is imparted to the labour interest as a whole by the extent and character of the divisions.

The Italian reforms

Italian unions demonstrated from the 1993 wage structure reform onwards a capacity to overcome the divisions among themselves ostensibly similar to those of the French. On the other hand, problems of vertical coordination remain a major hazard for any Italian organisation trying to achieve strategic capacity. Italian shop-floor militant movements, unlike the old shop-steward organisations in the UK, do not even formally form part of the official union structure but are quite autonomous associations. There is therefore a severe challenge for any Italian organisation engaging in shared reform initiatives with government and employers. Nevertheless, in both collective bargaining itself and pension reform the Italian experience during the 1990s has been more similar to the Dutch than to the French or even to the German. How can we explain this most unlikely case of divergence from what, on the basis of the German evidence, we might expect from a co-determinative social insurance system?

To some extent there has been the same shared economic vulnerability as in the Netherlands and France, though in fact the industries of the northern and midlands regions of the country have proved more resilient and adaptable to the new competitive environment than their opposite numbers in either of those countries. There has also been government determination to see reform, and following the collapse of the Christian Democratic Party Italy faces the theoretical possibility of periods of government by a more or less neo-liberal right. However, the main autonomous neo-liberal reform initiative that tried to bypass social partnership, by the Berlusconi government in the early 1990s, led to the fall of the government. Meanwhile, in reality the political system remains as fragmented and incapable of delivering decisive majorities as ever. It is difficult to see Italy having a higher level of governmental capacity than either France or Germany.

One answer might lie in the sheer absurdity that had been reached by the pension system, enabling able-bodied people in their early forties to leave the workforce on pensions that were not being funded by anything other than unsupportable public debt. The situation was similar to though more problematic even than the Dutch disability pensions. However, it is doubtful whether this would have been enough to force a concentration on reform without the final, crucial component of the Italian context of the 1990s: the widely shared determination of virtually all elites and a large proportion of the general population to see Italy remain at the core of the European Union and in particular to enter the single European currency. The reasons for this exceptional commitment to the European Union and the Euro can be variously interpreted: a desire to see the country achieve the status that its size and strength of its economy seemed to deserve, but which its political and bureaucratic practices seemed so often to let down; a desire to be rid of the constantly weakening lira; a preference for rule by foreigners in Brussels over rule by a political class that had been publicly demonstrated to be corrupt.

Whatever the combination of motives social research might reveal to us, the outcome was not in doubt and was fully, even exceptionally, shared by the labour movement and the business community: Italy must qualify for entry to the Euro. If this meant a tough central line on wage restraint in order to meet the Maastricht inflation criterion, so be it; if it meant a major onslaught on the early retirement scheme in order to meet the public deficit criterion, that too must be done. There were organisational costs for this assertion of a slender strategic capacity by labour leaders. The unofficial movement seems to have grown in strength. Other social partners seem to expect that it is enough if the unions deliver their own consent to an agreement; they cannot be expected to keep the unofficial movements in line too.

Keeping the energy of the reform wave moving now that Euro entry has been achieved and cannot be reversed has proved more difficult. Meanwhile, the system has not really been adapted to meet the needs of a multi-sector two-gender work force; the main achievement of reform has been getting rid of an early retirement system that had become impossible to maintain. However, the activities of the 1993–7 period show how only partially exogenous pressures can disturb what seems like the irresistible path dependency of the social insurance model.

Conclusions

One could examine other cases: for example, the way in which a prior strong employment and unionisation of women (mainly in the welfare state itself) prevented Danish social insurance ever developing the full-time, industrial male bias, despite very strong union involvement in the management of the unemployment system (Clasen 1998; Due *et al.* 1994; but see also the more pessimistic view of von Nordheim Nielsen (1996), who sees the relationship between the pension system and industrial relations leading to a fragmentation of the Danish pension system).

We have, however, seen enough to be able to draw some central conclusions. These concern the importance of examining agency as well as structure, of politics as well as sociology, of the micro- as well as the macro-level of action. Setting out the core characteristics of system types is not enough to enable us to predict how the actors in an individual case will respond. This is partly because real cases are extremely unlikely ever to be pure examples of one model, or of one ideal type. Empirical social structures are not only highly complex, but they embody a diversity of interests, legacies of past periods, and even some attributes which do not follow any organisational logic at all but just happen to be there. It is therefore possible for a component of a case that does not follow the logic of what we might have discerned as its core model suddenly to have an importance and determine change. Dutch departure from the German model of a primarily manufacturing-based economy would be one example; the priority of the single European currency for the Italians another.

Also, while all but the most determinist models will accept the notion of what economists call external shocks, it is only partially exogenous elements that have featured strongly in the above account. A determination to enter the Euro was not an external shock to the Italian system, but something which imparted a particular character to the normal interest calculations of the endogenous actors.

Notes

1 There is also the form of authoritarian corporatism. This is found only under non-democratic regimes. Although consideration of these would considerably extend the

interest of the analysis, for the purposes of this chapter I shall only consider forms which are compatible with democratic politics.

2 The analogy is defective at two points. First, the cost disciplines imposed on market actors are far more vague for political actors; theoretical attempts to impose strict cost-benefit calculations on them succeed only by removing from politics the capacity for subtle manoeuvring and goal displacement which are the heart of the activity. Second, actors in the pure market are under the constraint of anonymity, whereas overcoming of anonymity is a central task of political actors. (In reality, it is also an objective of economic actors, but at least the theory of economics can treat this as a special case, whereas it is fundamental to political life.)

3 Strictly speaking, any mechanism which interferes with pure market allocations is 'redistributive'. I here intend the more usual sense of the word as implying redistribution from rich to poor.

4 This term originates in eighteenth century chemistry, where it referred to an observed mutual attraction between two separate bodies based on the strong similarity of their characteristics (*affinitas electiva*). Goethe later used it as an analogy for individual human relationships, and later still Weber and other sociologists have used it to refer in a similar way to strong similarities which can appear between different social institutions.

5 This reservation opens a major question: are all different aspects of a welfare state somehow coherently related, or are their trade-offs at work within them? The tendency of contemporary analysis is to assume the former, but the latter may well be more informative. For example, the powerful role of publicly funded education in the USA not only contradicts assumptions of residualism in analyses of the role of public action in that country, but also directs our attention to a major aspect of the collectivist characteristics of that society.

6 The assumptions of perfect knowledge and perfect capacity to calculate risk which are at the heart of contemporary economic theory seem particularly to exclude the possibility of entrepreneurship. Entrepreneurship depends on the capacity to perceive possibilities for innovation which few others have anticipated. From this comes the scope for extracting temporary rents which make the risk-taking worthwhile. Where there is complete knowledge and discounted rational expectation, there can be no element of surprise and therefore no capacity to perceive opportunities for innovation.

References

Beer, S. H. (1982). *Britain against Itself: The Political Contradictions of Collectivism.* London: Faber.

Clasen, J. (1998). 'Unemployment Insurance and Varieties of Capitalism', Paper presented at the conference 'Varieties of Welfare Capitalism in Europe, North America and Japan'. Cologne: Max Planck Institute for the Study of Societies.

Crouch, C. (1993). *Industrial Relations and European State Traditions.* Oxford: Oxford University Press.

Crouch, C. (1999). *Social Change in Western Europe.* Oxford: Oxford University Press.

Due, J., Madsen, J. S., Jensen, C. S. and Petersen, L. K. (1994). *The Survival of the Danish Model.* Copenhagen: DJØF.

Ebbinghaus, B. and Hassel, A. (1999). 'The role of tripartite concertation in the reform of the welfare state', *Transfer* 1–2, 64–81.

Esping-Andersen, G. (1990). *The Three Worlds of Welfare Capitalism.* Cambridge: Polity Press.

Esping-Andersen, G. (1996). 'Welfare sates without work: The impasse of labour shedding and familialism in Continental European social policy', in G. Esping-Andersen (ed.), *Welfare States in Transition. National Adaptations in Global Economies.* London: Sage.

Finlayson, G. (1994). *Citizen, State, and Social Welfare in Britain 1830–1990*. Oxford: Clarendon Press.

Hemerijck, A. (1992). 'The historical contingencies of Dutch corporatism', DPhil thesis, University of Oxford.

Hemerijck, A. and Kloostermans, R. C. (1995). 'Der postindustrielle Umbau des korporistischen Sozialstaats in den Niederländern', in W. Fricke (ed.), *Jahrbuch Arbeit und Technik*. 287–96.

North, D. C. (1990). *Institutions, Institutional Change and Economic Performance*. Cambridge: Cambridge University Press.

OECD (Organisation for Economic Co-Operation and Development) (1994). *The OECD Jobs Study: Evidence and Explanations*. Paris: OECD.

OECD (1997). *The OECD Jobs Strategy: Making Work Pay. Taxation, Benefits, Employment and Unemployment*. Paris: OECD.

Visser, J. and Hemerijck, A. (1997). *'A Dutch Miracle': Job Growth, Welfare Reform and Corporatism in the Netherlands*. Amsterdam: Amsterdam University Press.

von Nordheim Nielsen, F. (1996). 'Danish occupational pensions in the 1980s: From social security to political economy', in M. Shalev (ed.), *The Privatization of Social Policy? Occupational Welfare and the Welfare State in America, Scandinavia and Japan*. Basingstoke: Macmillan, 241–60.

6 Social partnership, welfare state regimes and working time in Europe

Hugh Compston

Introduction

Working time is central to the political economy of any society: to live people must produce, and this takes time. Other things being equal, the volume of production is determined by the volume of aggregate working time, and for any given level of aggregate working time the number of people employed is determined by the average duration of individual working time. This implies that if there is not enough work to go around, unemployment will be lower if the available work is shared out among more people: the shorter individual working time is, the more people are employed. The idea is that a reduction in hours for those in employment will create a shortage of labour, so that employers will take on extra workers in order to maintain production – or at least avert dismissals if demand is low. Working time reduction as an anti-unemployment policy is thus a response to a situation in which either the volume of work is insufficient to employ everyone, or is not growing fast enough to maintain full employment (Blyton 1989: 161). To the extent that working time reduction can reduce unemployment, the political and economic dynamics of working time reduction are closely connected with what is arguably one of the principaldysfunctions of welfare capitalism in the 1990s: the persistence of mass unemployment. An effort to understand the political and economic dynamics of working time reduction as an employment policy is therefore important if we are to improve our understanding of the political economy of welfare capitalism as a whole.

Decisions on working time may be taken by employers acting unilaterally or in cooperation with individual employees; by collective bargaining at the firm, sectoral, regional or national level, with or without state involvement; or by the state. These are all important, but this chapter takes a public policy focus by concentrating on the politics of state initiatives to create or save jobs by reducing working time: state work-sharing initiatives, for short.

The question is, what are the determinants of the nature and incidence of state initiatives to reduce unemployment by reducing working time? In this chapter, I seek to illuminate this issue by examining the role of state interventionism, class, the welfare state and social partnership ideology. The methodology utilised is comparison of the experiences of nine West European industrial democracies: the four largest – Britain, France, Germany and Italy – plus Belgium, Denmark, Ireland, the Netherlands and Sweden. Although a larger number of cases would be desirable, the selection is limited by considerations of comparability, the availability of information and the author's understanding of individual countries in their historical contexts.

There are six main ways in which, in theory, jobs can be created and/or saved by reducing working time – overtime restrictions, shorter normal working time, short-time working, part-time work, long-term leave and partial early retirement – but to simplify the analysis I focus mainly on just two of these: reductions in normal working hours, and increasing the number of part-time jobs relative to full-time jobs.

Because reducing standard working hours can involve so many people, and so potentially free up a very large number of jobs, it is prima facie one of the most attractive forms of working time reduction. It does not always reduce unemployment – increased costs can endanger employment prospects by impairing competitiveness, reducing investment or calling forth restrictive economic measures from the government, and employers may choose not to recruit to replace the lost hours at all by letting production fall, dishoarding workers, increasing overtime, or taking advantage of productivity offsets – but most of these problems can be avoided by appropriate policy design. Leakage into overtime can be prevented by imposing restrictions on overtime. Cost problems can be offset by ensuring that cuts in working time are accompanied by proportionate cuts in wages. Such cuts can be reconciled with maintenance of employees' living standards by means of government wage subsidies or tax breaks for employees. Alternatively, employers could continue to pay the same wages and be compensated for the effective increase in hourly wages by subsidies or tax breaks, or trade off maintenance of wages against future wage restraint. Work reorganisation can create new job slots by putting together lost blocks of hours into job-sized packages. Training can help to ensure that there are enough appropriately skilled people to work the vacant hours and prevent wage rises due to skills bottlenecks. However, it is difficult to prevent productivity gains from limiting the employment dividend of reducing working hours: statistical studies suggest that this is the principal reason why the employment effect of reductions in working hours is unlikely to average more than 50 per cent of the positions that would be created if all the free hours were translated into jobs (Cette and Taddéi 1993: 562). This may seem disappointingly low, but it still means that cutting standard working hours can be an effective means of reducing unemployment (for reviews of the economics of working time reduction, see Compston (1997b) and earlier studies such as CEC (1980), Cuvillier (1984), Blyton (1985), Hart (1987) and White (1987)).

From an economic point of view, part-time work is the simplest and most effective form of work sharing because in general it neither increases employers' costs nor requires reorganisation. Increased utilisation of part-time jobs can create new positions where a full-time position is not justified on economic grounds, for instance in short peak periods and where work reorganisation yields less than a full-time job. Splitting full-time jobs into part-time jobs can also result in extra people in work. However, the employment yield of extending part-time work is likely to be limited by the higher productivity of part-time workers compared to full-time workers. There may be increased non-wage labour costs due to a bigger workforce doing the same work, although these are offset by these same productivity increases. As far as empirical evidence is concerned, there is wide agreement among economists that the extension of part-time work made a significant contribution to such employment growth as has taken place over the past decade (OECD 1994: 98).

The analysis begins with a brief review of the incidence of state work-sharing initiatives in historical context, then examines the role of the nature of state regulation of employment conditions, the logic of class interest, the influence of incentives and constraints created by welfare state structures, and the effects of the social partnership ideology of Christian and Christian-influenced trade unions. Somewhat unexpectedly, it is this last factor that seems to be the most important.

State work-sharing initiatives in Western Europe

Table 6.1 gives an overview of government measures to extend part-time work and reduce normal working hours according to information taken from monthly national reports in *European Industrial Relations Review* between 1979 and 1997. These reports are based on the answers to standardised questionnaires sent to respondents in each country. While there may have been some under-reporting of minor work-sharing initiatives, it seems reasonable to assume that most, if not all, major initiatives are covered.

It can be seen that most of these measures were introduced in times of recession: the early 1980s and early 1990s. This is consistent with the common-sense view

Table 6.1 State measures to reduce working hours, 1979–97

Country	*Extending part-time work*	*Reducing normal working time without pay cuts*	*Reducing normal working time with pay cuts*	*Initiatives to encourage work sharing via financial incentives (solidarity contracts)*
Belgium	1984, 1995		1983	1994
Britain	1982, 1986			
Denmark				
France	1981, 1983, 1985, 1990, 1993, 1994	1982		1982, 1984, 1985, 1986, 1990, 1993, 1996
Germany	1985, 1994			
Ireland				
Italy	1984, 1997			1983, 1984, 1993
Netherlands	1995		1983, 1994	
Sweden	1983			

Sources: EIRR (1979–97).

that new initiatives on employment are more likely when concern about unemployment is high.

Table 6.2 ranks the nine countries in order of the relative incidence of state work-sharing initiatives. While there is scope for dispute about the classification of borderline cases such as the Netherlands and Sweden, and the small size of the differences between most of the countries renders the classification vulnerable to measurement error and choice of period examined, the categorisation does provide a basis for comparative analysis.

The context of state work-sharing initiatives is a long-term decline in working hours: a study of sixteen Western industrialised countries found that between 1870 and 1970 average annual working hours virtually halved, from about 3,000 hours to 1,700–1,800 hours (Maddison 1979; cited in CEC 1980: 89–90). Between 1985 and 1990 average weekly hours in the European Union fell by a full hour, from 40 to 39, and between 1990 and 1994 by a further half hour, to 38.5 hours per week (CEC 1995a: 41). This trend is linked to a number of more specific trends: a gradual reduction in the normal working week, a significant increase in the number of part-time jobs relative to full-time positions, increased holiday entitlements and paid annual leave, a steep increase in the number of people in education, and a trend towards earlier retirement (OECD 1994: 81, 88–93; CEC 1995a: 10; Blyton 1989: 164).

Table 6.2 Incidence of state work-sharing initiatives

Relative incidence	*Work-sharing initiatives in general*	*Initiatives to expand part-time work*	*Initiatives to encourage work sharing via financial incentives (solidarity contracts)*
Very low	Sweden (1)[a] Denmark (0) Ireland (0)	n.a.[b]	n.a.
Low	Britain (2) Germany (2)	Denmark (0) Ireland (0)	Britain (0) Denmark (0) Germany (0) Ireland (0) Netherlands (0) Sweden (0)
Medium	Italy (5) Belgium (4) Netherlands (3)	Belgium (2) Britain (2) Germany (2) Italy (2) Netherlands (1) Sweden (1)	Belgium (1) Italy (3)
High	France (14)	France (6)	France (7)

Source: EIRR (1979–97).

Notes

a Figures in parentheses show the incidence of work-sharing measures 1979–97.

b Not applicable.

Table 6.3 Working time

Country	*Average annual hours, full-time employees, 1993*	*Country*	*Average weekly hours (without overtime), 1993*	*Country*	*Part-time employment in %of total employment, 1996*
Netherlands	1,451	Germany	36.4	Netherlands	36.5
Belgium	1,597	Britain	37.1	Sweden	23.6
Denmark	1,527	Netherlands	37.9	Britain	22.1
Germany	1,592	France	38.2	Denmark	21.5
Britain	1,668	Belgium	38.4	Germany	16.3
Italy	1,679	Italy	38.6	France	16.0
Sweden	1,630	Denmark	39.5	Belgium	14.0
France	1,768	Ireland	42.3m/36.9f	Ireland	11.6
Ireland	1,746	Sweden	40.7	Italy	6.6

Sources: EIRR 278: 14–20; 280: 16–21; OECD (1997).

Table 6.3 gives three measures of actual working time in the nine countries, although differences in data sources and measurement methods render the figures unsuitable for precise inter-country comparisons. It is therefore not surprising that there are no significant bivariate correlations between the incidence of state work-sharing initiatives and annual or weekly hours or between the incidence of state initiatives to expand part-time work and actual part-time employment.

Measurement problems notwithstanding, it is clear that part-time employment is by far the highest in the Netherlands, where it has risen very rapidly over the last decade. The incidence of part-time work is also considerably higher in Northern Europe than in Southern Europe. There is an even more striking correlation between levels of part-time work and the Protestant–Catholic cleavage: over 20 per cent of the workforce had a part-time job in all of the Protestant countries (Britain, Denmark and Sweden) but in none of the Catholic countries (Belgium, France, Ireland and Italy). Furthermore, all the Catholic countries surveyed had greater proportions of part-timers wanting to work full-time than all the Protestant countries (Dederichs and Köhler 1993; cited in Wedderburn 1995: 25–6).

Part-time work is heavily concentrated in low-skilled jobs and the service sector, and many full-timers fear that a transition to part-time work would lead to marginalisation and poorer career prospects. Conversely, part-time work is very scarce in skilled and management positions (Bosch *et al.* 1989; cited in Wedderburn 1995: 19, 20, 45). In every single country the overwhelming majority of part-time jobs are held by women (OECD 1996: table E).

Work sharing and government interventionism

The first determinant of the incidence and nature of state work-sharing initiatives is, not surprisingly, the extent to which the state customarily regulates conditions of employment, as opposed to leaving them to collective bargaining, individual negotiation or employer imposition.

Since the EU Working Time Directive came into force in 1996, regulation of working time at the national level has been constrained to operate within minimum standards set by the Directive. Among other provisions, this Directive sets a maximum 48-hour limit to the working week, including overtime, and stipulates a minimum period of four weeks annual leave (EIRR 282: 31–2). Within this framework, weekly working time is regulated by statute in all EU countries apart from Denmark, where collective bargaining provides a functional equivalent, and Britain, where company-level agreements set working time for most employees. In countries such as France, legislation regulates working time directly, while in countries such as Germany and Ireland it defines minimum standards that are often improved on by the provisions of collective agreements (EIRR 278: 14–20). In general the statutory working week in 1997 was 40 hours and the maximum working week 48 hours (ILO 1995: 112).

Part-time work is governed at the national level mainly by statute in France, collective agreement in Denmark, and statute supplemented by collective agreement in Belgium, Germany, Italy, the Netherlands and Sweden. In Britain and Ireland only some rights are governed by statute. Most EU states stipulate equal rights for, and treatment of, part-timers and full-timers, but social security treatment varies (Marullo 1995: 4). The trend is towards enhancing the rights of part-timers, as the British option – encouraging employers to take on part-time employees by deregulating employment conditions – has been closed off by passage of the Part-time Work Directive, which stipulates that discrimination against part-time workers must be removed and proposes measures to facilitate the development of part-time work in a manner that takes into account the needs of both employers and workers (Marullo 1995: 5; table A.1; EIRR 282: 31–2). In some countries, including Belgium, Denmark, France and Germany, part-time work is encouraged by financial incentives provided by the state.

That a tradition of state regulation is a prerequisite for state action in relation to working time reduction is demonstrated by comparing the incidence of work-sharing initiatives and two separate indicators of state regulation: the degree of regulation of normal working time in 1978 at the beginning of the period under investigation, and the degree of regulation of employment conditions in general (see Notes in Table 6.4 for details). The cross-tabulation (Table 6.4) reveals a clear pattern: state work-sharing initiatives were relatively common only in countries with highly developed state regulation of normal working time and employment.

Work sharing and class

Even if traditions of state regulation explain why governments in some countries tend not to take the lead on work sharing, much of the variation in the incidence of state work-sharing initiatives remains to be explained.

One obvious possibility is that class is important. The logic here is that the people most closely affected by government measures to encourage or enforce

Table 6.4 Work-sharing initiatives and regulation of working hours

Incidence of work sharing-initiatives	*Regulation of normal working hours*		*Employment regulation*		
	Low	*High*	*Low*	*Medium*	*High*
Very low	Denmark	Ireland Sweden	Denmark	Ireland Sweden	
Low	Britain	Germany		Britain	Germany
Medium		Belgium Italy Netherlands		 Netherlands	Belgium Italy
High		France			France

Sources: *Normal working hours*: CEC (1980: table 2.3); EIRR (280: 16). *Employment conditions*: *Belgium*: Blanpain and Engels (1990); Spineux (1990); Vilrokx and Leemput (1992); *Britain*: Bamber and Snape (1993); Edwards *et al.* (1992); Hepple and Freedman (1992); Sisson (1995); *Denmark*: Jacobsen (1989); Scheuer (1992); *France*: Despax and Rojot (1987); Goetschy (1993); Goetschy and Rozenblatt (1992); Segrestin (1990); *Germany*: Fürstenberg (1993); Jacobi *et al.* (1992); Weiss (1986); *Ireland*: Redmond (1991); *Italy*: Ferner and Hyman (1992); Pellegrini (1993); Regalia and Regini (1995); Treu (1991); *Netherlands*: Rood (1993); Visser (1990); *Sweden*: Adlercreutz (1990); Hammarström (1993); Kjellberg (1992); Martin (1995); Rehn and Viklund (1990).

Notes: Normal working hours: low = little or no regulation; high = regulation. Entries refer to the situation in 1978 apart from the Swedish entry, which refers to 1982. Employment conditions: low = some state regulation; medium = substantial state regulation; high = elaborate state regulation.

work sharing are employers and employees, who by virtue of their different positions in the production process have different objective interests the pursuit of which influences the political dynamics of work-sharing policies via their institutional representatives on the labour market (employer organisations and trade unions) and in Parliament (liberal/conservative parties and labour/socialist/social democratic parties). The relevant factors according to this view are thus (a) attitudes to work sharing based on the logic of class and institutional self-interest, and (b) the power resources of the various policy actors relative to one another.

To develop a class theory of work sharing, I set out Weberian ideal-types of the expected attitudes of organisations representing employees (unions, left parties) and employers (employer organisations, right parties) to government moves to expand part-time working and reduce normal working time.

In the case of employers, I start with the assumption that the views and actions of employer organisations and peak groups are determined largely by the interests of their constituents, since if the former diverge too far from the latter, problems of internal cohesion will arise. In the best economic tradition I take the interests of (private sector) employers to be the maximising of profit. Unemployment is not considered to be a concern to employers as employers except insofar as it is associated with a business downturn, and even here it is not unemployment itself that is the problem for employers but rather the lower profits and bankruptcies that recessions entail. Profitability can be improved by government moves to make it cheaper and easier to employ part-timers, as this can enable firms to deal more efficiently with varying workloads. On the other hand, employers may have reservations about expanding part-time work insofar as it involves additional fixed costs of employment (recruitment, training, etc). This implies that they would be unlikely to support measures that increase these costs, or the imposition of compulsory quotas of part-time employees. Putting this together, we would expect employers to welcome the expansion of opportunities to hire on a part-time basis provided that costs are controlled and full-time alternatives remain available. Conversely, we would expect employers to oppose reductions in normal working time that do not involve commensurate wage reductions because these would mean higher hourly wage costs. We would even expect employers to have reservations if wages were reduced if this imposed requirements to reorganise work that otherwise would not have been reorganised. Choosing part-time workers because their employment would be more advantageous than employing a full-timer is one thing; reorganising one's whole system of work to accommodate reductions in the working time for existing employees is quite another. For this reason we would expect employers to oppose all forms of reductions in normal working time, including solidarity contracts.

With trade unions it is also appropriate to start with the assumption that leaders are motivated in large part by the interests of their members. For the most part this means employees, although in the case of some trade unions, members who lose their jobs can retain their membership. To the extent that such members retain leverage within the organisation, we would expect union leaders to be concerned about unemployment. In addition, some employed members may fear losing their jobs, stimulating union leaders to be concerned about job protection if not job creation. However, this predisposition on the part of trade unions to support policies designed to curb unemployment would be expected to be limited. The fight against unemployment is likely to be a top priority for some or even many union members, but wages are likely to be a vital issue for most if not all members. The conclusion to be drawn from this is that where a proposed employment policy threatens wages, it would be expected to be opposed by trade unions. For this reason we would expect unions to oppose the extension of part-time work, as such jobs are lower paid than their full-time equivalents, and to try to limit its extent. Only if there is a clear demand for part-time work among union members, for example for family reasons, would this attitude be expected to soften. By the same token, we would expect trade unions to support reductions in normal working hours on the same pay as a benefit for employees. We would also expect unions to latch on to the new job-sharing rationale as an added justification for cutting hours but not pay. The problem is that for employment purposes the best form of shorter normal working hours is identical to part-time work: fewer hours on proportionately less pay, which we would expect trade unions to oppose. In times of high unemployment, when a large proportion of union members feel their jobs to be under threat, unions might compromise a little and accept some reduction in wages, but employment efficiency (i.e. proportionate cuts in costs for employers) and full-blooded union support would be expected to be combined only where wages are state-subsidised or employers compensated by the state for continuing to pay the same wages to employees on shorter hours.

In short, employers are expected to be for part-time work and against reductions in normal working time, while unions are expected to be against part-time work and for reductions in normal working time provided that living standards are maintained. We therefore expect state moves to extend part-time work to be more frequent where employers are relatively strong, and state moves to reduce normal working time to be more frequent where unions are strong. But this is not what we find in practice.

First, although the model is consistent with employer attitudes in the nine selected West European countries as recorded in the *European Industrial Relations Review* between 1979 and 1997 – all reported employer attitudes towards part-time work were positive, and all reported attitudes to shorter normal working hours were negative – it was only partly consistent with actual union attitudes. Attitudes to part-time work were negative in Belgium, Britain, Denmark, Germany and Italy, as expected, but Dutch unions supported the extension of part-time work as a means of creating jobs (there was insufficient information about the attitudes of unions in France, Ireland and Sweden). Similarly, while unions invariably supported reducing normal working hours provided wages were not cut, although often as an employee benefit rather than as an employment strategy and in the context of collective bargaining rather than legislation, in Sweden the union movement explicitly opposed reductions in normal working time as an employment strategy on economic grounds, and in Belgium, France, Germany and the Netherlands some unions were prepared to accept pay cuts in exchange for employment-creating reductions in normal working time.

Second, the model does not explain the relative incidence of state work-sharing initiatives in the nine countries examined. Measures of union power and party power (on the basis that left parties are the political allies of trade unions) were used to test whether moves to extend part-time work were more common where unions and left parties were relatively weak, and whether moves to provide financial incentives to employers and/or employees to reduce normal working time (solidarity contracts) were more common where trade unions and left parties were relatively strong.

To begin with, the incidence of work-sharing initiatives was cross-tabulated against the percentage of employees who are members of unions: union density, as measured by the results of a survey carried out for Eurobarometer in 1991 (EIRR 279). For Sweden, which was not an EU member in 1991, a figure for 1988 based on membership data provided by unions is used instead. This may be an overestimate, but even allowing for this it is clear that unionism in Sweden, at a reported 85.3 per cent of the employed labour force, is extremely high (Visser 1991). The 1991 survey found union density to be highest in Denmark (77.1 per cent) and lowest in France (9.4 per cent). In a middle category were

Belgium (36.7 per cent), Britain (29.5 per cent), Ireland (26 per cent), the Netherlands (25.5 per cent), Germany (23.9 per cent) and Italy (22.6 per cent). However, although the country with the lowest union density, France, has by far the highest number of state initiatives to expand part-time work, consistent with the class-power theory, no correlation is apparent for the other countries, and the number of solidarity contract initiatives was also highest in low union density France, contrary to predictions (Table 6.5).

The second indicator of union strength is the extent to which trade unions participate in economic policy making, for which an index has been devised recently that covers all nine countries for the period 1979–92 (see Compston 1997a: 738 for annual scores in each country).

However, union participation in economic policy making was not significantly lower in years when initiatives to extend part-time work were introduced than in other years (mean Union Participation Index score of 5.0 compared to the overall mean score of 5.1), and was not higher but lower in years when initiatives on solidarity contracts were introduced than in other years (4.7 compared with 5.1).

Table 6.6 cross-tabulates countries and work-sharing initiatives according to the mean level of union participation in policy making in each country over the period 1979–92. For this purpose the countries have been divided into three groups: *high* – Sweden (7.3), Italy (6.7), Ireland (6.3), Denmark (5.9) and the Netherlands (5.9); *medium* – Belgium (4.9) and Germany (3.9); and *low* – France (3.3) and Britain (1.6). However, no pattern is apparent.

To test whether class power, as expressed by the strength of left and right parties, is an influential factor, annual scores for the political complexion of parliament and government were obtained by applying a coding scheme devised by Woldendorp *et al.* (1993), ranging from 1 (right-wing dominance) to 5 (left-wing dominance; see Table 6.7 for details).

Table 6.5 Work-sharing initiatives and union density

Incidence of state initiatives	*Union density – Part-time work*			*Union density – Solidarity contracts*		
	Low	*Medium*	*High*	*Low*	*Medium*	*High*
Low		Ireland	Denmark		Britain Germany Ireland Netherlands	Denmark Sweden
Medium		Belgium Britain Germany Italy Netherlands	Sweden		Belgium Italy	
High	France			France		

Sources: Table 2; EIRR No. 279; Visser (1991).

Table 6.6 Work-sharing initiatives and union participation in economic policy making

Incidence of state initiatives	*Union participation in economic policy making–Part-time work*			*Union participation in economic policy making– Solidarity contracts*		
	Low	*Medium*	*High*	*Low*	*Medium*	*High*
Low			Denmark Ireland	Britain	Germany	Denmark Ireland Netherlands Sweden
Medium	Britain	Belgium Germany	Italy Netherlands Sweden		Belgium	Italy
High	France			France		

Sources: Compston (1997 a,b).

Note: Union participation in economic policy analysis, low: no/narrow consultation; medium: broad consultation; high: narrow/broad agreement.

Table 6.7 Work-sharing initiatives and the party complexion of government

Incidence of state initiatives	*Party complexion of government – Part-time work*			*Party complexion of government – Solidarity contracts*		
	Centre–left	*Centre–right*	*Right*	*Centre–left*	*Centre–right*	*Right*
Low		Denmark	Ireland	Sweden	Denmark Netherlands	Britain Germany Ireland
Medium	Sweden	Belgium Italy Netherlands	Britain Germany		Belgium Italy	
High	France			France		

Sources: Woldendorp, *et al.* (1993); Derksen (1998); EJPR Political Data Yearbooks (1992, 1993, 1994, 1996, 1997).

Notes: Party complexion of government – right: governing right parties have more than two-thirds of seats; centre–right: between one-third and two-thirds; centre–left: left and centre parties between one-third and two-thirds.

However, governments in years in which part-time work initiatives took place were more left-wing than usual, contrary to expectations (score 3.0 compared to the overall average of 2.4). Only in relation to solidarity contracts were results in accordance with expectations, with relatively more left-wing governments in place when initiatives took place than in other years (3.3 compared with the overall average of 2.4).

Table 6.7 cross-tabulates countries by the party complexion of government and the incidence of state initiatives on part-time work and solidarity contracts. For this purpose the countries have been divided into three groups: *centre–left* – Sweden (3.7) and France (3.6); *centre–right* – Denmark (2.7), Belgium (2.6), Italy (2.3) and the Netherlands (2.0); and *right* – Ireland (1.7), Germany (1.5) and Britain (1.2). Note that over this period the right has dominated, so the scale is relative rather than absolute. However, no clear pattern can be discerned apart from the fact that state initiatives on solidarity contracts never took place under right-wing governments.

Work sharing and the welfare state

Despite the limited explanatory value of an interest-based theory of class, a model of interests based on the incentives and constraints set up by welfare state structures has considerable explanatory force. In this way we can see a clear example of the strong structuring effects of welfare programmes on other areas of public policy.[1]

The basis of this model is that in relation to the welfare state the main motivation of individuals and organisations on the labour market is financial self-interest, while for the state financial self-interest in terms of fiscal costs and savings is joined as a postulated motivation by concern for policy efficacy: other things being equal, it is assumed that state policy makers prefer effective policies over ineffective policies. Accordingly, governments are not expected to be enthusiastic about introducing any work-sharing measures that involve the state in extra net expenditure. This implies that the most likely measures to be adopted, other things being equal, are those that either save money or are cost-neutral. To the extent that cutting working time succeeds in reducing unemployment, expenditure on unemployment benefits will fall, which would be expected to act as an incentive for government action, although because work sharing is not designed to create a greater volume of work, success in employment terms would not be expected to lead to increased revenue.

Two features of the welfare state have been chosen to illustrate the way in which welfare state structures appear to affect public policy on working time: the level of employers' social contributions and the level of unemployment benefits.

Cuts in employers' social contributions can help maximise the employment dividend of reductions in working time by ensuring that employers' hourly wage costs are kept constant even when wages are not reduced commensurately with hours. The extent to which state action in this area is possible, however, logically depends on the pre-existent level of employers' social contributions: only if levels are already high can large cuts in social contributions be made. State initiatives to encourage work sharing by reducing employers' social contributions would therefore be expected to be more frequent where the level of employers' social contributions is relatively high. Table 6.8 shows that this is indeed the case, although high social contributions are no guarantee of state action.

Table 6.8 Employers' social contributions and state work-sharing initiatives

Incidence of state measures to encourage work sharing by reducing employer's social contributions	*Level of employers' social contributions*		
	Low (0–3% of GDP)	*Medium (7–9% of GDP)*	*High (11–13% of GDP)*
Non-existent	Britain	Netherlands Denmark Ireland	Sweden
Low		Germany	
Medium		Belgium	Italy
High			France

Sources: EIRR, No. 60-286; Eurostat (1993, 1995).

Note: Ranked by average of employers' social contributions as per cent of GDP (1981, 1983, 1988, 1993).

The other example of the logic of self-interest at work comes from the interaction between unemployment benefit levels and the political dynamics of paid leave schemes implemented as anti-unemployment measures. This form of work sharing has not been discussed so far in this chapter, but it is useful to bring it in here to illustrate the way in which the fiscal effects of welfare states seem to affect state action on work sharing. The leave schemes concerned involve the state paying employees to take leave in order to open up temporary vacancies for previously unemployed people. Leave for educational purposes, leave to take care of children and sabbatical leave are the main possibilities here.

The logic of interest in this case demonstrates how high unemployment benefit payment levels can resolve a conflict of interest between employees and the state in relation to paid leave schemes and in so doing facilitate their introduction and operation. This conflict arises from the fact that, other things being equal, take-up of paid leave would be expected to be higher where employees on leave are paid well than where they are paid badly, but cost considerations would be expected to push governments into restricting payment levels. The existence of high payment rates for unemployment benefits can square this circle because to the extent that the positions of employees who take leave are filled by previously unemployed people, the net cost to the state of paid leave schemes depends on the relationship between the level of leave benefits paid to the employee and the level of unemployment benefits paid to the previously unemployed person: If the employee is paid at a higher level, there is a net cost to the state, other things being equal, but if he or she is paid less than the going unemployment benefit rate, the state saves money. Therefore one would expect that the combination of cost and efficacy considerations would mean that leave schemes would be most likely to be introduced where unemployment benefits are relatively high, since this enables relatively high benefits to be paid to the employee on leave at little or no net cost to the state.

Table 6.9 Unemployment benefit level and paid leave arrangements

State initiatives on paid leave	*Unemployment benefit level*		
	Low	*Medium*	*High*
Non-existent	Britain Ireland Italy	Germany	Netherlands
Existent		Belgium France	Denmark Sweden

Sources: EIRR (1979–97); CEC (1978, 1985, 1989, 1995b: 51; 1997, n.d.); Trehörning (1993: 75); and information from Swedish Embassy, London, 1998.

Cross-tabulation of countries by unemployment benefit payment rates and the incidence of state initiatives to encourage work sharing by introducing paid leave arrangements supports this theory (Table 6.9): governments moved to introduce or extend paid leave schemes only in countries in which unemployment benefit payment levels were high, although high unemployment benefit levels were no guarantee of state action.

Work sharing and social partnership

We have seen that a simple interest-based model of employer and union attitudes fails to explain the relative incidence of state work-sharing initiatives despite the fact that an interest-based model did have some explanatory power in the case of welfare state structures. Furthermore, the interest-based model could not predict accurately the expressed attitudes of trade unions. Since it was able to predict employer attitudes, this implies that the fault in the model lies in its construction of union attitudes. The argument to be put here is that this is indeed the case: if the interest component of union motivation in the model is supplemented by bringing in values and ideas that are not directly based on individual and institutional self-interest, the resulting model yields predictions that fit perfectly the observed incidence of state work-sharing initiatives.

Consider the conflict of interests between employers and unions over wages: employers want wages reduced if working time is reduced, but unions want to maintain existing living standards. For economic and cost reasons the state is also likely to want wages to be reduced. While these actors remain resolute, state action would be expected to be less likely than when one or both sides give ground because it is politically more difficult for governments to introduce legislative or regulatory measures against opposition from affected interests than when agreement has already been reached. Since it is the attitudes of unions that have been found to be inconsistent with their interests as defined in the model, a possible hypothesis is that where agreements are reached, this is because unions have shifted position, rather than employers or the state.

Why might unions give ground in this area, thereby acting in a way that is contrary to the interests of their members? One obvious possibility is that this occurs where unions are weak relative to employers, but we have already seen that union strength relative to employers does not appear to be significant. It is therefore necessary to look beyond self-interest to other motivations, that is, to motivations based on ideas and values that are not wholly attributable to self-interest. In short, we need to look at the role of ideology. After all, one of the main institutional cleavages within national union movements is based on ideology, namely the division between communist, social democratic and Christian trade unions. We do not have to assume ideological purity to acknowledge the existence of distinctive clusters of values and ideas in the rhetoric of each of these types of unions. In general, socialism was the first ideology to animate organised trade union movements, a number of which then split after First World War into communist and social democratic variants, while Christian trade unions were generally organised in explicit ideological opposition to the socialist unions (Fogarty 1957).

It is possible to identify numerous points of difference between the ideological rhetorics of these three types of unions, but for our purposes the relevant distinction is between the socialist conception of society as being divided into antagonistic classes and the Christian stress on the possibility and desirability of class cooperation in the interests of social harmony, because it is this ethic of social partnership that legitimates and indeed demands sacrifices on the part of Christian trade unionists in the interests of the greater good, in this case the reduction of unemployment. The official utterances of Christian unions place a high value on class cooperation, and prioritise inclusiveness and a sense that we are all in this together so that we ought to pull together and cooperate to solve problems, as opposed to disclaiming responsibility and leaving it to someone else (Fogarty 1957; Van Kersbergen 1994). Of course social democratic trade unions may also stress the value of cooperation, for example those in Scandinavian countries, but this is arguably a tactic rather than a basic commitment. For example, as late as the 1980s the 'moderate' social democratic blue-collar union confederations of Denmark and Sweden advocated the introduction of wage-earner fund schemes that would have had the effect of transferring control of the private sector from its present owners to huge investment funds controlled by trade unions (Tilton 1991: chapter 10; Pontusson 1987). This is hardly social partnership.

While the distinction between the social partnership ethic of Christian unions and the class antagonism of other unions is no longer as clear-cut as it has been in the past, the hypothesis advanced here is that it remains important enough to influence union attitudes towards state work-sharing initiatives. More specifically, the hypothesis is that Christian and Christian-influenced trade union confederations are more prepared than communist and social democratic union confederations to take the view that everyone is responsible for unemployment and for solving it. We would therefore expect these unions to be more prepared to compromise with employers on this issue and in so doing to agree to sacrifices on the part of their members in order to try to curb unemployment. In respect of working time this implies less resistance to the extension of part-time work, a greater preparedness to consider reductions in normal working time even if they involve wage cuts, and positive enthusiasm for solidarity contracts. Therefore state work- sharing initiatives would be expected to be more frequent in countries in which separate Christian and/or Christian-influenced trade union confederations are existent and significant.

Avowedly Christian trade union confederations are strongest in Belgium (ACV/CSC),[2] Italy (CISL) and the Netherlands (CNV). In the Netherlands the FNV, which is the result of a merger between the Catholic NKV and socialist NVV in 1982, explicitly accepts the religious heritage of the NKV. Although the DGB in Germany is also the result of a merger between socialist and Christian union confederations, this took place long ago just after the Second World War and since then the Christian element has been marginalised. The Irish ICTU is excluded due to its lack of any explicitly Christian tradition, based as it is on the British union model. Although the Catholic CFTC in France is rather small, the somewhat larger CFDT was formed when the original CFTC changed its name as a result of secularising in 1964 (the current CFTC is descended from those who objected to this move). After a militant period in the 1960s and 1970s, since 1979 the CFDT has reverted to a policy favouring compromise (Fogarty 1957; Kendall 1975: 67; Chubb 1982; Lange and Vannicelli 1982; Ross 1982; Pasture 1994).

Examination of the attitudes of Christian and Christian-influenced union confederations reveals that they are indeed more supportive than their socialist counterparts of work sharing as a means of curbing unemployment. In France, it is obvious that the CFDT has been the most enthusiastic proponent of work sharing as a way of combating unemployment, for example by explicitly not ruling out wage cuts as part of employment-creating packages of working time reductions (Notat 1997). In Belgium, the CSC/ACV is clearly more supportive of work sharing than the FGTB (H. Eyssen, Interview, 13 march 1998). In Italy the Catholic confederation CISL has always been more interested in work sharing in general and solidarity contracts in particular than either CGIL or UIL (E. Gualmini, personal communication, 1997). And in the Netherlands both the CNV and FNV support the extension of part-time work as a way not only of fighting unemployment but also of enabling members more easily to combine work and family responsibilities (FNV 1993; J. J. van Dijk, CNV, Interview, 31 July 1997).

The most persuasive evidence in favour of the social partnership hypothesis, however, is that there is a perfect correlation between Christian unionism and state action on work sharing: state work-sharing initiatives were more numerous in every single country in which one or more significant Christian or Christian-influenced union confederations exist than in any of the countries in which there is no such confederation (Table 6.10).

Table 6.10 Christian trade unionism and work sharing

Incidence of state work-sharing initiatives	*Strong Christian or ex-Christian trade union confederation(s)*	*No significant Christian or ex-Christian trade union confederation*
Very low		Denmark Sweden Ireland
Low		Britain Germany
Medium	Belgium Italy Netherlands	
High	France	

Sources: Fogarty (1957); Kendall (1975: 67); Chubb (1982); Lange and Vannicelli (1982); Ross (1982); and Pasture (1994).

Conclusion

If we assume for the moment that the correlations identified in this chapter reflect real processes of causation, we can construct a picture which in some ways is unremarkable: the incidence of state initiatives to curb unemployment by reducing working time is greater when unemployment is high and rising, and where employment conditions are customarily regulated directly by the state rather than by collective bargaining or the market. The nature and incidence of state work-sharing measures also appears to be influenced by the structure of national welfare states. These findings can probably be accepted without much question, and indeed their obviousness lends plausibility to the analysis as a whole.

Not so obvious, however, is the finding that class interest is inadequate as an explanatory factor until overlaid by an ideological model according to which the social partnership ideology of Christian and Christian-influenced trade unions facilitates state action in this area. The unexpectedness of this finding is partly attributable to the fact that political economists are often more accustomed to thinking in terms of interests rather than ideology, since interests are obviously important, can readily be elaborated into theories due to their clear logic, and dominate thinking in the important cognate field of economics. But it should also be kept in mind that there is legitimate room for doubt because by themselves the above findings are not conclusive due to the inherent limitations of the type of comparative analysis on which they are based: the data may be inadequate, the addition of more countries might change the result (although superficial examination of other West European countries has so far yielded no evidence of this), and we may be misled by spurious correlations caused by the absence of key causal factors from the analysis and/or by correlations between factors included in the analysis. For example, are state work-sharing initiatives rare in Britain because Britain lacks a Christian trade union movement, or because it has a tradition in which state regulation of employment conditions is relatively light, or both? With the above data and analytical method, we cannot tell.

The next step, then, is to subject the social partnership thesis to further testing using a different methodology, namely historical analysis. For example, if a case study found that the influence of the CFDT and/or CFTC was decisive in encouraging state work-sharing initiatives in France, the country in which they are by far most frequent, then we could be more confident that the theory fits reality.

In the meantime, the above analysis provides strong if incomplete evidence to support the proposition that the influence of Christian social thought is a significant factor in prompting governments to take steps to curb unemployment by encouraging or enforcing cuts in working hours – in fact the strongest evidence that purely comparative analysis can provide.

Notes

1 To some extent the countries with a high incidence of work sharing initiatives are the same as those 'Continental welfare states' identified by Esping-Andersen (1996) as utilising labour-force exit as a principal policy response to unemployment – Austria, Belgium, France, Germany and Italy – but work sharing measures are rare in Germany (and Austria), and it should be noted that work sharing as defined – part-time work and reductions in normal working time – does not involve exit from the labour force.

2 The full names of the trade union federations are as follows: ACV/CSC: Algemeen Christelijke Vakverbond van België/Confèderation des Syndicats Chrétiens de Belgiquep; CFDT: Confédération française et démocratique du travail; CFTC: Confèderation française des travailleurs chrétiens; CGIL: Confederazione Generale Italiana del Lavoro; CISL: Confederazione Italiana Sindacati Lavoratori; CNV: Christelijk Nationaal Vakverbond; DGB: Deutscher Gewerkschaftsbund; FGTB: Fédération du Travail de Belgique; FNV: Federatie Nederlandse Vakbeweging; ICTU: Irish Congress of Trade Unions; NKV: Nederlands Katholiek Vakverbond; NVV: Nederlands Verbond van Vakvereinigingen; UIL: Unione Italiana del Lavoro.

References

Adlercreutz, A. (1990). In R. Blanpain (ed.), *Sweden*, International Encyclopedia for Labour Law and Industrial Relations, Dordrecht: Kluwer.

Bamber, G. and Snape, E. J. (1993). 'Industrial relations in Britain', in G. J. Bamber and R. D. Lansbury (eds), *International and Comparative Industrial Relations*, 2nd edn. London: Routledge, 27–54.

Bastian, J. (1994). *A Matter of Time*, Aldershot: Avebury.

Blanpain, R. and Engels, C. (1990). In R. Blanpain (ed.), *Belgium*, International Encyclopedia for Labour Law and Industrial Relations, Dordrecht: Kluwer.

Blyton, P. (1985). *Changes in Working Time: An International Review*, London: Croom Helm.

Blyton, P. (1989). 'Working time reductions and the European work-sharing debate', in A. Gladstone, with R. Lansbury, J. Stieber, T. Treu and M. Weis (eds), *Current Issues in Labour Relations: An International Perspective*, Berlin: de Gruyter, 161–74.

Bosch, L. H. M., Eisendoorn, G. Th. and Nijsen, A. F. M. (1989). 'Stimulering van deeltijdarbeid (Stimulating part-time work)', *Tijdschrift voor Arbeidsvraagstukken* 5, 80–8.

CEC (Commission of the European Communities) (1978). *Comparative Tables of the Social Security Systems in the Member States of the European Communities*, 10th edn. Luxembourg: Office for Official Publications of the European Communities.

CEC (1980). 'Adaptation of working time: Impact of a reduction in the annual duration of work', *European Economy* 5, 87–119.

CEC (1985). *Comparative Tables of the Social Security Systems in the Member States of the European Communities*, 13th edn. Luxembourg: Office for Official Publications of the European Communities.

CEC (1989). *Comparative Tables of the Social Security Systems in the Member States of the European Communities*, 15th edn. Luxembourg: Office for Official Publications of the European Communities.

CEC (1995a). *Employment in Europe 1995*, Luxembourg: Office for Official Publications of the European Communities.

CEC (1995b). *Social Protection in Europe 1995*, Luxembourg: Office for Official Publications of the European Communities.

CEC (1997). *Social Protection in the Member States of the Communities: Situation on 1st July 1996 and Evolution*, Luxembourg: Office for Official Publications of the European Communities.

CEC (n.d.). *Social Protection in the Member States of the Communities: Situation on 1st July 1993 and Evolution*, Luxembourg: Office for Official Publications of the European Communities.

Cette, G. and Taddéi, D. (1993). 'The economic effects of reducing and reorganising working time', *Futures* 25(5), 561–77.

Chubb, B. (1982). *The Government and Politics of Ireland*, 2nd edn. London: Longman.

Compston, H. (1997a). 'Union power, policy-making and unemployment in Western Europe, 1972–1993', *Comparative Political Studies* 30(6), 732–51.

Compston, H. (1997b). 'The logic of work-sharing as an employment policy', unpublished manuscript.

Cuvillier, R. (1984). *The Reduction of Working Time*, Geneva: ILO.

Dederichs, E. and Köhler, E. (1993). *Part-time Work in the European Community: The Economic and Social Dimensions*, Dublin: European Foundation for the Improvement of Living and Working Conditions.

Derksen, W. (1998). *Elections Around the World*, Website. Available HTTP: http://www.agora.stm.it/elections/election.htm.

Despax, M. and Rojot, J. (1987). In R. Blanpain (ed.), *France*, International Encyclopedia for Labour Law and Industrial Relations, Dordrecht: Kluwer.

Edwards, P., Hall, M., Hyman, R., Marginson, P., Sisson, K., Waddington, J. and Winchester, D. (1992). 'Great Britain: Still muddling through', in A. Ferner and R. Hyman (eds), *Industrial Relations in the New Europe*, Oxford: Basil Blackwell, 1–68.

Esping-Andersen, G. (1996). 'Welfare states without work: The impasse of labour shedding and familialism in Continental European social policy', in G. Esping-Andersen (ed.), *Welfare States in Transition*, London: Sage, 66–87.

EIRR (*European Industrial Relations Review*) 60 (January 1979)–286 (November 1997).

EJPR (*European Journal of Political Research*) *Political Data Yearbooks* 1992, 1993, 1994, 1996 and 1997.

Eurostat (1993). *Taxes and Social Contributions 1980–1991*, Luxembourg: Office for Official Publications of the European Communities.

Eurostat (1995). *Taxes and Social Contributions 1982–1993*, Luxembourg: Office for Official Publications of the European Communities.

Ferner, A. and Hyman, R. (1992). 'Italy: Between political exchange and micro-corporatism', in A. Ferner and R. Hyman (eds), *Industrial Relations in the New Europe*, Oxford: Basil Blackwell, 524–600.

FNV (Federatie Nederlandse Vakbeweging) (1993). *Prospects for a Plural Society. The decisions of the 24th FNV Congress, 1993*, Amsterdam: FNV.

Fogarty, M. P. (1957). *Christian Democracy in Western Europe, 1820–1953*, London: Routledge and Kegan Paul.

Fürstenberg, F. (1993). 'Industrial relations in Germany', in G. J. Bamber and R. D. Lansbury (eds), *International and Comparative Industrial Relations*, 2nd edn. London: Routledge, 175–96.

Goetschy, J. (1993). 'Industrial relations in France', in G. J. Bamber and R. D. Lansbury (eds), *International and Comparative Industrial Relations*, 2nd edn. London: Routledge, 149–74.

Goetschy, J. and Rozenblatt, P. (1992). 'France: The industrial relations system at a turning point?', in A. Ferner and R. Hyman (eds), *Industrial Relations in the New Europe*, Oxford: Basil Blackwell, 404–44.

Hammarström, O. (1993). 'Industrial relations in Sweden', in G. J. Bamber and R. D. Lansbury (eds), *International and Comparative Industrial Relations*, 2nd edn, London: Routledge, 197–219.

Hart, R. A. (1987). *Working Time and Employment*, Boston: Allen & Unwin.

Hepple, B. and Freedman, S. (1992). In R. Blanpain (ed.), *Great Britain*, International Encyclopedia for Labour Law and Industrial Relations, Dordrecht: Kluwer.

ILO (International Labour Organization) (1995). *Conditions of Work Digest*, Geneva: ILO, Vol. 14.

Jacobi, O., Keller, B. and Müller-Jentsch, W. (1992). 'Germany: Codetermining the future?', in A. Ferner and R. Hyman (eds), *Industrial Relations in the New Europe*, Oxford: Basil Blackwell, 218–69.

Jacobsen, P. (1989). In R. Blanpain (ed.) *Denmark*, International Encyclopedia for Labour Law and Industrial Relations, Dordrecht: Kluwer.

Kendall, W. (1975). *The Labour Movement in Europe*, London: Penguin.

Kjellberg, A. (1992). 'Sweden: Can the model survive?', in A. Ferner and R. Hyman (eds), *Industrial Relations in the New Europe*, Oxford: Basil Blackwell, 88–142.

Lange, P. and Vannicelli, M. (1982). 'Strategy under stress: The Italian trade union movement and the Italian crisis in developmental perspective', in P. Lange, G. Ross and M. Vannicelli (eds), *Unions, Change and Crisis*, London: Allen & Unwin, 95–206.

Maddison, A. (1979). 'Long-run dynamics of productivity growth', *Banche Nazionale del Lavoro* 128, cited in CEC (Commission of the European Communities) (1980) 'Adaptation of working time: Impact of a reduction in the annual duration of work', *European Economy* 5, 89–90.

Martin, A. (1995). 'The Swedish model: Demise or reconfiguration?', in R. Locke, T. Kochan and M. Piore (eds), *Employment Relations in a Changing World Economy*, London: MIT Press, 263–96.

Marullo, S. (ed.) (1995). *Comparison of Regulations on Part-time and Temporary Employment in Europe: A Briefing Paper*, London: Department of Employment, Research Series No. 52.

Notat, N. (1997). 'Intervention de Nicole Notat', Conference de presse sur la RTT du mardi 24 juin 1997.

OECD (Organisation for Economic Co-Operation and Development) (1994). *The OECD Jobs Study: Evidence and Explanations*, Paris: OECD.

OECD (1996). *Employment Outlook*, July, Paris: OECD.

OECD (1997). *Employment Outlook*, July, Paris: OECD.

Pasture, P. (1994). *Christian Trade Unionism in Europe Since 1968*, London: Avebury.

Pellegrini, C. (1993). 'Industrial relations in Italy', in G. J. Bamber and R. D. Lansbury (eds), *International and Comparative Industrial Relations*, 2nd edn. London: Routledge, 126–48.

Pontusson, J. (1987). 'Radicalization and retreat in Swedish Social Democracy', *New Left Review* 165, 5–33.

Redmond, M. (1991). In R. Blanpain (ed.), *Ireland*, International Encyclopedia for Labour Law and Industrial Relations, Dordrecht: Kluwer.

Regalia, I. and Regini, M. (1995). 'Between voluntarism and institutionalisation: Industrial relations and human resource practices in Italy', in R. Locke, T. Kochan and M. Piore (eds), *Employment Relations in a Changing World Economy*, London: MIT Press, 131–64.

Rehn, G. and Viklund, B. (1990). 'Changes in the Swedish model', in G. Baglioni and C. Crouch (eds), *European Industrial Relations: The Challenge of Flexibility*, London: Sage, 300–25.

Rood, M. G. (1993). In R. Blanpain (ed.), *The Netherlands*, International Encyclopedia for Labour Law and Industrial Relations, Dordrecht: Kluwer.

Ross, G. (1982). 'The perils of politics: French unions and the crisis of the 1970s', in P. Lange, G. Ross and M. Vannicelli (eds), *Unions, Change and Crisis*, London: Allen & Unwin, 13–93.

Scheuer, S. (1992). 'Denmark: Return to decentralization', in A. Ferner and R. Hyman (eds), *Industrial Relations in the New Europe*, Oxford: Basil Blackwell, 168–97.

Segrestin, D. (1990). 'Recent changes in France', in G. Baglioni and C. Crouch (eds), *European Industrial Relations: The Challenge of Flexibility*, London: Sage, 97–126.

Sisson, K. (1995). 'Change and continuity in British industrial relations: "Strategic Choice" or "Muddling through"?', in R. Locke, T. Kochan and M. Piore (eds), *Employment Relations in a Changing World Economy*, London: MIT Press, 33–58.

Spineux, A. (1990). 'Trade unionism in Belgium: The difficulties of a major renovation', in G. Baglioni and C. Crouch (eds), *European Industrial Relations: The Challenge of Flexibility*, London: Sage, 42–70.

Tilton, T. (1991). *The Political Theory of Swedish Social Democracy*, Oxford: Clarendon Press.

Trehörning, P. (1993). *Measures to Combat Unemployment in Sweden*, Stockholm: Swedish Institute.

Treu, T. (1991). In R. Blanpain (ed.), *Italy*, International Encyclopedia for Labour Law and Industrial Relations, Dordrecht: Kluwer.

Van Kersbergen, K. (1994). 'The distinctiveness of Christian democracy', in D. Hanley (ed.), *Christian Democracy in Europe*, London: Pinter, 31–47.

Vilrokx, J. and Van Leemput, J. (1992). 'Belgium: A new stability in industrial relations', in A. Ferner and R. Hyman (eds), *Industrial Relations in the New Europe*, Oxford: Basil Blackwell, 357–92.

Visser, J. (1990). 'Continuity and change in Dutch industrial relations', in G. Baglioni and C. Crouch (eds), *European Industrial Relations: The Challenge of Flexibility*, London: Sage, 199–242.

Visser, J. (1991). 'Trends in trade union membership', *OECD Employment Outlook 1991*, Paris: OECD, 97–134.

Wedderburn, A. (1995). 'Part-time work', *Bulletin of European Studies on Time* 8, Dublin: European Foundation for the Improvement of Living and Working Conditions, 1–82.

Weiss, M. (1986). In R. Blanpain (ed.), *Germany*, International Encyclopedia for Labour Law and Industrial Relations, Dordrecht: Kluwer.

White, M. (1987). *Working Hours: Assessing the Potential for Reduction*, Geneva: International Labour Office.

Woldendorp, J., Keman, H. and Budge, I. (1993). 'Political data 1945–1990 – Party government in 20 democracies', *European Journal of Political Research* 24(1), 1–119.

7 The governance of the employment–welfare relationship in Britain and Germany

Anke Hassel

Introduction

One of the most pressing problems in advanced industrialised societies is the reorganisation of the relationship between the employment system and welfare provisions. After the Second World War and during the golden years of welfare state development, industrialised nations developed a level of functional and normative integration between the three social segments, i.e. employment, family patterns and welfare provisions. Each segment was closely tied to and complemented by the others, leading to a highly integrated framework. The gender division defined the complementary link between the family and employment, the employment-based funding of social security characterised the link between employment and welfare, and the population growth and birth rates were the basis on which the link between welfare and the family was defined.

The normative model of post-war employment envisaged a family with one permanently employed breadwinner whose employment generated income for the whole family and the accumulation of the funds out of which the social wage and other welfare state expenditures were to be paid. 'At the same time, the fact that people are normally employed and derive a family wage out of this employment limits the extent to which claims against the funds for the social wage will be made.' (Offe 1993: 222).

Today, the relationship between welfare and employment faces fundamental challenges due to changes in family and employment patterns. For instance, growing insecurity on the labour markets no longer allows for traditional family models with only one breadwinner. At the same time, the increase in female employment undermines the traditional division of labour within families. We also find that persistently high levels of unemployment and underemployment are putting pressure on social security budgets and unemployment funds. These pressures not only pose a challenge to the financing of existing social security systems, but also to the established balance between wage bargaining and social security payments. Social security systems are generally dependent on the availability of paid employment as the basis of taxation and contributions. Since the creation of employment is to some extent determined by the level of taxation on employment, we often see a vicious circle of low job creation leading to higher taxation of employment and vice versa. Independent changes in each segment – deriving from changed macroeconomic situations and changes in family values – have therefore introduced exogenous imbalances into the system.

At the same time, the tightness of fit of these systems makes adjustments to new patterns of employment very difficult. The interdependence between the individual segments reduces steering capacities, since changes in one aspect of the system alter the efficiency of other parts of the system (Freeman 1995: 17). Secondly, as the literature on the welfare state points out, welfare retrenchment follows different rules than welfare development, since it is highly influenced by its clientele (Pierson 1994). And thirdly, the governance structures of the employment–welfare relationship are very complex, given the country-specific evolution of trade union involvement in wage bargaining and welfare administration. The relationship between the state and societal actors turns the reform of the employment–welfare nexus into a highly path-dependent exercise.

In this chapter, I will try to tackle some aspects concerning the governance of the employment–welfare relationship by looking at the creation of low-productivity employment in two countries. Since employment creation remains at the heart of the employment–welfare nexus and since there is a strong assumption in the public debate that economic growth will not generate a sufficient number of high-productivity jobs, the only solution to this dilemma seems to be the creation of low-productivity employment. If this assumption is correct, the question arises as to why some countries are better than others at creating – or at least allowing for – low-productivity employment.

In the first section, I will explain how the notion of low-productivity employment is of crucial importance for the link between welfare and employment and will look at low-productivity employment in the context of the conflicting interests of different actors. Secondly, I will try to disentangle the employment–welfare nexus and identify three systematic links in the governance of welfare and employment. In the third section, using the examples of Germany and the UK, I will show how the link between employment and welfare has worked in the two countries and how policies have either created or inhibited incentives to take up low-productivity employment. Lastly, the experience of the two countries will be linked back to the general argument of the governance of the welfare–employment nexus.

Disaggregating welfare and employment: low-productivity employment

The main pressure which directly affects the relationship between the welfare state and the employment system is the need to accommodate low-paid employment in the employment and social security systems. Traditionally, the level of social security benefits presents a floor for minimum wages. At the same time, productivity in some economic sectors is too low to allow wage levels to be much higher than social security levels. In these sectors, such as certain areas of manufacturing (the textile industry), agriculture (for example, vine harvesting) and the service sector (private services), employment can only take place in the informal economy or not at all. With persisting unemployment levels and the maintenance of existing social security systems, there is an increasing development towards informal economies coinciding with a relatively high level of social security benefits, which again undermines the insurance base of many social security systems. While social security benefits have to be cut, the unemployed increasingly turn to informal employment opportunities.

This pressure is obviously linked to the overarching problem of unemployment and underemployment, but it is not the same thing. In the aftermath of the oil crisis of the early 1970s, labour markets in industrialised countries underwent two major developments. Firstly, a considerable portion of the unemployment rate proved to be a structural phenomenon on labour markets that was not affected by cyclical growth. While economic upswings and downswings had an impact on the size of the problem, the basic rate of unemployment gradually increased. Secondly, profound changes took place on the supply side of labour markets. On the one hand, female employment has risen persistently since the 1960s. This increase in female employment has broadened the notion of full employment to encompass all women and anyone who wishes to work (Kolberg and Esping-Andersen 1997: 11). On the other hand, other segments such as elderly employees were systematically encouraged to leave the labour market. As a consequence, we find a gender-specific shift in employment rates, with female employment rates generally increasing and male employment rates generally declining.

For these two reasons, the initial reasoning that an improvement in the unemployment problem could be the key to solving the growing dysfunctionalities of the welfare–employment relationship was misplaced. The structural changes in employment patterns require a much more thorough shift both in welfare funding and in welfare provisions. Pension schemes which are based on forty years of full-time employment are not viable if growing numbers of employees retire at the age of 55 or have patchy employment records.

Unemployment rates were therefore only part of the general problem of the employment–welfare relationship. In addition, the reduction of unemployment does not always solve the problem: even if the problem of unemployment could have been alleviated by an influx of unemployed people into early retiring, marginal employment or other forms of inactivity, the pressure on the welfare system would have been sustained. On the other hand, unemployment basically reflected a growing mismatch between job seekers and job opportunities.

A classical policy of reducing unemployment rates therefore does not necessarily provide an answer. The increase in the share of the working-age population in employment serves as a better policy goal for adjusting to the pressure on the employment–welfare relationship (see Scharpf, Chapter 12 in this volume). An increase in employment rates reduces the number of welfare recipients while at the same time enlarging the taxable base for the funding of social security systems. Taking this observation as a starting point, we find that the record on employment rates varies markedly between industrialised countries. In Anglo-Saxon and Nordic countries, in particular, employment rates have increased to a much greater extent than in Germany and other continental European countries, where employment growth is lagging behind. A closer inspection reveals that employment growth is sector-specific, with employment in the service sector accounting for the main differences between countries (see Scharpf, Chapter 12).

Assuming that employment growth will have to take place in these sheltered service sectors, we might be able to understand the problem more clearly if we look at employment growth from the perspective of labour costs. By doing so, we can classify these employment areas as employment segments with low productivity, implying that low productivity does not generate sufficient added value to make the workplace worthwhile in a competitive economic environment.[1]

This enables us to allocate the area of employment growth more specifically than a more descriptive allocation within the sheltered service sectors. Service sectors in general have lower productivity rates than the manufacturing sector. In addition, the type of employment which accounts for the different levels of employment growth refers primarily to low-productivity employment such as private and social services and only to a lesser extent to industrial and/or high-productivity services such as the banking sector. Because of the low level of productivity, this type of employment can only emerge if the costs are low. Somebody therefore has to pay the price for low-productivity employment – either employers, employees, the state or the social security funds (Table 7.1). In terms of governance, this perspective also helps to define the interests of the actors involved in the distribution of those costs.

As an illustration of how these different forms of paying for low productivity are linked to the general problem of decoupling and recoupling the relationship between welfare and employment, we can look at the issue of how companies and social security systems address the problem of workers with decreasing productivity

Table 7.1 Who pays for low productivity?

	Firms	*Labour*	*Government*	*Social security*
Form of payment	Cross-subsidising between departments and groups of employees	Accepting low pay	Subsidising of certain types of (state) companies, employees or sector	Benefits to low-productivity employees in the form of early retirement payments, unemployment benefits and social security benefits
Workplaces and labour market groups	Industry-related services, older and young employees	Private and industry-related services, low-skilled employees, young and old workers	Agriculture, steel and coal industries, state-owned manufacturing	Long-term unemployed, young unemployed, early retired
Form of regulation	Pay structure within the company	Wage bargaining	Direct subsidies	Benefits and training schemes

levels. One way of dealing with this in a number of countries, including Germany and the Netherlands, has been to use the instrument of early retirement (see Chapters 4 and 10). Early retirement schemes help to share the burden of the decrease in marginal productivity of elderly manual workers between the social security system and companies. Companies can use early retirement schemes to shed labour during times of recession, and labour market policy can transfer the problem of underemployment from young workers to older ones. While the exit from the labour market into social security was eased by lowering the retiring age, entry was still possible. This mechanism burdened a large proportion of the costs of decreasing productivity onto the social security system and therefore redistributed low-productivity costs from companies to social security funds.

The way in which the issue of low-productivity employment is framed here seems to imply a distributional problem in a zero-sum situation between companies, employees, government budgets and social security systems. The costs of lower productivity margins of workers and workplaces can be paid for by the company having some departments subsidise others. Large and vertically integrated companies along the Ford Rouge role model were only partially able to counterbalance relative productivity levels of departments and groups of workers against a bargained pay formula for the whole firm. This pay formula usually entailed a level of cross-subsidising of workplaces with a low level of productivity by other workplaces. Smaller companies that face a much narrower distribution margin and at the same time a broader range of investment decisions are much less able and willing to follow this path.

If, however, these workplaces and workers are not paid for by the company, they can be directly subsidised by the government. This is the case in agricultural employment in Europe, and also in other sectors, such as coal and steel, and in certain public utility companies. If a low-productivity sector is not directly subsidised by the government and a low-wage sector cannot develop because of minimum wage prescriptions, workers with low productivity potential have to be accommodated by social security funds. These can then either confine themselves to providing income maintenance for the unemployed or can engage in publicly funded employment creation and training schemes.

The problem of accommodating low-productivity employment in high-productivity economies has sharpened because the unequal impact of technological progress widens the gap between high and low productivity levels and because the internationalisation of the economy allows for a transfer of low-productivity production to countries with low labour costs. While productivity levels are steadily increasing across the economy and leave some room for redistribution, the issue of the relative increase in productivity levels between different segments of the economy and workplaces is increasingly coming under strain. The differences in productivity increases between sectors put more pressure on the wage structure and the existing balance between high- and low-productivity areas (Appelbaum and Schettkat 1995; Iversen and Wren 1998).

This directly relates to a central problem of the relationship between pay and workplace productivity. The internationalisation of the economy and technological progress give incentives to companies to focus on the marginal productivity of a workplace, since opportunity costs have risen so much faster than the reduction of transaction costs through a vertically integrated company. The structure of pay within a company and between different groups of employees therefore gains in importance compared to the absolute pay level. At the same time, pay structures are the most important mechanism of status differentiation within societies and are firmly enshrined in written agreements and pay formulas. It is therefore very difficult to alter pay structures, and in many cases this is only possible through company outsourcing and subcontracting. By doing so, these workplaces are moved to low-productivity companies (such as security, catering, private household services, etc.) which provide low-paid employment. The disintegration of previously vertically integrated companies therefore reduces the capacity for cross-subsidising groups of employees and shifts workers with a low level of productivity to separate companies, which then pay low wages.

On the other hand, the image of a distributional problem within a zero-sum situation is only partially accurate. One important counter-argument would be that social policy has an economically supportive function (Manow 1997), enabling companies to achieve high levels of productivity by providing a decent level of employability and flexibility of workers. Rather than having a purely risk-bearing function, social policy linked with labour market policy can also play a more active role by linking benefits to the acquirement of skills and hence giving incentives to employees to upgrade their qualifications.

Second, tightly defined wage structures force companies to counteract a lack of competitiveness by an increase in productivity rather than improving their competitiveness by lowering their labour costs. While the lack of low-paid employment might prevent the creation of employment in low-productivity segments, the existence of a constricting flat wage structure does not allow the gap in innovation between companies to become too large and provides incentives for structures at the plant level to develop uniformly and within acceptable periods of time in the plants (Bahnmüller and Bispinck 1995: 149). The argument therefore runs that the existing structures of the welfare model support the production model and that changes in the pattern of redistribution of costs might alter the setup in a way that could then undermine the production model. When following this line of argument, we need to be aware, however, that – ceteris paribus – it assumes that policy makers have agreed to accept low levels of employment growth in order to sustain a given production model.

However, keeping in mind the option of a possible win–win situation under the condition of economic growth, the productivity-enhancing effects of social policy are rarely a policy goal of the actors involved and cannot be used to explain the differences in governance structures in different countries. The adjustment pressures on the welfare–employment nexus therefore remain, and redistribution can be observed in different countries. In the following, I will take Germany and the UK as examples to analyse policy responses in very different institutional settings. Before doing so, I will lay the ground by framing the problem of governance of the welfare–employment relationship.

Modes of governance of the employment–welfare relationship

By formulating the reform of the employment–welfare relationship as a problem of governance, I refer to the totality of institutional arrangements that coordinate and regulate transactions inside and across the boundaries of different policy fields, in particular through the state and interest associations.[2] In real terms, the relationship between welfare and employment is highly interdependent but, at the same time, governance structures are highly particularised between different policy fields, in particular macroeconomic policy, social policy, labour market policy and industrial relations. These policy fields have over time become more departmentalised within state governments (Lehmbruch 1997). They are often directed by different ministries and are therefore determined by their sectoral discourse. For instance, there is a stark contrast between macroeconomic and labour market policies within government administrations.

In addition to the differentiation between governmental departments, the interpenetration between the self-regulation of labour markets by associations and by public policy is particularly strong in the area of welfare and employment, given the long-standing involvement of trade unions in welfare administration and the strict preservation of state-free collective bargaining.

While the governance structures of collective actors (associational governance) and public policy share some characteristics of the institutional structuring of policy making, there are also important differences between the two. Their commonalties entail the general structuring of policy agendas and veto points to decisions (Immergut 1992). As institutional approaches towards public policy have pointed out, the 'rules of the game' structure the competencies of collective action and shape the definition of self-interest strategies of collective action followed by the relevant policy actors, thereby critically influencing the nature or policy style of decision-making processes (Visser and Hemerijck 1997: 54).

Quite separate from the involvement of associations in public policy making, associational governance is characterised by a degree of decision-making autonomy that is not based on public force, but on the strength of the associational actors themselves. Under associational governance, associations are not only consulted in the process of decision making on public policy and play an advisory role when these decisions are implemented, they are also autonomous decision makers in areas which are explicitly not under the reign of public policy. However, the state can intervene in forms of purely associational governance by deciding on who should participate in negotiations and on the rules of the game, by supporting one actor, changing perceptions through information and intervening directly when decisions cannot otherwise be reached (Mayntz 1996: 160).

Associations act as governance mechanisms by defining and procuring public goods through organising and enforcing cooperative behaviour among their members, by engaging in collective contracts with other associations and by securing delegations of state authority to be used to the advantage of the members (Hollingsworth *et al.* 1994: 7). In this respect, associational governance per se entails the notion of a multi-level mediation process: associations mediate between their members and other actors in the policy field. As mediators, they can interpret the other side as well as using their positions to justify their actions. Associations can reject compromise proposals by arguing that members will not accept them, or they can put proposals to their members by arguing that the other actors will not concede to more.

Although we have placed public policy and associational governance at two ends of the spectrum of employment and welfare regulation, most regulatory issues are, however, interwoven and at least indirectly governed by a mixture of the two. Macroeconomic policy is clearly in the exclusive domain of public policy, but its regulatory capacity depends very much on the level of coordination of wage bargaining in the field of industrial relations. Similarly, wage bargaining is always constrained by macroeconomic policy decisions, in particular monetary policy. In the area of industrial relations, public policy generally only has direct interventionist power under very special circumstances. Here, public policy also provides a legal framework of substantive and procedural rules. This includes basic standards on the labour market, such as a minimum amount of paid holidays or a maximum working week, which are then topped up by collective bargaining. In addition, public policy also prescribes procedural rules, as in the cases of early retirement, dismissals and redundancies. For example, legislation prescribes not only the conditions under which dismissals can be carried out, but also that employees' representatives have to be consulted before they take place. In cases of complementary governance, public policy provides for a regulatory framework and financing conditions in which an administrative body made up of associations can influence particular policy decisions. The participation of associations in the administration of social security systems and labour market policy usually derives from the fact that these used to be exclusively governed by trade unions themselves prior to the introduction of state-governed social security systems.

The diversity of actors and governance structures across different countries indicates the wide variety of possible adjustment policies regarding the problem of employment growth and the great scope for diverging paths of development in different countries. This has far-reaching implications. For instance, the argument that increasing internationalisation puts pressure on companies in the exposed sector to reduce costs (Frieden and Rogowski 1996) does not necessarily imply that those costs then have to be borne by low-paid workers. They could also be paid by social security systems or by the state via subsidies. The question of which path a country will follow crucially depends on the position of individual actors within the given governance structures and the implications their actions have for other actors. Rather than implying a model of 'best practice' and a trend towards convergence, we can expect a whole range of different trajectories.

Governance structures and policy shifts in the employment–welfare relationship: Germany and the UK

Mechanisms of governance in Germany and the UK are frequently at opposing ends of the spectrum, both in terms of welfare state typologies and in terms of industrial relations regimes. The German welfare state has been characterised as 'conservative–corporatist' (Esping-Andersen 1990). Contrary to the more universal, egalitarian models of social-democrat regimes (as in Sweden), the German welfare state aims to maintain certain traditional differences in status by the differentiated treatment of social groups such as civil servants, farmers and the self-employed. In addition, the system of social security is based on the assumption of full employment and all benefits are related to work-based contributions, which leads from the start to discrimination against all those not in employment. The corporatist element of the German welfare state is characterised by the integration of a variety of different social interest groups (i.e. parties, welfare organisations, churches, trade unions, etc.) which are institutionally integrated in the organisational structure of social security systems. This is in stark contrast to the universal character of the British Beveridge model (in Esping-Andersen's classification, the British case is a deviant one but is closest to the liberal welfare regime), in which all groups are basically entitled to the same (low) level of benefits, regardless of their social position.

In terms of industrial relations, the German model of centralised wage bargaining and encompassing trade unions has enabled a degree of institutional integration of organised labour into the political system that differs strongly from the British features of fragmentation and voluntarism, which resulted in a very distant relationship between the government and trade unions (Crouch 1994). In Germany, the implementation of central collective agreements is based on strong and active associations that ensure the acceptance of agreements by their membership. A centralised structure of associations developed in Germany after the Second World War: industrial trade unionism was established in which the individual trade unions aimed at organising all employees of a particular industry, regardless of their politics and religion. Although union density in Germany never rose above 40 per cent, the trade unions affiliated to the DGB (*Deutscher Gewerkschaftsbund* German Federation of Trade Unions) succeeded in establishing a monopoly of representation massively supported by the involvement of these unions in social security functions and by court rulings.

The British system has always been characterised by a high degree of fragmentation and the inability to coordinate and stabilise the relationships between employers and trade unions. British trade unionism never lost its roots of being special interest organisations for occupational groups. Despite a comparatively high degree of unionisation in the post-war period, the mobilisation power of British trade unions remained at the level of members' activism and did not enable them to enter a neo-corporatist policy arrangement, as the ill-fated example of the Social Contract (1975–9) shows (Scharpf 1987).

The great differences in the position of organised interests in the two countries also had implications for the administration and policy formation in social security and labour market policies. In the German political system, organised interests have played a major role and taken on a range of public functions. The speciality of the German model of regulation is the interplay of an 'enabling state', which both defines and institutionally and legally secures the framework conditions and the steering capacities of organised interest associations: 'It is through state-enabled collective action and quasi-public, "corporatist" group self-government that the German political economy generates most of the regulations and collective goods that circumscribe, correct and underpin the instituted markets of *soziale Marktwirtschaft*.' (Streeck 1995: 11). In the UK, however, organised interests have traditionally remained in the position of 'pressure politics' and lobbying of the state. Although the degree of control of the British trade unions over the Labour Party was much higher than in the German case, this close relationship never achieved more than consultation and participation in tripartite bodies in which trade unions and employers were represented. The associations never gained either the importance or the autonomy of their German counterparts.

Economically, the interaction between the type of welfare governance, industrial relations and institutional integration of organised interest into policy making procedures has contributed to a dynamic process which turned out to follow opposing paths: the German model resulted in the virtuous circle of industrial peace, moderate wage developments and quality-competitive production (Streeck 1995), while the British model of the 1960s and 1970s followed the path of a vicious circle of industrial warfare, inflation and non-competitive manufacturing products. The two countries were therefore in a very different position when the first employment crisis of the early 1970s hit the welfare–employment nexus and set very different adjustment processes in motion.[3]

Germany: adjustment through supply-side reduction

The German mode of governance of welfare and employment (see Fig. 7.1) is based on a high level of associational governance of unemployment insurance in tripartite administrative bodies (*Bundesanstalt für Arbeit*, BfA (Federal Employment

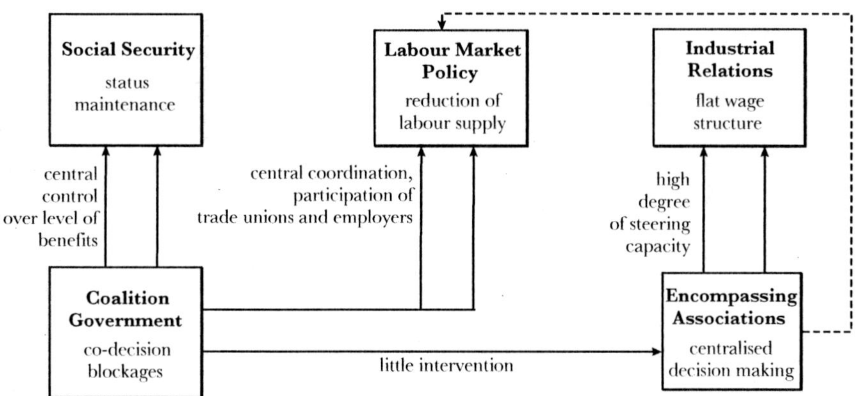

Figure 7.1 Governance structures of the employment–welfare nexus in Germany.

Institute)) and on centralised collective bargaining, complemented by a cooperative relationship of management and works councils at the plant level. This is combined with an incentive structure in which a high level of income maintenance is provided for those who are temporarily not in employment and a flat wage structure for those who are in employment. The combination of governance and incentive structure results in a situation in which company restructuring is facilitated by a high level of income maintenance for those who exit the labour market. As a consequence, the German adjustment pattern has been characterised by a tendency to reduce the supply side of the labour market (Schmidt 1988: 34; Esping-Andersen 1994, 1997).

The starting point for this pattern of supply-side reduction of the labour force is the German system of co-determination. Restructuring processes in companies facing turbulent environments were facilitated by the German co-determination system in which the works council and management jointly devised solutions for those workers whose workplaces would be eliminated – either through new technologies or through other processes of restructuring or downsizing. Management and works councils could basically use three mechanisms: The first was to upgrade the existing workforce for higher-productivity jobs which could use further vocational training provisions. This mechanism has come and gone in different phases with a tendency on the part of blue-collar employees to move into the positions of technicians. The second mechanism was the option of early retirement taken by elderly workers, and the third was voluntary redundancies. While the third option was aimed at the younger workforce, the second mechanism addressed all employees above the age of 59. The second and third solutions were often combined. For example, companies asked workers to take voluntary redundancy at the age of 57, to remain unemployed and then to enter early retirement schemes (Jacobs and Rein 1993). Companies would give extra payments to compensate for the loss in income for those who accepted voluntary redundancies and early retirement. Transferring elderly employees into unemployment followed by early retirement became the main instrument of downsizing the workforce in the 1980s.[4]

Both mechanisms, voluntary redundancies and early retirement, were only viable solutions because the level of benefits for those who then left the company was calculated on the basis of their pay and topped up by the companies. Until the early 1990s, the increasing abuse of these extra redundancy payments was not effectively monitored. Thus the wage-related benefit system was at the heart of the German pattern of downsizing.

The German form of company restructuring should, however, not be seen as a deliberate strategy of externalising costs to the social security system on the part of trade unions and employers (Oppen 1997), but instead as a gradual adjustment process to increasing pressures from below. In the late 1970s and early 1980s, industrial disputes against plant closures led to militant protests which had to be pre-empted if the general consensual system of labour cooperation was not to be destroyed.[5] This put pressure on works councils and management to find ways of adjustment that would not cause too much harm to these relations. As a consequence, works councils in the German manufacturing sector were extensively consulted on mass redundancies and played an important role by selecting who would be made redundant or go into early retirement.[6]

There were two preconditions for works councils to be able to participate actively in downsizing processes in companies: the flat wage structure and the high level of integration of works councils in the German trade union structures. The comparatively low level of wage differentiation in German industries is rooted in the basic structure of the German system of industrial relations. Centralised collective bargaining at the regional level determines the basic rate for wage differentials for different groups of employees within one industry. Changes in the wage structure usually occur when lower-paid workers catch up with higher-paid ones, e.g. low-paid women working in manufacturing in the early 1970s. A tight wage structure was important in two respects: (1) because it prevented competitive pressures between different groups of workers and therefore enabled a smooth relocation of tasks and jobs within a company, and (2) because it helped low-skilled workers to catch up with higher-skilled ones and offered career paths within a company. With regard to labour costs, the flat wage structure in German manufacturing also gave incentives to increase productivity levels for low-skilled workers. Productivity frequently increased as a result of the rapid introduction of new technology, which companies used in order to get rid of low-productivity workplaces. Tight wages therefore created pressure on companies for innovation but, at the same time, a level of trust and cooperation for employees who could see that investments in training and better performance would pay off.

The other precondition for a cooperative attitude on the part of works councils towards company restructuring was the high level of integration of works councils in the organisational structure of industrial trade unions (Streeck 1981) and their position within the system of benefit administration. The pressures from large manufacturing companies were able to feed directly into the administration of unemployment benefits, since works councils in these companies had a high degree of influence on trade union strategies. In industrial trade unions, the decisive policy making bodies are usually made up of the works council members of the most important companies.

Moreover, the tripartite setup of the unemployment benefit system enabled trade unions and employers to serve the needs of the companies for subsidising downsizing measures, which were also supported by the federal government. The government introduced legislation to facilitate early retirement by lowering the retirement age of the handicapped, by facilitating the 'unemployed pension' and by the early retirement law in 1984 (reformed in 1988), which entailed direct subsidies for a reduction in the working time of elderly workers (Jacobs and Rein 1993; Naschold *et al.* 1993).

The institutional design of the industrial relations and welfare regimes thus gave a high degree of incentives to use social security funds for downsizing and restructuring purposes. This resulted in a great number of redundant individuals on the labour market who were neither unemployed nor actively seeking employment. The main implication of the German way of reducing the supply side on the labour market is, however, that it is built on a stable wage structure, which has traditionally been safeguarded by the centralised collective bargaining system. The maintenance of a centralised and flat wage structure has therefore prevented any form of regulated low-paid employment on the labour market.

In this context, the restriction of the formerly generous early retirement option[7] tried to take away some of the most important adjustment mechanisms of the German employment–welfare nexus to worsen economic conditions and therefore created a more pressurised situation. Since the growth in employment in the public sector was always difficult for political reasons (Schmidt 1988: 35) and the pressures of internationalisation on German companies are high, the declining capacity of the welfare provisions to cut down labour supply has created substantial pressure on the rigid wage system.

In particular, the financial strain deriving from German unification (Czada 1998) has posed serious challenges to the established forms of conflict solutions through plant-level co-determination, centralised collective bargaining and the governance of labour market funds. The main effect has been that collective actors on both sides have experienced drastic membership losses and loyalty problems. The share of companies that are members of employers' confederations has been decreasing since the mid-1980s, with the pace of decline greater after 1990 (Hassel and Schulten 1998). Surveys covering companies in the former East Germany showed that 100 per cent of the companies with 500–1,000 employees were members of the employers' association, but only 78 per cent paid the going rate (Ettl and Heikenroth 1996: 150). There have been increasing examples of companies opting out of collective agreements and either openly or secretly making agreements with their workforce or works councils to do so (Hassel 1999). These processes indicate that the *governance capacity* of the associations has been seriously weakened.

The shrinking governance capacity of labour market associations has not yet been complemented by government action. While the federal government is increasingly engaged in proposing subsidies for low-paid employment,[8] the associations are still in a position to veto changes to the wage structure because of their strong position in the collective bargaining and benefit administration system. The difficulties which trade unions in Germany face in adjusting to new labour market pressures indicate that changes to the wage structure have serious implications for their role on the labour market. The strict pattern of institutionalisation of trade union organisation in the German political system has created very tight links between collective agreements, the position of trade unions in co-determination and their membership domains. Relatively minor changes in the collective bargaining and co-determination setup might lead to great changes in their bargaining position. The crucial question will therefore be whether and to what extent the German system of industrial trade unionism can accommodate a more flexible and open wage structure and internalise the conflicts which might come with it.

The British case: forceful deregulation

The British situation was very different to the German way of dealing with downsizing processes. Since the relationship between public policy and associational governance was traditionally much looser in the UK (see Fig. 7.2) than in other European countries (Shonfield 1965), trade unions and employers' confederations were not institutionally integrated in the political system and in the administration of social security functions to a comparable extent.[9] At the same time, the relationship at arm's length prevented the British government from intervening directly in the increasingly dysfunctional system of collective bargaining and workplace industrial relations. The government had to rely on indirect mechanisms to induce changes by either strengthening or weakening trade unions and by effectively using social funds to deregulate the labour market.

With regard to the employment regime, the fragmentation of workplace industrial relations in the UK in the 1950s and 1960s led to a pattern of localised and militant conflicts without any form of coordination or control by associations. In the British system of labour relations, there was no way of dealing in a cooperative way with the processes undertaken by companies to adjust to changing environments. Both downsizing and the introduction of new technology led to bitter struggles within the companies, which sometimes resulted in the relocation of whole industries, such as the printing industries in the mid-1980s. Technological progress and restructuring measures were therefore delayed, in particular in those cases where workforces were able to prevent changes in the work organisation or in downsizing processes. At the same time, the lack of competitiveness of British manufacturing required restructuring processes to a much greater extent than in most other OECD countries, and the structural change in the economy between 1970 and 1990 from manufacturing to service sector employment has been more profound than in many other countries. As early as the 1970s, labour turnover in British manufacturing was therefore comparatively high, but led to mass redundancies rather than to early retirement as it did in Germany.

The problem of conflictual restructuring processes was aggravated by three factors. First, the flat-rate system of unemployment benefits and social assistance

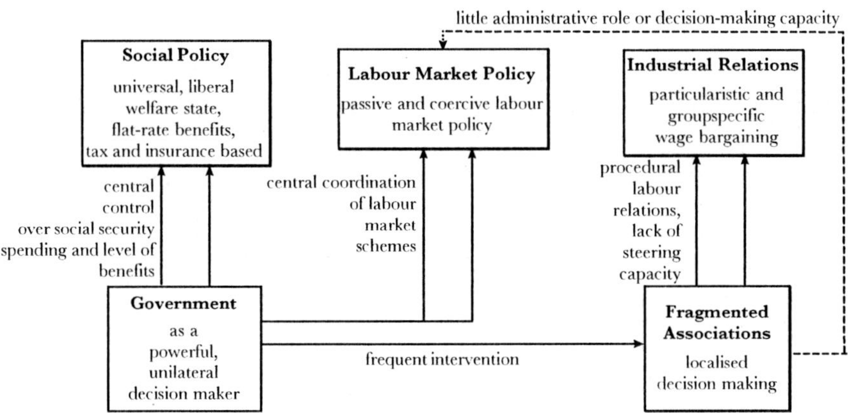

Figure 7.2 Governance structures of the employment–welfare nexus in Britain.

meant that job losses immediately turned into a direct threat of undermining the financial status of those employees who were made redundant. In terms of household income and employment relations, it was often worthwhile for low-skilled employees to engage in a long conflict with management to keep their present employment rather than to accept redundancy payments.[10] Second, the lack of workplace representation committees left a vacuum of interest representation which had to be filled by trade union activities (Terry 1995). As a consequence, the focus of trade union activities had to be on the workplace, which did not allow for a more coordinated strategy of trade unions and employers to regulate labour market conditions, but enhanced the already fragmented system of interest representation. This mechanism was further worsened by the legal promotion of trade union representatives in the workplace in 1975 (Employment Promotion Act 1975).

Third, the fragmented trade union structure traditionally tended to organise groups of workers on the basis of workshops or occupations. They bargained separate wages and introduced an element of wage competition at the workplace which again did not allow for coordinated wage bargaining. As a result, a pattern of localised conflicts at the workplace level evolved, leading to delays in the modernisation of production processes and to forced mass redundancies. In terms of low-productivity employment, this meant that, due to competitive wage bargaining, British companies had to pay wages that were too high for low-productivity employment without being able to put a ceiling on blue-collar wages through a centralised wage structure. On the other hand, for the British trade unions, workplace militancy against changes was often the only viable way to maintain the status of low-productivity workers.

The British government was unable to alter this ineffective form of problem solving directly, since collective bargaining was not in the public policy domain, and the neo-corporatist attempt of the mid-1970s clearly showed the limits to reform (Scharpf 1987). However, the government had two major tools which it used to indirectly govern the labour market from 1979 onwards: its direct access to social security and unemployment benefit funds and its means of regulating trade union activities.

The British system of income support for those who are not in employment was traditionally a combination of unemployment insurance and unemployment assistance, a two-tiered structure consisting of a flat-rate insurance benefit (paid subject to contributions and other conditions) supported by a second tier of income-tested assistance (Atkinson and Micklewright 1989).[11] This system did not undergo any radical changes during the 1980s, but the Conservative government introduced a gradual shift away from the insurance-based system towards a less generous assistance system. Important changes were the abolishment of the Earnings-Related Supplement (ERS) in 1980 and the introduction of taxation on unemployment benefit in 1982. The abolition of the Earnings-Related Supplement has put the UK in the position of being the only country in the EU in which unemployment benefits are not linked to earnings. Between 1979 and 1988, there have been seventeen significant changes in the system of National

Insurance unemployment benefit (UB) alone, most of which were unfavourable for the unemployed. Similarly, income support measures and supplementary benefits were gradually reduced (Dilnot and Walker 1989; Lister 1991; Pierson 1994). With regard to collective bargaining, the government abolished wages councils, which used to set minimum wages in the low-paid sector, although these wages were already very low (Gregg and Wadsworth 1995; Rubery 1994). In the area of labour law, dismissal procedures were loosened, and the period of job tenure before regulations concerning protection against unfair dismissals could apply was lengthened (Deakin 1990). Institutional constraints on the labour market – which were perceived as rigid – were gradually removed.

The social policy of the British government therefore initially put more pressure on the already conflictual restructuring processes of companies, since the unemployed had to expect even harsher conditions during unemployment than before. A thorough reform of the industrial relations system was a precondition for a deregulation of the labour market in order to prevent further blockages in company restructuring by trade union representatives at the workplace. In other words, the trade unions had to be weakened, since they would try to resist the changes in social policy reforms and to have a greater incentive to resist job losses under the new social policy conditions. The trade union reform programme consisted of a range of measures: the abolition of the closed shop, the interference in union decision-making procedures and the regulation of strike activities, which made it very difficult for trade unions to recruit members, to enter into collective bargaining and to go on strike (Edwards *et al.* 1998). Over time, the frequent government interventions led to an institutional erosion of trade union representation at the workplace, in particular in the private sector.

Consequently, wage bargaining by trade unions initially became even more particularistic and *ad hoc*. Sectional wage bargaining was able to be sustained for the most part of the 1980s, and wages for blue-collar workers continued to rise despite relatively minor productivity increases (Brown *et al.* 1995). However, since the fragmented system of pay bargaining only covers those who are involved in it, the employment growth in the service sector has not experienced any spillover effects from pay bargaining in manufacturing, and wages in the service sector were able to be kept low. The breakdown in institutional wage coordination during the 1980s and 1990s is reflected in the increasing wage inequalities, with the UK having the highest increase in wage inequality in the OECD (OECD 1996). A low level of flat-rate unemployment and social security benefits combined with the severe weakening of trade union representation have contributed to the development of a low-productivity–low-wage labour market, which again forced the unemployed to adjust to new economic segments in the services sector. The British reaction to the economic and labour market crisis of the 1970s was therefore the opposite one to the German solution of consensual restructuring processes and supply-side reduction. The government chose the route of increasing workplace conflicts and employment insecurity in order to speed up adjustment processes in the labour market. The means of adjustment was the strong downward pressure on wages of those groups which were not represented in institutionalised trade union organisations and the forceful erosion of collective organisation. The major weaknesses of the British employment regime of trade union fragmentation, weak representation rights and weak social provisions for the unemployed have not been resolved, and the reform initiatives of the Conservative government have not led to a new form of institutional stability of the welfare and employment linkage, but instead to a temporary, institutionally insecure cooling-off period.

In terms of the welfare–employment nexus, the increase in labour market flexibility has not eased the pressure on welfare financing. There are two main reasons for this: (1) because employment creation has not increased at the speed that was expected, given the massive interference in the incentive structure and the decline in labour market regulation, and (2) because of the poverty trap, which has become a major problem due to the increase in low-paid employment.

The average employment rate in the UK in the 1980s and 1990s was below the level of the early 1970s and was unable to keep up with the trend in the USA (Fig. 7.3). This is somewhat surprising, given the strong incentives deriving from low benefits, hard eligibility criteria for unemployment benefits and the low potential of organised labour to resist restructuring processes. In the German case, a decrease in the employment rate was to be expected, since the German answer to the employment crisis tended to reduce the labour supply. The most likely reason for the slow speed of employment creation is the low level of skills of British blue-collar workers, which makes it difficult to transfer elderly workers to newly emerging service sectors. In this sense, the fast pace of structural change in the British economy from manufacturing to services has offset a higher dema nd for labour against the unskilled. 'The consequence of this is that Germany is able to respond to the relative demand shift in favour of the skilled with less dislocation.' (Nickell 1997: 23).

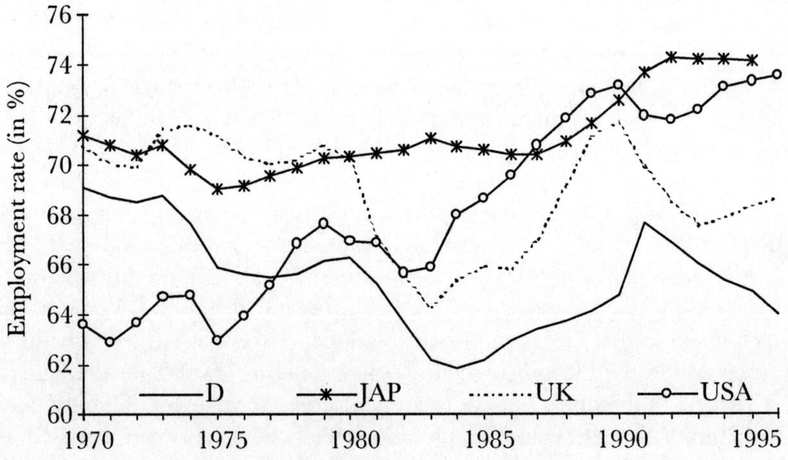

Figure 7.3 Employment rates in Germany, UK, USA and Japan.

Sources: OECD Labour Force Statistics (various years).

The second reason, which is related to the first, is that social spending has hardly decreased despite the massive cuts in the level of transfer payments to the individual unemployed (Pierson 1994). The increase in earnings inequality has partly been offset by transfer payments through income supplements, housing benefits and social assistance schemes due to the increasing poverty traps of the unemployed and the retired. Since low pay also keeps people in low-productivity jobs and does not enable training initiatives, there is a danger that a poverty trap will become cemented at the bottom end of the labour market.

Thus, in contrast to the situation in Germany, where the danger increasingly lies in the lack of *governance capacity* of the associations, the high level of governing capacity of the British government has led to decisive changes in the employment–welfare relationship, which have however not yet proven to be very effective instruments for employment creation. Here, we find a policy shift that is contingent with the governance structure of fragmented associations and an interventionist state that has not developed an *effective policy* in order to break out of the pattern of low trust, low productivity and low pay.

Conditions and outcomes of governance structures in the welfare–employment nexus

What are the implications of the different governance structures for the employment– welfare nexus? There are three conclusions that can be drawn from these two cases: The first relates to the *employment–welfare nexus*. The British case charges the costs of low productivity to the low-paid employee, who has little possibility of rejecting low-paid work. This does not solve the problem of welfare financing, as long as transfer payments still continue to rise due to rising poverty. In Germany, the major share of the costs are borne by social security systems, which provide better conditions for the unemployed and might give more incentives for upgrading rather than taking any job available on the labour market. Governance problems of the employment and welfare relationship therefore have to take into account the repercussions of training and qualification systems. It seems that the relevant question is not only employment creation per se, but that the governance of the employment–welfare relationship also entails the transformation of employment structures from blue-collar manufacturing employment into white-collar service sector employment. In Germany, middle-aged employees who leave manufacturing jobs exit the labour market, while in the UK they become unemployed or find comparable work in the low-productivity segment. Neither country seems to have managed to find solutions for the transfer from one segment to the other. As the German case also shows, the generation of skills depends on a fine balance of individual gains in training by employers and employees and a certain level of coercion to provide and engage in training.[12] The issue of the generation of skills is therefore a systematic intervening force when evaluating the potential of employment creation in emerging economic sectors.

The second conclusion refers to the relationship between *public policy* and *associational governance*. Compared to the situation in Germany, the British government had far more effective means to intervene in wage setting and social policy, although its relationship with trade unions and employers was more distant. Effective intervention was only used to introduce more market elements into the labour market and less coordination and constraints. It therefore created more competition, but less trust and less willingness to engage in insecure investments in training and cooperative relations. The German government was prevented from interfering substantially in the employment regime by the high level of associational governance and governance capacity. The federal government had to take into account the interests of the associations because of their general institutionalised strength within the German political system. Given the decrease in *governance capacity* of the associations, the German government seems to underestimate the efforts necessary to provide functional equivalents in the future. While encompassing associations can prevent a major deregulation of the labour market, they have increasing problems in reproducing the preconditions for their governance structure.

Third, the two cases indicate a *high level of contingency* of governing structures and policy changes. The history of the relationship between the state and interest associations and the form of integrating organised interests into the political system of advanced industrialised societies still determines to a remarkable extent the scope of government action and other forms of governance. While there is no doubt about the ideological commitment to labour market deregulation of the British Conservative government during the 1980s, the question remains whether governance structures and sets of problems in the UK would have allowed for a more cooperative and mutually beneficial strategy to solve the deadlocks at plant level in British manufacturing. Looking back at the major crisis of British politics starting with the ill-fated Industrial Relations Act 1971 and ending with the winter of discontent in 1979, we have to realise the scale of the problem and the conflict between local fragmented actors who did not have the means to coordinate their strategies.

On the other hand, the German case indicates the limited room for manoeuvre of the government and encompassing interest associations to deregulate institutional rigidities on the labour market. High trust and cooperative relationships between employers and works councils could easily be disturbed by harsh policy measures. The tight links of welfare, employment and training between the industrial relations model, the employment regime and the welfare state in Germany run counter to the potential for striking policy changes.

Notes

1 The notion of low-productivity employment can only serve as a heuristic tool, not as an analytical concept in itself. Looking at national statistics on sector-specific labour productivity, it can be seen that, in many public and semi-public services, output is calculated on the basis of wages. In these cases, low productivity derives from low wages, and from a purely statistical point of view, higher wages will lead to higher productivity.

2 *Governance* as a mode of social coordination should also be seen as distinct from the notion of *governing*, which implies a greater level of steering capacity by the state (Mayntz 1993: 11).

3 However, the relevance of welfare and labour market institutions in this process should not be overstated. Other factors, such as the relationship between banks and companies (Lane 1989), the vocational training system (Steedman and wagner 1987) and corporate governance systems (Lash and Urry 1987), played a crucial role as well (Cox and Kriegbaum 1980).

4 A fourth method was the reduction of working time, which started as a trade union campaign in 1984, but finally became an instrument of employment security and company restructuring in the 1990s after the pioneering agreement at Volkswagen in January 1994.

5 For example, the massive protests at Videocolor in Ulm (1982), Heckel in Saarland (1983) and the shipyards HDW and AG Weser (1983), which led to occupation of the factory buildings, contributed to a more cooperative style of crisis management of works councils and management in German manufacturing (for a list of militant protests, see Däubler 1990: 366).

6 The forerunner of this mechanism was the steel industry, where works councils and management already started to draw up early retirement plans in the 1960s, leading to a general retirement age of 59 (Russig 1982: 237).

7 The Pension Reform of 1992 aimed at raising retirement ages and increased the costs of early retirement by reducing benefits by 3.6 per cent per year. It also introduced a part-time pension scheme from the age of 62 (Naschold *et al.* 1993: 176).

8 Proposals on subsidies for low-paid employment have been made by the German Conservative party (Christlich-Demokratische Union Deutschlands, CDU) and by employers' confederations and have become a major issue under the new 'Alliance for Jobs' project after the change of government in 1998.

9 The Social Contract tried to institutionally integrate trade unions to some extent by co-opting trade union representatives into the newly established arbitration system (Advisory, Conciliation and Arbitration Service, ACAS) and the training authority (Manpower Service Commission). Nevertheless, British trade unions were not involved in the administration of either the pension scheme or the unemployment scheme (Hepple and Fredman 1992).

10 This mechanism could still be observed even in the late 1990s, e.g. in the dock-workers' dispute in Liverpool.

11 This was introduced by the Unemployment Act 1934, which was supplemented by a third earnings-related tier (Earnings-Related Supplement) in 1966.

12 On a similar line, it is argued that Germany should not and cannot follow the Anglo-American example of deregulated labour markets, since this would undermine the basic pillars of the German model. This argument assumes that low-paid employment in deregulated labour markets and a high level of skill production are incompatible (Carlin and Soskice 1997; Hancké 1998).

References

Appelbaum, E. and Schettkat, R. (1995). 'Employment and productivity in industrialized economies', *International Labour Review* 134(4–5), 605–23.

Atkinson, T. and Micklewright, J. (1989). 'Turning the screw: Benefits for the unemployed 1979–88', in A. Dilnot and I. Walker (eds), *The Economics of Social Security*. Oxford: Oxford University Press, 17–50.

Bahnmüller, R. and Bispinck, R. (1995). 'Vom Vorzeige-zum Auslaufmodell? Das deutsche Tarifsystem zwischen kollektiver Regulierung, betrieblicher Flexibilisierung und individuellen Interessen', in R. Bispinck (ed.), *Tarifpolitik der Zukunft*. Hamburg: VSA, 137–72.

Brown, W., Marginson, P. and Walsh, J. (1995). 'Management: Pay determination and collective bargaining', in P. Edwards (ed.), *Industrial Relations*. Oxford: Blackwell Publishers.

Carlin, W. and Soskice, D. (1997). 'Shocks to the system: The German political economy under stress', *National Institute Economic Review* 159: 57–76.

Cox, J. and Kriegbaum, H. (1980). *Growth, Innovation and Employment. An Anglo-German Comparison.* London: St. Stephens House.

Crouch, C. (1994). *Industrial Relations and European State Traditions.* Oxford: Clarendon Press.

Czada, R. (1998). 'Vereinigungskrise und Standortdebatte. Der Beitrag der Wiedervereinigung zur Krise des westdeutschen Modells', *Leviathan* 26(1), 24–59.

Däubler, W. (1990). *Arbeitsrecht 1 und 2.* Reinbek b. Hamburg: Rowohlt.

Deakin, S. (1990). 'Equality under a market order: The Employment Act 1989', *Industrial Law Journal* 19(1), 1–19.

Dickens, R., Gregg, P., Machin, S., Manning, A. and Wandsworth, J. (1993). 'Wages councils', *British Journal of Industrial Relations* 31(4), 515–30.

Dilnot, A. and Walker, I. (eds) (1989). *The Economics of Social Security.* Oxford: Oxford University Press.

Edwards, P., Hall, M., Hyman R., Marginson, P., Sisson, K., Waddington, J. and Winchester, D. (1998). 'Great Britain: From partial collectivism to neo-liberalism to where?', in A. Ferner and R. Hyman (eds), *Changing Industrial Relations in Europe.* Oxford: Basil Blackwell, 1–54.

Esping-Andersen, G. (1990). *The Three Worlds of Welfare Capitalism.* Oxford: Polity Press.

Esping-Anderson, G. (1992). 'Post-industrial class structures: An analytical framework', Working Paper, Madrid: Centro de Estudios Avanzados en Ciencias Sociales.

Esping-Anderson, G. (1994). 'After the Golden Age: The future of the welfare state in the new global order', Geneva: UNRISD, Word Summit For Social Development, Occasional Paper No. 7.

Esping-Anderson, G. (1997). 'The three political economies of the welfare state', in J. E. Kolberg (ed.), *The Study of Welfare State Regimes.* New York: M.E. Sharpe, 92–123.

Ettl, W. and Heikenroth, A. (1996). 'Strukturwandel, Verbandsabstinenz, Tarifflucht: Zur Lage der Unternehmen und Arbeitgeberverbände im ostdeutschen verarbeitenden Gewerbe', *Industrielle Beziehungen* 3(2), 134–50.

Freeman, R. B. (1995). 'The large welfare state as a system', *American Economics Association Papers and Proceedings* 85(2), 16–21.

Frieden, J. A. and Rogowski, R. (1996). 'The impact of the international economy on national policies: An analytical overview', in R. O. Keohane and H. Milner (eds), *Internationalization and Domestic Politics.* Cambridge: Cambridge University Press, 25–47.

Gregg, P. and Wadsworth, J. (1995). 'A short history of labour turnover, job tenure and job security, 1975–93', *Oxford Review of Economic Policy* 11(1), 73–90.

Hancké, B. (1998). 'Deregulierung und Flexibilität als Wunderheilmittel. Fragen zur Übertragbarkeit des flexiblen Modells', *WSI-Mitteilungen* 51(4), 255–8.

Hassel, A. (1999). 'The erosion of the German system of industrial relations', *British Journal of Industrial Relations* 37(3), 484–505.

Hassel, A. and Schulten, T. (1998). 'Globalisation and the future of central collective bargaining: The example of the German metal industry', *Economy and Society* 27(4), 486–522.

Hepple, B. and Fredman, S. (1992). *Labor Law and Industrial Relations in Great Britain.* Deventer and Boston: Kluwer.

Hollingsworth, J. R., Schmitter, P. C. and Streeck, W. (1994). 'Capitalism, sectors, institutions, and performance', in J. R. Hollingsworth, P. C. Schmitter and W. Streeck (eds), *Governing Capitalist Economies. Performance and control for Economic Sectors.* Oxford and New York: Oxford University Press, 3–16.

Immergut, E. (1992). 'The rules of the game: The logic of health policy making in France, Switzerland and Sweden', in S. Steinmo, K. Thelen and F. Longstreth (eds), *Structuring Politics. Historical Institutionalism in Comparative Analysis.* Cambridge, MA: Cambridge University Press, 57–89.

Iversen, T. and Wren, A. (1998). 'Equality, employment and budgetary restraint: The trilemma of the service economy', *World Politics* 50, 507–46.

Jacobs, K. and Rein, M. (1993). 'Early retirement: Stability, reversal or redefinition', in F. Naschold and B. de Vroom (eds), *Regulating Employment and Welfare: Company and National Policies of Labour Force Participation at the End of Worklife in Industrialised countries.* Berlin and New York: de Gruyter, 19–50.

Kolberg, J. E. and Esping-Andersen, G. (1997). 'Welfare states and employment regimes', in J. E. Kolberg (ed.), *The Study of Welfare State Regimes.* New York: M.E. Sharpe, 3–36.

Lane, C. (1989). *Management and Labour in Europe. The Industrial Enterprise in Germany, Britain and France.* Aldershot: Edward Elgar.

Lash, S. and Urry, J. (1987). *The End of Organized Capitalism.* Cambridge: Cambridge University Press.

Lehmbruch, G. (1995). 'Der Beitrag der Korporatismusforschung zur Entwicklung der Steuerungstheorie', *Politische Vierteljahresschrift* 37(4), 735–51.

Lehmbruch, G. (1997). 'Zwischen Institutionentransfer und Eigendynamik: Sektorale Transformationspfade und ihre Bestimmungsgründe', in G. Lehmbruch and R. Czada (eds), *Transformationspfade in Ostdeutschland. Beiträge zur sektoralen Vereinigungspolitik.* Frankfurt: Campus, 17–57.

Lister, R. (1991). 'Social Security in the 1980s', *Social Policy and Administration* 25(2), 91–107.

Manow, P. (1997). 'Cross-class alliances in welfare reform: A theoretical framework', draft, prepared for the workshop 'The new politics of welfare', Center for European Studies, Harvard University, 5–7 December 1997.

Mayntz, R. (1993). 'Governing failures and the problem of governability', in J. Kooiman (ed.), *Modern governance. New Government–Society Interactions.* London: Sage, 9–20.

Mayntz, R. (1996). 'Politische Steuerung: Aufstieg, Niedergang und Transformation einer Theorie', in K. von Beyme and C. Offe (eds), *Politische Theorien in der Ära der Transformation,* Sonderheft 26 der Politischen Vierteljahresschrift (PVS). Opladen: Westdeutscher Verlag, 148–68.

Naschold, F., Oppen, M., Peinemann, H. and Rosenow, J. (1993). 'Germany: The concerted transition from work to welfare', in F. Naschold and B. de Vroom (eds), *Regulating Employment and Welfare. Company and National Policies of Labour Force Participation at the End of Worklife in Industrial Countries,* Berlin and New York: de Gruyter, 117–82.

Nickell, S. (1997). 'Structural changes and the British labour market', in H. Siebert (ed.), *Structural Changes and Labour Market Flexibility: Experiences in Selected OECD Economies.* Tubingen: Mohr, 3–28.

OECD (1996). 'Earnings inequality, low paid employment and earnings mobility', in OECD, *Employment Outlook 1996.* Paris: OECD, 59–103.

Offe, C. (1993). 'A non-productivist design for social policies', in H. Coenen and P. Leisink (eds), *Work and Citizenship in Europe.* Aldershot: Edward Elgar, 215–33.

Oppen, M. (1997). 'Concerted cooperation and immobilism: Labour policy and the regulation of early exit', in F. Naschold and M. Muramatsu (eds), *State and Administration in Japan and Germany: A Comparative Perspective on Continuity and Change.* Berlin and New York: de Gruyter, 247–80.

Pierson, P. (1994). *Dismantling the Welfare State? Reagan, Thatcher, and the Politics of Retrenchment.* Cambridge: Cambridge University Press.

Rubery, J. (1994). 'The British production regime: A societal-specific system?', *Economy and Society* 23, 3.

Russig, H. (1982). 'Sozialversicherungs- und arbeitsrechtliche Rahmenbedingungen für die Ausgliederung älterer und/oder leistungsgeminderter Arbeitnehmer aus dem Betrieb', in U. Jürgens, K. Dohse and H. Russig (eds), *Ältere Arbeitnehmer zwischen Unternehmensinteresse und Sozialpolitik*. Frankfurt: Campus, 237–87.

Scharpf, F. W. (1987). *Sozialdemokratische Krisenpolitik in Europa. Das 'Modell Deutschland' im Vergleich*. Frankfurt: Campus.

Schmidt, M. G. (1988). 'The politics of labour market policy', in F. G. Castles, F. Lehner and M. G. Schmidt (eds), *Managing Mixed Economies*. Berlin and New York: de Gruyter, 4–53.

Shonfield, A. (1965). *Modern Capitalism. The Changing Balance of Public and Private Power*. Oxford: Oxford University Press.

Steedman, H. and Wagner, K. (1987). 'A second look at productivity, machinery and skills in Britain and Germany', *National Institute Economic Review* 4, 84–95.

Streeck, W. (1981). 'Qualitative demands and the neo-corporatist manageability of industrial relations', *British Journal of Industrial Relations* 14, 149–69.

Streeck, W. (1995). 'German capitalism: Does it exist? Can it survive?', MPIFG discussion paper 95/5. Cologne: Max Planck Institute for the Study of Societies.

Terry, M. (1995). 'Trade unions: Shop stewards and workplace', in P. Edwards (ed.), *Industrial Relations*. Oxford: Blackwell Publishers.

Visser, J. and Hemerijck, A. (1997). *'A Dutch Miracle': Job Growth, Welfare Reform and Corporatism in the Netherlands*. Amsterdam: Amsterdam University Press.

Part III

Pension regimes and financial systems

8 Between financial commitment, market liquidity and corporate governance

Occupational pensions in Britain, Germany, Japan and the USA

Gregory Jackson and Sigurt Vitols

In this chapter we examine the linkages between pension regimes and national financial systems.Welfare state regimes shape the accumulation of pension savings by shaping the mix of public and private pension provision, as well as by regulating investment policies of private pension capital. We compare *market-based pension regimes* in Britain and the USA (combining low public pensions and externalised private pension provision) with *solidaristic regimes* in Germany and Japan (combining high public pensions and organisationally embedded private pensions). The theoretical background concerns the distinction between bank-based (Germany–Japan) versus securities-based financial systems (UK–USA) in different 'varieties of capitalism' (Albert 1993; Crouch and Streeck 1997), as well as stakeholder- versus shareholder-oriented corporate governance.

In this chapter we look at welfare state regimes as an *independent variable* shaping political economy, particularly financial systems and corporate governance. This perspective is common in studying labour markets, by looking at how welfare state policies impact labour force participation and other labour market outcomes. Despite many econometric studies on pension finance, the literature on welfare states offers no general formulation of how pension regimes impact national financial systems and hence different varieties of capitalism (Davis 1995). The linkages between pension regimes and corporate finance are manifold. Policy choices balancing the three pillars of pension regimes (public, occupational and individual) impact the *supply side* of national savings. The regulation of private pensions (second and third pillars) shape how savings are channelled into capital markets through investments in stocks, bonds, loans or internal company reserves. Conversely, pension regimes impact the *demand side* for different financial assets by shaping the personal sector's portfolio distribution between bank deposits and securities. We will specify major dimensions along which pension regimes differ that, in turn, impact financial systems.

Pension regimes and financial systems: interactions and interdependence

The largest source of savings in economies is generally the household sector and the largest deficit sector is the productive (or non-financial company) sector. Whereas in pre-industrial societies the household and productive sectors were directly fused (e.g. through obligations and privileged of serfdom or the lack of separation between 'firm' and 'household' in the case of the artisan), industrialisation involves the development of an autonomous financial system comprised of specialised institutions for mediating the flow of household savings into productive investment. Financial systems have offered two major alternative modes of financial mediation (Gerschenkron 1962; Zysman 1983). One alternative is *bank-based finance* – i.e. mediation through a banking system which takes deposits from households and channels these savings into loans made directly to companies. Another alternative is *market-based finance*, in which households directly or indirectly invest in securities issued by companies. These securities generally can be exchanged on the market without the express permission of the issuer and, in the ideal case, have a high degree of liquidity (i.e. can be sold with little or no losses in price).

One of the most striking differences between countries – despite liberalisation and the globalisation of capital markets – is the large variation in the structure of national financial systems. When examining the US, UK, Germany and Japan, one can see a broad distinction between the first and the last two countries in terms of basic measures of financial system structure, corporate liabilities and household savings patterns (Table 8.1). Banks in the US and UK are only one of a plurality of financial institutions, accounting for about one-quarter of total financial system assets, whereas banking systems in Japan and Germany account for the majority of financial system assets (64 and 74 per cent). In contrast, stock market capitalisation, a rough measure of the importance of external equity finance for companies, is higher in both the US and UK (122 and 152 per cent of GDP) than in Germany and Japan (27 and 63 per cent of GDP).

Furthermore, the distinction between market-based and bank-based financial systems can be seen in both the structure of company liabilities and household assets. The relative importance of equity market finance versus non-securitised

Table 8.1 Financial system characteristics, 1995 (in per cent)

	USA	*UK*	*Germany*	*Japan*
Banking sector assets as a percentage of total financial system assets	24.6	ca. 25.0	74.3	63.6
Stock market capitalisation as a percentage of GDP	122.0	152.0	27.0	63.0
Securitised liabilities as a percentage of total non-financial enterprise liabilities	61.0	66.9	21.1	15.4
Currency and deposits as a percentage of total household sector assets	20.9	25.3	43.3	62.3

Sources: Bank of Japan (1996); Deutsche Bundesbank (1997).

finance (mainly bank loans) is reflected in the relative proportions of total company liabilities. In both the US and UK, securitised liabilities make up a majority of company sector liabilities (61 and 67 per cent, respectively), whereas in Germany and Japan they account for a minority (21 and 15 per cent, respectively). The household sector, which provides the bulk of savings, also shows wide variation. In the US and UK, currency and bank accounts total 21 and 25 per cent, respectively, of total household sector assets versus 43 and 62 per cent in Germany and Japan.

In the past decade, a growing literature has explored linkages between financial systems and corporate governance regimes (Jackson 2002). This literature suggests that bank-based systems are better able to provide stable long-term finance to the corporate sector, which in turn enables companies to make long-term commitment to employees. Market-based systems, in contrast, subject companies to more pressure for short-term profits and less secure employment policies, but may be more supportive of radical innovations and science-based industry (Vitols *et al.* 1997).

The 'savings side' of financial systems, the link between the household sector and types of financial systems, remains under-researched (Vitols 1996). This is an important 'black box' to open, since the household sector is generally the largest net saver in economies. Household savings levels and patterns – particularly longer-term savings motivated by provision for retirement – and the policies that influence them are thus crucial in determining: (1) which type of savings vehicles and financial institutions receive 'preferential' access to household savings, and (2) the incentives and investment policies of financial institutions (including pension funds). These factors influence corporate governance through the capacity of financial systems to provide different kinds of finance. Finally, since pension assets constitute a large portion of household financial claims and since pensions often differ in their coverage of different groups, (3) pension policies are a key factor influencing the 'politics of reform' in capitalist economies, including the reform of financial systems, corporate governance systems and, ultimately, welfare state policies.

We explore three hypotheses regarding the links between pension regimes and financial systems with regard to Germany, Japan, Britain and the US:

(1) *Pension regimes with a greater emphasis on public pension provision are more supportive of bank-based financial systems; pension regimes stressing private (both occupational and personal) pension provision favour market-based financial systems.*

While the aggregate impacts of pension systems on levels of national savings are difficult to estimate, pension regimes influence the structure of savings and capital investment portfolios (Mackenzie *et al.* 1997). Public pensions are usually pay-as-you-go (PAYG) systems financed by employer/employee contributions or taxes; thus, the financial assets accumulated by public pension systems are generally small. Second and third pillar private pensions, on the other hand, are generally funded and accumulate considerable financial assets. Public and private pillars are interdependent, such that generous public pensions tend to 'crowd out' private pensions. Strong public provision will, other things equal, channel fewer financial assets to institutional investors such as pension funds and thus increase the relative proportion administered directly by the household.

The public–private mix, in turn, exerts a strong indirect effect (or 'conditional causal linkage') on financial systems by altering the distribution of financial assets between households and financial intermediaries. This mix is so significant due to the differences in the portfolio preferences of households relative to institutional investors. The differences are evident by comparing the asset portfolios of pension funds (Table 8.2) and households (Table 8.3).[1] Pension funds tend to hold greater levels of long-term and risky assets, such as corporate stocks, than households. Households favour more liquid and less risky assets due to their shorter time horizons. These different portfolios reflect the fact that large institutional investors have a greater capacity to effectively diversify investment risks across different types of assets and pool risks on their liabilities side that might require unexpected payments. Thus, private pension provision increases the supply of finance to capital markets, particularly to equity markets. Conversely, the more significant public

Table 8.2 Pension funds portfolio, 1994 (in per cent)

	Pension funds portfolio (in %)				*Real returns 1967–90*	
	Equity	*Bonds and loans*	*Property*	*Liquidity and deposits (% foreign)*	*Mean*	*Standard deviation*
Germany	11	75	11	3 (6)	5.1	4.4
Japan	27	61	2	3 (7)	4.0	9.0
UK	80	11	6	3 (30)	5.8	12.5
US	48	38	0	7 (10)	2.2	11.9

Sources: Davis (1996; 1995: 150).

Note: Mean and standard deviation over 1967–90 of annual real total returns on the portfolio in local currency.

Table 8.3 Gross financial assets of households by type of financial instrument (in per cent), 1975 and 1994

Country	*Year*	*Equities*	*Bonds*	*Institutional investors*	*Deposits*
Germany	1975	7	9	15	62
	1994	6	14	28	45
Japan	1975	15	6	13	59
	1994	7	6	25	62
UK	1975	16	8	26	40
	1994	12	1	54	26
USA	1975	24	13	26	36
	1994	19	12	44	18

Source: Davis (1996: 49).

Note: Categories do not total 100 per cent due to other components not referred to in the table.

pension provision is, and thus the direct accumulation of savings by households, the greater the supply of liquid assets to the banking system will be.

(2) *Private pension regimes that are large, externally administered and/or have defined-contribution obligations are more supportive of market-based financial systems; conversely, private pension regimes that are smaller, internally administered and/or have defined-benefit obligations are less supportive of market-based financial systems.*

Several dimensions of private pension schemes are relevant to financial systems: their size, form of administration and benefit scheme. First, converse to the argument above, large private pension schemes accumulate more assets and channel them into equity markets. Second, private pension schemes differ as to whether they are internally administered by the sponsoring company (for example, through book reserve methods) or externally administered by independent organisations. Private funds face 'moral hazard' problems associated with the danger of default on pension obligations due to company bankruptcy. Pension reserves, insofar as they were reinvested in company assets, could be considered a direct loan from employees or a form of employee equity in the company. However, regulators have increasingly forced companies to establish fully funded pensions that lessen the dependence of employees upon their employer. Therefore, internal or external administration reflects the degree of employer–employee trust in industrial relations, as well as different strategies for institutionalising risks. Third, private pension schemes differ as to whether obligations are defined-contribution or defined-benefit. Private pension claims historically have been defined-benefit, although in a number of countries such as the US, a shift toward defined-contribution plans can be seen in the past two decades. Whereas defined-benefit plans tend to invest in fairly conservative investments with a safe minimum return (such as real estate or municipal bonds), defined-contribution plans appear to put a higher emphasis on marketable securities and are more willing to invest in higher-risk assets such as equities.

External funds tend to increase the demand for liquid financial assets. The existence of independent pension funds also tends to encourage a dynamic of competition between potential fund managers, who are often reappointed annually on the basis of their short-term (one year) performance. To the extent that pension schemes are funded on a defined-contribution basis, the demand for high-return equities is likely to grow, as well as shifting the capital market risks associated with pension savings further from firms to employees. Pension regimes with a greater emphasis on private provision thus tend to support market-based financial systems in general and a higher-risk, shorter-term investment orientation. A feedback effect of defined-contribution schemes is to, in turn, pressure companies for higher short-term returns and become less willing to collectivise pension risks of their employees.

(3) *Solidaristic pension regimes support political alliances between the lower- and middle-income groups to a greater extent than systems with a higher degree of private pension provision, which are more supportive of alliances between middle- and upper-income groups. Differences in alliances are significant in influencing the direction of political reform, including financial system, corporate governance and welfare state policies.*

The group most affected by differences in pension regimes is the middle-income group.[2] Lower-income households in all systems are almost entirely dependent upon public pensions. Similarly, upper-income households in all systems rely more upon private provision for retirement income. The mix of retirement income sources for middle-income households, by contrast, varies greatly with the nature of the pension regime.[3] Retirement income for middle-income households in solidaristic regimes is mainly financed by taxes or employer/employee contributions, thus aligning the interests of middle-income and lower-income households regarding the viability of welfare states and the rights of employees. Retirement income for the middle-income group in private pension regimes, however, tends to come from capital income (particularly equity income), thus creating a sort of 'people's capitalism' aligning the interests of middle- and upper-income groups. This coalition has an interest in increasing the profitability of companies through reducing taxes and social contributions and through the introduction of shareholder value (and the associated weakening of employee rights).

The public–private mix

A basic distinction exists between Germany and Japan as countries with pension regimes emphasising the public dimension in pension funding, and the US and UK, where private pensions play a more significant role. Actually, the distinction between public and private pension provision is a difficult one that involves many dimensions (Shalev 1996; Kangas and Palme 1992; Rein and Rainwater 1986). The public versus private distinction may be made according to the different *carriers* of pension provision such as the state, firms, families, labour unions, insurance companies, etc. Here only state-administered funds would be considered public, but neglect statutory schemes administered by the social partners. Others distinguish according to the sort of *benefits* received, such as the degree to which market principles versus social entitlements are involved or the degree to which pensions orient toward minimum social standards versus replacing past labour market earnings beyond that minimum. Finally authors distinguish according to the *regulation* of pension regimes, i.e. whether schemes are mandatory versus voluntary, entail universal versus selective coverage, or have a statutory versus contractual basis. Most real-world pension regimes use a complex combination of principles such as the market, distributive justice and the insurance of risks. Self-organisation by the private sector often occurs in the shadow of state hierarchy, and subjected to public standards and oversight. Given the focus here on financial systems, we define public pensions in relation to state versus private control over pension savings.

International differences in public versus private pension provision can be summarised by several measures. First, levels of *expenditures* are largely determined by demographic structures, as well as the generosity of benefits. For this reason, we measure the relative shares of public and private sources in total expenditure. Table 8.4 shows a higher share of public expenditures in Germany and Japan (roughly 80–20 per cent), than in Britain and the US (roughly 60–40 or 70–30 per cent).[4] Table 8.4 also shows that private schemes account for

Table 8.4 The balance of private and public pension expenditures

	Benefits as % of GDP (% of pension benefits), 1980			*Contributions as % of labour costs (% of pension contributions), 1984*		
	Total	*Private*	*Public*	*Total*	*Private*	*Public*
Germany	13.2	2.6	10.6	21.0	5.0	16.0
	(100%)	(20%)	(80%)	(100%)	(24%)	(76%)
Japan[a]	5.0	0.9	4.1	13.5	4.7	6.8
	(100%)	(18%)	(82%)	(100%)	(18%)	(82%)
UK	10.9	4.6	6.3	15.0	7.0	8.0
	(100%)	(42%)	(56%)	(100%)	(47%)	(53%)
USA	10.2	3.3	6.9	18.0	9.0	9.0
	(100%)	(32%)	(68%)	(100%)	(50%)	(50%)

Sources: Compiled from OECD (1988); Davis (1995); Shinkawa and Pempel (1997); Rein (1996).

Note
a Contributions data: 1978.

Table 8.5 Public and private pension income

	Target replacement rates of public system (in %)	*Social-security replacement rate (1992), based on final salary of $20,000 and $50,000 (in %)*	*Percentage of gross household income (in %)*[a]	
			Private pensions	*Public pensions*
Germany	70	70–59	12.8	68.0
Japan	68	54[b]	n.a.	n.a.
UK	25	50–26	22.0	48.7
USA	40	65–40	14.4	33.0

Sources: OECD (1998c, 1988); Davis (1995: 43).

Notes
a Percentages do not total 100 per cent due to income from other sources. Relates to households headed by those between ages 65 and 75 (UK and USA: 1986; Germany: 1981).
b Ratio to average earnings in 1986.

higher shares pension contributions in Britain and the US. Second, based on *income*, Table 8.5 shows replacement rates of pension schemes based on two income levels.[5] Germany has the highest replacement rate, representing the most generous of the public pension systems. The US is also generous at lower salary levels, but less comprehensive at higher income levels. Public pensions in Britain are the least generous. Table 8.5 also shows that elderly households in Germany rely more on public pensions for the overall income than either Britain or the USA. Third, given the less comprehensive public system, a higher percentage of employees are covered by private schemes in Britain and the US (see Table 8.6).

Table 8.6 Private pension fund assets, 1995

	Assets of pension funds as % of GDP[a]	*Private pension fund coverage as % of employees*	*Assets of life insurance companies as % of GDP*
Germany	2.7	42	19.4
Japan	6.0[b]	37	33.9
UK	68.8	70	63.4
USA	59.8	50	30.1

Sources: OECD (1998a: 10; 1998b: 30; 1997).

Notes
a 1994.
b For Germany and Japan, data do not include the large reserve funded pension plans with assets held directly on the sponsoring firm's balance sheet.

Four systems

In Germany, nearly all employees are covered by a compulsory general PAYG pension insurance system. Contributions from employers and employees each amount to 8.85 per cent of gross earnings, up to a DM 6,500 maximum. A number of different insurers with parity representation for employers and employees administer the system: the Federal Insurance Agency for White Collar Employees, 18 regional state insurance institutes, and other special institutions for seamen, railway employees, farmers and coal miners.[6] Insurers are regulated by either the Federal Insurance Agency (*Bundesversicherungsanstalt*) and the Minister of Labour and Social Affairs, or directly by the *Länder*. In addition to earnings-related contributions, a general subsidy is paid from the general budget of the federal government amounting to 20 per cent of expenditures in 1995. Together, the Association of Pension Insurance Carriers (*VDR*) administer a reserve fund. The fund has shrunk from 9.3 to 1.5 months expenditures between 1972 and 1994 – amounting to 1.1 per cent of GDP (VDR 1994). The reserve fund portfolio consists primarily of bank deposits (72 per cent), short-term loans (15 per cent) and short-term securities (4 per cent). The public system accumulates little capital and contributes to the financial system via bank deposits.

In Japan, the public pension system makes a major contribution to the bank-based financial systems. The Pension Insurance Amendments of 1985 transformed the existing National Pension Plan into a national retirement system for all employees. Employees receive a flat-rate benefit from the National Pension Plan, and participate in an additional statutory plan with an earnings-related scheme (the Employees' Pension Insurance System, or EPS). The EPS is funded exclusively through equal employer–employee contributions totalling 16.5 per cent of gross earnings in 1995 (Clark 1998: 106). These statutory pensions are *partially funded*. The programme evolved from full funding to partial funding, but still has substantial reserves. Funds collected under both the NPS and EPS plans are deposited in the Trust Fund Bureau of the Ministry of Finance (see Chapter 9 by Estevez-Abe in this volume).[7] In 1999, both funds totalled roughly 139 trillion yen or roughly 28 per cent of GDP. The funds receive an interest rate set by the Ministry of Finance (MOF), and are then pooled with postal savings as part of the Fiscal Investment and Loan Programme (FILP). Public pension assets are managed as a tool of extended fiscal policy by ensuring the availability of large sums of capital to finance public works investment.

In Britain, state pensions historically aimed at compensating voluntary pension schemes in providing minimum social security for the poor (see Manow 1997). Unlike welfare models oriented to upgrading the earnings-related component for mainstream workers in Germany and Japan, British welfare sought to provide basic minimum income. Pension policy was linked to the goals of reducing poverty among the elderly and thus targeted to populations outside the mainstream wage earners. The Social Security Pension Act in 1975 introduced a state earnings-related pension scheme (SERPS) alongside the basic pension, but also gave the option of contracting out to an occupational scheme provided a minimum guarantee of benefits. In light of the degenerating contribution ratio that creates financial troubles under a PAYG system, the Thatcher government cut benefits provided by SERPS. The past two decades have been characterised by increasing 'opting out' from the public system.

In the US, the first national pension system (Social Security) was established in 1935 as part of the New Deal. Unlike tax-financed flat-rate schemes, Social Security is an earnings-related system financed by payroll taxes. President Franklin D. Roosevelt favoured the earnings component in order to ensure a vested interest among the broad wage earning public and thus mass political support for Social Security. Initial benefits were not particularly generous, and one of the major demands of the trade unions and the progressive wing of the Democratic party since the New Deal has been to increase Social Security. Due to the strength of the conservative opposition (in part related to the disproportionate strength of small rural states in the US Senate), trade unions focused on establishing and extending pension benefits through collective bargaining in the 1940s and 1950s. Although the generosity of Social Security has considerably increased, the system remains less comprehensive at upper-middle income levels. Since around 1984, social security has gradually moved from PAYG to a partially funded system in anticipation of demographic changes. In 1997, the Old-Age and Survivors Insurance (OASI) and Disability Insurance (DI) trust funds had surplus assets of $655 billion or around 8.4 per cent of GDP. This sum remains relatively small compared to Japan. Fund assets are invested entirely in low-yield government bonds, and have little direct impact on the financial system.

In sum, the public–private mix of pension provision has both direct and indirect impacts on financial systems. The *direct effects* of state system relate to the size and structure of assets accumulated by the state. Here the major differences are between pay-as-you-go systems (Germany, Britain) and partially funded systems (Japan and the United States). Partial or full funding potentially gives the state increased control over financial markets. However, as the US example shows, the impact of accumulated pension reserves can be limited to general fiscal effects by financing public debt. While this reduces the supply of government debt offered to the private sector, the impacts on the financial system are small and consistent with the market mechanism, since no state intervention in the allocation of credit exists. Japan is more similar to Sweden, where the state plays an active role in credit allocation. State allocation of credit occurs through the use of a public banking system, and hence creates a source of patient capital for private industry, in addition to sponsoring public works.

An *indirect impact* of the public–private mix relates to the 'crowding out' effect on private pensions through generous public schemes. Cross-national research has demonstrated a strong negative correlation between the levels of private and public pension expenditures (see Kangas and Palme 1992; Esping-Andersen 1987). Strong negative correlations exist between the replacement rates and the level of private expenditures, suggesting that public pensions 'crowd out' private pensions by reducing the demand for private funds. Where public pensions display weak income gradation, earnings-related pensions components have been provided in the private sector. This pattern is illustrated across the four cases examined here: private pensions are low in Germany and Japan (corresponding to high levels of public pensions) and high in Britain and the US (corresponding to lower levels of public provision) especially for higher-income groups. Such demand-side effects may be partially countered by other state incentives such as tax breaks to implement private pension plans.

Private pension accumulation: organisationally embedded versus market-based regimes

Unlike public schemes implicitly guaranteed by the state's power of taxation, private schemes rely on contractual mechanisms and insurance to guarantee that pension benefits will be paid. Thus, most private pension regimes are fully or partially funded and accumulate large sums of capital. With the ageing populations of OECD countries, pension capital has become a fast-growing source of savings and investment capital. For example, Table 8.6 compares the assets of private pension funds. Converse to their less comprehensive public sectors, British and US private pensions assets are large relative to Germany and Japan.[8] As already shown in Table 8.2, pension fund portfolios are dominated by equities. Their importance to domestic stock markets can be shown by the fact that 33 per cent of UK and 25 per cent of US stocks were owned by pension funds in 1995, compared to only 1 per cent in Germany and around 2 per cent in Japan.

In this section we compare institutional differences in the organisation and regulation of private pension accumulation. These factors influence who controls private pension resources and how they are channelled into national financial systems. Company-sponsored pensions were historically an element of welfare that served to transform workers into members of a paternalistic firm-community. Company insurance systems created risk pools at the company level, creating an organisationally bounded community of fate among members that might reinforce company rather than class identification. Employers used pension benefits as a selective incentive to reward company loyalty and reduce the problems of labour turnover. Yet financially, pension benefits remained at risk through the employer's default or subject to breach of trust. For this reason, most pension regimes secure assets in separate funds, or sometimes guarantee direct commitments by compulsory insurance as in Germany. The principle of separation can also be found in the regulation of investments. Pension funds usually have formal or informal portfolio rules, as well as limits on self-investment in sponsoring firms. Last, along with regulating risks, pension regimes vary in the control rights individual beneficiaries have over their pension assets, particularly the surplus funds generated by investment. Historically, international differences have arisen in the institutional arrangements to address the financing methods, as well as rights and obligations of private pension funds.

Our typology groups private pension regimes according to whether assets are *internalised in organisationally embedded* forms of investment or *externalised in market-based* forms of investment. Ideal-typically, organisationally embedded regimes internalise capital allocation within the firm (e.g. through the internally held pension reserves) or indirectly through the self-investment by formally external funds or through networks of firms linked by implicit contracts, such as Japanese life insurance firms. These systems are often associated with direct claims by employees on their sponsoring companies. Market-based regimes externalise capital accumulation outside the sponsoring firm or group of firms. These regimes are administered by company or independent pension funds, as well as through group insurance provided by life insurance firms. Pension claims thus normally fall on a legally independent organisation who hold the assets. These regimes are considered external because they are regulated to serve the best *financial* interests of policy holders by maximising market returns to capital.

In Germany, private pensions are voluntary supplements to the public system. In 1990, 32 per cent of firms provided occupational pensions covering 65 per cent of their employees (Statistisches Bundesamt 1995: 157). Defined-benefit plans dominate, while only 2 per cent of firms offered defined-contribution plans (Schmähl and Böhm 1994: 14). The accumulated assets of private schemes totalled 486 billion DM or 14.6 per cent of GDP in 1994. These assets are divided among four different types of schemes: 57 per cent of assets were in the form of direct commitments, 8 per cent support funds, 12 per cent direct insurance and 22 per cent pension funds (Spengel and Schmidt 1997).

The majority of pension assets can be classified as organisationally embedded through *direct commitments* and *support funds*. Direct commitments involve direct obligations by the employer, and hence the firm bears insurance risks directly. These are widespread among large firms, who calculate pension liabilities through book reserve methods and use reserves as internal finance for capital investments. Besides the strong tax advantages they offer (Manow 2000), firms are obligated to calculate pension liabilities at an interest rate of 6 per cent (Wartenberg 1992), thus being attractive for corporate finance when real interest rates are high. The building and diminishing of reserves can also be used by firms as a form of profit smoothing to minimise taxable profits over time[9] or sustain shareholder profits during temporary downswings. Support funds are held externally, but not supervised by the federal insurance agency. Thus, support often make loans to sponsoring firms although these plans are the least widespread sort of pension scheme. Market-based forms of pension accumulation, such as direct insurance and pension funds, constitute only a minority of assets and are widespread among small firms.

Direct insurance involves employer sponsorship of a plan through an independent life insurance company. The advantages for smaller firms are simple administration, low costs, and the bearing of risks by an external insurer. However, funds are channelled outside the firm, thereby lowering firm liquidity and reducing the level of funds available for internal investment. Most insurance assets are invested in credit markets to finance housing and public debt.[10] Pension funds are organised by external mutual insurance associations financed by employer and employee contributions. Pension funds are allowed to loan a maximum of one-third of their assets to sponsoring firms if strict collateral requirements are met. Further pension funds are restricted to investing 30 per cent of their assets in stock and other equity, as well as owning a maximum of 5 per cent of the total capital of any one company. In practice, pension funds invest below the legal maximums in equities (see Table 8.2).

In Japan, three sorts of private pension schemes exist: lump severance payments, employee pension funds (EPF) and tax-qualified pensions (TQP). Japanese firms have traditionally provided lump sum severance payments equal to 3–4 years of salary. As in Germany, firms created book reserve liabilities to pay future pensions and used the interim cash as internal finance. However, reserves are tax exempt only up to 40 per cent of their total value. Tax-exempt reserves totalled 10.9 trillion yen in 1989, and total pension reserves was estimated at around 27 trillion yen (Clark 1991). A growing number of firms have introduced two main types of private pensions.[11] EPFs pay a contracted-out portion of the public pension system, plus at least 30 per cent above the public benefit. They are managed by outside organisations such as trust banks and life insurance firms. In 1996, around 1,900 EPFs existed covering 12.1 million people and with assets of 41.6 trillion yen (roughly 7 per cent of GDP). TQPs are separate from the public system, existing in 91,000 companies, covering 10.7 million members, and holding assets of 17.8 trillion yen. Pensions benefits are paid through either lump sum severance payments, annuities or both.

Assets of TQPs and EPFs must be administered by a life insurance company or trust bank licensed by the Ministry of Finance. Pension funds are thus politically channelled to a relative small set of highly regulated organisations. Pension capital is strongly linked to both the horizontal corporate networks or *keiretsu*. The Japanese life insurance industry is the world's largest, with over twelve times as many assets as the UK or Germany (see Estevez-Abe, Chapter 9; Table 8.6). The life insurers remained highly concentrated, given the MOF restricted market entry and guaranteed minimum interest rates. Trust banks had to follow 5:3:3:2 investment rules (low risk assets, stocks, currency related and real estate). Thus, a smaller proportion of assets went into securities markets, and given the smaller size of trust funds themselves, pension funds have not yet had a dramatic impact on the Japanese financial system. Such regulations have now been abolished as part of the financial 'Big Bang'. Pension funds are managed by parity employer–employee representatives, and surpluses can only be withdrawn with approval of the Ministry of Health and Welfare.

In Britain, occupational pensions are coupled with the statutory system through the option of contracting out the earnings-related benefit under SERPS. Contracting out is allowed when particular conditions are met to assure beneficiaries of higher benefits than under the state scheme (Blake 1992; Davis 1997).[12] Around 92 per cent of members in occupational schemes are covered by defined-benefit systems, with the remaining 8 per cent in defined-contribution schemes. British occupational pension funds must be set up as *trusts*, having several important implications. Occupational schemes must be funded rather than PAYG, with the exception of state employees. Furthermore, funds must be separate from the employer. As shown in Table 8.2, their assets are primarily invested in marketable equities following diversified portfolios. The 1990 Social Security Act capped self-investment by pension funds into their sponsoring companies at 5 per cent of all fund assets (Blake 1995: 318). Trustee law dictates that trustees have the fiduciary responsibility to act in the best interests of their beneficiaries. The *Megarry Judgement* in a 1982 dispute over investments of a mineworkers' pension fund showed that the financial interests of the beneficiaries took precedence over other sorts of interests (Blake 1995: 319–20). In the judgement of the High Court:

> When the purpose of the trust is to provide financial benefits for the beneficiaries, as is usually the case, the best interests of the beneficiaries are normally their best financial interests. In the case of a power of investment, as in the present case, the power must be exercised so as to yield the best return for the beneficiaries, judged in relation to the risks of the investments in question.
> (Blake 1995: 319–20)

Taken together, the British regulatory environment discourages organisationally embedded pension accumulation as hostile to the interests of beneficiaries. A conflict of interest is construed between the best interests of the sponsoring company and the financial interests of future pensioners for high capital market returns.

In the US, occupational pensions are particularly widespread to supplement statutory social security. Given the low replacement rates of social security among upper-middle income groups, private coverage spread from 19 per cent of private sector employees in 1945 to 46 per cent in 1987 (OECD 1990). Private pension assets are roughly evenly divided between defined-benefit and defined-contribution schemes. However, defined-contribution schemes have been growing rapidly since the 1980s due to the widespread popularity of 401 k plans. Roughly two-thirds of pension assets are operated by trust-fund plans, while the remaining one-third of assets are held by life insurance firms.

Since 1974, private sector plans are governed by ERISA, the Employee Retirement Income Security Act of 1974. ERISA does not recognise direct commitments for tax benefits, but forces separation of assets onto separate funds and established duties for pension trustees: loyalty of beneficiaries, prudence, asset diversification, and various prohibitions of self-investment or transactions involving potential conflicts of interest. The prudent-man concept limits self-investment in sponsoring firms at 10 per cent of fund assets and mandates that assets are broadly diversified. However, no other concrete restrictions are applied. In practice, rules on underfunding lead to a high level of investment in fixed-interest securities to guarantee fund liquidity.[13] As in Britain, fund managers are viewed as having fiduciary duties to act in the financial interests of their beneficiaries. Further incentives to maximising financial returns are institutionalised by the diffusion of defined-contribution schemes that place the risks and rewards of pension asset returns with the beneficiaries themselves. Pension funds thus form a major pillar of the contemporary market-oriented financial system.

Pension regimes and varieties of capitalism: institutional complementarity with financial systems, corporate finance and corporate governance

Organisationally embedded versus market-based regimes of pension accumulation have wide-ranging impacts on financial systems, corporate finance and corporate governance. Beyond contributing to the bank-based or market-based nature of the financial systems, these effects also have consequences for corporate finance and corporate governance. In particular, organisationally embedded pension regimes increase the financial autonomy of corporations and limit pressures to generate shareholder returns relative to market-based systems. Such regimes create the supply of 'patient' capital relative to liquid capital, and provide sources of financial commitment to enterprises in Germany and Japan. Such patterns of ownership and control, in turn, have institutional complementarities with 'stakeholder'-oriented management or non-liberal patterns of corporate governance as discussed in Germany and Japan (Jackson 2002). Conversely, the liquidity orientation of UK and US pension funds increase stock market pressures on companies, and help give voice to shareholder interests and reinforce the exclusive focus on shareholder value found in those national systems of company law.

Sources of financial commitment

In Germany and Japan, substantial private pension assets are accumulated as internal reserves on the balance sheets of large firms and used as a means of internal company finance.[14] Internal reserves can be used either to reduce external liabilities (capital substitution) or finance new investments in physical capital or financial instruments. Thus, pension reserves increase the long-term financial autonomy of firms, reducing their dependence on external equity finance. Book reserves can be particularly effective for new, growing companies since liabilities won't mature for several decades. In Germany, pension reserves accounted for 19.9 per cent of corporate liabilities in 1990, compared to just 9.5 per cent in 1970 (Wartenberg 1992). Over the same period, equity declined from 26.7 per cent to just 18.5 per cent.

Likewise, the absence of large pension funds[15] reinforces the existing patterns of financial commitment among corporate owners. German and Japanese stock markets are dominated by banks and inter-corporate shareholding motivated by strategic organisational interests (Jackson 2001), while individual and portfolio-type institutional investors remain relatively small. In Japan, life insurance companies play a key role as stable shareholders, protecting firms from the threat of hostile takeovers. Japan has an additional feature in that the pension assets held in external pension funds or life insurers are linked to the system of cross-shareholding within company groups. Here, 'external' pension capital again becomes re-embedded within the company group as a source of stable, committed finance.

Sources of financial liquidity

Pension capitals in the UK and the US are largely accumulated and controlled by external pension funds. Pension funds pool household savings and function to diversify risks in providing funds to financial markets. They channel large amounts of capital into equity markets (see Table 8.2), increasing the long-term supply of equity capital, but also increasing volatility and capital market pressures on companies. Given their institutional trustee relation, pension funds pursue maximum shareholder returns in the interests of their members, subject to prudent rules concerning the diversification of assets. Institutional investors thus have a fundamental interest in market liquidity, the ability to transact in large size without moving the price against them and at low transaction costs. Pension funds also favour market-oriented regulatory institutions, such as market-based accounting rules, stringent disclosure requirements, takeover codes, restrictions on insider information, limiting special share voting rights, etc. Large pension funds and insurance companies have greatly improved capital market efficiency: liquidity is increased, prices better reflect market values, and pension funds largely hold to professional standards of trading.

Despite their strengths, pension funds have been criticised for contributing to the problem of *short-termism* of UK–US financial markets (Blake 1995). First, large pension funds tend not to invest in small companies (Blake 1995; Davis 1997), both because the costs of information gathering are greater and due to restrictions on holding maximum levels of equity in single firms (these limits are quickly reached with smaller firms). Second, pension funds invest little in venture capital markets, as these markets are characterised by direct investment rather than the portfolio approach of pension funds. Third, pension funds also increase the short-term volatility of securities markets. Fund trading strategies can easily lead to cascading sales or purchases, causing markets to bubble or crash. Derivates trading may also have reinforcing effects on price swings. Volatility also results from the 'herd mentality' of investors: the performance checks of fund managers against the market that may induce similar behaviour among investors who fear performing worse than the 'average' fund, or infer information from each others' trades. Fourth, pension funds also create their own interests and may lead to inefficient practices, such as the churning of stocks to raise fees with the further consequence of increasing stock market volatility. Also, contestation arises over the often ill-defined ownership of funds surpluses during mergers and takeovers.

Market-oriented pension investment shapes corporate governance by increasing pressures toward shareholder value on British and American corporations. Paradoxically, the growing size of private pension funds has helped partially overcome the fragmented nature of corporate ownership and increase the use of shareholder 'voice' in corporate governance. Pension funds own nearly 20 per cent of all stock in the US, compared to less than 1 per cent in both Germany and Japan (Jackson 2002). Due to their indexing strategies and large size, the liquidity of pension fund investments is sometimes quite limited. Furthermore, recent legal interpretations in the US suggest that fiduciary duties may include balancing indexing strategies with active monitoring and relationship investing. Shareholder activism has formalised corporate governance practices. Thus, while increasing the commitment of shareholders, it is important to remember that pension funds interests differ substantially from the *strategic organisational interests* pursued by banks and life insurers in Germany and Japan.

It remains to be seen whether the maturing of private pension funds will have destabilising impacts on capital markets. Stock market booms in both Britain and the US were fuelled by dramatic increases in pension funding. The inflow of new funds may slow, and over time fund liabilities will come due. As pension funds mature, their optimal investment portfolio changes – funds need guard against the risks of default on liabilities, and may increase their share of fixed-interest securities. Portfolios may no longer easily be re-balanced by new inflows. A large-scale shift from equities to bonds may have a destabilising impact on asset prices, and hence the value of the pension funds themselves.

Conclusion

National pension regimes are an important factor shaping financial markets, as well as corporate finance and corporate governance. German pensions have the smallest impact on their financial system, since the public system is generous and organised on a PAYG basis, but contribute to providing patient capital to firms through small private schemes financed primarily through company book reserves. Japanese pensions also contribute to bank-based and 'patient' finance, both through the public trust funds and private provision through life insurance firms. British and US pension funds are largely organised around external pension funds that invest high proportions of their assets in equities. Pension funds thus increase the size of equity markets, as well as aggregating share ownership and providing some degree of institutional shareholder 'voice' within corporate governance.

Just as pension regimes displayed institutional complementarity with national patterns of financial markets and corporate governance in the past, the changes in pension regimes during the 1980s and 1990s have wide-reaching consequences for these national models of capitalism. The growth of pension funds is closely linked to the growing size stock markets and the increased pressures for 'shareholder-value'-oriented corporate governance. Companies now face pressures to improve shareholder returns that have far-reaching consequences for corporate organisation and the balance of power among stakeholders within the firm. Until recently, weaker pressures for shareholder value in Germany and Japan were associated with their smaller and organisationally embedded regimes of private pension accumulation. Welfare state reform may be one of the driving forces changing patterns of corporate governance.

Notes

1 For example, UK pension funds held 69 per cent of their assets in equities compared to 13 per cent for households.
2 We are grateful to Ron Dore for an extended note outlining these differences.
3 For example, German households in the top three income groups are three times more likely to receive private pensions than those in the lowest quintile, and only half as likely to depend entirely upon the statutory system (BMA 1998).
4 These shares may be sensitive to the relative maturity of the public versus private pension systems or categories used. For example in Germany during 1995, 78 per cent of pensions paid came from the public schemes, only 5 per cent from private schemes and the remaining from occupational and civil service schemes (BMA 1998).
5 Replacement rates differ greatly by salary level. Given the different distributive effects of pension regimes, it is difficult to evaluate the generosity of public pensions with a single measure.
6 Details for the funding and contribution rates differ for these occupationally specific schemes.
7 A major reform of FILP is planned for the year 2001 that would end mandatory deposit of pension reserves as part of FILP (see http://www.mof.go.jp).
8 In addition to public pensions, the size of private pensions is influenced through tax policies, the rates of return on pension assets, and the maturity of pension schemes.
9 This practice may be viewed as a way of delaying tax payments and hence incurring an uncollateralised loan from the state. Real tax savings occur by way of minimising taxable assets (through incurring a liability).
10 According to the Association of Life Insurers, corporate stock accounts for only 2 per cent of the assets of life insurance companies (Wartenberg 1992: 149).
11 In 1993, 92 per cent of firms with over 30 employees offered private pension plans (Clark 1998). Around 58 per cent of EPI insured employees were covered by either an EPF or TQP in 1989 (Clark 1991: 86).
12 In 1991, 9.7 million employees were contracted out of SERPS, while 1 million were 'contracted in' where occupational pension benefits are paid only on top of the SERPS scheme (Davis 1997: 12).
13 Minimum funding standards were established for defined-benefit schemes. The law has greatly improved the funding status of pensions: the proportion of private pension funds with sufficient assets to cover liabilities increased from fewer than 35 per cent in 1974 to nearly 75 per cent in 1985 (OECD 1990). The Pension Benefit Guarantee Corporation (PBGC) was established to insure defined-benefit schemes against default.
14 Some important differences do exist: German employees do not customarily contribute to occupational pension schemes, which would imply a financial participation on the direct commitments of the firm, whereas in Japan firms and employees contribute equally to the schemes.
15 In Germany, pension funds and life insurers invest in equities below the legal maximums. However, German equities have not underperformed. But the small differences in returns between German bonds and stocks may not be large enough to justify the extra risk involved.

References

Albert, M. (1993). *Capitalism versus Capitalism*. New York: Four Wall Eight Windows.

Bank of Japan (1996). *Comparative Economic and Financial Statistics: Japan and Other Major Countries*. Tokyo: Bank of Japan.

Blake, D. (1992). *Issues in Pension Funding*. London: Routledge.

Blake, D. (1995). *Pension Schemes and Pension Funds in the United Kingdom*. Oxford: Clarendon Press.

Clark, R. L. (1991). *Retirement Systems in Japan*. Boston: Irwin.

Clark, R. L. (1998) 'Pensions in transition in the U.S. and Japan: Parallels and contrasts', in T. Marmor and P. De Jong (eds), *Ageing, Social Security and Affordability*. Aldershot: Ashgate, 99–118.

Crouch, C. and Streeck, W. (eds) (1997). *The Political Economy of Modern Capitalism: Mapping Convergence and Diversity*. London: Sage.

Davis, E. P. (1995). *Pension Funds. Retirement-Income Security, and Capital Markets. An International Perspective*. Oxford: Clarendon Press.

Davis, E. P. (1996). 'The role of institutional investors in the evolution of financial structure and behaviour', Special Paper No. 89, Financial Markets Group, London School of Economics.

Davis, E. P. (1997). *Private pensions in OECD Countries – The United Kingdom*. Paris: Organisation for the Economic Co-operation and Development.

Deutsche Bundesbank (1997). 'Die Aktie als Finanzierungs- und Anlageinstrument', *Deutsche Bank Monatsberichte* 49, 1.

Esping-Andersen, G. (1987). 'State and market in the formation of social security regimes', Working Papers No. 87/281. Florence: European University Institute.

Gerschenkron, A. (1962). *Economic Backwardness in Historical Perspective. A Book of Essays*. Cambridge, MA: Belknap.

Jackson, G. (2001). 'The origins of non-liberal corporate governance in Germany and Japan', in W. Streeck and K. Yamamura (eds), *The Origins of Non-Liberal Capitalism: Germany and Japan*, Ithaca, NY: Cornell University Press (forthcoming).

Jackson, G. (2002). 'Corporate governance in Germany and Japan: Liberalization pressures and responses', in W. Streeck and K. Yamamura (eds), *Germany and Japan: The Future of Nationally-Embedded Capitalism in a Global Economy* (forthcoming).

Kangas, O. and Palme, J. (1992). 'The private–public mix in pension policy', in J. E. Kolberg (ed.), *The Study of Welfare State Regimes*. Armonk, NY: M.E. Sharpe, 199–236.

Mackenzie, G. A., Gerson, P. and Cuevas, A. (1997). *Pension Regimes and Saving*, Washington, DC: International Monetary Fund.

Manow, P. (1997). *Cross-Class Alliances in Welfare Reform. A Theoretical Framework*. Cologne: Mimeo.

Manow, P. (2000). 'Crisis and change in pension finance: Germany and Japan compared', unpublished paper.

OECD (Organisation for Economic Co-operation and Development) (1988). *Reforming Public Pensions*. Paris: OECD.

OECD (1990). 'Private pensions in OECD countries. The United States', *OECD Social Policy Studies* 10. Paris: OECD.

OECD (1997). *Institutional Investors Statistical Yearbook 1997*. Paris: OECD.

OECD (1998a). 'The macroeconomics of ageing, pensions and savings: A survey', Working Paper AWP 1.1. Paris: OECD.

OECD (1998b). 'Private pensions systems: Regulatory policies', Working Paper AWP 2.2. Paris: OECD.

OECD (1998c). 'Retirement income systems: The reform process across OECD countries', Working Paper AWP 3.4. Paris: OECD.

Rein, M. (1996). 'Is America exceptional? The role of occupational welfare in the United States and the European Community', in M. Shalev (ed.), *The Privatization of Social Policy? Occupational Welfare and the Welfare State in America, Scandinavia and Japan.* Houndsmills, UK: Macmillan, 27–43.

Rein, M. and Rainwater, L. (eds) (1986). *Public/Private Interplay in Social Protection.* Armonk, NY: M.E. Sharpe.

Schmähl, W. and Böhm, S. (1994). 'Occupational pension schemes in the private and public sector in the Federal Republic of Germany – an overview', ZeS-Arbeitspapier 5/94. Bremen: University of Bremen, Centre for Social Policy Research.

Shalev, M. (1996). *The Privatisation of Social Policy? Occupational Welfare and the Welfare State in America, Scandinavia and Japan.* London: Macmillan.

Shinkawa, T. and Pempel, T. J. (1996). 'Occupational welfare and the Japanese experience', in M. Shalev (ed.), *The Privatization of Social Policy? Occupational Welfare and the Welfare State in America, Scandinavia and Japan.* Houndsmills, UK: Macmillan, 280–326.

Spengel, C. and Schmidt, F. (1997). *Betriebliche Altersversorgung, Besteuerung und Kapitalmarkt. Ein Vergleich der Verhältnisse in Deutschland, Frankreich, Großbritannien, den Niederlanden und den USA.* Baden-Baden: Nomos.

Statistisches Bundesamt (1995). 'Betriebliche Altersversorgung 1990 im früheren Bundesgebiet', *Wirtschaft und Statistik,* Band 2.

VDR (Verband deutscher Rentenversicherungsträger) (1994). *VDR Geschäftsbericht für das Jahr 1994.* Frankfurt: VDR.

Vitols, S. (1996). 'Modernizing capital: Financial regulation and long-term finance in the postwar U.S and Germany', Dissertation, Department of Sociology, University of Madison-Wisconsin, Madison, WI.

Vitols, S., Casper, S., Soskice, D. and Woolcock, S. (1997). *Corporate Governance in Large British and German Companies: Comparative Institutional Advantage or Competing for Best Practice* London: Anglo German Foundation.

Wartenberg, L.-G. von (1992). 'Zur Bedeutung der betrieblichen Altersversorgung für die Finanzierung deutscher Unternehmen', in W. Förster (ed.), *Betriebliche Altersversorgung in der Diskussion zwischen Praxis und Wissenschaft.* Cologne: Verlag Dr. Otto Schmidt.

Zysman, J. (1983). *Governments, Markets and Growth: Financial Systems and the Politics of Industrial Change.* Ithaca, NY: Cornell University Press.

9 The forgotten link

The financial regulation of Japanese pension funds in comparative perspective

Margarita Estevez-Abe

Introduction: the welfare–finance nexus, a forgotten link?

To the extent that the literature on the varieties of capitalism has taken notice of welfare state arrangements, it has done so by focusing upon the impact of such arrangements on employment relations (Esping-Andersen 1990; Estevez-Abe *et al.* 1999; Manow 1997a,b; Mares 1997; Huber and Stephens 1997; Wood 1997). In the literature, however, employment relations constitute just one of the features that define a specific model of capitalism (Aoki and Dore 1994; Berger and Dore 1996; Crouch and Streeck 1997; Hall 1986; Hall and Soskice, forthcoming; Boyer 1989; Hollingsworth and Boyer 1997; Kitschelt *et al.* 1999). The nature of financial markets and the relations between firms and suppliers of capital are every bit as important. The ability of corporations to form long-term commitments, such as lifetime employment, depends on the availability of patient, far-sighted capital. The longer the time horizon of capital suppliers, the greater the autonomy of corporate managers. The time horizon of capital is, in short, one of the most significant determinants of variation between different types of capitalism.

It is necessary to look more closely at the way welfare programmes affect the financial market. The central contention of this chapter is that welfare programmes can be designed to create large sums of patient, far-sighted capital, thereby giving rise to a distinctive type of capitalism. Just as some welfare programmes 'de-commodify' labour, some 'communalise' capital. For instance, while pay-as-you-go pension systems only raise sufficient money to pay for the benefits incurred in a given period, others raise a surplus that can be pooled. Pooled money must be administered (which is to say, invested). This gives rise to further important variations in terms of social protection beyond those studied traditionally. Some welfare programmes keep money under state control, directing it to key economic sectors, while others do not. In short, the design of welfare programmes affects not just the savings rate – i.e. capital accumulation – but the flow of capital.[1] Whoever administers these welfare funds determines where the money goes.

The case of Japan will be used here to demonstrate one way in which welfare programmes play critical roles in the flow of capital within the economy.

More specifically, it will be argued that Japan employed welfare funds to sustain a low level of taxation and to foster a long-term relationship between capital and firms during the post-war period. This chapter focuses on the period between the 1950s and the 1960s, when a distinctive finance nexus developed in Japan. During this period, private and public pension programmes were designed that managed to produce a large volume of long-term or patient capital in Japan. Welfare funds provided much needed capital for industry via the indirect financial market and also functioned as patient capital, as a buffer against potentially hostile shareholders. The combination of these two factors helped to produce and sustain a unique corporate governance structure in Japan. In the following decades, welfare funds continued to stabilise mutual corporate shareholding. Welfare funds in the private sector were channelled into bank shareholdings, thereby granting major Japanese banks a degree of independence from their shareholders. The government used the welfare funds it controlled to fund public projects without additional taxation, thereby enabling Japan to have one of the lowest levels of taxation in advanced industrial societies.[2]

The purpose of this chapter is to present a new way of understanding linkages between welfare programmes and the structure of a political economy as a whole. More specifically, an attempt will be made to link the two important bodies of literature in comparative politics on advanced industrial economies, namely the welfare state literature and the varieties of capitalism literature.

These two bodies of literature have rarely acknowledged each other in the past. Scholars in each genre pursued fundamentally different issues. The welfare state literature, primarily concerned with the question of social rights, was interested in why some countries protected social rights of their citizens more than others. The varieties of capitalism literature, in turn, dealt with the problem why economic behaviour and relations took on a long-term cooperative nature in some countries, while in others they remained oriented toward maximising profits over the short term.

Scholars interested in qualitative differences among welfare states eventually began to ask whether these differences had any economic implications. Gøsta Esping-Andersen's pioneering work on different models of welfare capitalism indeed set a new research agenda for exploring the role of welfare programmes in the economy. Nonetheless, the traditional emphasis on social rights left a deep imprint on the new efforts. Taxonomies of welfare states tended to be based upon the size of the public programmes and the extent to which they 'de-commodified' labour. As a consequence, countries have been grouped into social democratic and non-social democratic camps, with non-social democratic welfare states further categorised into liberal and conservative Bismarckian types. As it is well known, Esping-Andersen (1990) has called these three types 'social democratic', 'conservative-statist' and 'liberal' welfare capitalism.[3] In their inquiries into the relationship between the welfare state and the broader economy, scholars have focused primarily on the implications of social policy for the labour market.

This chapter does not focus exclusively on social rights in exploring welfare–capitalism linkages. It gives more weight to the contributions of varieties of capitalism literature in reassessing the linkages. The relative neglect of non-social, rights-related designs of welfare programmes, it is argued here, has blinded us from acknowledging the possibility that there may be commonalties and differences across the 'three worlds of welfare capitalism'. For instance, Esping-Andersen (1990) categorised Japan and the Anglo-American countries as liberal regimes because they all have large private pension sectors relative to the continental European countries. At first glance, this categorisation might seem plausible to scholars who generally think of the United States and Japan as 'weak labour welfare laggards'. But to those who study the varieties of capitalism, this categorisation will seem strange because Japan and the United States are commonly thought of as polar opposites.

The varieties of capitalism literature have drawn attention to the fact that, while economic transactions in the United States tend to be short-term, in some countries the government and economic actors establish long-term commitments among themselves. Japan and Germany have been recognised as coordinated market economies, in contrast to Anglo-American liberal market economies (cf. Soskice 1994, 1999). Esping-Andersen's taxonomy is not suitable for those interested in examining qualitative differences that are not based on degrees of social rights protection or status preservation. His framework, by design, does not capture specific differences between pension programmes that arise from divergences in the financial market. For example, differences between American and Japanese designs of corporate pensions affect the behaviour of pension funds in the two countries. Japanese corporate pension plans, by law, can only be managed by life insurance companies or trust banks. These financial institutions are subject to numerous regulations by the government as to what they can do with the funds. This contrasts with the situation in the United States, where the pension funds are subject to market forces and fund managers are guided by the prudent-man rule. To use the label 'liberal welfare regime' for both Japan and the United States is thus misleading. The flow of money in the Japanese pension mix[4] is constrained to a much greater extent than in the United States.

The importance of financial designs of welfare programmes is obvious when we look at the varieties of capitalism literature. The flow and character of capital affect state and corporate finance, which in turn shape different patterns of economic behaviour. This is why the role welfare programmes play in the financial market and corporate finance becomes highly important in understanding welfare capitalism.

In short, the aim of this chapter is to highlight a different side of the welfare–capitalism nexus, namely the financial implications of different welfare arrangements. It is argued here that the design of a welfare programme matters greatly in facilitating state and market actors to engage in long-term, cooperative transactions. The contention is that welfare funds provide institutional safeguards to consolidate the key financial relations that define a particular brand of capitalism.

The second section of this chapter offers a general discussion of the interests and preferences of key actors – corporations, financial institutions and the government – and of the five categories of pension designs. The third section examines the Japanese case during the 1950s and 1960s, as explained in the introduction. The final section discusses the comparative implications of the Japanese case.

The welfare–finance nexus

All governments in advanced industrial societies design public pension programmes and encourage various private ones. Programmes in areas such as pensions and housing have an impact on the financial market because programmes designed to pool funds increase the amount of savings in a country, regardless of whether they are private or public. The government encourages savings and regulates the management of accumulated welfare funds as part of its overall financial market regulation. Welfare funds form a critical element of what might be termed the 'finance nexus between the firm and the provider of capital' because these funds are a source of long-term capital. The regulatory framework governing the accumulation and management of these funds has a major impact on economic interactions between the government, the financial sector, corporations and their employees.[5] Nowhere is this more true than in Japan, where welfare funds provide the basis for patient, far-sighted capital, which makes Japanese capitalism significantly different from the Anglo-American model of a liberal market economy.

The core of the finance nexus lies in the relationship between the provider of capital and the corporate manager. To illustrate this, we can develop a simple model of this relationship by employing the 'principal/agent model'. The provider of capital is the 'principal' and the corporate manager his 'agent', the former has a stake in the latter's performance and an interest in monitoring the latter's activities. Given the asymmetry of information available to the principal concerning the 'agent's' actions, potential investors will refrain from investing unless some safeguards are in place to check, discourage and punish moral hazards by the 'agent'.

Corporate governance by shareholders – in which the 'principal's' position as the owner of the firm is legally protected – provides one example of the capital–firm relation. But it is not the only form (cf. Aoki 1994; Berglof 1990; Mayer 1998; Roe 1994). For instance, corporate governance by shareholders is an essential component of the finance nexus in an equity-based financial market (such as the United States), while it may be less relevant in a system where debt finance is the dominant source of capital (such as Germany and Japan).[6] Furthermore (while perhaps unthinkable to American investors), investors may not themselves be interested in monitoring company performance if other mechanisms exist to hedge against potential investment risks.

This means that the interests and preferences of each actor are critical for an adequate understanding of the arrangements that emerge. The precise design of welfare state arrangements becomes central because it affects the possibilities of bargaining and cooperation between the key actors, namely the providers of capital, corporations and the government.

Before going further, we need to consider each actor's interests in more detail, and relate those interests to the emergence of specific welfare state arrangements (i.e. different designs of welfare funds).

Capital providers[7]

The providers of capital include financial institutions, non-financial corporations, institutional and individual investors.[8] While the importance and cost of monitoring corporate actions differ greatly for large institutional and small individual investors, all investors have an interest in reducing the risk of moral hazards and the cost of monitoring. To this end, they seek to establish and sustain an effective monitoring system. Preferences regarding the precise shape of the corporate governance structure will vary significantly from one type of investor to another, depending on such factors as vulnerability to risk, time horizon, and bargaining strength relative to other actors.

Corporations[9]

While corporate managers are constrained by the demands of capital suppliers and the regulations of governmental agencies, corporate managers themselves will try to shape the finance nexus between the corporation and the provider of capital to their advantage. Corporate managers thus are not wholly constrained. They have both market and political means to pursue their interests. Moreover, they have some leverage in choosing suppliers of capital; they can opt either for equity financing or debt financing and can select from various types of capital suppliers in each category. Corporate managers can also negotiate to persuade large non-financial corporations and financial institutions to become major shareholders. Similarly, they can borrow money from public agencies, private banks and insurance companies.

Corporate managers have different interests from capital suppliers. Investors seeking short-term profits have no stake in the long-term profitability of particular firms. Some organisational needs (e.g. long-term employment relations and big capital investments) make corporate managers seek out investors who are more patient during temporary slacks in corporate earnings. Corporations committed to long-term contracts cannot, for instance, resort to layoffs to improve corporate profit levels according to short-term business cycles. Factors such as the nature of recruitment and remuneration systems will affect the behaviour of corporate managers. Those managers whose careers are tied to their firm, for instance, will have a greater stake in the long-term profitability of the corporation. To this end, corporate managers will try to avoid the impact of investors' threats of 'voice' and 'exit'.[10] Therefore, while corporations are primarily interested in 'cheap capital', corporate managers also try to maximise their autonomy from capital suppliers. They will seek 'friendly' capital suppliers, whose interests and time horizons are similar to their own. Whether corporations can get investors to make long-term commitments depends on what they can offer in exchange and the range of investment strategies potential investors can reasonably tolerate. Agreement reached between the firm and the investor will affect the type of corporate governance structure that will develop.

The government

While some financial institutions and individual investors have the market power and resources to negotiate the terms of the transactions with firms, monitoring remains too costly for ordinary individual investors. Development of indirect and direct financial markets thus requires governmental involvement to reduce the cost of monitoring in order to stimulate the market. The government acts as a provider of a public good; it intervenes as a regulatory and legal overseer to reduce the costs of monitoring and the risks of moral hazards, which in turn are caused by the information asymmetry between the investor and the firm. Since the government is held accountable and sanctioned for poor national economic performance, it has an incentive to make sure there is enough capital for economic growth.[11]

Ensuring the availability of funds in the economy, however, does not necessarily require a well-developed capital market. If the government can provide capital on its own, for instance, it will see little need to develop institutional arrangements for capital markets. To the contrary, if government officials are interested in controlling the flow of capital within the economy, they will have a disincentive to stimulate an equity market where firms can raise capital on their own. Instead, governmental officials will try to increase the importance of governmental and indirect financing.[12] Transactions in the indirect financial market are easier for the government to control than those in the capital market, which more closely approximate a 'pure' marketplace. Governments can, for instance, favour the indirect financial market by making transactions in the equity market costly for small investors, thereby limiting the latter's investment opportunities to financial products offered by the government or indirect financial institutions. The government also has an incentive – and the sole authority – to raise the overall level of capital available to the economy by enforcing savings promotion policies.

The precise nature of funded welfare programmes will depend on the interests and political influence of actors included in the negotiation. Most analyses of welfare politics only examine labour, capital and the political parties, and consider 'capital' to be employers. Yet more sensitivity is required in identifying *who* the *capitalists* are when studying the politics involved in designing the funding/fund management aspects of a welfare programme. It is necessary to include corporate managers, owners of capital, financial institutions and others who provide the capital. The relationship among these sub-categories of capital and the government affects the design of welfare programmes.

Let us discuss five potential categories of pension programmes in order to identify who prefers and benefits from which specific welfare programme design.

Market-based pension programmes

When the government is interested in promoting savings (capital accumulation) but is indifferent to controlling the flow of capital, the management, i.e. investment, of accumulated funds will be determined by the market factors, such as the rate of return and the degrees of risk. In this case, governmental regulation centres around the protection of investors – employers and employees, or individuals. The government acts as the umpire of fair competition, regulates and punishes those who violate the rules. It intervenes to reduce potential costs of moral hazards for every investor. Thus, as a rule, the government does not regulate selectively; for instance, it does not control entry into a specific product market. In the absence of barriers to new entrants into the market, the emergence and growth of new pension markets lead to an increasing number of service providers and greater competition among financial institutions to attract these funds. In any case, once the money is invested via the capital market, it is very difficult for the government to control the flow of the money. Financial institutions capable of offering a wider range of portfolio and products will do better in the market for they can cater to a wider range of clients' (in this context, investors') needs.[13]

The next four categories are all cases in which the government steps in to control the flow of capital either by selecting *who* manages the funds or by targeting *where* the money goes.

Fund management by the government

The government exercises control over the flow of welfare funds by putting them directly under the control of the state. Funds are invested into the economy by public banks and public corporations or invested in public bonds to finance the government. The social security system in the United States, the Japanese Public Pension and other public income maintenance products (e.g. Postal Life Insurance, Postal Pension Plan, etc.) are examples of programmes in this category (Anderson 1990; Calder 1990; Patashnik 1995). The French Caisse de Depots is a corollary of this group.

Fund management by corporations (employers)

The government can directly siphon the funds to corporations by allowing corporations to administer their own corporate pension and retirement plans. This facilitates corporate access to cheap capital without being subject to pressures from outside shareholders. When used to shield corporate managers from the short-term profit-oriented demands of shareholders, these programmes can serve the interest of employees by stabilising employment. In this case, corporate programmes may take the form of book reserve or independent funds. The accumulated pension funds thereby become part of the capital available to the firm for further investment. German corporate book reserve pension funds are an example (Edwards and Fischer 1994; Hauck 1994).

Fund management by designated financial institutions

A government can design welfare programmes, such as public or corporate pensions, that are exclusively managed by designated financial institutions, and it can even set the terms of contract between financial institutions and specific funds. This scenario creates very attractive rents for those financial institutions allowed to handle and manage the funds. The government gains significant leverage *vis-à-vis* the financial sector, since business opportunities for these institutions depend upon government policies that influence, for example, the size of the potential 'captive market' as well as the content of products and services. In other words, a significant portion of corporate profits depends upon public policy. This category may even be termed an illiberal option in contrast to the very liberal first category. The Japanese Tax Qualified Corporate Pension and Employee Pension Funds – the contracted-out portion of the National Employee Pension Programme – fall into this category.[14]

Fund management by the insured (labour)

This is an arrangement whereby the insured have a say about how their contributions are invested. Programmes in this category include labour-managed pension plans and mutual assistance associations. Contributory social insurance programmes, in which the representatives of the insured – labour representatives – take part in fund management decisions, also belong in this category. The Swedish ATP (National Supplement Pension Scheme) is an example of such an arrangement.

The five categories of welfare design confirm that there are significant differences across welfare regimes that have not been exhausted. These differences, in turn, generate important political and economic implications. The following section will discuss the situation in Japan.

Pension mix and the finance nexus in Japan

In order to understand the origin of the post-war finance nexus in Japan, we need to go back to the early post-war period. The 1950s and 1960s saw the creation of the basic characteristics of the financial market and relations between business and capital providers. Key pension programmes were created during the same period. In many ways, the design of funded welfare programmes shaped and was shaped by prevailing financial relations at the time. Different sectors of the financial industry, corporations and government were all parties to the political and economic negotiations that occurred during this period.[15] The arrangements institutionalised during this period have persisted intact until recently, thereby constituting crucial components of the renowned Japanese model of capitalism.

This section demonstrates how welfare funds were employed to create a bank-based system rather than an equity-based system like the one that developed in the United States. In Japan, welfare funds both in governmental and private accounts were siphoned into the banking sector at critical junctures. Furthermore, welfare funds in the private sector enabled a significant volume of shares to be concentrated in the hands of just a few financial institutions (life insurance companies and trust banks). Since those shares were heavily regulated and protected, it was pointless for the companies that owned the pension funds to get involved in monitoring them. The absence of monitoring enabled financial institutions to use welfare funds – including individual pension plans – as they saw fit. Since the owners of pension funds did not exercise their demands as 'principals', the 'agents' (life insurance companies and trust banks) had little incentive to be aggressive about their investments. Thus, welfare funds became the source of patient capital for life insurance companies and trust banks, which were by law put in charge of private pension fund management. These financial institutions also became shareholders of large corporations and major city and local banks in Japan, thereby becoming patient shareholders themselves. This linkage is critical in understanding the main bank system and mutual corporate shareholding, features that shape the Japanese finance nexus between the firm and the capital provider.

Need for capital accumulation and welfare funds

The post-war period in Japan did not begin ex nihilo. The government, the corporate sector and the financial sector all had specific pre-existing preferences. The economy faced a grave shortage of capital in the 1940s, 1950s and 1960s. The US Occupation Government originally restricted the role of the Japanese government in finance, as a way of creating an equity-based financial market there. But the stock market crash in 1949 aborted the American plan (Miyawaki 1995: 30). The US Occupation Government rescinded the restrictions they had imposed on the Savings Bureau (later reorganised to become the Trust Fund Bureau) in the Ministry of Finance (MOF). As a result, the Bureau began directing money into the banking sector to alleviate a capital shortage in the private sector.[16]

Furthermore, in the 1950s, various public financial corporations were founded to provide yet another way of channelling funds into the private sector (Miyawaki 1995: 31). These included the Japan Development Bank (JDB) and the Japan Export and Import Bank. Loans by the JDB amounted to 17 per cent of loans by the entire banking sector in 1955. As several authors have pointed out, the JDB funded various large-scale projects together with groups of private banks. The participation of JDB as a capital supplier in addition to the private long-term credit banks such as the Industrial Bank of Japan (IBJ) thus reduced significantly the risk and cost of prior project evaluation. This, in turn, enabled the smooth supply of capital from the private financial sector into the industrial sector, which might have been delayed had it not been for the mechanism to channel money under state control into the banking sector.[17] These policies benefited the banking sector because they established a credit-based system and helped banks finance industry at a discounted risk.

Welfare funds played a role in this process. During the 1950s and the 1960s, private and public welfare funds became vehicles for the government's capital accumulation policy (see Anderson 1990; Calder 1990; Shinkawa and Pempel 1996). In the absence of well-developed social insurance programmes in the 1950s, Postal Life Insurance, Postal Pension and Postal Savings Programmes were among the few options citizens had to secure income for their old age. These programmes raised capital for the government. As part of the social insurance plans, an Employees' Pension Programme – introduced during the war – and a comprehensive National Pension Programme (1960), both of which were contributory, were established.[18] The pension programmes supplemented the postal programmes and further accumulated money. Employees' Pension Programmes, as Fig. 9.1 shows, have been particularly important sources of funds. All public welfare funds were then placed in the Trust Fund Bureau of the Ministry of Finance, which managed these funds, investing them in economic and public enterprises through the Fiscal Investments and Loan Programmes (hereafter, FILP) of the Trust Fund Bureau.

The government also promoted the private side of the pension mix. The growth of the life insurance industry, for instance, was systematically promoted by public policy. The government privileged the industry as a semi-public one because of the nature of its products, which complemented social security programmes: life insurance products offered means to maintain one's old age income and income for survivors (Asahi Seimei Sogo Kikakubu 1986: 47). The introduction of various preferential tax treatments in the 1950s and early 1960s stimulated the growth of the life insurance market (Usami 1984: 268).

The government also created 'captive' markets for favoured financial institutions. It licensed life insurance companies in 1947 to sell group insurance plans to corporations to cover their employees. It introduced the Tax Qualified Corporate

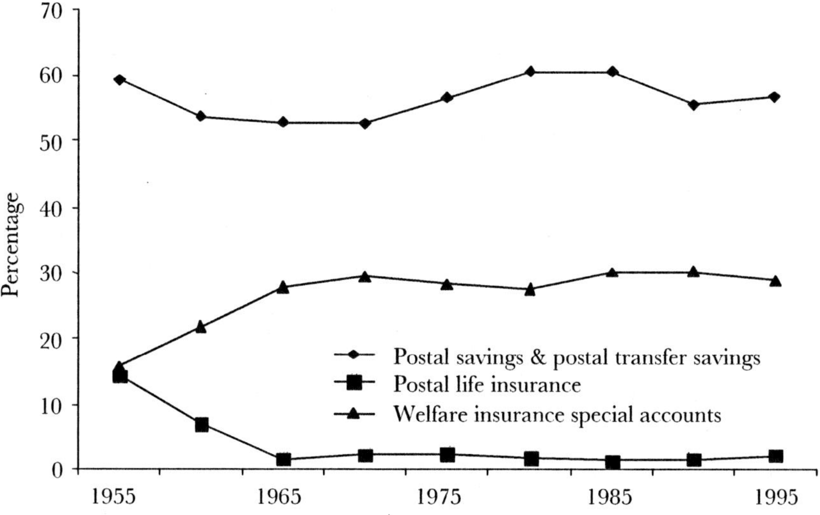

Figure 9.1 Japanese welfare funds deposits in per cent of the fiscal investment and loan programme.

Pension Plans in 1962 and the Employee Pension Fund in 1966, which only life insurance and trust banks were licensed to handle. As a result, the industry grew steadily throughout the 1960s, giving Japan one of the largest life insurance businesses in the world. Furthermore, the Ministry of Finance restricted new entries to the trade and thereby kept the number of life insurance companies constant until the 1990s. The life insurance industry was guaranteed a market with promising growth potential. In exchange, however, the government often requested the industry to cooperate with governmental investment priorities.[19]

Life insurance companies were very important suppliers of the long-term credit needed by the economy. In the 1950s, the life insurance companies lent large amounts of capital to corporations in core industries and worked closely with the Bank of Japan (BJ). Indeed, a section in the BJ coordinated life insurance loan syndicates to fulfil capital demands not met by banks (Yamanaka 1982: 27). The government also instructed life insurance companies to provide loans to the four core sectors – electricity, steel, maritime and coal (Yamanaka 1982: 30). In 1961, about 39 per cent of the overall funding was managed as loans to industry (Komiya 1994: 464). In the 1960s, the government began requesting the life insurance sector to increase its public investment, which it did from 1963 onwards. In 1964, public investments represented 8 per cent of life insurance assets. In the same year, more than 30 per cent of all the loans made by life insurance companies were concentrated in the aforementioned four sectors. The government not only requested the life insurance industry to invest in the core industries, but also to cooperate in funding the activities of the Japan Housing Public Corporation (Nihon Jutaku Kodan) (Usami 1984: 346–7). The life insurance industry responded positively by loaning large sums to this public corporation. As a consequence of this cooperation between the industry and the government, more than 40 per cent of loans made by the life insurance industry as a whole were prompted by various governmental requests (Usami 1984: 347–8; Seimei Hoken Kyokai (1973) contains records of numerous instances of cooperation between the government and the life insurance industry).

In the relative absence of national industries and any strong extractive taxation capacity in the state, the Ministry of Finance relied on its control over the financial market to direct capital to sectors it considered to be vital for economic growth. The MOF even had two budgets in addition to the general budget: the FILP as the 'second budget', and pension funds in life insurance and trust banks as the 'third budget'. As the allocation of FILP resources did not require Diet approval, funds in the FILP – not to mention the 'third budget' – provided a very important source of political capital for the Ministry of Finance.[20] In sum, welfare funds served to expand the financial means of the government well beyond its tax capacity.

The creation of patient capital

Although most governments regulate corporate pension programmes, the extent of regulation over pension management in Japan was pervasive. The government restricted the range of financial institutions that were allowed to participate in the pension market, imposed restrictive instructions on the content of investments (known as the '5.3.3.2 Rule'), and even set the expected rate-of-return by law at 5.5 per cent. This rate, which was set when the Employee Pension Fund was introduced in 1964, remained unchanged until 1996.[21] Moreover, life insurance companies were not required to create separate accounts for each of the corporate funds they were managing, making it difficult for corporate clients to evaluate the performance of their own funds. Neither were fund-managing institutions required to disclose the current value of assets they possessed, and the accounting was based on the value at purchase (Murakami 1996; Okumura 1996). Thus the regulatory framework, instead of making financial institutions more accountable, had precisely the reverse effect. As a consequence, regulations did not strengthen the position of investors but merely shielded financial institutions from monitoring by investors. This, more than anything else, contributed to the patient character of the welfare funds managed by private financial institutions.

In relation to the model of capitalism, the large volume of patient capital in these two sectors proved crucial in making banks more autonomous *vis-à-vis* their shareholders. The 1960s were a critical period for Japan's corporate finance sector. Japan was to embark on the first phase of financial liberalisation in the mid-1960s, and Japanese corporations feared takeovers by foreign capital (Ministry of Finance 1991: 682–4; Kasahara 1968: 385–6). Financial strengthening of domestic banks was necessary to prevent such a wave of takeovers. Japanese life insurance companies expanded their ownership of banking shares during the first phase of financial liberalisation in the mid-1960s and thus became some of the largest shareholders of city banks and major local banks (Yamanaka 1982: 43–4; Kasahara 1968: 390–1; see Table 9.1).[22] As a consequence, city banks managed to consolidate the ownership of their shares into the hands of *keiretsu* member corporations and life insurance companies (for more on *keiretsu*, a Japanese term for a conglomeration of businesses linked together by cross-shareholdings, see Gerlach 1992). In most cases, life insurance companies and trust banks are by now the largest shareholders for large banks in Japan. Therefore, the banks – critical providers of short-term capital – are themselves owned by large institutional stockholders who do not press for short-term profits, enabling the banks to concentrate as well on creating patient capital.

Patient welfare funds were also critical for non-banking corporations. As Table 9.2 shows, this was the period when life insurance companies increased their investments, thereby becoming large shareholders and helping Japanese business consolidate mutual corporate shareholding.

Group Life Insurance plans, the Tax Qualified Pension and the Employee Pension Funds laid the groundwork for stable shareholding by life insurance companies by creating a close, barter-and-exchange business relationship between client firms and life insurance companies (Nihon Hokengyoushi Hensankai 1968b: 293). According to Hiroshi Yamanaka, president of Meiji Life Insurance, corporate clients would contract life insurance companies to manage their pension programmes or would purchase group insurance programmes, and in exchange would ask life insurance companies to invest in their stock (Yamanaka 1982: 36).[23]

Table 9.1 Bank shares held by Japanese life insurance and mutual holding companies (in per cent)

	1964	*1965*	*1966*	*1967*
Mitsui Bank				
Mitsui Life Insurance	10.0	10.6	11.3	11.3
Mutual holdings	31.2	31.9	31.8	32.3
Mitsubishi Bank				
Meiji Life Insurance	17.0	16.8	19.4	18.7
Mutual holdings	27.9	28.8	28.6	30.3
Sumitomo Bank				
Sumitomo Life Insurance	5.8	5.5	6.3	8.8
Mutual holdings	34.6	36.1	35.9	38.4
Fuji Bank				
Yasuda Life Insurance	0.0	9.5	10.2	10.5
Mutual holdings	20.9	23.9	22.3	22.5
Dai-ichi Bank				
Asahi Life Insurance	6.6	7.4	12.0	10.7
Mutual holdings	27.3	24.3	24.5	17.2
Sanwa Bank				
Daido Life Insurance	0.0	5.9	6.5	7.6
Mutual holdings	22.5	23.8	24.0	24.9

Sources: Keizai Chosa Kyokai, annuals (1965, 1966, 1967, 1968).

Table 9.2 Life insurance companies as shareholders: The cases of Toyota and Nissan

	Shareholdings		*Increase in shares from previous year*	
	(in thousands)	*(in % of total)*	*(in thousands)*	*(in % of total)*
Total Toyota stocks[a]	*765,000*			
All insurance companies	84,900	11.1	28,170	33.2
Nippon Life Insurance	21,500	2.8	1,200	5.6
Daiwa Bank	19,110	2.5	2,270	11.9
Dai-ichi Life Insurance	13,000	1.7	6,400	49.2
Meiji Life Insurance	10,000	1.3	10,000	100.0
Asahi Life Insurance	10,000	1.3	4,000	40.0
Mitsui Trust Bank	12,210	1.6	640	5.2
Total Nissan stocks[b]	*796,000*			
All insurance companies	91,110	11.9	16,220	17.8
Industry Bank of Japan	43,230	5.7	6,280	14.5
Nippon Life Insurance	22,750	3.0	1,300	5.7
Dai-ichi Life Insurance	22,540	2.9	7,540	33.5
Yasuda Trust Bank	19,840	2.6	2,950	14.9
Toyo Trust Bank	16,360	2.1	3,020	18.5
Yasuda Life Insurance	7,000	0.9	1,380	19.7
Asahi Life Insurance	6,500	0.8	2,600	40.0

Source: Compiled from data in Kasahara (1968: 533) by the author.

Notes

a November 1966.

b September 1966.

From 1955 to the 1960s, the importance of shareholding by life insurance companies rose significantly. To understand the impact of the scope of shareholding by life insurance companies, however, one needs to look beyond the aggregate numbers. Although the position of the life insurance industry in the overall financial market might appear small in Table 9.3, one needs to take the size of each firm into consideration.

In contrast to the United States and European countries, where the numbers of life insurance companies total more than 2,000 and 100, respectively, in Japan the number has been kept around twenty for most of the post-war period. In the late 1980s, twenty-five life insurance companies came to hold 12.8 per cent of the stock of the major corporations. Although the figure is smaller than the total stockholdings by the banking sector (22.2 per cent), the size of the holdings of each life insurance company becomes significant when the small number of companies in this business sector is taken into consideration (Komiya 1994: 365). Moreover, the three largest life insurance companies own half the shares on the market.[24] For instance, Nihon Seimei, the largest life insurance company in Japan, is the largest stockholder of more than 100 of the largest corporations in Japan (Komiya 1994: 380–1). Even medium-sized life insurance companies are usually the largest – or at least among the top ten largest – stockholders of a significant number of large corporations (Komiya 1994: 365–6).

As a result, the post-war shift of emphasis from individual shareholders to institutional shareholders was accelerated in the mid-1960s (Ministry of Finance

Table 9.3 Relative size of shareholding by sector (in per cent)

	1961	*1966*	*1971*	*1976*	*1981*	*1986*
Financial institutions						
Banks and trust	8.9	10.9	15.1	16.8	17.3	20.5
Investment trust	9.9	4.3	1.3	1.4	1.3	1.8
Pension funds	—	—	—	—	0.4	0.9
Life insurance	7.2	10.9	11.3	11.8	12.6	13.3
Non-life insurance	3.5	3.5	4.4	4.7	4.9	4.4
Securities financial companies	0.3	0.4	0.9	0.7	2.2	2.6
Others	—	—	1.0	1.0	—	—
Total	30.0	29.8	33.9	36.5	38.7	43.5
Securities companies	2.8	5.4	1.5	1.4	1.7	2.5
Non-financial corporations	18.7	18.6	23.6	26.5	26.3	24.5
Individuals and others	46.7	44.1	37.2	32.9	28.5	23.9
Government	0.2	0.3	0.3	0.2	0.2	0.9
Foreigners	1.7	1.8	3.6	2.6	4.7	4.8

Sources: Compiled from data in *Nikko Securities*, annuals, by the author.

1991: 683). Table 9.4 illustrates how Japan developed a distinctive pattern of shareholding in which the insurance companies played an important role as institutional investors.

Life insurance companies are, in short, large owners of Japanese corporations. Since most Japanese life insurance companies are mutual companies, they themselves are not owned by shareholders, but rather by their policy holders. This feature has proved critical in making life insurance companies desirable partners from the perspective of corporate managers trying to secure bases for stable shareholding. Two reasons account for this. First, other financial institutions and corporations were expensive shareholders compared with life insurance companies because they would normally request investment in their own shares in exchange. Life insurance companies were largely exceptions to the rule since most were mutual companies and had no shareholders to worry about. Because they did not press other corporations to buy their own shares in exchange for being stable shareholders, life insurance companies came to be much cheaper allies for firms trying to consolidate corporate shareholding. Second, life insurance companies did not exploit their position as dominant shareholders to influence the actual management of other corporations and chose instead to remain silent partners (Komiya 1994; Hashimoto and Takeda 1992). The patience and silence of life insurance companies was enhanced by the fact that these companies owned shares in firms that were their own policy holders.

In sum, the particular designs of pension funds and the government regulation of these funds contributed to the consolidation of a bank-based financing system and stable stockholding patterns. Shareholding by the life insurance industry was not only pivotal in strengthening the stability of mutual shareholding, but was also directly involved in supporting the long-time horizon of Japanese banks (Kasahara 1968: 381–575). Life insurance companies and trust banks became the largest shareholders of Japanese banks and strengthened the bank management's position *vis-à-vis* 'outside' shareholders.[25] The role of life insurance companies and trust banks as silent shareholders of major corporations also strengthened banks' position *vis-à-vis* the corporations. Life insurance companies and trust banks, by remaining silent, delegated their monitoring role to main banks.

Financial institutions, corporations, governments and welfare funds

A look at the struggle over the control of corporate pensions provides a useful insight into the nature of politics between financial institutions, corporations and the government. Throughout the earlier post-war period – until the government finally introduced the contract-out option in the Employee Pension Programme – corporations and their employees complained about the exclusive use of their pension funds by the government.[26] They objected to the pooling of their money by the Employee Pension Programme. They argued that the government should not absorb so much capital from the private sector even in the name of welfare, and that the Trust Fund Bureau should not manage funds. From the late 1950s,

Table 9.4 Patterns of stockholding in Germany, Japan and the United States (in per cent)

	Germany				*Japan*				*United States*		
	1970	*1980*	*1990*		*1970*	*1980*	*1990*		*1970*	*1980*	*1990*
Individuals	28	19	17	Individuals	39.9	29.2	23.1	Individuals	79.4	70.8	54.4
Public sector	11	10	5	Public sector	0.3	0.2	0.6				
Private corporate sector	41	45	42	Private corporate sector	23.1	26.0	25.2				
				Financial institutions	30.9	37.3	41.6				
Banking	7	9	10	Banks/ trust banks	—	17.7	22.5	Banks	0.6	0.5	0.5
Insurance/ pension funds	4	6	12	Insurance companies	—	17.4	17.3	Insurance companies	3.2	5.0	5.5
				Others	—	2.2	1.8	Pension funds	9.0	17.0	26.5
				Investment trust	1.4	1.5	3.6	Mutual funds	4.6	2.7	6.6
				Brokerage firms	1.2	1.7	1.7				
Foreigners	8	11	14	Foreigners	3.2	4.0	4.2	Foreigners	3.2	4.0	6.4
Total	100	100	100	Total	100	100	100	Total	100	100	100

Source: Takahashi (1995).

large corporations demanded a third-tier corporate pension and tax concessions to support corporate pensions. They eventually called for a contract-out option with the intention of having more control over the overall cost of post-retirement income for their employees. The government conceded to the contract-out option while retaining its influence over the funds. Corporations thus were not allowed to manage the funds themselves as they had initially hoped. The financial sector – life insurance and trust banks – had also been lobbying the government for such an option. The government designed both the Tax Qualified Pension and the contracted-out Employee Pension Fund to be managed by trust banks and life insurance companies. Employers and employees gained little in terms of control over fund management, even after the introduction of the contract-out option. Moreover, the government continued to regulate the funds in the contracted-out segment.

The upshot of all this is that corporations in Japan have less control over the pension funds than their German and American counterparts. In Germany, large corporations manage the corporate pension funds internally. In the United States, the government monopolises the control of Social Security Funds. But as far as corporate and individual pensions are concerned, the government refrains from interfering with the flow of money. Instead, the government provides investor protection in the form of the 'prudent-man rule' or the Employee Retirement Income Security Act (ERISA).

To what extent did Japanese post-war welfare fund arrangements benefit the corporate sector? Why did corporations permit their money to be used by a few financial institutions? As I explained earlier, government regulation did not allow corporations to 'voice' their preferences over the investment of their pension plans. Furthermore, since life insurance companies and trust banks competed among themselves, they were willing to purchase shares (what they call 'sales-related investments') and make loans to keep their clients content. Although the internal management of their own pension funds would have been a simpler solution, corporations did benefit from their close relationships with these financial institutions during the period of capital shortage.

Corporations in the 1950s and the 1960s were not very concerned with any potential pension liabilities in the future. Throughout the business world, employees were young on the whole, which meant that corporate pension plans did not face a large number of pensioners entitled to full benefits. Until 1996, the Japanese government legally mandated that corporate pension programmes generate 5.5 per cent return. Since this was not a difficult target to hit in those days, corporate managers simply relied on governmental regulation and their fund managers. They simply did not worry about corporate pensions, despite the fact that the defined benefit design of corporate pension programmes contained potential problems that would actually lead to trouble in the 1990s.

As far as corporate managers were concerned, pensions programmes were something that the fringe benefit department of the corporation could take care of. From their perspective, it was good enough that they had gained access to the funds via life insurance and trust banks. In other words, corporate leaders could ignore the issue since it did not affect the annual corporate balance sheets. Moreover, in those days, corporate welfare issues were more important from the point of view of labour management. Corporations were more concerned about the design of welfare programmes that affected labour incentives.[27]

Corporations and financial institutions developed mutual interests, as the former needed 'friendly capital' and the latter required clients. In exchange for long-term capital, financial institutions gained long-term clients. For instance, banks became main banks and took care of corporate accounts and coordinated loans. Insurance companies expected corporations to be their customers. Such long-term mutual commitments helped financial institutions build secure bases of clientele, even in years when there was an excess of capital. For corporations, welfare funds in life insurance and trust bank sectors helped finance stable mutual corporate shareholding: first, by becoming the largest shareholders themselves and, second, by becoming the largest shareholders of major banks, which, in turn, became large key shareholders and major lenders (i.e. main banks) to corporations. The expansion of corporate-based housing plans, pensions and survivor's plans further strengthened the ties between firms and life insurance companies/trust banks. The welfare funds thus shielded Japanese firms and banks from pressure by investors and from the chances for hostile takeovers.

Comparative implications

A case study of Japan demonstrates how the design of a pension mix matters greatly in creating and consolidating a brand of capitalism, in which the long-term finance nexus has been critical. It also helps us see that political struggles and alliances over welfare programmes do not solely involve labour, employers, and leftist and conservative parties. Alliances between capital and labour and between corporations and financial institutions matter considerably. State involvement as a facilitator of firm–capital cooperation also plays a crucial role.

The finance-mediated welfare–capitalism nexus is not unique to Japan. The Swedes designed ATP funds in order to stimulate industrial investment. Even in the United States, social security funds are used to finance the government's budget so as to maintain a liberal tax policy and a low level of taxation. Private pension plans in the United States (e.g. Individual Retirement Accounts and 401k Employee Pension Funds) have been designed to increase savings and to stimulate investment. Yet while the US government encourages private plans without controlling the flow of welfare funds in the private sector, in Japan, public policy influences the flow of welfare funds (even in private welfare programmes) and shields these funds from market forces.

A large volume of welfare funds can stimulate the capital market, finance fiscal deficits and/or stabilise stockholding. Hence, the welfare–finance nexus described here helps identify an important area of welfare–capitalism linkage beyond the case study of Japan. Some countries have designed their pension programmes in a fund-pooling manner, while others have not. Welfare arrangements that create large volumes of welfare funds make the welfare state an important source of capital. These funds – themselves shaped by strategic interactions among political and economic actors – not only change the volume of capital available for the economy, but also affect the economic relationship among corporations, financial institutions and government. More importantly, these funds shape corporate governance and corporate behaviour either by enhancing patience or encouraging short-sightedness.

Some models of capitalism are known for the long-term nature of key economic relations (i.e. the employment relations between employees and employers, and the financial relations between corporations and suppliers of capital). Germany and Japan are both representative cases of this category of long-term models of capitalism, in contrast to the United Kingdom and the United States, where there are no key long-term relations. German and Japanese corporations operate within an institutional environment very different from what their British and American counterparts face. The welfare–finance nexus described in this chapter constitutes part of the institutional environment that produces cross-national differences of corporate behaviour. Pension programmes in Germany and Japan share a common feature when compared with the United Kingdom and the United States: they are designed *not to* stimulate short-term transactions in the stock market. Welfare funds are generally protected – by design – from market forces. Of course, the German and Japanese pension mixes are not identical. The German social insurance schemes for pensions are pay-as-you-go programmes and hence do not accumulate capital. In contrast, the Japanese social insurance schemes are partially funded. Nonetheless, the corporate pension programmes in Germany and Japan are similar in the sense that the funds are used to stabilise corporate finance. In Germany, internal book reserve pension plans helped corporations accumulate capital and also become investors supporting other firms. This arrangement, while institutionally different, resembles the Japanese arrangement functionally (Edwards and Fischer 1994; Hauck 1994; Kubler 1994). Both Germany and Japan differ from the Anglo-American liberal welfare systems, which deliberately release welfare funds into the market.[28]

Similarly, the Swedish ATP funds provide another case of a non-liberal use of welfare funds (Esping-Andersen 1985; Pontusson 1984, 1992). Unions and employers in Sweden agreed to use the second-tier pensions to finance industrial investment as part of the full employment policy. It is true that the active labour market policy was more significant in Sweden's commitment to full employment. We cannot, however, ignore that the structure of the welfare–finance nexus in Sweden was also conducive to achieving the goal of full employment.

In sum, the study of the welfare–finance nexus possesses three theoretical and practical implications for comparative studies:

1 Welfare states constitute crucial pillars of political economies. The link between welfare programmes and the flow of capital improves our understanding of the institutional infrastructure that sustains some models of capitalism. The preceding paragraphs have shown that the welfare–finance nexus itself is not unique to Japan. What we need to explore is how different systems of welfare provision reinforce or inhibit competitive market forces in

the realm of corporate finance, and how they may support low levels of taxation in some countries.

2 An understanding of the existing welfare–finance link is particularly important in assessing the impact of the environmental changes (such as financial liberalisation, demographic ageing) that advanced industrial countries are going through today. It is important to note that the welfare–finance nexus that develops during one period may or may not survive demographic and economic changes. A system that has favoured capital accumulation may well outlive its shelf life (Estevez-Abe 1998). Without understanding the micro-level link between welfare funds and the key financial relations in a particular political economy, we cannot fully appreciate how vulnerable a specific model of capitalism – and welfare system – is to different kinds of socioeconomic changes.[29]

3 The ongoing debate concerning the future forms of public and private pension programmes both within the United States and elsewhere should take micro-level issues of corporate finance and their implications for the overall nature of capitalism more seriously. While the World Bank's recommendation for a three-tier pension mix focuses on macroeconomic implications of privatised second- and third-tier pension programmes (see World Bank 1994), the discussion concerning what type of capitalism public policy should encourage is missing from the debate. The findings in this chapter suggest that there is more to pension funds than merely increasing the national savings levels or the volume of capital invested in the capital market. Different ways in which the funds are used can affect public and corporate finance, enabling or preventing specific types of corporate behaviour.

Notes

1 For a concise review of economic issues concerning the relationship between social security and saving, see Davis (1995: chapter 1).

2 At 14.3 per cent and 22.2 per cent in 1965 and 1990, respectively, Japanese overall taxation levels, measured as the percentage of total taxation over GDP, have consistently been one of the lowest among OECD countries (OECD 1996: table 4).

3 I am aware of further variations within the 'liberal' camp. There are important differences between the US, the UK, and 'wage earner welfare states' in Australia and New Zealand as demonstrated by John Stephens, Francis Castles and others (Castles and Mitchell 1991; Huber and Stephens 1997). I have no intention of arguing that my framework should replace others or that it is exhaustive of all possible variations. Unlike some other criticisms of Esping-Andersen's taxonomy (Esping-Andersen 1990), I am not taking issue with his 'clusters' per se. It suffices to say here that I am interested in bringing to the fore a very important aspect of welfare arrangements that has been long overlooked in the welfare state literature. For a critical view of Esping-Andersen's cluster analysis, see Ragin (1994: 320–45).

4 By 'pension mix', I mean public pensions, corporate pension programmes, individual and other old age plans supported by public policy.

5 O'Higgins' insightful study (1986) of pension politics is one of the few studies that has considered financial actors to be participants of 'welfare politics'.

6 Zysman (1983) is one of the first people to note the important differences between equity-based systems and credit-based systems in shaping distinctive, political economic systems.

7 The government provides capital, too. Nonetheless, here I refer to non-governmental investors and creditors.
8 Importantly, banks in some regulatory environments are by law prohibited from directly investing in shares or offering brokerage services.
9 I distinguish owners/investors of corporations from their managers. Here, I am talking about managers.
10 The worst threat for corporate managers is a hostile takeover.
11 This takes us back to the old debate about the pro-capital nature of the modern state, which cannot be explored here (cf. Lindblom 1977; Block 1977).
12 Zysman (1983) distinguished between credit-based financial systems and broker-based systems. As his work has demonstrated, the state was an important actor in shaping these different financial systems.
13 Programmes such as the Individual Retirement Account or 401k Employee Pension Funds are good examples of welfare programmes of this category.
14 As I will discuss in greater detail later in this chapter, these two programmes are both designed as 'fund-pooling' programmes. The government designates which subsectors of financial institutions can offer fund-managing services. Thus, there is less room for choice for pension fund owners. Moreover, regardless of the needs of pension funds, the government restricts the content of investments.
15 Labour was not totally irrelevant. Nonetheless, in terms of pension politics, labour did not play a leading role in Japan. A more wide-ranging analysis in my dissertation includes labour among the actors (Estevez-Abe 1999).
16 In 1949, the Bureau began depositing some of its funds in private banks. It also started purchasing banking shares, which were issued by long-term credit banks such as the Industrial Bank of Japan (IBJ) and the Japan Long-Term Credit Bank. In 1950, the Bureau absorbed 38.5 per cent of newly issued banking bonds. The figure rose to 59.8 per cent in 1951. The Bureau bought 59.4 per cent of newly issued IBJ bonds in 1951, too. As a result, the percentage of banking bonds in the total of the funds managed by the Bureau rose from 7 per cent in 1950 to nearly 18 per cent in 1953 (Miyawaki 1995: 31; Ishikawa and Gyoten 1977: 43–4; Nihon Kogyo Ginko 1982: 222–4; Fukushima *et al.* 1973: 165).
17 Of course, there were other mechanisms at play such as the 'over-loan' to city banks by the Bank of Japan. I am arguing that welfare funds were the only sources or mechanisms used to channel capital into the banking and core industrial sectors.
18 Campbell (1992: chapter 3) provides a very detailed account of pension politics during the 1950s and the 1960s. While Campbell focuses more on politics over public pension benefits, I focus on the financial aspect of public and private pension programmes.
19 In the early 1990s, Japanese life insurance companies had assets of 175,700 billion yen, more than any other OECD country (Seimeihoken Bunka Senta 1993): American companies ranked second (71.2 per cent of Japanese assets), followed by French (13.9 per cent), German (8.3), British (8.0), Canadian (7.8), Korean (4.5), Dutch (3.8) and Australian life insurance companies (2.7 per cent).
20 The volume of the FILP relative to the general budget continued to grow during the post-war period: from around one-third of the budget in the 1950s, it rose to more than 45 per cent in the latter half of the 1960s. It is currently over 50 per cent of the general budget. These figures are based on State of Central and Local Public Finance data in Bank of Japan (ed.), Economic Statistical Annual.
21 Not only Employee Pension Funds but also all the other financial pension and income maintenance products were subject to various detailed regulations by the Ministry of Finance.
22 Life insurance companies are still prominent shareholders for financial institutions. Nenpo Keiretsu no Kenkyu annually publishes the list of the largest shareholders of publicly traded corporations.

23 Life insurance companies call this type of deal an 'Eigyou Toushi' (sales-related investment). This has been a very common practice even for the largest life insurance companies. The same happened with non-life insurance companies that sold products for corporate clients. There are reports that suggest that a large decrease in the shareholding of a particular client would translate to a reduction of sales to that particular corporation.
24 While there were many life insurance companies in the pre-war period, the number of life insurance companies in the post-war period has been kept small by the MOF's deliberate control over new entry into the trade. The new insurance law passed in 1995 liberalised the entry into the life insurance sector.
25 Since the case for trust banks is similar to that of life insurance companies, I have avoided going into detail about trust banks in this chapter.
26 The government, while allowing corporations to have a 100 per cent book reserve for a lump sum retirement payment in the immediate post-war period, retracted from that position in the 1950s.
27 For recent changes in corporate managers' approach to pension programmes, see Estevez-Abe (1998).
28 I do not mean that the governments in liberal welfare capitalism do not interfere with welfare funds. They do encourage the buildup of funds by tax policies and legally intervene to maintain a fair competitive environment (see Dobbin and Boychuk 1996).
29 In the context of Japan, the welfare–finance nexus that proved highly effective during the economic growth period may not necessarily continue to be effective in the era of financial liberalisation. The legacy of success may even be a hindrance in a new environment (Estevez-Abe 1998).

References

Anderson, S. (1990). 'The political economy of Japanese saving: How postal savings and public pension support high rates of household saving in Japan', *Journal of Japanese Studies* 15(1), 61–92.

Aoki, M. (1994). 'Main characteristics of the Main Bank System: An analytical and developmental view', in M. Aoki and H. Patrick (eds), *The Japanese Main Bank System*. Oxford: Oxford University Press, 109–41.

Aoki, M. and Dore, R. (eds) (1994). *The Japanese Firm: The Sources of Competitive Strength*. Oxford: Oxford University Press.

Asahi Seimei Sogo Kikakubu (ed.) (1986). *Seimei Hoken Saishin Jijo* (New Trends in Life Insurance Industry). Tokyo: Tokyo Keizai Shinpo.

Berger, S. and Dore, R. (eds) (1996). *National Diversity and Global Capitalism*. Ithaca: Cornell University Press.

Berglof, E. (1990). 'Capital structure as a mechanism of control: A comparison of financial systems', in M. Aoki, B. Gustafsson and O. E. Williamson (eds), *The Firm as a Nexus of Treaties*. London: Sage, 237–62.

Block, F. (1977). 'The ruling class does not rule', *Socialist Revolution* 7(3), 6–28.

Boyer, R. (1989). 'The transformation of modern capitalism: By the light of the regulation approach and other political economy theories', Paper presented at the Comparative Governance of Economics Sectors Conference, Bellagio, 29 May to 2 June, 1989.

Calder, K. (1990). 'Linking welfare and the developmental state: Postal savings in Japan', *Journal of Japanese Studies* 16(1), 31–59.

Campbell, J. C. (1992). *How Policies Change: The Japanese Government and the Ageing Society*. Princeton, NJ: Princeton University Press.

Castles, F. and Mitchell, D. (1991). 'Three worlds of welfare capitalism or four?', Discussion paper, the Australian National University (Canberra), Graduate Programme in Public Policy.

Crouch, C. and Streeck, W. (eds) (1997). *Political Economy of Modern Capitalism: Mapping Convergence and Diversity*. London: Sage.

Davis, E. P. (1995). *Pension Funds: Retirement-income Security and Capital Markets*. Oxford: Oxford University Press.

Dobbin, F. and Boychuk, T. (1996). 'Public policy and the rise of private pension: The US experience since 1930', in M. Shalev (ed.), *The Privatization of Social Policy*. New York: St. Martin's Press, 104–35.

Edwards, J. and Fischer, K. (1994). *Banks, Finance and Investment in Germany*. Cambridge: Cambridge University Press.

Esping-Andersen, G. (1985). *Politics Against Market: The Social Democratic Road to Power*. Princeton, NJ: Princeton University Press.

Esping-Andersen, G. (1990). *The Three Worlds of Welfare Capitalism*. Princeton, NJ: Princeton University Press.

Estevez-Abe, M. (1996). 'The welfare-growth nexus in the Japanese political economy', Paper presented at the Annual Meeting of the American Political Science Association, San Francisco.

Estevez-Abe, M. (1998). 'Challenges to the Japanese model of capitalism and its welfare state: Becoming more like the US?', Paper presented at the Annual Meeting of the American Political Science Association, Boston.

Estevez-Abe, M. (1999). 'Welfare and capitalism in postwar Japan', Ph.D. dissertation, Government Department, Harvard University.

Estevez-Abe, M., Iversen T. and Soskice, D. (1999). 'Social protection and skill formation', Paper presented at the Annual Meeting of the American Political Science Association, Atlanta, 1999.

Fukushima, R., Mitsuhide, Y. and Shuu, I. (1973). *Zaisei Toyushi* (Fiscal Investment and Loan Programme). Tokyo: Okura Zaimu Kyokai.

Gerlach, M. (1992). *Alliance Capitalism: The Social Organization of Japanese Business*. Berkeley: University of California Press.

Hall, P. A. (1986). *Governing the Economy: The Politics of State Intervention in Britain and France*. Oxford: Oxford University Press.

Hall, P. A. and Soskice, D. (eds) (forthcoming). *Varieties of Capitalism*. New York: Oxford University Press.

Hashimoto, J. and Takeda, H. (eds) (1992). *Nihon Keizai no Hatten to Kigyo Shudan* (The Development of Japanese Economy and Corporate Groupings). Tokyo: Tokyo University Press.

Hauck, M. (1994). 'The equity market in Germany and its dependency on the system of old age provisions', in T. Baums, R. Buxbaum and K. Hopt (eds), *Institutional Investors and Corporate Governance*. New York: de Gruyter, 555–64.

Hollingsworth, J. R. and Boyer, R. (eds) (1997). *Contemporary Capitalism: The Embeddedness of Institutions*. Cambridge: Cambridge University Press.

Huber, E. and Stephens, J. D. (1997). 'Welfare state and production regimes in the era of retrenchment', Paper presented at the Workshop 'The New Politics of Welfare', Harvard University, Center for European Studies, 5–7 December 1997.

Ishikawa, S. and Gyoten, T. (eds) (1977). *Zaisei Toyushi* (Fiscal Investment and Loan Programme). Tokyo: Kinyu Zaisei Jljo Kenkyukai.

Kasahara, N. (1968). 'Kinyu Shihon Keiretsu-ka no Sokushin to Hokenkaisha no Yakuwari' (The Role of Life Insurance Industry in the Formation of Financial Keiretsu), in Nihon Hokengyoushi Hensankai (ed.), *Nihon Hokengyoushi: Soron* (History of Japanese Insurance Industry). Tokyo: Hoken Kenkyujo, 381–575.

Keizai Chosa Kyokai (ed.) (1965). *Nenpo Keiretsu no Kenkyu*. Tokyo: Keizei Chosa Kyokai.

Keizai Chosa Kyokai (1966). *Nenpo Keiretsu no Kenkyu.* Tokyo: Keizei Chosa Kyokai.

Keizai Chosa Kyokai (1967). *Nenpo Keiretsu no Kenkyu.* Tokyo: Keizei Chosa Kyokai.

Keizai Chosa Kyokai (1968). *Nenpo Keiretsu no Kenkyu.* Tokyo: Keizei Chosa Kyokai.

Kitschelt, H., Lange, P., Marks, G. and Stephens, J. D. (1999). *Continuity and Change in Contemporary Capitalism.* Cambridge: Cambridge University Press.

Komiya, R. (1994). 'The life insurance company as a business enterprise', in K. Imai and R. Komiya (eds), *Business Enterprise in Japan: Views of Leading Japanese Economists.* Cambridge, MA: The MIT Press, 365–86. Originally published as Komiya, R. (1989) 'Kigyo toshiteno Seiho' (The life insurance company as a business enterprise), in K. Imai and R. Komiya (eds), *Nihon no Kigyo* (Business Enterprise in Japan). Tokyo: Tokyo University Press.

Kubler, F. (1994). 'Institutional investors and corporate governance: A German perspective', in T. Baums, R. Buxbaum and K. Hopt (eds), *Institutional Investors and Corporate Governance.* New York: de Gruyter, 565–79.

Lindblom, C. (1977). *Politics and Markets: The World's Political-Economic Systems.* New York: Basic Books.

Manow, P. (1997a). 'Cross-class alliances in welfare reform: A theoretical framework', Paper presented at the Workshop 'The New Politics of Welfare', Harvard University, Center for European Studies, 5–7 December 1997.

Manow, P. (1997b). 'Social insurance and the German political economy', MPIFG discussion paper 97/7, Cologne: Max Planck Institute for the Study of Societies.

Mares, I. (1997). 'Interwar responses to the problem of unemployment: A game-theoretic analysis', APSA Annual Meeting, Washington, DC, 28 August–1 September 1997.

Mayer, C. (1998). 'Financial systems and corporate governance: A review of the international evidence', *Journal of Institutional and Theoretical Economics* 154(1), 144–65.

Ministry of Finance (1991). *Showa Zaiseishi: 1952–1973.* Tokyo: Tokyo Keizai Shinposha, Vol. 10.

Miyawaki, A. (1995). *Zaisei Toyushi no Kaikaku* (Reforming the Fiscal Investment and Loan Programmes). Tokyo: Tokyo Keizai Shinposha.

Murakami, K. (1996). 'Teikinri to Kosei Nenkin Kikin' (Low interest rate and employees' pension funds), *Seimei Hoken Keiei* 64(3), 3–20.

Nihon Hokengyoushi Hensankai (ed.) (1968a). *Nihon Hokengyoushi: Soron* (History of Japanese Insurance Industry). Tokyo: Hoken Kenkyujo.

Nihon Hokengyoushi Hensankai (ed.) (1968b). *Nihon Seimei Hokengyoushi: Kaisha hen Gekan* (History of the Development of Life Insurance Industry in Japan). Tokyo: Hoken Kenkyujo.

Nihon Kogyo Ginko Nenshi Hensan Iinkai (ed.) (1982). *Nihon Kogyo Ginko 75 nenshi* (A 75 Year History of the Industrial Bank of Japan). Tokyo: Nihon Kogyo Ginko.

OECD (Organisation for Economic Co-operation and Development) (1996). *Revenue Statistics, 1965–1995.* Paris: OECD.

O'Higgins, M. (1986). 'Public/private interaction and pension provision', in M. Rein and L. Rainwater (eds), *Public/Private Interplay in Social Protection: A Comparative Study.* New York: M.E. Sharpe, 99–148.

Okumura, K. (1996). 'Kigyo nenkin wo meguru shomondai to shikin unyo kadai' ('On corporate pension and its asset management issues'), *Seimei Hoken Keiei* 64(6), 1177–92.

Patashnik, E. (1995). 'The growing importance of trust funds in federal budgeting', chapter delivered at the 1995 APSA conference, Chicago, 31 August–3 September 1995.

Pontusson, J. (1984). *Public Pension Funds and the Politics of Capital Formation in Sweden.* Stockholm: Arbetslivscentrum.

Pontusson, J. (1992). *The Limits of Social Democracy: Investment Politics in Sweden.* Ithaca, NY: Cornell University Press.

Ragin, C. C. (1994). 'A qualitative comparative analysis of pension systems' in T. Janoski and A. Hicks (eds), *The Comparative Political Economy of the Welfare State.* Cambridge: Cambridge University Press, 320–45.

Research Dept., Nikko Securities Co., Ltd, *Toushi Geppou.* Tokyo: Nikko Securities Co., Ltd, monthly.

Roe, M. (1994). *Strong Managers Weak Owners: The Political Roots of American Corporate Finance.* Princeton, NJ: Princeton University Press.

Seimeihoken Bunka Senta (1993). *Seimeihoken Fact Book.* Tokyo: Seimeihoken Bunka Senta.

Seimei Hoken Kyokai (ed.) (1973). *Showa Seimei Hoken Shiryo* (Insurance Documents from Showa-period). Tokyo: Seimei Hoken Kyokai, Vol. 6.

Shinkawa, T. and Pempel, T. J. (1996). 'Occupational welfare and the Japanese experience', in M. Shalev (ed.), *The Privatization of Social Policy?: Occupational Welfare and the Welfare State in America, Scandinavia and Japan.* New York: St. Martin's Press, 280–326.

Soskice, D. (1994). 'Advanced economies in open world markets and comparative institutional advantages: Patterns of business coordination, national institutional frameworks and company product market innovation strategies', unpublished paper.

Soskice, D. (1999). 'Divergent production regimes: Coordinated and uncoordinated market economies in the 1980s and 1990s', in H. Kitschelt, P. Lange, G. Marks and J. D. Stephens (eds), *Continuity and Change in Contemporary Capitalism.* Cambridge: Cambridge University Press.

Takahashi, T. (ed.) (1995). *Koporeto Gabanansu: Nihon to Doitsu no Kigyo Shusutemu* (Corporate Governance: Corporate Systems in Japan and Germany). Tokyo: Chuo Keizaisha.

Usami, N. (1984). *Seimei Hoken Hyakunenshiron* (One Hundred Years of Life Insurance Industry). Tokyo: Yuhikaku.

Wood, S. (1997). 'Choice and constraint in the fight against unemployment: Contemporary labour market policy in Sweden, Germany and Britain', Paper presented at the Workshop 'The New Politics of Welfare', Harvard University, Center for European Studies, 5–7 December 1997.

World Bank (1994). *Averting the Old Age Crisis: Policies to Protect the Old and Promote Growth.* Cambridge: Cambridge University Press.

Yamanaka, H. (1982). *Seiho Kinyu no Mado kara: Seiho Kinyu 50nen no Ayumi* (From the Window of Life Insurance Finance: A Fifty-year History). Tokyo: Sangyo Noritsu Daigaku.

Yuka-shouken Houkokusha. Tokyo: Ministry of Finance.

Zysman, J. (1983). *Government, Markets and Growth: Financial Systems and the Politics of Industrial Change.* Ithaca, NY: Cornell University Press.

Part IV

The political economy of welfare state reform

10 The experience of negotiated reforms in the Dutch and German welfare states[1]

Anton Hemerijck and Philip Manow

Contrasting success with failure

It is fair to say that the key to international acclaim of the Dutch model is its job miracle (Visser and Hemerijck 1997). Job growth has been at 1.6 per cent per year since 1983, which is four times higher than the European Union average. The Netherlands cut the unemployment rate from almost 14 per cent in 1983 to just over 3 per cent in 2000, far below the dismal 10 per cent average for the European Union. These are impressive figures indeed.

At the same time, the once highly acclaimed performance of the 'Modell Deutschland' has worsened substantially. German unemployment is high at around 9.7 per cent, job creation and overall employment is low. Due to a 'negative supply-side policy' (Claus Offe) that induces people to leave the labour force through various social policy measures, the ratio between welfare state contributors and recipients has become increasingly unfavourable (Esping-Andersen 1996b). Hence, even steady efforts to contain costs have not brought social insurance contributions significantly down (Schmidt 1998: 154; BMA 1998; Alber 1998a,b). On the contrary, the welfare costs imposed on labour have constantly increased in the recent past.

Generally, what has made the Dutch experience of negotiated social policy reform attractive is that it seems to prove that there is still considerable scope for welfare state reform without sacrificing values like social equality and social protection. Unlike the Dutch example, the German *Reformstau* (literally reform congestion) *vis-à-vis* high and persisting levels of unemployment seems to be the classic example of how the Continental model of social policy has reached a dead end in its ability to reduce the labour supply and maintain the 'family- or productive-wage' (Esping-Andersen 1996b; see Scharpf, Chapter 12 in this volume).

We admit that in making this Dutch–German comparison we are running the risk of being too close to time-bound perceptions of success and failure: the 'sick man of Europe' is celebrating his recovery without recognising that in many respects (e.g. employment rates) he has merely caught up with the OECD average. And the 'motherland of the economic miracle' is now suffering from a post-unification melancholy that may distract us from seeing that the German model is still alive and kicking, while the considerable decline in economic performance might be mainly attributable to the exceptional burdens of unification (Czada 1998). Considering the most recent developments in both countries, Germany's policy stalemate seems to have been – at least partially – overcome now that the government has enacted a major tax reform and is undertaking a profound pension reform, while the Dutch success story has run up against its first limitations in having produced de facto full employment with a residue of long-term unemployed who resist any attempt to bring them back from welfare to work. Yet, striking differences in the reform record and economic performance of both countries remain, and while unification certainly posed a massive external shock to the German model, the predominant response pattern of a radical reduction of labour supply (Manow and Seils 2000) conforms to the routine response of Continental welfare states to economic shocks. Moreover, Germany's employment dilemma began long before 1990, since the employment performance has been deteriorating continuously since the early 1970s (Siegel and Jochem 1999: 11–12). If Germany is now undergoing a crisis comparable to the Dutch one of the late 1970s and early 1980s, one might ask whether the lesson learnt from the Dutch experience, namely that the dilemma of 'welfare without work' is not inevitable for Continental welfare states, might not also apply to the German case.

What makes Germany and the Netherlands interesting cases for a comparative study? We would like to emphasise in particular the similarities between the welfare state regimes and the structures of economic governance in both countries. Both welfare states belong to the Continental regime type (Kersbergen 1995; Esping-Andersen 1996b, 1990; Castles and Mitchell 1993; Huber and Stephens 1999),[2] and both countries represent sectorally 'coordinated' market economies (cf. Soskice 1990; Kitschelt *et al.* 1999) with 'intermediate' collective bargaining systems (OECD 1994; Iversen 1998). The Netherlands and Germany are committed to open trade, and in both countries the disinflationary policy pursued by their respective central banks has hindered the governments to use Keynesian deficit spending or strategic currency depreciation to stimulate the economy. Collective wage bargaining predominantly takes place at the industry-sector level (OECD 1994: 175–7). The coverage of collective bargaining is high. Coordination between trade unions and employers' associations is considerable. Industrial conflict occurs rarely, yet if it takes place, then it is highly organised. Both German and Dutch industrial relations are deeply entrenched in a complex institutional framework in which their social security systems play a prominent, maybe even a predominant, role. Because social security is mainly financed out of payroll taxes, the interdependence between production and protection is particularly strong. Social policy belongs to a 'corporatist complex' in which the state cannot intervene autonomously, but is bound to a negotiated consensus with organised labour and capital.

Yet within the domains of industrial relations and social security, the German and Dutch central actors enjoy very different degrees of autonomy. Thus, the institutional context within which unions, employers and the government can choose and coordinate their strategies to overcome the 'welfare-without-work' dilemma is very different. We argue that this has important consequences for the fate of negotiated social policy reform in the two countries.

Due to the *tight coupling* between capitalist production and social protection, welfare reforms in Germany and the Netherlands have often tended to safeguard the particular interests of unions and employers and were dependent on the de facto consent of the 'social partners'. For capital and labour, the welfare state offers the valuable opportunity to externalise the costs of economic adjustment. Hence, the welfare state functions both as a 'productivity whip' – due to the considerable non-wage costs imposed on labour in the form of social insurance contributions – and as an 'inactivity trap' – due to the various pathways out of employment that the Continental welfare state so generously provides. Thus, the main problem in managing the production–protection interplay in both countries is the essentially political task of balancing between *productivity* and *inactivity*. Apparently, they have fared differently in this respect. In order to understand this difference, despite the striking similarities in the society-wide organisation of work and welfare, we have to take a look at the incentive structure established by the welfare state *cum* industrial relations system. We hold that an examination of these incentive structures will enable us to better assess the *prospects for* and *dynamics of* welfare reform in Germany and the Netherlands.

In the next section we will explain what we mean by the notion of *tightly coupled* welfare states. Thereafter we will identify the adjustment logic prevalent in Continental welfare states that gives rise to what we label the 'productivity–inactivity dilemma'. We will then describe in more detail the patterns of success and failure in reforming the systems in the Netherlands and Germany. We conclude with some general remarks on the institutional and political preconditions for successful social policy reform.

The predicament of social policy reform in 'tightly coupled' welfare states

Different welfare states face different problems of sustainability or vulnerability under conditions of greater international economic interdependence and endogenous social change (Scharpf 1998). More than ever, the level of social protection seems to depend on and to affect the competitive advantage of individual nations. The proficiency of social policy relies very heavily on the international competitiveness of the economy to generate jobs, wealth and a tax base to finance adequate standards of social protection. As increased economic interdependence is likely to intensify competition among countries in product and investment markets, for mobile taxable resources this may pose serious constraints on social policy at the national level (Garrett 1998). Economic internationalisation constrains the effectiveness of national macroeconomic management and national labour market policies. Together with technological change, the internationalisation of product markets has reduced the demand for unskilled labour in the advanced political economies. As a result, long-term unemployment and rising poverty is concentrated among those who lack effective educational standards. Increased capital mobility critically reduces the capacity of national governments to tax capital assets and incomes (Genschel 2000). With the internationalisation of firms and the proliferation of exit options for employers, national systems of industrial relations come under pressure to adapt. In short, economic internationalisation impacts four key – interrelated – social and economic policy areas: macroeconomic policy, industrial relations, social security and labour market policy (Hemerijck 1998).

From nation to nation, the four policy areas are governed according to very different rules of policy making within very different institutional settings. Drawing on insights from organisational theory, we distinguish between the 'loose' and 'tight' coupling of policy areas (Weick 1976; Freeman 1995; Hemerijck 1998). Loose coupling stems from the 'mutual indifference' among policy domains, while 'tightly coupled' systems entertain strong interdependencies between different policy areas. Loose coupling allows for incremental, flexible, decentralised adjustments to environmental pressures. *Many* agents flexibly adapt to a changed environment via 'local maximisation'. In tightly coupled systems, only a *few* agents have to try to maximise globally, while the higher costs involved in achieving such global coordination correspond to the higher costs should coordination fail. Loose coupling displays a trade-off between the positive effect of flexible local adjustment and the negative effect of a lack of a global management of change. Moreover, loose coupling may engender processes of differentiation between policy domains, leading to sectoral fragmentation.

Policy change follows highly 'path-dependent' trajectories in tightly coupled political systems. Change is likely to proceed – if at all – in a sequential-diachronic rather than in a parallel-synchronic manner (Hemerijck and Kersbergen 1998). If not coordinated, efficiency gains attained in one area may incur severe efficiency losses elsewhere. Often these dire consequences make politicians simply shy away from any major tinkering with the status quo. Another risk-averse strategy is the 'negative coordination' between policy domains, in which only those changes will be made that are not likely to negatively affect other policy domains (Scharpf 1997). Change thus proceeds slowly, if at all. If policies are tightly coupled, the mode of managing the policy interdependencies is crucial: are interdependencies managed overtly and consciously, or coordinated covertly and negatively? It is our contention that herein lies the critical difference between our two cases.

How exactly are production and protection coupled in the Dutch and German political economies? We will briefly address this question in the next section.

The vicious and virtuous cycles in Continental welfare states

The Continental welfare state comes very close to what Titmuss has called the industrial achievement–performance model of social policy (Titmuss 1974). The strict adherence to the insurance principle means that entitlements closely follow the income distribution generated by the market. This means that the welfare state puts a premium on steady working careers, that it benefits workers with relatively high skills and thus high incomes, and that it discriminates against part-time work and consequently against the participation of women in the labour market.

Take the case of pensions. If pension entitlements are based strictly on the length and level of previous contributions, employees are unwilling to engage in part-time work and try to avoid short-term labour contracts. Hence, specific welfare state regulations support full-time, life-long employment – the so-called 'standard employment relationship'. Yet, the norm of the 'standard worker family' (Esping-Andersen 1996b: 76), in which a male breadwinner earns a 'family wage', increasingly hinders significant job creation in the service sector and the proliferation of more flexible employment patterns.

The main beneficiary of the Continental welfare state has been the skilled male worker in the manufacturing sector – not to mention special occupational groups like civil servants, miners and farmers, who often enjoy special privileges in separate schemes. Since pensions are designed to preserve one's standard of living during retirement, Continental welfare states often do not allow for a gradual transition from work into retirement. Given the strict adherence to the insurance principle and generous early retirement schemes, employers have no interest in creating part-time jobs to allow for a slower passage to retirement, nor do unions have an interest to push for the creation of those jobs. Early retirement has been quite generous in order to help adjust and increase the flexibility of the labour market within economies that put a strong emphasis on stable career paths, long-time engagements, mutual trust, the protection of acquired skills, etc. For instance, in both Germany and the Netherlands, disability was defined as a 'social risk', namely as a worker's particular incapacity to find a (part-time) job matching his or her qualifications. Early retirement is particularly attractive for employers who seek to downsize their workforce without stirring up major unrest within the firm. It has been extensively used in economic downturns, but is generally attractive to employers since it fosters wage flexibilisation if wages follow seniority. Moreover, early retirement may improve a workforce's skill level, since firms can substitute older with younger workers who have been trained in the most advanced technologies.

A stylised account of the interplay between a high-wage production regime and the Continental welfare state would highlight the following pattern: under increased competitive pressure, firms in high-wage economies like the Dutch and German can only survive by increasing labour productivity. This is most commonly achieved by offering high-quality vocational training, making labour-saving investments, and laying off less productive or 'too expensive', that is usually older, workers. These strategies are costly and drive up taxes and payroll contributions to social security. An increase of non-wage labour costs prompts a reassessment of the remaining workforce in terms of its level of productivity, which most often leads to another round of dismissals. In this way, a virtuous cycle of productivity growth could turn into a vicious cycle of high-wage costs, an exit of less productive workers, and an increase in social security contributions, which in turn would require further productivity increases in competitive firms, elicit yet another round of reductions in the workforce, and so on. The economy finds itself in a pathological spiral of 'welfare without work'. Jobs disappear in sectors where productivity gains stagnate and where the prices of goods and services cannot be easily raised. Moreover, high non-labour costs may frustrate job growth in the labour-intensive public and private services sectors, especially at the low-productivity end of the labour market. This creates a new class of non-employed, low-skilled, permanently inactive, welfare-dependent citizens. These citizens are unable to gain access to the formal labour market because of the prohibitively high costs of job creation resulting directly from the transfer-based and payroll-financed welfare state. A new cleavage between the insiders and outsiders of the labour market emerges (Esping-Andersen 1996a).

The particular production–protection interplay in Continental welfare states thus leads to

- overall low employment and high structural unemployment
- low participation of women in the labour market (OECD 1996: 196–7)
- low participation of older employees (OECD 1996: 187–9
- below-average employment in the service sector.

This 'low-employment equilibrium' has an especially unfavourable impact on the contribution-financed Continental welfare state: While firms may remain internationally competitive due to their high productivity, the economy as a whole might prove unable to defend welfare state objectives like high levels of employment and encompassing social protection. Yet, the comparison of the incidence of part-time work in Germany and the Netherlands (Table 10.1) and of the development of unit labour costs between 1970 and 1996 in both countries (Fig. 10.1) reveals that the low-employment equilibrium is not inevitable. In the following

Table 10.1 Incidence and composition of part-time employment (percentages)

	Part-time employment as a proportion of employment							
	Men				*Women*			
	1973	*1983*	*1993*	*1995*	*1973*	*1983*	*1993*	*1995*
Germany	1.8	1.7	2.9	3.6	24.4	30.0	32.0	33.8
Netherlands[a]	—	6.9	15.3	16.8	44.0	50.3	64.5	67.2
United States[b]	8.6	10.8	11.0	11.0	26.8	28.1	25.5	27.4
	Part-time employment as a proportion of total employment				*Women's share in part-time employment*			
	1973	*1983*	*1993*	*1995*	*1973*	*1983*	*1993*	*1995*
Germany	10.1	12.6	15.1	16.3	89.0	91.9	88.6	87.4
Netherlands[a]	—	21.2	35.0	37.4	—	78.4	73.7	73.6
United States[b]	15.6	18.4	17.6	18.6	66.0	66.8	66.0	68.0

Source: OECD (1996: 192).

Notes

a Break in series after 1985.

b Break in series after 1993.

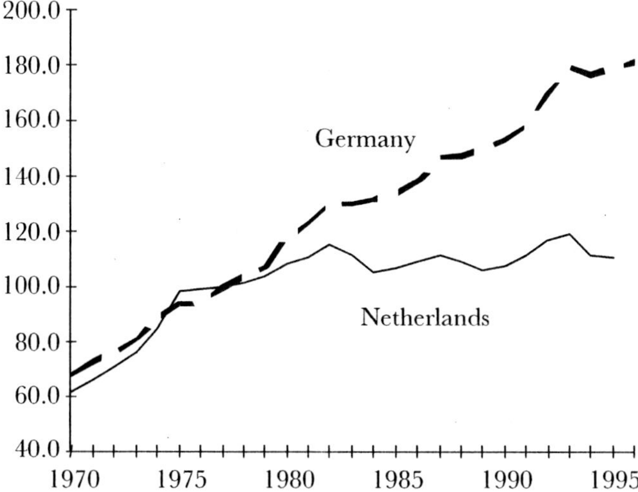

Figure 10.1 Unit labour costs in the Netherlands and Germany, 1970–96 (in national currency; 1977 = 100).

Source: Bureau of Labour Statistics (1997), calculations by the authors.

Note: The comparison of unit labour costs should be interpreted with caution. It may overstate changes in competitiveness, since labour costs are only a (small) part of overall costs and value added.

paragraphs we will investigate the political-institutional preconditions for such a trend reversal. We will start by analysing the resurgence of effective, negotiated adjustment in the Netherlands, and then describe the failure of centralised economic coordination in Germany.

The Netherlands

The resurgence of corporatist adjustment in the Netherlands

In the Netherlands, the government responded initially to the first oil crisis by pursuing an expansionary policy that soon resulted in wage hikes and soaring inflation. By the mid-1970s, the Dutch experiment with Keynesian reflation had been aborted. Like Austria, the Netherlands adopted a fixed exchange rate to the Deutschmark, de facto in 1979 and de jure in 1983. The centre-right coalition (Christian democrats and conservative liberals), which came into power in 1982 under leadership of the Christian democrat Ruud Lubbers, threw its support behind a deflationary programme. Although the 'hard currency policy' provided greater macroeconomic stability, it also meant that changes in the international political economy had to be adapted to by voluntarily moderating wages, increasing productivity or reforming the structure of welfare. The shift to restrictive macroeconomic policy in the Netherlands pushed up the level of unemployment to unprecedented levels. With unemployment soaring to a post-war record, the trade union movement, having lost almost 20 per cent of its membership in less than a decade, was in no position to engage in industrial conflict. After a decade of failed tripartite encounters based on Keynesian premises, the Dutch crowned the new coalition's entry into office with a bipartite social accord in December 1982, known as the Wassenaar Accord. In this accord, the unions recognised that it was necessary to achieve a higher level of profitability in order to have a higher level of investment, which in turn was essential to create more jobs and to fight against unemployment. The accord marked the resurgence of overt corporatist adjustment based on a commonly understood 'supply-side' diagnosis of the crisis (Visser and Hemerijck 1997). Subsequently, the accord encouraged overt cooperation between the social partners based on two factors: (1) with regard to policy content, wage moderation was exchanged for a reduction of working hours; (2) with regard to the institutional structure, a process of 'organised decentralisation' was established in the Dutch system of industrial relations that combined sectoral bargaining with effective input from the national level (Traxler 1996).

The Wassenaar Accord inaugurated an uninterrupted period of wage restraint until the mid-1990s. All agreements since 1982 have reconfirmed the need for wage restraint. Nominal wage increases have fallen to zero, and since the 1980s the anticipated increase in inflation has been the basis for sectoral negotiations. Only in 1992 and 1993 did the average negotiated wage increase exceed the inflation rate by half a percentage point. Estimations are that over 40 per cent of job creation in the last decade must be contributed to prolonged wage moderation (Centraal Plan Bureau 1995: 268), and a remarkable degree of social and political consensus is organised in its support.

While wage restraint in itself helps to preserve and create jobs, an additional payoff was required to make corporatist adjustment tangible for the trade union rank and file. Over the last decade the average work week has been shortened from 40 to 37.5 hours. In those sectoral agreements in which the work week was shortened, wage increases have been the smallest. The process of reducing work hours across-the-board has been gradually replaced by the introduction of part-time work as the main instrument for redistributing work. Between 1983 and 1993, the share of workers with part-time jobs (less than 35 hours per week) increased from 21 to 35 per cent. Part-time jobs are filled particularly by the increased number of married women who have entered the job market (see Table 10.1).

In the 1990s, wage restraint was increasingly compensated by lower taxes and social charges, made possible by improved public finances and a broader tax base through the creation of more jobs in domestic services. This helped to maintain spending power and to boost domestic demand.

Although the appreciation of the guilder (linked to the Deutschmark since 1983) has made exports more expensive, the overall decline in wage costs compensated for the competitive losses due to changes in the exchange rate. Moreover, the appreciation of the guilder has stimulated a low level of inflation, which, in turn, has had a favourable effect on domestic wage trends.

Institutionally, the corporatist agreements have evolved from comprehensive package deals to so-called central framework agreements that generally voice non-binding recommendations to be worked out in more detail at the sectoral level. Since the Wassenaar Accord, there has been no political intervention in wage setting. The role of the peak organisations has remained limited to that of directing negotiating parties on the sectoral level toward tacit, economy-wide, wage restraint. The greater the degree of consensus at the highest level, the smoother the bargaining at the intermediate level (Heertum-Lemmen and Wilthagen 1996).

Although the state plays a considerably less dominant role in collective bargaining, it still exercises extensive political power. Based on pre-war laws, the Minister of Social Affairs and Employment has the authority to declare collective bargaining agreements legally binding for all employees and employers in certain branches of industry, whether they are unionised or not. This provision has remained a treasured policy instrument and is crucial for securing wage restraint throughout the economy. Although in practice, the minister routinely implements this mandatory extension of collective bargaining agreements, he or she has the right to refuse a request for extension when the content of the agreement is not in line with policy interests. Under the 'shadow of hierarchy', meaning the threat of state intervention (Scharpf 1997), Dutch governments thus have been effective in encouraging labour and capital to reach agreements that concur with their central policy goals.

Reversing the 'welfare-without-work' dilemma

Organised capital and labour, under the shadow of hierarchy, have managed to find a responsible and mutually rewarding solution to problems of economic adjustment. It consists of a payoff between wage moderation and a shorter work week. Early on, however, the return to responsive corporatism was facilitated in a perverse way, by offering less productive, mainly older employees a generous enticement to take early retirement. Eventually, a crisis of inactivity spilled over into a general crisis of governability in the social security system, which then prompted major policy and institutional changes, particularly in the sickness and disability insurance schemes.

Until the 1960s, the expansion of social protection in the Netherlands lagged behind most advanced European countries, in part as a result of organisational fragmentation in provisions of social policy. By the 1970s and 1980s, there was a complete turnaround: the take-up rate of social benefits in the Netherlands now surpassed that of all European welfare states except Sweden (Flora 1986). The Dutch social security system is largely based on social insurance that is financed through compulsory payroll taxes. Eligibility for insurance depends on the number of years one has contributed to it. Unemployment, sickness and disability insurance schemes are administered by bipartite Industrial Boards (Bedrijfsverenigingen) and run by the unions and the employers' organisations. Because of their quasi-monopoly, the Industrial Boards have a high degree of institutional power over social policy in general, independent of the state.

The 1990s crisis of the Dutch welfare state revolved around the disability scheme, which had become increasingly an instrument for early retirement and industrial restructuring. Four features marked the idiosyncrasy of the Dutch scheme (Aarts and De Jong 1996). First, risk of disability was defined as a social rather than solely an occupational risk. Second, the provision known as the 'labour market consideration' stipulated that in assessing the degree of disability, the diminished labour market opportunities of partially disabled persons should be taken into account. As a consequence, disability as the basis for entitlement was redefined as a worker's particular incapacity to find a job similar to his former job. If the probability of not finding an 'appropriate' job was assessed to be great, the degree of disability would also be correspondingly high. Third, disability and sickness insurance benefits were closely related in that a person would receive sickness insurance benefits during the first full year and then qualify for the disability scheme. The funding of the schemes, however, was dissimilar. Sickness insurance was primarily financed by employers while disability benefits were entirely financed by employee contributions. Fourth, employee contributions were set at uniform nationwide rates and were unrelated to the particular risk factors in different industrial branches. Most firms supplemented sickness insurance benefits up to a level equalling 100 per cent of former earnings, and many even supplemented disability benefits to a comparable level for a year or longer. The combination of the low threshold for entitlement, the blurring of social and occupational risks, the generous level and duration of benefits, together with the primacy of bipartite self-regulation by the Industrial Boards, explains why the sickness insurance and disability schemes developed into a convenient method for reducing the supply of labour.

The result was a steep rise in the number of recipients and the exhaustion of the scheme's financial resources. A scheme that originally was meant to support no more than 200,000 people was paying benefits to over 900,000 in 1990. Estimates indicate that between 30 and 50 per cent of those receiving disability benefits should have been considered unemployed (Aarts and de Jong 1996). To the generous disability scheme were added early retirement options, and these also rapidly became popular exit routes out of the labour market. As a result, the percentage of older men gainfully employed (aged 60–64) dropped dramatically from about 70 per cent in 1973 to 22 per cent in 1991 (Hemerijck and Kloosterman 1995).

In due course, the scheme became a vicious welfare trap: once officially recognised as partially disabled, an employee acquired a permanent handicap on the labour market. The labour market consideration was interpreted in such a way that an employee whose productivity was below the wage earned in his or her job would be considered fully incapacitated to work. Furthermore it was assumed that such a person would not be able to find another job.

Political attempts were made to reduce the demand for the schemes. In 1987, the second centre-right Lubbers government cut replacement rates from 80 to 70 per cent, restricted entitlements, cancelled the indexation of benefits to wages, and shortened the duration of disability and unemployment benefits. Also the labour market consideration was repealed. However, these measures had little effect on spending because the number of social security beneficiaries continued to rise. By 1989, the number of people receiving disability benefits was rapidly approaching 1 million, and costs were exploding. This added to an already emerging sense of emergency among most social and political actors, notably among social democrats who had entered a coalition with the Christian democrats. In a dramatic *cri de coeur*, Prime Minister Lubbers proclaimed that the Netherlands had become a 'sick country' and that 'tough medication' was required. Given this diagnosis, the government proposed more radical reforms in order to discourage the misuse of sickness insurance and disability benefits and to close off other labour market exit routes. In spite of the emergency and the widespread conviction that radical changes had to be made, the reform proposal was highly controversial, politically risky and stiffly resisted. The Labour Party was internally divided; party leader Wim Kok almost fell over this issue. The social democrats were largely held responsible for what the electorate saw as an attack on established rights. The party did not recover in time, and in the 1994 elections it was punished with a historic defeat.

Notwithstanding popular resistance, the reforms were enacted. A complete synopsis of all measures cannot be included in this comparative analysis; we can only highlight the general character of the reform efforts of the 1990s in which financial incentives were introduced through the partial privatisation of social risks and social policy administration, and the institutional structure governing social security underwent a fundamental redesign. The government has in part marketised the system of social security in an attempt to improve incentives and efficiency and to minimise moral hazard. The right to unemployment benefits has been made more dependent upon the willingness of the beneficiary to accept a job offer or to participate in training programmes. The privatisation of sickness insurance became effective in 1996 with the Act on the Enlargement of Wage Payment during Sickness. Employers are now legally obliged to continue to pay their employees for a year, have a direct stake in reducing absenteeism, and seek private insurance against this risk. The new measures do not necessarily lead to a deterioration of protection. Replacement rates are 70 per cent of earnings, and benefits are commonly upgraded to 100 per cent in collective agreements. With respect to the disability scheme, the duration of the benefit has been substantially shortened. This has especially affected employees with an income substantially above the statutory minimum wage. Benefits for persons younger than age 50 have been reduced, and these now decline gradually over time to 70 per cent of the statutory minimum wage plus an additional age-related allowance. Finally, medical re-examinations of beneficiaries were undertaken on the basis of more stringent rules, and the legal stipulation requiring partially disabled employees to accept alternative employment was strengthened. A new definition of disability now forces beneficiaries to accept all 'normal' jobs. The result of these reforms is that the costs of sickness and disability insurance have effectively become elements in collective bargaining, further reinforcing incentives to reduce absenteeism due to sickness and disability at the level of individual companies and industrial sectors.

The institutional overhaul of the Dutch welfare state was critically enhanced by an in-depth parliamentary inquiry into the functioning of the organisation and administration of social security in the Netherlands. The Buurmeijer Commission (1993) conclusively brought to the fore the most problematic aspect in the institutional design of the social security system, namely an ambiguous distribution of power and responsibility. The major recommendation of the parliamentary commission was to have social security monitored by a government agency that could operate fully independently of the 'social partners'. The Buurmeijer Commission also advised that the Industrial Boards be replaced by regional agencies that would closely work together with the Public Employment Services in order to link passive and active labour market policies. The Kok government (social democrats, progressive democrats and conservative liberals, i.e. the first government since 1918 without any of the religious parties) has largely followed the recommendations of Buurmeijer. In 1994, the Social Insurance Council was dismantled. It was replaced by an independent supervisory institution, the Supervisory Board for Social Insurance (CTSV). A separate institution was created for the implementation of social security legislation, the Temporary Institute for Coordination (TICA), which remained tripartite. In 1997, the Industrial Insurance Boards were dismantled. The TICA board was reorganised into the permanent National Institute for Social Insurance (LISV) and made responsible for contracting the administration of social security out to privatised delivery agencies. The trade unions and employers' associations were granted an advisory status in the LISV. Institutional reform, however, remains unfinished business. In June 1998, the social partners agreed in the Social and Economic Council, SER, to fully privatise the administration of the social security system, including both the acceptance of claims and the implementation of social security provisions. However, the second, newly formed Kok government maintained that the acceptance of claims could not be left to market forces, but would be best kept under political control. It took until January 2000 before an informal compromise could be reached. The Minister of Social Affairs promised the social partners that they would continue to play a role in the new social security structure. The current solution is that a newly formed public agency is to be responsible for the execution of social security arrangements, whereas the tasks of prevention and reintegration of the unemployed and disabled are to be executed by private agencies.

While it is still too early to assess all of the above reforms, it does need to be pointed out that the disability rate remains comparatively high. After 1994, there was a significant drop in the number of disabled persons from a peak of 925,000 in 1994 to 861,000 in 1995, and a decrease in absenteeism due to illness. Since 1997, disability has again begun to rise with younger working women constituting the largest group of new claimants. A major result of the recent reform efforts is the institutional breakthrough, whereby the 'social partners' are forced to accept independent supervision and control over social security.

Germany

Adjustment by 'covert coordination': payoffs and trade-offs

Wage restraint has rarely been a serious problem for German unions. Since the principle of *Tarifautonomie*, the autonomy of employers and unions in collective bargaining, governs German industrial relations, collective bargaining does not take place in 'the shadow of hierarchy', i.e. under the threat of state intervention, but in 'the shadow of the independent Bundesbank'. The German central bank – strictly committed to a non-accommodating monetary policy since the end of the Bretton Woods system – has sufficiently proven in the past its eagerness to instantly punish any inflationary wage settlement by 'retaliatory interest rate increases' (Soskice *et al.* 1998: 41). This lesson was painfully learnt by the unions in the mid-1970s (cf. Scharpf 1987), and subsequently the 'signalling game' between the German central bank and the unions has worked fairly smoothly (Iversen 1999; Hall and Franzese 1998). Within this system of 'institutionalised monetarism' (Streeck 1994: 118; cf. Hall 1994), wages are set through industry-sector collective bargaining, in which the metalworker union, the IG Metall, most often has taken the lead. Pilot agreements in key branches and regions of the metalworking sector are then taken over by other regions and industries as well. IG Metall's wage demands usually remain within the limits set by increases in productivity plus the 'natural' rate of inflation. Wage demands thus essentially mirror the publicly announced growth in the money supply to which the Bundesbank commits itself each year by taking into account exactly these two factors (Streeck 1994: 123; Kreile 1978). Given this relatively efficient coordination (Hall 1994; Iversen 1999), Germany's inflation rate in the wake of the 1970s' oil crisis did not even come near the Dutch figures, while employment losses in Germany were more severe compared to those in countries that had followed a less restrictive monetary policy.

Centralised, concerted action had no real place and rationale within this functioning framework of 'industrial self-government' (Flanagan *et al.* 1983: 276), and Keynesianism could never really take hold in Germany even during its heyday in the late 1960s and early 1970s (Allen 1979). The same is true for corporatism as it is conventionally conceptualised, namely as a nationwide, tripartite exchange between the central associations of capital and labour and the state in which labour exercises wage restraint, the state commits itself to an expansionary fiscal and monetary policy in order to secure economic growth and full employment, and capital promises to reinvest the profits stemming from moderate wage growth and in this way to expand employment. In spite of the broader public and scholarly attention that was paid to such attempts at macroeconomic coordination like the Concerted Action, or more recently the Solidarity Pact (*Solidaritätspakt*; cf. Sally and Webber 1994) or the Alliance for Jobs (*Bündnis für Arbeit*; cf. Lehmbruch 1996; Bispinck 1997), these concerted actions did not exert much economic impact and were essentially symbolic exercises.

However, covert economic coordination cannot fully substitute for the lack of explicit and overt political management of the various policy interfaces in Germany's tightly coupled political economy. Given the high productivity in manufacturing, the leading role of the IG Metall in the collective wage agreements, the compressed wage structure and the relatively high minimum wage as defined by the level of social assistance, even economically 'responsible' wages in the manufacturing sector are usually too high to allow for significant job growth in the lower segments of the labour market, in particular in the service sector.

Workers who lost their jobs in these segments due to the high-wage and non-wage labour costs were not channelled, as in Sweden, into other, more productive sectors of the economy via active labour market programmes. The German welfare state is passive in nature, providing those out of employment with transfer payments as a substitute for the lost market-income. The public sector is too small to compensate for the lack of jobs in the private service sector by expanding public sector employment (see Scharpf, Chapter 12). As long as the Continental welfare state could take care of (the limited number of) the unemployed and the good export performance secured strong employment in manufacturing,[3] the strategy coupling high wages and high productivity was viable. Yet increasingly it came to be a problem for German industrial relations and the welfare state alike. Industrial self-governance proved to be especially ill-suited to addressing the problems of poor job growth, high unemployment, and the spiralling costs of social spending caused by subsidising various forms of non-employment through the welfare state.

Due to the principle of *Tarifautonomie*, direct state intervention into collective bargaining is not an option that promises to solve the 'welfare-without-work' dilemma. Neither can a substantial social reform, which would break with the collusive practices of organised labour and capital by which they externalise the costs of economic adjustment at the expense of the welfare state, be expected to result from corporatist negotiations in which everything depends on the consent of exactly those 'social partners' who profit most from the status quo.[4] Yet, given their organisational and political strength, given the social partners' strong involvement in the administration of the welfare state, and given the material interests at stake for them, a government risks severe political conflict and industrial strife if it enacts reforms against the – possibly joint – resistance of unions and employers (see Alber 1989; Wood 1997; Thelen 2000). Not surprisingly, the reform record of both social democratic and Christian democratic governments in the last thirty years has been far from impressive in all those areas where social policy directly affects employment and the labour market. In particular, governments of both colours have shied away from reforming the 'negative supply-side' labour market policy, which has become the standard response to economic shocks. Where the government did decide to act, as in the sick pay reform of 1996 or in the reform of early retirement in the first half of the 1980s, the unions and employers often engaged in 'implementation sabotage' and watered down in practice what they had not been able to prevent from becoming law (Mares 1996). While the German social partners were clearly less autonomous in the administration of the social insurance schemes than their Dutch counterparts, their privileged role at least offered them the opportunity to minimise the effects of reforms that they perceived as going against their interests.

Thus, it was not only union strength that stood in the way of welfare reforms, and, conversely, it is not the decrease in unionisation that might endanger the stability of *Modell Deutschland* (Thelen 2000). More important for the functioning of the German political economy has been 'business density', that is, the impressive ability of employer associations to organise the firms of their industry, to coordinate the strategies of their members, and to effectively sanction them when they fail to comply with the rules that have been laid down (Soskice 1990). To the extent that welfare retrenchment could potentially endanger the fragile capital–labour compromise, employers themselves have been quite unenthusiastic about it. Since the German production model is highly dependent on the buffering and moderating capacity of the Continental welfare state model, welfare cutbacks do not translate necessarily into cost advantages for firms and do not automatically improve their competitiveness (Manow 2000). On the contrary, such cutbacks may even entail the risk of deteriorating the comparative advantages of German firms if they result in industrial strife, in the weakening of the unions' capacity to bind their members to jointly reached agreements, or in the erosion of 'solidarity' between employers that collective bargaining at the industry-sector level forces upon them (Hall 1997). The failed co-determination reform in the 1980s (Wood 1997), the ambiguous position of employers with respect to opening clauses in collective bargaining contracts and to the reform of the traditional territorial wage treaties (*Flächentarifvertrag*), and the spectacular failure of sick pay reform in 1996 all hint at the critical fact that it is the German employers who cannot bring themselves to dismantle the German model (Thelen 2000). Well aware of both the positive payoffs and increasing costs of the status quo, employers are frequently undecided whether to call for major reforms or to adapt themselves to things as they are. Moreover, since costs and benefits of reforms are unevenly distributed between small and big enterprises and between firms and employees in the 'exposed' or the 'sheltered' sectors, coalition building within the employers' camp is very complicated (Thelen 2000), especially since German industrial relations lack an arena in which side-payments or package deals could balance losses and gains.

The double bind of welfare reforms: cost containment or cost externalisation

Recent reforms of old-age insurance testify to the two partly conflicting economic functions of the German welfare state. On the one hand, the pension system is an important instrument to ease the transition from work to retirement, to reduce the unemployment among older workers, and to enable employers to flexibly adjust their workforce to the business cycle in a relatively inexpensive and 'painless' way. On the other hand, the high cost of pensions (and other social spending) increases non-wage labour costs and therefore intensifies the pressure on firms to dismiss employees. Here again, pressures target especially older workers, due to the seniority wages and relatively strict employment protection for older workers. Early retirement enables firms to increase productivity, to import new skills through the 'rejuvenation' of the workforce, *and* it permits greater flexibility in a firm's wage structure and personnel policy (Gatter and Schmähl 1996). For unions, the welfare exit from the labour market has been attractive since it is primarily the members of the core workforce, that is union members with many years of job tenure, who are the chief beneficiaries.

The major roads into early retirement in the German pension insurance, namely disability pensions and long-term unemployment pensions (Jacobs *et al.* 1991; Jacobs and Schmähl 1989; Gatter and Schmähl 1996), were reformed only half-heartedly in the 1980s and 1990s, although unfavourable economic and demographic trends have put pension finances under increasing pressure. The pension insurance contribution rate today is at a record high of 20.2 per cent of gross wages, which amounts to nearly half of the 40 per cent of gross wages paid into the social insurances as a whole. Yet, the increase in contributions is not simply due to the government's lack of political activity in the field of pension policy. Rather it reveals that the government has not been overly successful in its numerous attempt to stop the trend towards an ever earlier retirement. Let us briefly discuss some of the major reforms since 1982.

As one of the first cost-containment laws of the Kohl government, the 1984 budget law (*Haushaltsbegleitgesetz* '84) restricted the access to disability pensions with immediate and significant effects especially for women. Their take-up rate of disability pensions dropped by 50 per cent (172,888 disability pensions for women in 1984 as compared to 85,938 disability pensions in 1985; VDR 1997: 53). At the same time, however, the *Haushaltsbegleitgesetz* broadened the eligibility to the standard old-age pension (pension age for men 63/65, for women 60), leading to a significant rise in the take-up rate especially of women for standard old-age pensions (from 90,904 pensions for women in 1985 to 147,246 in 1986; VDR 1997: 53). For men, entry into early retirement via the disability pathway remained an attractive option despite the reform, and the number of those retiring with a disability pension decreased only slightly (163,017 in 1984 as compared to 142,729 in 1985 and 129,029 in 1986; VDR 1997: 52).

Disability pensions developed into an attractive retirement option mainly because of rulings by the Federal Social Court (*Bundessozialgericht*) in 1969 and 1976 that held that even minor reductions in working capacity could entitle a person to a full pension if he or she finds no 'appropriate' part-time employment. Through these rulings, the pension insurance became responsible for genuine labour market risks, and it is no surprise that this so-called 'concrete interpretation' (*konkrete Betrachtungsweise*), i.e. an interpretation that takes the current situation on the labour market into account, became particularly important during the economic recession of the 1980s and especially following German unification.

While the 1984 budget law was only moderately successful in reducing the overall number of disability pensions, the Pre-Retirement Act (*Vorruhestandsgesetz*) of the same year was supposed to reverse the trend with respect to the second major pathway into early retirement, a sequential combination of long-term unemployment benefits and pre-retirement pensions (see Mares, forthcoming). The Pre-Retirement Act tried to end the practice, especially of larger firms, of letting employees go at the age of 59 while matching their unemployment benefits to the level of their previous net wage for the period of one year (so-called 59er rule), until they reached age 60 and were eligible to a full pension because of long-term unemployment (without actuarial reductions for the longer period in which pensions are drawn). The Pre-Retirement Act introduced the opportunity to retire at the age of 58 (so-called 58er rule) with employers paying retirees between two (women's retirement age: 60) and five years ('flexible retirement' age for men: 63) at least 65 per cent of their last net wage. At the same time, the law offered a public subsidy of at most 35 per cent to this retirement wage if the open position would be filled by a registered unemployed or a trainee for at least two years. However, pre-retirement did not stir up a lot of excitement. The take-up rate was rather modest with only about 165,000 employees going into retirement between 1984 and 1988, when the Pre-Retirement Act expired. The substitution rate, meaning the rate at which vacated positions were refilled, has been estimated to have been about 80 per cent, thus leading to a maximum of 135,000 new jobs (cf. Jacobs *et al.* 1991; Frerich and Frey (1993) report lower figures). These rather low numbers did not increase even though in 1982 the government had introduced rules that forced firms to reimburse the government for unemployment benefits that were paid out to formerly long-term employed workers who were dismissed at age 59. These rules were tightened in 1984 to include also the pension and sickness insurance contributions paid by the Labour Office for each unemployed. This was just another attempt to render the 59er rule less attractive and to motivate employers and employees to use the 58er rule of the Pre-Retirement Act instead. However, firms were quick in challenging this new reimbursement provision before the courts. Ultimately the employers' repayments were rather insignificant. Thus, while the 59er rule is still a frequently used pathway into retirement, the Pre-Retirement Act expired in 1988 and has been succeeded only by an even less successful programme, the *Arbeitsteilzeitgesetz* (Part-time Labour Law), the effects of which have been negligible.

All in all, the Pre-Retirement Act was an unsuccessful attempt by the Kohl government to regain control over the work–welfare interface. The attempt failed not only because the employers battled the act in court and employees and important unions (like the IG Metall) were unwilling to fight for attractive pre-retirement clauses in collective bargaining. It also failed because the government itself took a very ambivalent stance toward early retirement, which is especially evident with respect to the considerable extension of eligibility for unemployment benefits that was introduced at exactly the same time that the government tried to diminish the attractiveness of the 59er rule (cf. Jacobs *et al.* 1991: 193). Initially, the maximum period of eligibility for 'unemployment pay' (*Arbeitslosengeld*) as the first and most important (generous) unemployment benefit had been twelve months. In a series of 'quite turbulent legislative changes' (Jacobs *et al.* 1991: 193), this period was extended within only two years (between 1985 and 1987) to no less than thirty-two months for workers aged 54 and over! At the same time, the law relieved these older workers from the obligation to prove that they were still actively searching for employment.[5] What Jacobs *et al.* have labelled a 'purely passive and resigned adaptation to labour market shortcomings' (Jacobs *et al.* 1991: 193) made early retirement through the unemployment pathway more and not less attractive. By significantly extending the period of eligibility for unemployment benefits, the government quite intentionally increased the scope of the 59er rule. As a consequence, the 59er rule has today 'effectively become a 57er rule' (Jacobs *et al.* 1991: 203).

At the same time, the number of unemployment pensions has steadily grown since the mid-1980s and has skyrocketed since the early 1990s (from 40,000 in 1985 to nearly 300,000 in 1995 for both men and women; the 1995 number is for East and West Germany). Annually, early retirement costs the pension insurance more than 20 billion DM.

Both the government's ambivalence and the interest fragmentation among employers and unions explain this very mixed reform record. With respect to the latter, small and medium firms as well as the crafts are highly critical of the current practice of big employers to externalise the costs of economic adjustment onto the social insurance schemes. While they supported the attempt of the Labour Ministry to substitute the 59er rule with the less inexpensive 58er rule of the Pre-Retirement Act (see Mares, forthcoming), this attempt ultimately failed not the least because the government followed this strategy half-heartedly at best. Unions were also divided over the best strategy to lower unemployment. While the IG Metall put its main thrust into the campaign for the 35-hour week, the more moderate IG Chemie preferred to have the labour supply reduced by lowering the retirement age and therefore supported the Pre-Retirement Act. Neither employers nor unions were able to outbalance these internal divisions of interest. Hence, any profound reform would have triggered the formation of a cross-class alliance between unions and employers of either camp. Since the government itself followed a rather indecisive strategy, employers and unions could continue to pick their most preferred choice out of a rich variety of options that existed for the transition from work to retirement.

Conclusions

This chapter has compared two very similar 'social systems of production' and welfare state regimes. The comparative literature on political economy and on the welfare state usually puts the Netherlands and Germany into the same category of having sectorally organised or coordinated market economies and of having a Continental model of social policy, respectively. This is justified by the striking similarity of the institutional features of the production system and the welfare regime in both countries. It is also substantiated by the very similar socioeconomic response patterns in both countries to economic crisis, namely labour force reductions via early retirement and disability pensions, low female participation rates, etc. However, the subsequent *political* response patterns to the 'welfare-without-work' crisis were very different in both countries. This chapter investigated the causes for this difference.

Our central claim is that the political management of the many interdependencies between the 'sphere of production' and the 'sphere of protection' in both tightly coupled welfare states differs critically. While management has been overt and deliberate in the Dutch case, the German system of covert coordination did not allow for issue linking and a sequential reform dynamic. Our analysis has at least two broader implications. In substantive terms, the Dutch case shows that the pathologic 'welfare-without-work' equilibrium is not inevitable for Continental welfare states. In more theoretical terms, the German–Dutch comparison reveals that an understanding of the adaptive dynamics in tightly coupled welfare states depends critically on an analysis of the economic as well as political effects of the production–protection interplay. In tightly coupled welfare states, in which the social insurance system is well integrated into a 'corporatist complex', the investigation into the different trajectories of welfare state reform makes it necessary to study the system of industrial relations.

Notes

1 Anton Hemerijck would like to thank Jelle Visser and Kees van Kersbergen for their contribution of many of the ideas presented here in a number of recent collaborative projects (Visser and Hemerijck 1997; Hemerijck and van Kersbergen 1998). Both authors would also like to thank Fritz Scharpf, Vivien Schmidt, and Torben Vad for their encouragement to further develop the dynamic consequences of 'tightly coupled' welfare states for processes of welfare reform, as a central theme of the Conference Project 'The Adjustment of National Employment and Social Policy to Economic Internationalization', Max Planck Institute for the Study of Societies (MPIfG), Cologne, 1997–9. Philip Manow would like to thank Eric Seils and Christina van Wijnbergen for many helpful discussions and valuable information.

2 In the following we will speak of the Continental welfare state model. There is some indeterminacy regarding Esping-Andersen's classification of the Netherlands, which is sometimes grouped with the social-democratic regimes, sometimes classified as a conservative regime (cf. Alber 1998a). We follow the work of Huber and Stephens, van Kersbergen and also Castles and Mitchell who have shown that Germany and the Netherlands can be grouped together as conservative or Continental welfare states based on 'similar levels of expenditures, comparable degrees of equality, and analogous characteristics of political configurations' (van Kersbergen 1995: 56).

3 Although the German employment ratio in manufacturing is the highest in the OECD world, it fell by a third from 33.4 per cent in 1970 to 20.12 per cent in 1990. The worst drop occurred in response to the recession in the early 1980s. The unification shock led to a further decline by three percentage points.

4 Not to speak here of the lack of institutional preconditions necessary to strike broad package deals across different policy domains: Unions are sectorally fragmented. The union peak association is weak. The business community is heterogeneous. Employers' interests are divided between small and medium enterprises, on the one side, and big industry on the other. Employer representatives are incapable of making binding agreements concerning the reduction of overtime work or the creation of new jobs – two central union demands in the *Bündnis für Arbeit* (Alliance for Work) (Lehmbruch 1996; Bispinck 1997).

5 Employees have to prove their 'availability' by showing up at the local unemployment offices every three weeks. Local unemployment offices themselves do not offer job placements to employees aged 54 and over. These employees are de facto 'retired', but are paid until the age of 60 by the unemployment insurance, not by the old-age insurance.

References

Aarts, L. and de Jong, P. (eds) (1996). *Curing the Dutch Disease*. Aldershot: Avebury.

Alber, J. (1989). *Der Sozialstaat in der Bundesrepublik 1950–1983*. Frankfurt: Campus.

Alber, J. (1998a). 'Der deutsche Wohlfahrtsstaat im Lichte international vergleichender Daten', *Leviathan* (25), 199–227.

Alber, J. (1998b). 'Recent developments in Continental European welfare states: Do Austria, Germany, and the Netherlands prove to be birds of a feather?', Paper presented at the 14th World Congress of Sociology, Montreal, 29 July 1998.

Allen, C. S. (1979). 'The underdevelopment of Keynesianism in the Federal Republic of Germany', in P. A. Hall (ed.), *The Political Power of Economic Ideas*, 264–89.

Bispinck, R. (1997). 'The chequered history of the alliance for jobs', in G. Fajertag and P. Pochet (eds), *Social Pacts in Europe* Brussels: ETUI, 63–78.

BMA (Bundesarbeitsministerium) (1998). 'Statistisches Taschenbuch', http://www.bma.de/

Bureau of Labor Statistics (1997). Data, http://stats.bls.gov.

Castles, F. G. and Mitchell, D. (1993). 'Worlds of welfare and families of nations', in F. G. Castles (ed.), *Families of Nations: Patterns of Public Policy in Western Democracies* Dartmouth: Aldershot, 93–128.

Centraal Plan Bureau (1995). *Centraal Economisch Plan 1996.* The Hague: CPB.

Czada, R. (1998). 'Vereinigungskrise und Standortdebatte. Der Beitrag der Wiedervereinigung zur Krise des westdeutschen Modells', *Leviathan* (25), 24–59.

Esping-Andersen, G. (1990). *The Three World of Welfare Capitalism.* New York: Polity Press.

Esping-Andersen, G. (ed.) (1996a). *Welfare States in Transition. National Adaptations in Global Economies.* London: Sage.

Esping-Andersen, G. (1996b). 'Welfare states without work: The impasse of labour shedding and familialism in Continental European social policy', in G. Esping-Andersen (ed.), *Welfare States in Transition. National Adaptations in Global Economies.* London: Sage, 66–87.

Flanagan, R. J., Soskice, D. W. and Ulman, L. (1983). *Unionism, Economic Stabilization, and Incomes Policies.* Washington, DC: The Brookings Institute.

Flora, P. (ed.) (1986). *Growth to Limits*, 4 volumes. Berlin: de Gruyter.

Freeman, R. (1995). 'The large welfare state as a system', in *American Economics Association, Papers and Proceedings* 84(2), 16–21.

Frerich, J. and Frey, M. (1993). *Handbuch der Geschichte der Sozialpolitik in Deutschland, Bd. 3: Sozialpolitik in der Bundesrepublik Deutschland bis zur Herstellung der deutschen Einheit.* München: Oldenbourg.

Garrett, G. (1998). *Partisan Politics in the Global Economy.* New York: Cambridge University Press.

Gatter, J. and Schmähl, W. (1996). 'Vom Konsens zum Konflikt – Die Frühverrentung zwischen renten- und beschäftigungspolitischen Interessen', in Bremer Gesellschaft für Wirtschaftsforschung (ed.), *Massenarbeitslosigkeit durch Politikversagen?* Frankfurt: Peter Lang, 183–204.

Genschel, P. (2000). 'Der Wohlfahrtsstaat im Steuerwettbewerb', MPIfG Working Paper 00/5. Cologne: Max Planck Institute for the Study of Societies.

Hall, P. A. (1994). 'Central bank independence and coordinated wage bargaining: Their interaction in Germany and Europe', *German Politics and Society* 31, 1–23.

Hall, P. A. (1997). 'The Political Economy of Adjustment in Germany', in F. Naschold, D. Soskice, B. Hancké and U. Jürgens (eds), *Ökonomische Leistungsfähigkeit und institutionelle Innovation. WZB-Jahrbuch.* Berlin: Sigma, 293–317.

Hall, P. A. and Franzese, R. J. (1998). 'Mixed signals: Central bank independence, coordinated wage bargaining, and European Monetary Union', *International Organization* 52(3), 505–35.

Heertum-Lemmen, A. H. and Wilthagen, A. J. C. M. (1996). *De Doorwerking van de Aanbevelingen van de Stichting van de Arbeid.* The Hague: SDU.

Hemerijck, A. C. (1998). 'Recasting the postwar equilibrium', Paper presented at the opening workshop of the conference project 'The Adjustment of National Employment and Social Policy to Economic Internationalization', Max Planck Institute for the Study of Societies, Cologne, 12–14 March 1998.

Hemerijck, A. C. and Kloosterman, R. (1995). 'Der postindustrielle Umbau des korporatistischen Sozialstaats in den Niederlanden', in W. Fricke (ed.), *Jahrbuch Arbeit und Technik 1995. Zukunft des Sozialstaates.* Bonn: Verlag J.H.W. Dietz, 287–96.

Hemerijck, A. C. and van Kersbergen, K. (1998). 'Negotiated change: Institutional and policy learning in tightly coupled welfare states', Paper prepared for the ECPR Joint Sessions, Workshop 22 'The Role of Ideas in Policy-Making', Warwick University, 23–28 March 1998.

Huber, E. and Stephens, J. D. (1999). 'Welfare state and production regimes in the era of retrenchment', Occasional Papers. Princeton, NJ: Institute for Advanced Studies.

Iversen, T. (1998). 'Wage bargaining, hard money and economic performance: Theory and evidence for organized market economies', *British Journal of Political Science* 28, 31–61.

Iversen, T. (1999). *Contested Economic Institutions: The Politics of Macroeconomics and Wage Bargaining in Advanced Democracies.* New York: Cambridge University Press.

Jacobs, K., Kohli, M. and Rein, M. (1991). 'Germany: The diversity of pathways', in M. Kohli, M. Rein, K. Jacobs and A.-M. Guillemard (eds), *Time for Retirement.* Cambridge: Cambridge University Press, 181–221.

Jacobs, K. and Schmähl, W. (1989). 'The process of retirement in Germany: Trends, public discussion and options for its redefinition', in W. Schmähl (ed.), *Redefining the Process of Retirement.* Berlin: Springer, 13–38.

Kersbergen, K. van (1995). *Social Capitalism. A Study of Christian Democracy and the Welfare State.* London and New York: Routledge.

Kitschelt, H., Lange, P., Marks, G. and Stephens, J. (1999). 'Convergence and divergence in advanced capitalist democracies', in H. Kitschelt, P. Lange, G. Marcks and J. Stephens (eds), *Continuity and Change in Contemporary Capitalism.* New York: Cambridge University Press, 427–60.

Kreile, M. (1978). 'West Germany: The Dynamics of Expansion', in P. Katzenstein (ed.), *Between Power and Plenty.* Madison, WI: University of Wisconsin Press, 191–224.

Lehmbruch, G. (1996). 'Crisis and institutional resilience in German corporatism', Paper prepared for presentation at the 8th International Conference on Socio-Economics, SASE, Geneva, 12–14 July 1996.

Manow, P. (2000). 'Comparative institutional advantages of welfare state regimes and new coalitions in welfare state reforms', in P. Pierson (ed.), *The New Politics of Welfare.* New York: Oxford University Press, 146–64.

Manow, P. and Seils, E. (2000). 'The unemployment crisis of the German welfare state', in M. Rhodes and M. Ferrera (eds), *Restructuring European Welfare States,* West European Politics, special issue. London: Frank Cass, 138–60.

Mares, I. (1996). 'Firms and the welfare state: The emergence of new forms of unemployment', WZB discussion paper FS I 96-308. Berlin: Social Science Research Center.

Mares, I. (forthcoming). 'Business (non) coordination and social policy development: The case of early retirement', in P. Hall and D. Soskice (eds), *Varieties of Capitalism.* New York: Oxford University Press.

OECD (Organisation for Economic Co-Operation and Development) (1994). 'Collective bargaining: Levels and coverage', in *Employment Outlook.* Paris: OECD, 167–94.

OECD (1996). *OECD Employment Outlook.* Paris: OECD.

Sally, R. and Webber, D. (1994). 'The German solidarity pact: A case study in the politics of the unified Germany', *German Politics* 3, 18–46.

Scharpf, F. W. (1987). *Sozialdemokratische Krisenpolitik in Europa.* New York: Campus.

Scharpf, F. W. (1997). *Games Real Actors Play. Actor-Centered Institutionalism in Policy Research.* Boulder, CO: Westview Press.

Scharpf, F. W. (1998). 'Negative and positive integration in the political economy of European welfare states', in M. Rhodes and Y. Mény (eds), *The Future of European Welfare: A New Social Contract?*. Houndsmill: MacMillan, 155–177.

Schmidt, M. G. (1998). *Sozialpolitik in Deutschland. Historische Entwicklung und internationaler Vergleich*, 2nd edn. Opladen: Leske + Budrich.

Siegel, N. A. and Jochem, S. (1999). 'Zwischen Sozialstaats-Status quo und Beschäftigungswachstum. Das Dilemma des Bündnisses für Arbeit im Trilemma der Dienstleistungsgesellschaft', ZES Arbeitspapier Nr. 17/99, Bremen: University of Bremen, Center for Social Policy Research.

Soskice, D. (1990). 'Wage determination: The changing role of institutions in advanced industrialized countries', *Oxford Review of Economic Policy* 6, 36–61.

Soskice, D., Hancké, B., Trumbull, G. and Wren, A. (1998). 'Wage bargaining, labour markets and macroeconomic performance in Germany and the Netherlands', in L. Delson and E. de Jong (eds), *The German and Dutch Economies: Who follows Whom?* Berlin: Physica, 39–51.

Streeck, W. (1994). 'Pay restraint without incomes policy: Institutionalized monetarism and industrial unions in Germany', in R. Dore, R. Boyer and Z. Mars (eds), *The Return to Incomes Policy.* New York: Pinter, 118–40.

Thelen, K. (2000). 'Why German Employers cannot bring themselves to Dismantle the German Model', in T. Iversen, J. Pontusson and D. Soskice (eds), *Unions, Employers and Central Banks.* New York: Cambridge University Press, 138–69.

Titmuss, R. M. (1974). *Social Policy: An Introduction.* London: Allen & Unwin.

Traxler, F. (1996). 'Farewell to labor market associations? Organized versus disorganized decentralization as a map for industrial relations', in C. Crouch and F. Traxler (eds), *Organized Industrial Relations in Europe: What Future?* Aldershot: Avebury, 3–20.

VDR (Verband der Rentenversicherungsträger) (1997). *Rentenversicherung in Zeitreihen*, Frankfurt: VDR.

Visser, J. and Hemerijck, A. (1997). *A Dutch Miracle: Job Growth, Welfare Reform and Corporatism in the Netherlands.* Amsterdam: Amsterdam University Press.

Weick, K. E. (1976). 'Educational organizations as loosely coupled systems', *Administrative Science Quarterly* 21(1), 1–20.

Wood, S. (1997). 'Weakening codetermination? Works council reform in West Germany in the 1980s', WZB discussion paper FS I 97–302. Berlin: Social Science Research Center.

11 The challenge of de-industrialisation

Divergent ideological responses to welfare state reform

Anne Wren

The welfare state and the challenge of de-industrialisation

The close links between industrial and welfare state development have long been recognised in the political economy literature. Some authors attach primal causal weight to the 'logic of industrialism' in explaining welfare state expansion. Through its simultaneous creation of economic growth and destruction of traditional social networks and support systems, it is argued, industrial development created both a demand for state welfare policies and an opportunity for their provision (Wilensky 1975). Others have emphasised political factors such as the development of a coherent and solidaristic social democratic movement in explaining variations in welfare state effort within the group of advanced industrial nations. However, despite their more political logic, these accounts also recognise the links between welfare state development and the expansion of the industrial working class (Stephens 1979; Korpi 1983; Esping-Andersen 1985).

In recent years, increasing attention has been devoted to the implications of the *decline* of traditional industrial sectors for welfare state development (Esping Andersen 1993, 1994, 1996; Wren and Iversen 1997; Iversen and Wren 1998; Iversen and Cusack 2000; Scharpf 1999). In sharp contrast with the rapid expansion which took place in the 1950s and 1960s, the last two decades have witnessed significant reductions in manufacturing employment rates in most advanced industrial economies, as demonstrated in Table 11.1.

While opinion as to relative causal weights differs, it appears that several factors have contributed to this decline. Some authors emphasise the effects of increased global economic integration, for example, arguing that low wage competition from developing countries has exerted downward pressure on low-skilled wages and manufacturing employment in their more economically developed trading partners (Wood 2000; Saeger 1999). However, considerable controversy surrounds the issue of the size and significance of these effects, and a growing consensus suggests that while trade with the developing world may have played a role in accelerating the de-industrialisation process, it has not been the dominant factor (Freeman 1995; Rowthorn and Ramaswamy 1997, 1998).[1]

Table 11.1 Employment growth in manufacturing (annual averages in per cent), 1960–94

	1960–9	*1970–9*	*1980–9*	*1990–4*
USA	2.3	0.5	−0.7	−1.8
Canada	—	1.7	0.8	−2.8
Germany	0.6	−0.7	−0.3	−1.9
France	—	0.1	−1.9	−2.0
Italy	1.6	1.3	−1.7	−2.2
UK	−0.1	−1.4	−3.3	−4.2
Australia	1.3	−0.7	−0.3	−1.6
Netherlands	—	−1.9	−0.9	−1.4
Denmark	−0.4	−1.1	0.6	−1.5
Norway	0.8	0.3	−2.2	−2.6
Sweden	—	−0.7	−0.8	−5.0
Average	0.9	−0.2	−1.0	−2.5

Source: OECD (1996a).

Instead it is argued that de-industrialisation stems primarily from long-term development processes within the advanced economies themselves, and is related to significant changes which have occurred in the structures of production and consumption over the last quarter of a century. In the so-called 'golden age' of industrial expansion in the 1950s and 1960s, the spread of Fordist mass-production methods resulted in rapid increases in productivity in many industrial sectors. Price reductions associated with these improvements triggered high levels of demand as a whole range of manufactured items (in particular consumer durables) came within reach of average consumer budgets for the first time. In other words, in these relatively unsaturated markets, demand for a wide range of mass-produced items was price elastic. It was also income elastic. As incomes rose, people tended to spend proportionately less money on necessities such as food and shelter and more on more 'luxurious' items such as consumer durables.[2] This combination of characteristics of production and consumption facilitated the emergence of a virtuous circle of productivity increases, rising real wages, falling prices, and the expansion of demand and employment. As long as wage increases did not absorb the entire improvement in productivity in the most dynamic sectors of manufacturing, the resulting reduction in relative prices could support an expansion of employment in those sectors. In turn, rapid productivity growth permitted real wages to grow and thus secured expanding markets and rising employment. In this environment, the labour-saving effects of manufacturing productivity increases were more than compensated for by the dynamic process of demand expansion.[3]

As time progressed, however, markets became more saturated with manufactured goods. Just as the proportion of household budgets devoted to basic agricultural products had declined previously, the demand for basic manufactures also became less responsive to price reductions and rising incomes. Increasingly wealthy and choosy populations began to place less emphasis on quantity and more on the quality and distinctiveness of manufactured goods when making their consumption choices. Under these conditions the price reductions associated with productivity increases no longer produced demand expansions of a sufficient size to compensate for their labour-saving effects. Thus, Appelbaum and Schettkat (1995), for example, have shown the existence of a significant *negative* relationship between manufacturing productivity growth and employment during the 1980s, and a similar result is found in Iversen and Wren (1998).

Along with these changes, complementary shifts have occurred in modes of industrial production. The decline of Fordism has been associated in many countries with a new emphasis on the production of more specialised goods for smaller and more fluid niche markets. Operating in small and constantly changing markets requires above all a high degree of flexibility in production, however, and adaptability of this kind in turn requires high levels of skill if employees are to be able to adjust to constantly changing working environments (Piore and Sabel 1984).

The consequence of these changes has been a decline in the demand for labour in the manufacturing sectors of the advanced industrial economies, with a heavy concentration of employment loss among the unskilled. The worsening labour market position of the low skilled is indicated in Table 11.2. According to estimates by Nickell and Bell (1995), unemployment rates among the unskilled were at least double that of high-skilled workers in all of the countries shown except Italy in the mid to late 1970s. Moreover, over the next decade this gap

Table 11.2 High- and low-skilled unemployment rates (male), 1975–78 and 1987–90

	1975–8		*1987–90*	
	High skill[a]	*Low skill*	*High skill*	*Low skill*
USA	2.2	8.6	2.1	9.8
Canada	2.6	8.2	3.4	11.3
Germany	1.6	3.1	2.9	7.6
France	2.1	6.5	2.6	10.8
Italy[b]	12.3	4.4	13.1	8.1
UK	2.0	6.4	4.0	13.5
Australia[c]	3.5	8.3	3.9	10.0
Netherlands[b]	2.1	4.7	4.6	16.9
Norway	0.8	2.2	1.5	6.0
Sweden	0.8	2.4	1.0	2.4
Average	3.0	5.5	3.9	9.6

Source: Nickell and Bell (1995).

Notes

a For all countries except Germany, skill is measured by educational attainment. For Germany, according to ILO occupational definitions.

b Male and female.

c 1979–82 in Australia.

widened significantly in many places, with average unskilled unemployment rates almost doubling, while average unemployment rates among skilled workers increased by only 25 per cent.

The release of large numbers of (largely unskilled or semi-skilled) workers from previously secure employment in the manufacturing sectors of the advanced industrial economies creates a new set of challenges for the welfare state. Increasing dependency ratios associated with the loss of manufacturing employment clearly place additional pressure on welfare state budgets (Scharpf 1999). In addition, it has been argued that the increased labour market risks associated with de-industrialisation and the disappearance of stable lifelong manufacturing employment create pressure for further expansions of welfare state entitlements as citizens turn to the state for protection from the increased uncertainty of their environment (Iversen and Cusack 2000).[4] Furthermore, these additional pressures arise at a time when the number of external restrictions on government spending is commonly attested to be increasing (see for example Scharpf 1991; Kurzer 1993).

Significantly, however, both the extent of the increase in dependency ratios and the nature of the labour market risk associated with de-industrialisation are closely related to developments in the service sector. It is clear, for example, that de-industrialisation poses a more serious threat to dependency ratios where service sector development is limited, as there is little alternative to welfare state compensation for the loss of a manufacturing sector job. We would expect the threat to dependency ratios to be less where either private or public service sector expansion creates opportunities for the re-absorption of shed labour. However, the nature of the labour market risk associated with manufacturing job loss is also likely to vary depending on the structure of service sector development. For example (for reasons which we shall discuss later), public service sector employment has tended to be associated with higher rates of pay and greater levels of employment security than private.[5]

In fact, patterns of service sector development vary significantly across countries. Table 11.3 shows average rates of service sector employment as a percentage of the working age population in the 1970s and early 1990s in a range of countries, as well as of the percentage of this employment located in the public sector. The final two columns show the change in these measures between the two periods.

From column 6 we can see that the importance of the service sector as an employer has increased in all countries except Germany over the last two decades. In fact, by the first half of the 1990s it employed close to half of the working age population in the majority of the countries shown. In some countries service sector expansion was more limited, however. In Italy and the Netherlands, as in Germany, for example, less than a third of the population was engaged in service sector activities by the later period. In addition, the composition of service sector expansion has varied significantly across countries. Thus while the US and Norway exhibited similarly high rates of expansion (at 10 and 11 points, respectively), in the US this expansion was associated with a sharp decline in the public sector component of service employment, while in Norway the public sector component *increased* similarly sharply. In fact, service sector

Table 11.3 Service sector employment as a percentage of the working population (ages 15–64)

	1970–9		*1990–4*		*Change*[a]	
	Service employment	*% public*	*Service employment*	*% public*	*Service employment*	*% public*
Sweden	42	47	49	50	7	3
Denmark	37	45	44	50	7	5
Norway	38	37	49	43	11	6
Germany	26	34	23	35	−3	1
Netherlands	28	25	31	21	3	−4
Italy	18	43	23	40	5	−3
France	30	44	36	43	6	−1
UK	36	39	43	30	7	−9
USA	36	28	46	22	10	−6
Canada	38	34	45	33	7	−1
Australia	42	21	48	21	6	0
Average	34	36	40	35	6	−1

Source: OECD (1996a).

Note

a Change is the difference between the two periods.

employment became increasingly public in all three Scandinavian countries, although this performance contrasts notably with the general trend. The most extreme example of the trend towards the privatisation of service sector employment is observed in the UK. Thus while total service sector employment in the UK increases from 36 to 43 per cent of the adult population, the percentage of this employment located in the public sector falls from 39 to 30 per cent.

De-industrialisation thus poses a challenge to the welfare state. But the nature and magnitude of that challenge are closely related to developments in the service sector. It is ironic, therefore, that (as the next section will describe) the structure and extent of service sector development is itself significantly affected by welfare state institutions and policies: the relationship between welfare states and varieties of capitalism is in this instance a two-way street.

The trilemma of the service economy[6]

The connection between public service sector development and welfare state policy is straightforward. Welfare states have traditionally guaranteed their citizens a range of legal and material rights (including, for example, rights to employment protection in the face of labour market insecurity and to income protection in the face of job loss, disability or old age). However they have also played an active role in the provision of services, of which education, health and child care are probably the most obvious examples. Of course, the range of services for which governments have assumed responsibility, as well as the degree of responsibility which they have assumed, varies significantly across countries and across welfare state regimes. Thus while traditionally social democratic welfare states have been associated with the provision of a wide range of public services to citizens, Christian democratic regimes have tended to eschew state provision and to rely more heavily on social networks such as the family or church organisations. Meanwhile in neo-liberal regimes, the notion that services, like all goods, are most efficiently provided in market, has led to minimal government involvement in service provision (Esping-Andersen 1990). Clearly the degree of responsibility assumed by governments in the provision of services directly affects the public private mix in service provision and the extent of public service sector employment. The connection between welfare state policies and private service sector development, however, while perhaps less immediately obvious, is no less real.

To state the relationship in its starkest terms, private service sector employment expansion is inhibited by policies which tend to compress wage structures. Thus in an age of de-industrialisation, solidaristic wage policies can create an obstacle to employment expansion where previously their employment effects were considered to be at worst insignificant, at best positive. In fact the famous Rehn–Meidner model of industrial development showed that in the 'golden age' of industrial expansion, policies aimed at reducing market inequalities tended to complement the existing virtuous circle of falling prices, real wage increases, and the expansion of production and employment (Meidner 1974; Rehn 1985). This complementary relationship existed because solidaristic policies had the effect of restraining relative wages in the most productive industries, thus magnifying the positive effects of productivity increases on demand and employment in these sectors; at the same time, by raising relative wages in the least dynamic sectors where the scope for productivity increases was smallest, firms in these sectors were forced either to innovate or perish. Either way, the net effect was to shift production and employment to the more productive firms which enjoyed the greatest capacity for dynamic expansion. Especially if complemented with active labour market policies, there was therefore no inherent contradiction between reducing wage equality and increasing demand.

There is a crucial difference between the industrial expansion of the 'golden age' and current expansions in service production, however. While manufacturing expansion occurred in the most dynamic and internationally integrated sectors of the economy (facilitating international specialisation), current service sector expansion has predominantly come about in sheltered sectors such as personal services, health care, education and what Esping-Andersen (1990) has called 'food and fun' services where productivity growth tends to be slower and where international specialisation is low. Although it is notoriously difficult to measure productivity in services, and although there are obviously important differences across branches, there is broad consensus among economists that most services are inherently less conducive to rapid productivity growth.[7] Teachers can serve more students, nurses more patients, and waiters more customers, but this is not easily achieved without a decline in the quality of the service.[8] Thus OECD estimates of total factor productivity show a continuing gap in productivity growth between private services and manufacturing of around 2.5 per annum between 1970 and 1994 (Iversen 1998).

It will be recalled that the virtuous circle which allowed real wages and employment to expand simultaneously in the 'golden age' depended on high levels of productivity because it enabled prices to fall while real wages and demand increased. At low levels of productivity, similar price reductions can only be achieved through higher levels of wage restraint. If wages in services are linked with wages in more highly productive manufacturing sectors, therefore, at least some private service production will be priced out of the market, and expansion of employment will be inhibited. Hence, in the context of rising demand for low productivity services, the Rehn–Meidner model has been turned on its head: solidaristic wage policies tend to inhibit employment because relative wages are kept high in the *least* productive sectors where demand is the most price elastic.

This effect is illustrated in Fig. 11.1, which plots the relationship between earnings equality (measured by the D1/D5 ratio – the ratio of the income of a worker in the lowest decile of the earnings distribution to that of the median worker) and private service sector employment expansion.[9] Stronger statistical evidence in support of the negative relationship between earnings and equality and private service sector employment growth, controlling for a range of economic and institutional factors, is offered in Glyn (1997) and Iversen and Wren (1998).

Of course, as an alternative to private service sector expansion, the government can assume the responsibility for employing workers at wages that are more consistent with a solidaristic wage policy. This option has been heavily favoured by social democratic governments which have used welfare state

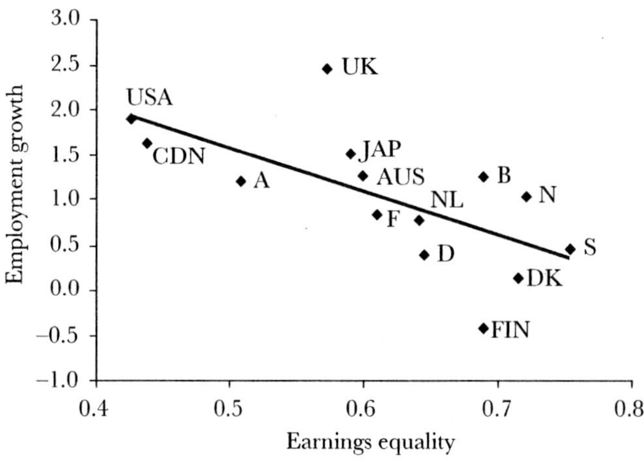

Figure 11.1 Earnings equality and private service employment growth, 1974–93.

Sources: Data on private service sector employment was obtained from the OECD International Sectoral Database (1996); on D1/D5 ratios from the OECD Employment Outlook (1991, 1996).

Notes: The horizontal axis shows average annual growth rates in levels of private service sector employment as a percentage of the working age population between 1974 and 1993; the vertical axis shows the average D1/D5 ratio over the same period.

expansion as a means not only of increasing the range of publicly provided services, but also of incorporating large numbers of workers into welfare state employment at relatively high wage rates. Figure 11.2 demonstrates the obvious drawback of this strategy. Higher levels of public service employment expansion are accompanied by larger public sector wage bills. Since this wage bill must be financed from the public purse, the implication is that low levels of spending, taxation and deficits are more difficult to combine with earnings equality and high employment today than in the 'golden age' of manufacturing.

De-industrialisation thus brings to the fore a new set of trade-offs in economic policy which Iversen and Wren (1998) label the trilemma of the service economy. Since solidaristic wage policies tend to inhibit private service employment expansion, their continued pursuit entails sacrifices in terms of either employment creation or budgetary restraint (that is, low levels of spending, taxation and/or public debt). A combined emphasis on the goals of equality and budgetary restraint will tend to constrain both private and public sector employment expansion, entailing increasing costs in terms of overall employment in the context of de-industrialisation. By contrast, the simultaneous pursuit of the goals of equality and employment creation requires higher levels of spending, and with it higher levels of debt and/or taxation. Meanwhile, the cost of private service sector expansion (the alternative strategy for combining budgetary restraint with employment creation) is the relaxation of welfare state protection at the lower

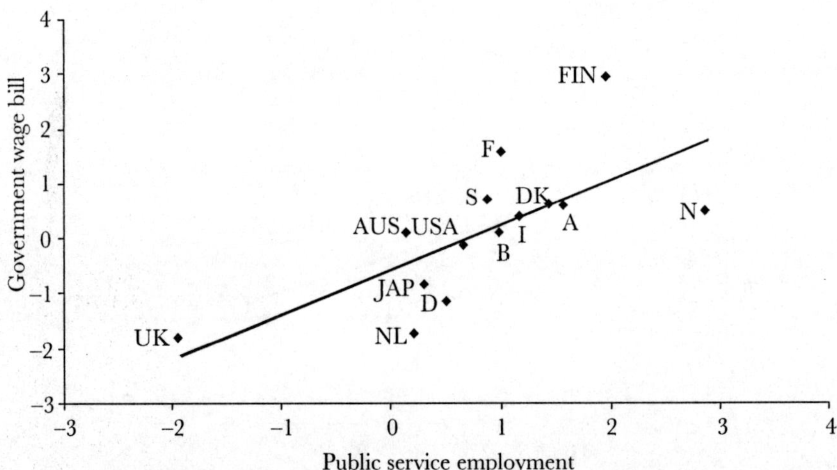

Figure 11.2 Change in public service employment and the government wage bill (annual growth rates in per cent), 1975–94.

Source: Public Employment and Wages data set compiled by T. R. Cusack, Science Centre, Berlin (1998).

Notes: The horizontal axis shows annual average growth rates in public service employment as a percentage of the working age population between 1975 and 1994; the vertical axis shows annual average growth rates in the government wage bill as a percentage of GDP over the same period.

end of the wage scale and increased levels of income inequality. Hence the trilemma: at most two of the policy goals of equality, employment creation and budgetary restraint may be pursued successfully at any one time.

Responding to the trilemma

What determines how welfare states respond to this new set of trade-offs? Wren (2000) and Iversen and Wren (1998) argue that governments representing the three chief ideological traditions in Western political thought – social democracy, Christian democracy and neo-liberalism – possess distinct sets of preferences with respect to the distributional choices implied by the trilemma, and that their response to the challenge of de-industrialisation will be conditioned by these preferences.

Social democratic ideology, for example, traditionally combines a strong egalitarian ethos with a work ethic that emphasises employment as the origin of collective identity and individual fulfilment. Moreover, it conceives of the state as the appropriate tool to use in order to achieve its egalitarian and full employment objectives. Thus, it is argued that when faced with a three-way choice between the policy goals of employment creation, equality and fiscal restraint, social democratic governments will place a heavy emphasis on the goals of equality and high employment and display a willingness to finance the pursuit of these goals through high levels of state spending and taxation.

Neo-liberal ideology, by contrast, centres on the belief that freely operating markets are inherently welfare maximising whereas state involvement in the economy leads to organisational inefficiencies and a misallocation of resources (due to 'rent-seeking' behaviour by special interest groups). Market wages are considered to accurately reflect the contribution of individuals to overall welfare – reflected in the neo-classical economic concept of marginal productivity – while competition between private firms in decentralised markets is believed to lead to the spread of 'best practices' that will maximise efficiency and employment opportunities. This economic ideology is combined with a work ethic which underscores self-reliance through active labour market participation. The role of the government is to ensure that competition is indeed fair, and that individuals have equal access to the opportunities that industrious participation in the economy affords them. It is *not* the business of government to guarantee that such participation leads to equality of outcomes. Neo-liberal governments, therefore, are expected to emphasise the minimisation of spending and taxation and embrace higher levels of inequality in the pursuit of private sector employment.

Christian democratic ideology also underscores the minimisation of direct state participation in the economy, but it places greater weight on equality and less on individual self-reliance and free markets than neo-liberalism. In corporatist and Christian democratic thought community, church and family are seen as bulwarks against the de-humanising and alienating effects of unfettered markets, as well as against the potential encroachments of state power on the independence and freedom of associational life (Van Kersbergen 1995). Although society is recognised as inherently hierarchical and status-differentiated, stark market-generated inequalities are seen as a potential danger to the social order. High employment levels, on the other hand, are a relatively low priority in this model because women are viewed as the guardian of the traditional family, and hence not encouraged to participate in the labour market. Although women are free to work, they may pursue equally important functions outside the labour market caring for children and spouse, and it is not the responsibility of the government to ensure that women are afforded the same job opportunities as men. Thus, Christian democrats emphasise both equality and low spending and taxation, and tend to be more accepting the low levels of employment which this implies. While the political acceptability of policies based on minimising female labour market participation has declined over time, the idea of sharing available work opportunities through policies aimed at minimising the labour supply – such as early and disability retirement schemes and job sharing – remains prominent in Christian democratic platforms.

Iversen and Wren's analysis of national responses to the trilemma shares with the path-breaking work of Esping-Andersen (1990) a concern with the impact of the three dominant ideologies in Western political thought – social democracy, Christian democracy and neo-liberalism – on the welfare state. The role which these two arguments accord to ideology in explaining post-industrial employment trajectories, however, is subtly different. For Esping-Andersen, ideology and government partisanship play a significant role in explaining initial patterns of welfare state development. At a certain point, however, welfare state institutions appear to become 'locked-in', so that national responses to the crisis of de-industrialisation, for example, are largely conditioned by inherited welfare state structure.[10] While institutions are expected to evolve and adapt to changing circumstances, the political mechanisms underlying this evolution are left unexplored. Thus the explanation of change becomes essentially functionalist in nature, with its impetus arising from the particular economic pressure to which each welfare state regime type is subject, and little scope for independent *political choice* over competing distributional objectives remains.

Iversen and Wren (1998) and Wren (2000), by contrast, emphasise the continued political power of governments of differing ideological hues to direct policy and influence institutional change in line with their distributional preferences.[11] This is not to imply that inherited institutional structures place *no* constraints on government action. Pierson (1994, 1996) provides a convincing *political* logic for the resilience of welfare state policies and institutions, demonstrating how, over time, electoral support coalitions build up around existing policies, tending to raise the costs of change and creating an institutional bias towards the status quo. Pierson's account thus underlines the 'path-dependent' nature of many aspects of welfare state development. However, his close examination of the political mechanisms underlying policy change also highlights the fact that the costs of change can vary both with the policy itself and with the institutional environment. Thus, for example, the political costs of altering the terms of a government-imposed incomes policy are likely to be significantly less than those involved in the enforced dismantling of wage setting institutions which are controlled by union and employer organisations.

All of which suggests, therefore, that national responses to the trilemma are likely to be determined by the interaction of the political preferences of elected governments and the institutional environment in which they find themselves. But what of *external* constraints on government action? One well-known line of argument is that the globalisation of capital and goods markets leads to pressure for a cross-national convergence of social policy along neo-liberal lines. In an era of globally integrated financial markets, it is argued, a lack of fiscal restraint, symbolised by increasing deficits, will be punished by the markets through the imposition of high interest rate premia. Meanwhile the threat of capital flight reduces the capacity of governments to finance social policy through taxation. High rates of corporate taxation eat into company profits; while taxes on labour, where they are passed on to real wages, pose a threat to competitiveness. Since mobility increases the power of capital owners to sanction such policies, it also tends to reduce the capacity of governments to engage in tax-financed expansions (Pfaller *et al.* 1991; Kurzer 1993; Rodrik 1996, 1997). In fact, recent research has challenged the importance of these constraints in practice (Krugman 1996; Garrett 1998; Mosley 1999). For participants in the European Monetary Union, however, restrictions imposed on deficit spending by the Maastricht convergence criteria constitute more tangible institutional constraints on fiscal expansion.

In the context of the trilemma, increased restrictions on public spending make the simultaneous pursuit of the goals of equality and employment creation more difficult, since they reduce the capacity of governments to finance large public sector wage bills. Furthermore, insofar as low levels of service employment creation imply increased levels of dependency on welfare state budgets, a reduction in governments' fiscal resources may also create increased pressure to trade off equality for private service sector employment creation. In general, therefore, theoretical arguments about the effects of globalisation on national economic policy suggest that we should expect increases in openness to be associated with a convergence in social policy towards increased flexibility in wage setting and the promotion of private rather than public service sector expansion.

In spite of increased economic openness, however, empirical studies continue to find evidence of significant effects of partisanship on distributional policies over the last two decades. Garrett (1998), for example, provides strong evidence in support of the argument that big government, countercyclical fiscal policies and progressive taxation remained important elements of a distinctive social democratic socioeconomic strategy in the 1980s, while Boix (1997, 1998) finds a relationship between left government and levels of spending on human and physical capital formation in this period. Of more direct relevance to the service economy trilemma are findings of significant effects of partisanship on levels of government consumption of goods and services (Cusack 1997; Iversen and Cusack 2000), public employment (Wren and Iversen 1997; Wren 2000), and wage structures (Wren and Iversen 1997; Wren 2000) which also persist throughout the decade. The following section describes the evolution of wage and public employment policies in a range of OECD countries over the 1980s and early 1990s.

The evolution of public employment and wage policy: 1979–94

Table 11.4 charts the evolution of public employment policy in a range of OECD countries over the 1980s and early 1990s. Numerical columns 1 and 6 show the proportion of the working age population engaged in public service sector employment at the start and end of the period. The remaining columns record average annual growth rates in this ratio.

At the start of the period, relatively clear regime effects are visible here. Thus the Scandinavian social democratic regimes exhibit average growth rates in public sector employment ratios of around 3 per cent in the four years following the second oil crisis, while the public sector contracts in three out of the four neo-liberal welfare states – the UK, Australia and the US. In contrast, the Christian democratic regimes displayed moderate levels of public sector growth over this period, but in general this expansion occurred from a significantly lower base. In fact, at the start of the period, the proportion of the working age population engaged in the public service sector was significantly lower in Germany, the Netherlands and Italy than most of the neo-liberal regimes, this figure of course reflecting the bias in Christian democratic welfare states towards low levels of labour market participation.

These patterns begin to break up in the mid-1980s, to be replaced by a general trend towards the curtailment of public sector expansion, and at the start of this decade, in many cases, by cutbacks in public sector employment. Thus we see some evidence here of a general tightening of fiscal constraints on public employment policy making over the last decade. There remain exceptions to this trend,

Table 11.4 Public service sector employment as a percentage of the population (ages 15–64), 1979–94

	Level[a] *1979*	*Average annual employment growth (in %)*				*Level*[a] *1994*
		1979–82	*1983–6*	*1987–90*	*1991–4*	
Sweden	22	3	1	0	−3	22
Denmark	19	4	0	0	−1	21
Norway	15	3	2	2	2	21
Germany	8	1	1	0	−3	8
Netherlands	6	1	−1	−1	1	6
France	12	1	2	0	2	13
Italy	8	1	0	1	1	8
UK	14	−1	0	0	−8	9
Australia	10	−1	2	−1	−2	10
USA	9	−1	0	2	1	10
Canada	13	0	1	1	−1	14
Average	12	1	1	0	−1	13

Source: OECD (1996a).

Note

a Public employment in per cent of total employment.

however – the most notable being the continued expansionary policies of socialist governments in France and Norway. These observations are consistent with statistical results suggesting that while government partisanship remains an important determinant of levels of public employment and of government consumption of goods and services, the *size* of observed partisan effects may have decreased somewhat during the 1980s (Cusack 1997; Wren and Iversen 1997; Wren 2000).

Table 11.5 shows the evolution of income differentials over the 1980s and early 1990s. Since we are interested in barriers to wage flexibility among low-paid, low-skilled workers, the D1/D5 ratio (measuring the ratio of the gross earnings of a worker at the top of the 10th (that is, the lowest) earnings decile to that of the median worker) is of particular relevance. The first thing to notice from the table is that there is no indication of a convergence in wage structures across countries over this period – or even a notable trend towards increased flexibility. In fact, as measured by the D1/D5 ratio, inequality increased in only four countries – the US, Canada, the UK and Sweden. In all other countries the level of equality either increased significantly – as in Norway, Germany and Italy – or remained relatively constant – as in Denmark, the Netherlands, France and Australia.

Neither levels of equality nor directions of movement can be explained purely by welfare state regime type. While the Scandinavian economies display significantly higher and the North American economies significantly lower levels of equality throughout the period, the distinctions between other countries and patterns of movement are less clear. The UK and Australia – neo-liberal welfare states in Esping-Andersen's categorisation – begin the decade with wage structures similar to that of the Christian democratic regimes – Germany, the Netherlands and France. Over the course of the decade, equality does decrease significantly in the UK, but not in Australia. Among those countries classified as social democratic, Norway exhibits a significant increase in equality, while levels of equality start to decline in the most egalitarian of all – Sweden.

Table 11.5 Evolution of income differentials (D1/D5 in per cent), 1979–94

	1979–82	*1983–6*	*1987–90*	*1991–4*	*Change*[a]
Sweden	76	76	75	74	−2
Denmark	71	71	72	—	+1
Norway	71	73	69	76	+5
Germany	61	62	65	68	+7
Netherlands	—	64	64	64	0
France	60	62	61	61	+1
Italy	55	59	66	60	+5
UK	59	58	56	56	−3
Australia	60	60	59	61	+1
USA	45	42	40	—	−5
Canada	45	41	42	44	−1

Sources: OECD (1991, 1996b).

Note

a Change is the difference between the two periods.

Thus concepts of permanent welfare state regime type are at best only partially capable of explaining the dynamics of change in wage structures over the last decade and a half. Neither is there any evidence, however, that the pressures of increased economic openness or a spreading neo-liberal orthodoxy have caused a convergence of wage structures across countries.[12] In order to understand these patterns of movement, therefore, we need to look more closely at the policies and institutions which underlie them.

Wage structures and welfare state policies

Recent research has established the close links between wage structures and the structure of collective bargaining (Rowthorn 1992; Iversen 1996, 1999; Wren and Iversen 1997; Pontusson 1999; Rueda and Pontusson 2000; Wallerstein 1999). In particular, it has been argued that highly centralised wage bargaining systems tend to increase the bargaining power of lower paid workers, with positive effects on equality (Rowthorn 1992; Iversen 1996, 1999; Pontusson 1999). The strength of this relationship is demonstrated in Fig. 11.3, which plots the average level of centralisation of bargaining[13] in the period from 1973 to 1993 against average D1/D5 ratios over the same period.

If wage bargaining configurations explain a significant part of the variation in wage structures across countries and over time, what is the mechanism which links government ideology to these outcomes? In fact, there are numerous ways in which governments can and do influence patterns of income distribution. In the first place, partisanship has historically played a significant role in the development and support of centralised bargaining systems. The important role

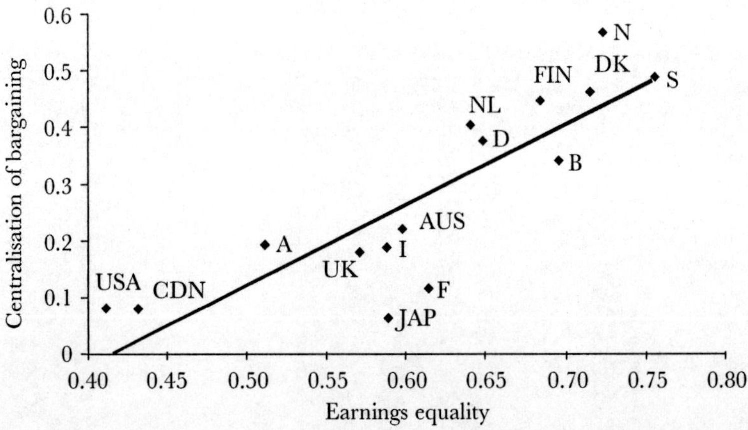

Figure 11.3 Earnings equality and the centralisation of wage bargaining, 1973–93.

Notes: The horizontal axis shows the average value of the D1/D5 ratio between 1973 and 1993; the vertical axis shows the average value of Iversen's (1999) index of centralisation of wage bargaining.

played by social democratic governments as 'guarantors' of a labour- friendly policy environment is often emphasised in analyses of the political preconditions for the successful conclusion of centralised agreements between unions and employers' organisations. The pursuit of fiscal and monetary policies aimed at promoting the goal of full employment, and the introduction of tax and subsidy packages designed to encourage high levels of domestic reinvestment of corporate profits, reduced the uncertainty associated with the returns to wage restraint for unions, and formed a critical element of the social democratic corporatist model (Cameron 1978, 1984; Przeworski and Wallerstein 1982; Lange 1984; Scharpf 1987; Garrett and Lange 1991). In addition, it has been argued that a key element of the class compromise embodied in the social democratic model involved more direct compensation for union wage restraint in the form of expansions of the social wage through benefit improvements and new social programmes (Cameron 1978, 1984; Esping-Andersen 1990).

Meanwhile, while the collapse of centralised bargaining in Sweden and Denmark in the 1980s may be primarily attributed to splits within the union and employer organisations themselves,[14] it has been argued that partisanship continued to play a significant role in accelerating or retarding this process (Iversen 1996, 1999). Thus, while the neo-liberal government in Denmark actively encouraged the disintegration process through the pursuit of austere macroeconomic policies, the Swedish social democrats continued their attempts to shore up the traditional social democratic contract through the pursuit of full employment policies until a fiscal and currency crisis forced a change in the monetary regime at the end of the decade.

Moreover, the Swedish case is the only example we have of a social democratic government presiding over a substantial decentralisation of bargaining procedures and a significant increase in levels of inequality in this period. In Norway, Austria and Australia, social democratic governments were actively engaged in instituting the increased centralisation of bargaining, resulting in significant increases in equality in the Norwegian case in particular (Kyloh 1989; OECD 1994; Wallerstein *et al.* 1997; Hawke and Wooden 1998). Meanwhile, in the UK, in sharp contrast, Thatcher's neo-liberal government embarked on a radical programme of deregulation accompanied by tight macroeconomic policies and direct legislative attacks on the unions, which dramatically reduced their organisational and bargaining power (Crouch 1990; Brown and King 1988; Ward 1988; Hall 1986).

Thus governments can exert an *indirect* influence on wage structures by choosing to support or undermine the institutions of wage bargaining. Moreover, they also possess a wide array of instruments with which they are capable of influencing the structure of wages more *directly*. One area where there is significant scope for government intervention is in determining the extent of coverage of collective agreements. In general, in highly centralised bargaining systems, union organisations tend also to be relatively centralised, and union density rates are high. As a result, collective agreements struck in these systems cover a high proportion of workers. In less centralised systems, however, the correlation between centralisation and coverage rates is not so strong. In particular, where rates of union density are low, external mechanisms may be necessary if collective agreements are to be transferred to larger proportions of the workforce. In several countries mandatory extension laws ensure that levels of collective bargaining coverage are high even where rates of union density are low or declining. This has most notably been the case in France and the Netherlands where extension laws have significantly affected the structure of wages (Freeman 1996; Visser 1998). Again in the UK several important legal extension mechanisms were removed under the neo-liberal government in the 1980s.[15]

Other legal mechanisms which impact wage structures directly are equal pay and minimum wage legislation, the latter affecting the relative wages of low wage workers in particular. The decline in the real value of the minimum wage has been cited as an important factor influencing the rise in earning dispersion in the 1980s in the US (Freeman 1996; Mishel and Bernstein 1994; Dinardo *et al.* 1994) and in Britain (Machin and Manning 1994). In the US, federal statutory minimum wages were frozen between January 1981 and April 1990 under the neo-liberal Republican government, while in Britain the independent wages councils, responsible for setting a minimum wage in the most vulnerable industries (many of them low productivity service sectors such as retailing and catering), saw their powers removed by the conservatives. In sharp contrast, the social democratic government in Australia instituted regular increases in minimum wages throughout the 1980s (Belchamber 1996), and the indexation of legal minimum wages to wage and price developments has contributed to a relatively high degree of earnings equality in the bottom half of the earnings distribution in France and the Netherlands.

Where minimum wage legislation is nominally absent, high levels of replacement rates on unemployment benefits can act in an identical fashion to place a floor on low wages. Thus in Denmark, extremely high replacement rates tend to act as a functional equivalent to minimum wage regulation (which is relatively weak). According to OECD estimates, the generosity of unemployment benefits (based on a summary indicator taking account of replacement rates for three different types of family circumstances and durations of unemployment) in Denmark is significantly higher than almost all other countries (OECD 1994). Thus Denmark scores 53 on the OECD's index in 1981, compared with scores of 24 and 29, respectively, in Sweden and Norway, the other social democratic regimes. This fact may go some way in explaining the persistently high D1/D5 ratios recorded in Denmark in the face of significant decentralisation of bargaining. Interestingly, while neo-liberal governance is reflected in declines in the generosity of unemployment benefits in the UK case,[16] Norway, Sweden and France all record significant increases[17] in the generosity of benefits under the social democratic governments of this period.

Government-imposed incomes policies have also been used extensively to influence wage structures. In Denmark in the 1970s, for example, the automatic linkage of wage increases to a cost of living index had a considerable dampening effect on wage inequality due to the combination of high inflation and flat-rate wage increases (Flanagan *et al.* 1983; Iversen and Thygesen 1998), while the similarly constructed *Scala Mobile* in Italy was also associated with significant increases in equality in that country in the late 1970s and early 1980s (as can be seen from Table 11.5). Meanwhile, governments in both Belgium and the Netherlands have traditionally used their power to intervene directly in the wage setting process to structure relative wages (Wolinetz 1989; Hancké 1991; Visser 1998; Visser and Hemerijck 1997). The imposition of egalitarian incomes policies in Denmark ceased with the election of a neo-liberal government at the start of the 1980s. In Italy, increased flexibility was introduced into the *Scala Mobile* in the mid-1980s, but it was not finally removed until the early 1990s, when the era of Christian democratic hegemony was ended by the collapse of the political and party systems.

Finally, a key policy initiative which introduced greater flexibility into service sector wage setting in the UK case was the widespread service privatisation programme undertaken by the neo-liberal government. The transfer of large numbers of workers from the most unionised sector of the economy (public services) to the least unionised (private services) had the effect of severely reducing the bargaining power of low-skilled workers.

Thus aside from their capacity to support or attack the institutions of wage bargaining, governments also possess considerable power to influence wage structures more directly. This power is evidenced by research indicating that partisan governments have regularly manipulated wage structures in pursuit of their distributional goals (Wren and Iversen 1997; Iversen and Wren 1998; Wren 2000). In particular, Wren (2000) shows that, irrespective of the structure of wage bargaining, Christian democratic and social democratic strength in government were associated with positive effects on levels of equality over the 1980s and early 1990s, while the observed relationship between neo-liberal parliamentary strength and equality was negative (Wren 2000).

Thus it appears that, in spite of the constraints imposed on their actions by inherited institutional structures and increased economic openness, governments retain a considerable ability to influence wage structures. In the case of public employment policy there is more evidence of the effects of a tightening of international macroeconomic constraints. Nevertheless, effects of partisanship also remain visible in this area. This suggests that governments should possess a significant degree of power to orchestrate strategic responses to the challenge of de-industrialisation and the trilemma of the service economy. The following section will discuss how governments from each of the three ideological traditions discussed – neo-liberalism, social democracy and Christian democracy – have responded to these challenges during the 1980s and early 1990s.[18]

Strategic responses to the trilemma

The neo-liberal response: Britain under Thatcher

When Thatcher's neo-liberal government came to office in the UK at the start of the 1980s, it inherited a situation of rapidly rising unemployment, public deficit problems and considerable industrial conflict. The Labour government, in office from 1974 to 1979, had attempted to institute a typically social democratic response to the first oil crisis. Their 'Social Contract' with the unions proposed an exchange of union wage restraint for the pursuit of government policies favourable to worker interests. These included the imposition of legal recognition of unions, equal pay legislation and the continued expansion public sector services (Ward 1988). The Contract foundered in the face of economic recession and continued militancy in union wage demands. As in many countries in this period, the government responded to the social actors' failure to reach non-inflationary wage agreements by imposing wage controls. Their failure to impose levels of restraint on certain groups of private employees equivalent to those forced on the public sector led to increased militancy on the part of the strong public sector unions, however, and the 'winter of discontent' of public strike action, combined with a crisis of confidence caused by the debt and currency crises and the resort to borrowing from the IMF, resulted in the Labour government's electoral defeat in 1979 (Hall 1986).

The new neo-liberal government responded to the crisis by instituting a radical course of deregulation, designed to reorganise the economy and to permanently reduce the political power of the unions. No attempt was made to shore up the failed 'Social Contract'. Instead, union power was undermined by the introduction of the Employment and Trade Union Acts of 1980, 1982 and 1984. Procedures for establishing union recognition and enforcing generally recognised norms of pay and working conditions on low-paying employers were abolished. Rights to industrial action were restricted to those unions directly involved in a conflict and then only when mandatory secret balloting of union members had occurred. In addition the creation of 'closed shops' which placed restrictions on the hiring of non-union members was made considerably more difficult (Crouch 1990; Brown and King 1988; Ward 1988; Hall 1986). The Acts had the effect of substantially reducing union organisational capacity and labour market power, and under these circumstances it became virtually impossible to negotiate over wage and working conditions at anything other than a highly decentralised level.

Meanwhile, all institutional obstacles to flexibility in wage setting and employment contracts came under attack. Unemployment benefits and entitlement were significantly cut back, while the power of the Wage Councils, responsible for setting a minimum wage in the most vulnerable industries (many of them low productivity service sectors such as retailing and catering), was substantially reduced. Important legal extension mechanisms on collectively bargained agreements were also removed, resulting in a decline in collective bargaining coverage from 70 to 47 per cent over the 1980s (OECD 1994). These included the Fair Wage Resolution, which had obliged all employers working on government contracts to follow industrial level agreements on wages and working conditions, and provisions in the Employment Protection Act (introduced by the Labour government in 1975) under which firms could be obliged to follow industry level collective bargains.[19]

Substantial public sector cutbacks had the dual effect of combating the fiscal crisis and reducing the power of the public sector unions (which had been clearly demonstrated during the 'winter of discontent'). Under the government's privatisation scheme, a wide range of previously publicly provided services were offered up for competitive tender and contracted out. This had the effect of transferring large numbers of low-skilled workers from the most highly unionised sector in the economy to the private services sector, where unions were weakest. This action alone removed one of the most significant obstacles to the introduction of wage flexibility at the lower end of the wage scale, and the effects could be immediately seen in the low wages paid to subcontracted private sector workers compared to their public sector predecessors. According to one estimate, the wages of hospital cleaners, for example, were reduced by between 30 and 40 per cent when cleaning jobs were 'contracted out' to the private sector (Ward 1988).

The results of the Thatcherite reforms are striking. All measures of inequality in Britain show significant increases over the 1980s. We can see from Table 11.5 that the D1/D5 ratio fell from 59 to 56, and the D1/D9[20] ratio also fell from 35 to 30 per cent over this period (OECD 1991, 1996). This increase was accompanied by a significant expansion (from 15 to 21 per cent between 1979 and 1993) in the proportion of the working age population engaged in the private provision of personal and social services (OECD 1996).[21] At the same time, as shown in Table 11.4, the proportion of the adult population employed in the public service sector fell back from 14 to 9 per cent (OECD 1996).

The Christian Democratic response?: the Netherlands

Like the British conservatives, the Christian democrat–neo-liberal coalition government which came to power in the Netherlands at the end of the 1970s, inherited a situation of rapidly rising unemployment and fiscal crisis. The preceding government (a coalition between social and Christian democrats) had pursued notably egalitarian incomes policies. Social benefits were extended and formally linked to the statutory minimum wage (at high replacement rates). Meanwhile, the minimum wage itself was linked to developments in average private sector wages, as were public sector wages (Wolinetz 1989; Visser 1998; Visser and Hemerijck 1997). These changes added to the automatic flat-rate price escalator clauses which had been included in collective agreements since the late 1960s, to create serious obstacles to flexibility at the lower end of the wage structure.

When unemployment rates doubled in the wake of the second oil shock, the linkage of benefits with private sector wages began to create severe fiscal problems. Considerable conflict existed within the new coalition government as to the best way out of the crisis. The neo-liberal VVD[22] argued that the system of wage and benefit indexation was destroying the competitiveness of Dutch industry by increasing wage costs and taxation, and called for the removal of all labour market rigidities and substantial cutbacks in public expenditure. The Christian democratic CDA,[23] meanwhile, also sought methods to reduce expenditure, but was resistant to the idea of substantial cutbacks in income protection for low wage groups. Its proposed solutions to the joint unemployment and budgetary crisis therefore emphasised wage restraint and job sharing policies within a context of continued welfare state protection for low income groups (Wolinetz 1989; Visser 1998; Visser and Hemerijck 1997).

After the election of 1982, when the VVD significantly increased its representation in the cabinet,[24] the coalition's policy stance became more neo-liberal. The new government imposed a strict austerity package, suspended wage and price indexation, and imposed freezes on minimum wages, benefits and the salaries of public sector workers. Faced with the threat of radical intervention, the social partners reached a bipartite agreement on wages and working conditions for the first time in ten years – the Wassenaar Accord – under which unions agreed to surrender the jealously guarded wage–price linkage mechanism in return for concessions from employer organisations on the reduction of working time.

Thus increased flexibility began to be introduced into Dutch wage setting procedures in the 1980s. Nevertheless, low wage incomes remained extremely heavily protected in comparative terms. While cutbacks in real benefit levels did occur, they were small compared with those observed in Britain. According to OECD estimates, the average generosity of Dutch unemployment benefits remained substantially higher than most other countries (and was only outstripped by Denmark) during the 1980s (OECD 1994).[25] Equally significant, during this period, was the continued widespread reliance on generous disability benefits as an alternative to redundancy by firms seeking to restructure, which led to 13 per cent of the labour force being listed as disabled by the end of the decade (Jones 1998).

Meanwhile, while the linkage of benefits, wage minima and average wages was suspended during most of the 1980s, it was re-established in 1989 with the replacement of the VVD by the social democrats as coalition partners of the CDA. This government introduced some flexibility into the mechanism with the passing of the Conditional Linking Act in 1992, which made linkage contingent on dependency ratios and average wage growth. However, it continues to provide a significant degree of protection for low incomes. Protection is also provided by the continued presence of legal extension mechanisms on collective agreements. By law, Dutch governments have the power to declare agreements binding on the entire sector in which they were negotiated, and it is estimated that around three-quarters of sectoral agreements are extended in this way (European Industrial Relations Review 1995).[26] This policy profile stands in significant contrast with that of Britain over this period which saw substantial cutbacks in benefit and the removal of virtually all legal and institutional obstacles to low wages. Also in sharp contrast with the British case, no attempt was made to legally restrict union power.

One area in which the neo-liberal (VVD) and the Christian democratic (CDA) coalition partners were united was in their opposition to the social democratic idea of an active role for the state as an employer and provider of services. As a result of this ideological commitment on the part of the Christian democratic parties, there has been little expansion of public employment in the Netherlands, even in periods (such as the 1970s) when the social democrats formed part of the governing coalition. Instead, the Dutch response to low levels of employment creation has been the expansion of programmes aimed at minimising labour supply. As the political acceptability of policies aimed at discouraging female labour market participation has decreased, Christian democrats have been forced to devise other methods of labour supply reduction. In the 1980s Dutch governments relied heavily on disability retirement programmes (as well as more common early retirement programmes) to achieve this effect. The overuse of disability programmes created its own fiscal crisis in the late 1980s and early 1990s and has since been substantially cut back. However, an emphasis on 'sharing' restricted employment opportunities through working time reduction and job sharing schemes remains.

The evolution of wage structures in the Netherlands and the UK in this period reflects the distinction between wage policies in these two countries. Over the 1980s, de-indexation and the suspension of wage and benefit linkages have resulted in some divergence between public and private sector wages, and between average wages and statutory minima in the Netherlands. However, in relative terms, levels of equality in the Netherlands have remained high and remarkably stable. Thus, as we can see from Table 11.5, the D1/D5 ratio remained unchanged at 64 between the early 1980s and early 1990s (compared with a decline from 59 to 56 in the UK). The D1/D9 ratio, meanwhile, declined by only one point, from 40 to 39, over this period (compared with a decline from 35 to 30 in the UK; OECD 1991, 1996).

These high levels of wage equality have been associated with a relatively small expansion in the proportion of the Dutch population engaged in the private provision of personal and social services. Employment in these sectors increased from 14 to 16 per cent of the working age population between 1979 and 1993, compared with an expansion from 15 to 21 per cent in the UK (OECD 1996). Moreover, it is estimated that, between 1985 and 1990 at least, 75 per cent of total service sector employment creation was part-time,[27] indicating that work sharing has played a substantial role in overall employment creation (Meulders, *et al.* 1994).[28] Meanwhile, referring to Table 11.4, we can see that, throughout the period, only 6 per cent of the Dutch working age population were employed in the provision of *public* services – an extremely low figure in comparative terms (OECD 1996).

The parliamentary socialist response: France

At the beginning of the 1980s, France's new socialist government embarked on a full-scale Keynesian response to the recession. Government spending programmes aimed simultaneously to reflate the economy and effect a substantial redistribution of income. As part of this policy, minimum wages, unemployment benefits, pensions, housing and family benefits were all increased significantly (Cole 1999; Hantrais 1996; Lombard 1995; Hall 1986). Meanwhile, a large-scale nationalisation initiative greatly expanded the size of the public sector. While the emphasis in this period was on the promotion of the state-led industrial sector as the engine of growth, public service sector employment was also expanded substantially.

Thus, while public service sector employment remained constant between 1981 and 1985 in the UK, in France it grew by 10 per cent (OECD 1996).

In the midst of a global recession and the pursuit of deflationary policies in most countries, the French reflation led to growing current account deficits and, ultimately, strong pressure on the franc. Given the government's commitment to remain in the European Monetary System, there was little alternative to a tightening of fiscal and monetary policy if the situation was to be stabilised. By 1983, the government had switched towards a policy of macroeconomic austerity. Public spending was cut back, industrial subsidies reduced, and severe measures were undertaken to restrain prices and incomes. Wage and price increases were decoupled, increases in benefits and minimum wages were slowed down, and high levels of wage restraint were imposed on public sector workers (Lombard 1995; Boyer 1994; Halimi *et al.* 1994; Segrestin 1990).

The switch towards a policy of austerity marked the end of Mitterand's ambitious programme of redistributive Keynesianism based on state-led industrial development. Its demise was cemented by the election of a conservative government under Chirac in 1986. The new government was fully committed to the pursuit of a neo-liberal deregulatory response to the economic crisis. Fiscal and monetary policy were sharply reigned in and plans for the widespread privatisation of nationalised industries were instituted (Schmidt 1996; Hall 1994; Ross 1991). Price controls were removed and measures to increase flexibility in employment contracts were introduced (Boyer 1994; Hall 1994; Segrestin 1990). Minimum wages and benefits were further cut back and public service sector employment expansion was sharply curtailed.[29] 'Cohabitation' with a socialist president and the shortness of conservative tenure curtailed the implementation of a full neo-liberal deregulatory programme, however. In 1988 a new socialist government was elected, and while several important aspects of the conservative programme (such as the industrial privatisation and financial deregulation programmes) were retained under the new government, substantial continuities with the socialist policies of the early 1980s also remained. As a result the contrast between the French and British experiences over the period as a whole remains stark.

In the area of industrial relations, for example, the Auroux laws, introduced in the early 1980s, sought to strengthen union organisation and collective bargaining procedures. While British unions were seeing their rights to recognition, representation and negotiation legally removed, French unions saw their rights extended and annual negotiations on wages and working conditions at the company and industry level made compulsory. At the same time, the laws sought to extend the coverage of industry level agreements on wages and working conditions, setting comprehensive coverage as their objective (Segrestin 1990; Goetschy 1998). As a result of the Auroux laws, there has been a significant increase in the importance of company level bargaining (often associated with less egalitarian outcomes) over the last fifteen years in France. However, while the pace of industry level bargaining has slackened, coverage has increased – from 85 to 95 per cent between 1980 and 1994, compared with a *decline* from 70 to 47 per cent in the UK, according to OECD estimates (OECD 1994). Since bargains set at this level tend to act as a minimum in company level agreements, they therefore continue to have a particularly important effect in protecting the income of low-paid workers (Goetschy 1998).

Meanwhile, while rates of increase slowed from the initial period of socialist rule in the early 1980s, no attempt was made to remove the statutory protection of minimum wages (Boyer 1994). Rather the national minimum wage remained indexed to consumer prices and was also periodically increased by government decree (European Industrial Relations Review 1997). Similarly, while benefit levels were cut and eligibility criteria tightened after the switch towards fiscal austerity, the cutbacks were insufficient to completely erase the expansions of the early 1980s (Tálos and Falkner, 1994). Increases in unemployment benefits, coupled with the introduction of new and extended minimal benefits in the framework of unemployment insurance in 1982 and 1985, resulted in a significant overall increase in the generosity of unemployment benefits between 1981 and 1991, according to OECD estimates (OECD 1994).[30] In addition, on their return to office in 1988, the socialists introduced a new guaranteed minimum income policy for the unemployed. Under the *revenue minimum d'insertion* (RMI), all unemployed people over the age of 25 were guaranteed a minimum income provided they agreed to join state-financed vocational training and educational schemes (European Industrial Relations Review 1988). By 1991, there were close to 2 million RMI recipients (Hantrais 1996).

Table 11.5 shows that the outcome of these policies has been the persistence of relatively high levels of equality in France. By the early 1990s, the French D1/D5 ratio stood at 61, slightly higher than at the beginning of the 1980s. Meanwhile the D1/D9 ratio remained unchanged at 31 per cent. It is unsurprising, therefore, that in France, as in the Netherlands, the percentage of the population engaged in the private provision of personal and social services has remained low, expanding only slightly from 10 to 11 per cent between 1979 and 1993. It will be recalled that in the UK this figure increased from 15 to 21 per cent of the population in the same period under Thatcher's neo-liberal regime.

French socialists also chose to pursue distinctly different policies with respect to public service sector employment in this period. While Mitterand's ambitious plans for the nationalisation of industry were frozen after the currency crisis of 1983, and subsequently reversed through successive privatisations, the protection of the welfare state remained a constant priority (Ross 1991). As a result, public service employment continued to expand in France in a period which saw cutbacks in many countries (see Table 11.4). Moreover successive French socialist governments continued to use the areas of local government and public service production to artificially create employment opportunities for young people (Cole 1999; Goetschy 1998; Ross 1997, 1991). As a result, between 1981 and 1985, under socialist rule, public service sector employment grew by 2.3 per cent per annum on average, compared with 0.8 per cent in the years of conservative cohabitation between 1986 and 1987. Growth remained low during the first couple of years of socialist governance at the end of the decade, but began to expand again in the early 1990s, reaching a peak of 3.1 per cent in 1993, before a return to conservative government saw a further deceleration (OECD 1996).[31]

Finally, the continued distinctiveness of French socialist policies is illustrated by the policy platform of the Jospin government, which came to power in 1997. Upon its election, the government raised the national minimum wage by 4 per cent (the largest increase for fifteen years), and reasserted its aim to extend the coverage of collective agreements to 100 per cent. Moreover, within six months it had provided for the creation of 350,000 jobs for young people in the public sector (European Industrial Relations Review (various issues); Cole 1999; Ross 1997). Meanwhile, along more Christian democratic lines it reduced the basic working week from 39 to 35 hours (Cole 1999; Goetschy 1998; Ross 1997; European Industrial Relations Review 1997).[32]

Conclusions

De-industrialisation poses a common challenge to all the advanced economies. The release of large numbers of low-skilled workers from relatively stable manufacturing employment tends to increase dependency ratios and, with them, the financial burden on the welfare state. Moreover, depending on the conditions of 'non-employment', it threatens to increase levels of social exclusion and discontent (the social effects of early retirement at generous replacement rates, for example, are likely to differ substantially from those of long-term unemployment). Distributional outcomes will also vary, however, depending on the extent to which excess labour can be absorbed into the developing service sector, and the nature of service sector development. Public service sector expansion tends to create relatively well-paid and secure employment, but requires higher levels of deficits and/or taxation to finance the wage bill. The expansion of low-skilled employment in the private service sector, by contrast, can reduce the pressure on welfare state budgets, but at a cost of increasing inequality and social divisions between well-paid labour market insiders and the 'working poor'.

In this chapter I have suggested that, in spite of growing economic pressures, the choice between these distributional outcomes remains ultimately a political one. A critical linkage exists between the welfare state policies which a nation pursues and the 'variety' of service sector development which it experiences. Patterns of public spending on health, education, child care etc. clearly directly affect the rate of public service sector expansion. Additionally though, the rate of *private* service sector expansion is influenced by welfare state policies which affect the structure of wages. Specifically, policies which compress wage structures tend to inhibit employment expansion in the private service sector. I have argued here, and elsewhere, that in spite of the constraints imposed by the external economic environment and by their inherited institutional context, governments possess considerable power to direct policy in these areas and thus to influence both the structure of service sector development and the distributional costs incurred as a result of the de-industrialisation process.

Accordingly, we continue to see distinct variation in the strategic responses of governments to the new set of challenges associated with de-industrialisation, which are reflective of their distributional preferences and underlying ideological goals. In the 1980s and early 1990s neo-liberal governments favoured the pursuit of a 'private sector' route to service sector development, focusing on the introduction of increased flexibilisation in wage setting to facilitate private sector expansion, eschewing public sector investment and, in some instances, embarking on ambitious privatisation plans in the service sector.

In contrast, in the same period, both social democratic and Christian democratic governments continued to support a wide range of institutions and policies designed to protect the wages of workers at the lower end of the income distribution, at a cost of low private service sector employment expansion. On the public sector side, there is some evidence that economic openness and the requirements of participation in the European Monetary System and European Monetary Union may have acted to increasingly constrain policy choices. However, the institution of significant programmes of public sector expansion in Norway and France in particular in this period indicates that where economic and political conditions allow, social democratic governments continue to favour strategies aimed at compensating for employment loss and shortfalls in private service sector development through public sector expansion.[33]

Notes

1 See Rowthorn and Ramaswamy (1997, 1998) for a review of the evidence.
2 A condition known as Engel's Law.
3 See Salter (1960) and Appelbaum and Schettkat (1994, 1995) for convincing empirical documentation of these relationships.
4 This argument has much in common with earlier analyses of welfare state expansion as resulting from attempts by the state to compensate citizens for economic dislocations and insecurity arising from exposure to an uncertain international economic environment (see for example Cameron 1978; Ruggie 1983; Katzenstein 1985) as well as with more recent proponents of this argument (Rodrik 1997; Garrett 1998). Where it differs is in its estimation of the primary source of increased labour market uncertainty as arising from long-term processes of economic development at the domestic level rather than the increased integration of international markets for capital and trade.
5 See Gornick and Jacobs (1998) for recent evidence of public sector wage premiums.
6 The argument in the following section is presented in more detail in Iversen and Wren (1998). The term 'trilemma' (denoting a three-way choice) is borrowed from Swenson (1989).
7 See especially the path-breaking studies Baumol (1967) and Baumol and Bowen (1966).
8 Having said this, it is important to note that productivity in services is not a moot issue. Organisational and sometimes technological factors can inhibit or advance the efficiency of service provision, and with manufacturing employment in decline, the question of how to promote service productivity is in a sense more important than ever.
9 It is interesting to note that the UK case is clearly an outlier here, displaying particularly high rates of private service sector employment expansion over the period. It is unsurprising that this strong private service sector growth performance occurred in the 1980s and early 1990s in the midst of the radical reform efforts of Thatcher's neo-liberal government. The dramatic changes which occurred in the structure of earnings (and in the British economy in general) in this period cannot be adequately captured in the average figures reported in this graph, but will be discussed in more detail later in this chapter.
10 See Esping-Andersen (1990, Part II, 1993, and 1996).

11 Wren (2000) also shows the continued significance of divergences in preferences over these issues in determining patterns of electoral support for social democratic, Christian democratic and neo-liberal parties.
12 Of course, D1/D5 ratios are only one measure of income inequality. It is worth noting, however, that D1/D9 ratios show almost identical patterns of variation across countries and over time in this sample.
13 As measured by Iversen's (1999) index.
14 Iversen (1996) describes how increased integration into international markets and changes in the structure of industrial production resulted in the formation of cross-class 'flexibility coalitions' in favour of a return to decentralised bargaining. An increasing number of employers engaged in 'diversified quality production' based on new technology and scarce highly skilled labour came to favour flexibility in wage setting in order to increase labour productivity and competitiveness, and to encourage long-term company loyalty (Streeck 1991; Soskice 1999). Their demand found allies among high-skilled workers, possessing high levels of market power, who were increasingly frustrated at the restraint placed on their incomes by centralised bargaining outcomes and high levels of taxation.
15 As will be discussed in more detail in the following section.
16 From 23 to 18.
17 From 29 to 39 in Norway, from 24 to 29 in Sweden, and from 30 to 37 in France.
18 A period in which the international economic and institutional environment arguably placed particularly strong constraints on European governments' room to manoeuvre in policy making.
19 On the content of and effects of Thatcherite reforms in Britain, see Hall (1986), Ward (1988), Jessop (1988), Brown and King (1988), Lane (1989), Talos and Falkner (1994).
20 Measuring the ratio of the gross earnings of a worker at the top of the 10th (that is, the lowest) earnings decile to that of a worker in the 9th decile.
21 Encompassing restaurants and hotels, wholesale and retail trade, community, social and personal services.
22 The Liberal party.
23 Christian Democratic Appeal.
24 From one-third to just under a half. Data from the *Comparative Welfare States Data Set* compiled by Huber *et al.* (1997).
25 Increasing from a score of 48 to 51 between 1981 and 1991 on the OECD's 'index of generosity' compared with a reduction from 23 to 18 in the UK.
26 Collective bargaining coverage declined only slightly over the 1980s from 76 to 71 per cent, compared with a fall from 70 to 47 per cent in the UK (OECD 1994).
27 With the exception of Belgium, no other country recorded a percentage of more than 43 per cent (Germany).
28 Employment creation in this period has also been aided by extremely high levels of average wage restraint. Both average real wages and unit labour costs are estimated to have remained roughly constant throughout the 1980s (Visser 1998).
29 Public sector employment expanded at an annual average rate of 0.8 per cent in 1986 and 1987, compared with 2.4 per cent between 1982 and 1985.
30 France shows an increase from 30 to 37 in the OECD's index of generosity in this period, compared with a decline from 23 to 18 in the UK.
31 On average, therefore, between 1981 and 1993, public service sector employment increased by 1.8 per cent per annum in France (in spite of low recorded growth rates in the years of conservative 'cohabitation' between 1986 and 1987). These figures may be contrasted with an annual average growth rate of 0.1 per cent per annum in the Netherlands and a *negative* annual average growth rate of −1.6 in the UK over the same period.
32 In fact, work sharing strategies have been increasingly emphasised in France since the early 1980s and have been an important component of parliamentary socialist as well

as neo-liberal platforms. Mitterand's labour market programme contained important measures aimed at reducing labour supply. The legal retirement age was reduced and early retirement encouraged. Meanwhile working time was reduced through the extension of annual leave entitlements, overtime ceilings and reductions in the working week (Lombard 1995). While the high cost of early retirement schemes has reduced their attractiveness as a method of labour supply reduction over time (Goetschy 1998), significant financial incentives have been offered to employers to reduce their employees' working time.

33 This tendency is further evidenced by the policy initiatives of the Blair and Jospin governments (in the UK and France, respectively) at the end of the 1990s. Both governments have increased levels of income protection for the low-paid – in Blair's case through the reinstitution of the minimum wage; in Jospin's through significant increases in its value. In addition, both have increased the commitment of state budgets to employment in public services – in Jospin's case through deliberate employment creation programmes targeted at the young; in Blair's through plans for large-scale increased investment in the public health and education sectors.

References

Appelbaum, E. (1995). 'Employment and productivity in industrialized countries', *International Labour Review* 134(4–5), 605–23.

Appelbaum, E. and Schettkat, R. (1994). 'The end of full employment? On economic development in industrialized countries', *Intereconomics* 29, 122–30.

Baumol, W. (1967). 'The macroeconomics of unbalanced growth', *American Economic Review* 57(3), 415–26.

Baumol, W. and Bowen, W. G. (1966). *Performing Arts: The Economic Dilemma.* New York: The Twentieth Century Fund.

Belchamber, G. (1996). 'Disappearing middle or vanishing bottom? A comment on Gregory', *The Economic Record* 72(218), 287–93.

Boix, C. (1997). 'Political parties and the supply-side of the economy', *American Journal of Political Science* 41(3), 814–45.

Boix, C. (1998). *Political Parties, Growth and Equality.* Cambridge: Cambridge University Press.

Boyer, R. (1994). 'Wage reforms imposed by the state: Some paradoxes in French incomes policies', in R. Dore, R. Boyer and Z. Mars (eds), *The Return to Incomes Policy.* London: Pinter, 47–70.

Brown, A. and King, D. (1988). 'Economic change and labour market policy: Corporatist and dualist tendencies in Britain and Sweden', *West European Politics* 11, 75–91.

Cameron, D. (1978). 'The expansion of the public economy: A comparative analysis', *American Political Science Review* 72, 1243–61.

Cameron, D. (1984). 'Social democracy, corporatism, labor quiescence, and the representation of economic interest in advanced capitalist society', in J. H. Goldthorpe (ed.), *Order and Conflict in Contemporary Capitalism.* Oxford: Oxford University Press, 143–78.

Cole, A. (1999). 'French Socialists in office: Lessons from Mitterand and Jospin', *Modern and Contemporary France* 7(1), 71–87.

Crouch, C. (1990). 'United Kingdom: The rejection of compromise', in G. Baglioni and C. Crouch (eds), *European Industrial Relations: The Challenge of Flexibility.* London: Sage, 326–55.

Cusack, T. (1997). 'Partisan politics and public finance: Changes in public spending in the industrialized democracies, 1955–1989', *Public Choice* 91, 375–95.

Cusak, T. (1998). Public Employment Data set. Update of original data from Cusack, T. R., T. Notermans, and M. Rein (1989). 'Political-Economic Aspects of Public Employment', *European Journal of Political Research* 17, 471–500.

Dinardo, J., Fortin, N. and Lemieux, T. (1994). 'Labor market institutions and the distribution of wages, 1973–1992: A semi-parametric approach', University of Montreal, CRDE Cahier 0894.

Esping-Andersen, G. (1985). *Politics against Markets: The Social Democratic Road to Power.* Princeton, NJ: Princeton University Press.

Esping-Andersen, G. (1990). *The Three Worlds of Welfare Capitalism.* Princeton, NJ: Princeton University Press.

Esping-Andersen, G. (1993). *Changing Classes: Stratification and Mobility in Postindustrial Societies*, London: Sage.

Esping-Andersen, G. (1994). 'The eclipse of the democratic class struggle? European class structures at fin de siècle', Paper presented to the study groups on 'Citizenship and Social Policies and State and Capitalism', Harvard University, Center for European Studies.

Esping-Andersen, (1996) (ed.). *Welfare States in Transition: National Adaptations in Global Economies.* London: Sage.

European Industrial Relations Review (1988). Vol. 176, September 1988.

European Industrial Relations Review (1995). Vol. 254, March 1995.

European Industrial Relations Review (1997). Vol. 283, August 1997.

Flanagan, R. J., Soskice, D. W. and Ulman, L. (1983). *Unionism, Economic Stabilisation and Incomes Policies: European Experience.* Washington, DC: Brookings Institution.

Freeman, R. B. (1995). 'Are your wages set in Bejing?', *Journal of Economic Perspectives* 9(3), 15–32.

Freeman, R. B. (1996). 'Labor market institutions and earnings inequality', *New England Economic Review* (May/June), Proceedings of a symposium of the Federal Reserve Bank of Boston on *Spatial and Labor Market Contributions to Earnings Inequality*, 17 November 1995, 157–68.

Garrett, G. (1998). *Partisan Politics in the Global Economy.* Cambridge: Cambridge University Press.

Garrett, G. and Lange, P. (1991). 'Political responses to interdependence: what's "left" for the Left?', *International Organization* 45(4), 539–64.

Glyn, A. (1997). 'Low pay and the volume of work', typescript, Corpus Christi College, Oxford.

Goetschy, J. (1998). 'France: The limits of reform', in A. Ferner and R. Hyman (eds), *Changing Industrial Relations in Europe.* Oxford, UK: Blackwell Publishers, 357–394.

Gornick, J. and Jacobs, J. A. (1998). 'Gender, the welfare state and public employment: A comparative study of seven industrialized countries', *American Sociological Review* 63(5); 688–710.

Halimi, S., Michie, J. and Milne, S. (1994). 'The Mitterand experience', in J. Michie and J. G. Smith (eds), *Unemployment in Europe.* London: Academic Press, 97–115.

Hall, P. A. (1986). *Governing the Economy.* Oxford: Oxford University Press.

Hall, P. A. (1994). 'The state and the market', in P. A. Hall, J. Hayward and H. Machin (eds) *Developments in French Politics.* London: Macmillan, 171–87.

Hancké, B. (1991). 'The crisis of national unions: Belgian labor in decline', *Politics and Society* 19(4), 463–87.

Hantrais, L. (1996). 'France: Squaring the welfare triangle', in V. George and P. Taylor-Gooby (eds), *European Welfare Policy: Squaring the Welfare Circle.* London: Macmillan, 51–71.

Hawke, A. and Wooden, M. (1998). 'The changing face of Australian industrial relations: A survey', *The Economic Record* 74(224). 74–88.

Huber, E., Ragin, C. and Stephens, J. D. (1993). 'Social democracy, Christian democracy, constitutional structure, and the welfare state', *American Journal of Sociology* 99(3), 711–49.

Huber, E., Ragin, C. and Stephens, J. D. (1997). 'Comparative Welfare States Data Set', University of North Carolina, Chapel Hill, NC.

Iversen, T. (1996). 'Power, flexibility, and the breakdown of centralized bargaining: The cases of Denmark and Sweden in comparative perspective', *Comparative Politics* 28, 399–436.

Iversen, T. (1998). 'The choices for social democracy in comparative perspective', *Oxford Review of Economic Policy* 14(1), 59–76.

Iversen, T. (1999) *Contested Economic Institutions*. Cambridge: Cambridge University Press.

Iversen, T. and Cusack, T. (2000). 'The causes of welfare state expansion: Deindustrialisation or Globalization?', *World Politics* 52(3), 313–49.

Iversen, T. and Thygesen, N. (1998). 'Denmark: From external to internal adjustment', in E. Jones, J. Frieden, and F. Torres (eds), *Joining Europe's Monetary Club: The Challenge for Smaller Member States*. New York: St. Martin's Press, 61–83.

Iversen, T. and Wren, A. (1998). 'Equality, employment and budgetary restraint: The trilemma of the service economy', *World Politics* 50(4), 507–74.

Jessop, B. (1988). *Thatcherism: A Tale of Two Nations*. Cambridge: Polity Press.

Jones, E. (1998). 'The Netherlands: top of the class', in E. Jones, J. Frieden and F. Torres (eds), *Joining Europe's Monetary Club: The Challenge for Smaller Member States*. New York: St. Martin's Press, 149–71.

Katzenstein, P. (1985). *Small States in World Markets*. Ithaca, NY: Cornell University Press.

Korpi, W. (1983). *The Democratic Class Struggle*. London: Routledge.

Kurzer, P. (1993). *Business and Banking*. Ithaca, NY: Cornell University Press.

Krugman, P. (1996). *Pop Internationalism*. Cambridge, MA: MIT Press.

Kyloh, R. H. (1989). 'Flexibility and structural adjustment through consensus: Some lessons from Australia', *International Labour Review* 128(1), 103–23.

Lane, C. (1989), 'From "welfare capitalism" to "market capitalism": A comparative review of trends towards employment flexibility in the labour markets of three major European societies', *Sociology* 23(4), 583–610.

Lange, P. (1984). 'Unions, workers and wage regulation: the rational bases of consent', in J. H. Goldthorpe (ed.), *Order and Conflict in Contemporary Capitalism*. New York: Oxford University Press, 98–123.

Lombard, M. (1995). 'A re-examination of the reasons for the failure of Keynesian expansionary policies in France, 1981–1983', *Cambridge Journal of Economics* 19, 359–72.

Machin, S. and Manning, A. (1994). 'Minimum wages, wage dispersion and employment: Evidence from the UK wages councils', *Industrial and Labour Relations Review* 47, 319–29.

Meidner, R. (1974). *Co-ordination and Solidarity: An Approach to Wages Policy*. Stockholm: Prisma.

Meulders, D., Plasman, O. and Plasman, R. (1994). *Atypical Employment in the EC*. Brookfield, Vt. USA: Dartmouth Publishing Co.

Mishel, L. and Bernstein, J. (1994). *The State of Working America, 1994–1995*. New York: M.E. Sharpe.

Mosley, L. (1999). 'Room to Move: International Financial Markets and National Welfare States', unpublished manuscript, duke University.

Nickell, S. and Bell, B. (1995). 'The collapse in demand for the unskilled and unemployment across the OECD', *Oxford Review of Economic Policy* 11(1), 40–62.

OECD (Organisation for Economic Co-Operation and Development) (1991) *Employment Outlook.* Paris: OECD.

OECD (1994). *The OECD Jobs Study: Evidence and Explanations.* Paris: OECD.

OECD (1996a). *OECD International Sectoral Database.* Paris: OECD.

OECD (1996b). *Employment Outlook.* Paris: OECD.

Pfaller *et al.* (1991). In A. Pfaller, I. Gough and G. Therborn (eds). *Can the Welfare State Compete?: A Comparative Study of Five Advanced Capitalist Countries.* London: Macmillan.

Pierson, P. (1994). *Dismantling the Welfare State? Reagan, Thatcher and the Politics of Retrenchment.* Cambridge: Cambridge University Press.

Pierson (1996). 'The new politics of the welfare state', *World Politics* 48(2), 143–179.

Piore, M. J. and Sabel, C. F. (1984). *The Second Industrial Divide: Possibilities for Prosperity.* New York: Basic Books.

Pontusson, J. (1999). 'Labor market institutions and wage distribution in Sweden and Austria', in T. Iversen, J. Pontusson and D. Soskice (eds), *Unions, Employers and Central Banks: Macroeconomic Coordination and Institutional Change in Social Market Economies.* Cambridge: Cambridge University Press, 292–330.

Przeworski, A. and Wallerstein, M. (1982). 'The structure of class conflict in democratic capitalist societies', *American Political Science Review* 76, 215–38.

Rehn, G. (1985). 'Swedish active labor market policy: Retrospect and prospect', *Industrial Relations* 24, 62–89.

Rodrik, D. (1996). 'Why do more open economies have larger governments ?', NBER Working Paper No. 5537.

Rodrik, D. (1997) *Has Globalization gone too far?*, Washington, DC: Institute for International Economics.

Ross, G. (1991). 'The Changing Face of Popular Power in France', in *Labour Parties in Postindustrial Societies.* Cambridge: Polity Press, 71–100.

Ross, G. (1997). 'Jospin so far', *French Politics and Society* 15(3), 9–19.

Rowthorn, B. (1992). 'Corporatism and labour market performance', in J. Pekkarinen, M. Pohjola and B. Rowthorn (eds), *Social Corporatism.* Oxford: Clarendon Press, 44–81.

Rowthorn, R. and Ramaswamy, R. (1997). 'Deindustrialization: Causes and implications', Washington, DC: IMF Working Paper 97, 42.

Rowthorn (1998). 'Growth, trade and deindustrialization', Washington, DC: IMF Working Paper 98, 60.

Rueda, D. and Pontusson, J. (2000). 'Wage inequality and varieties of capitalism', *World Politics* 52(3), 350–83.

Ruggie, J. G. (1983). 'International regimes, transactions, and change: Embedded liberalism in the postwar economic order', in S. D. Krasner (ed.), *International Regimes.* Ithaca, NY: Cornell University Press, 195–232.

Saeger, S. (1996). 'Globalization and economic structure in the OECD', unpublished Ph.D. dissertation, Harvard University.

Salter, W. E. G. (1960). *Productivity and Technical Change.* Cambridge: Cambridge University Press.

Scharpf, F. W. (1987). 'A game-theoretical interpretation of inflation and unemployment in Western Europe', *Journal of Public Policy* 7, 227–57.

Scharpf, F. W. (1991). *Crisis and Choice in European Social Democracy.* Ithaca, NY: New York University Press.

Scharpf, F. W. (1999). 'The viability of advanced welfare states in the international economy: Vulnerabilities and options', MPIfG Working Paper 99/9. Cologne: Max Planck Institute for the Study of Societies.

Schmidt, V. A. (1996). *From State to Market: The Transformation of French Business and Government*. Cambridge: Cambridge University Press.

Segrestin, D. (1990). 'Recent changes in France', in G. Baglioni and C. Crouch (eds), *European Industrial Relations: The Challenge of Flexibility*. London: Sage, 97–126.

Soskice, D. (1999). 'Divergent production regimes: Coordinated and uncoordinated market economies in the 1980s and 1990s', in H. Kitschelt, P. Lange, G. Marks and J. D. Stephens (eds), *Continuity and Change in Contemporary Capitalism*, Cambridge: Cambridge University Press, 101–35.

Stephens, J. D. (1979). *The Transition from Capitalism to Socialism*. London: Macmillan.

Streeck, W. (1991). 'On the institutional conditions of diversified quality production', in E. Matzner and W. Streeck (eds), *Beyond Keynesianism: The Socio-economics of Production and Full-Employment*. Aldershot: Edward Elgar, 2–61.

Swenson, P. (1989). *Fair Shares: Unions, Pay and Politics in Sweden and Germany*. Ithaka, NY: Cornell University Press.

Tálos, E. and Falkner, G. (1994). 'The role of the state within social policy', in W. Muller and V. Wright (eds), *The State in Western Europe Retreat or Redefinition? Western European Politics* July. Special Issue, 52–76.

Van Kersbergen, K. (1995). *Social Capitalism: A Study of Christian Democracy and the Welfare State*. London: Routledge.

Visser, J. (1998). 'Two cheers for corporatism, one for the market: industrial relations, wage moderation, and job growth in the Netherlands', *British Journal of Industrial Relations* 36 (2) 269–292.

Visser, J. and Hemerijck, A. (1997). *A Dutch Miracle: Job Growth, Welfare Reform and Corporatism in the Netherlands*. Amsterdam: Amsterdam University Press.

Wallerstein, M. (1999). 'Wage-setting institutions and pay inequality in advanced industrial societies', *American Journal of Political Science* 43(3), 649–80.

Wallerstein, M., Golden, M. and Lange, P. (1997). 'Unions, employers' associations, and wage-setting institutions in Northern and Central Europe, 1950-1992', *Industrial and Labor Relations Review* 50(3), 379–401.

Ward, T. (1988). 'From mounting tension to open confrontation: The case of the UK', in R. Boyer (ed.), *The Search for Labor Market Flexibility: The European economies in transition*. Oxford: Clarendon Press, 58–79.

Wilensky, H. (1975). *The Welfare State and Equality*, Berkeley. CA: University of California Press.

Wolinetz, S. B. (1989). 'Socio-economic bargaining in the Netherlands: Redefining the post-war policy coalition', *West European Politics* 12(1), 79–98.

Wood, A. (1994). *North–South Trade, Employment and Inequality*. Oxford: Oxford University Press.

Wren, A. (2000). 'Distributional trade-offs and partisan politics in the post-industrial economy', unpublished Ph.D. dissertation, Harvard University.

Wren, A. and Iversen, T. (1997). 'Choosing paths: Explaining distributional outcomes in the post industrial society', Paper presented to the 93rd American Political Science Association Meeting, Washington, DC.

12 Employment and the welfare state

A continental dilemma

Fritz W. Scharpf

Estimates of the comparative health of the North American and Western European economies and societies have had their fashion cycles – from Servain-Schreiber's warnings that Europe was falling behind, rather than catching up with, American technological leadership in the 1960s, to European exasperation over American trade and budget deficits in the 1970s, to anxieties over Eurosclerosis in the early 1980s and over the American loss of international competitiveness in the late 1980s. At present, by all accounts, the sick man is again Europe, which has been experiencing higher unemployment and much lower rates of job creation over the last two decades or so. The main problem is a rising level of long-term unemployment that mainly affects unskilled workers and, in most countries, young job seekers with low levels of schooling.

When seeking an explanation, most commentators see little need to search beyond the usual suspects – institutional rigidities, union power and the burdens of the welfare state. In an age of intensified global competition, so it is argued, government regulations and collective-bargaining agreements can no longer be considered 'beneficial constraints' but have become fetters that prevent European firms from achieving the flexibility and innovativeness that allow American firms to compete successfully at the cutting edge of high-tech markets. In addition, the European economies are labouring under the dead weight of bloated public sectors – which are claiming more than 50 per cent of GDP in Sweden and Denmark and more than 40 per cent in France, Germany and other Continental countries, compared to less than 30 per cent in the United States and Japan – and of overextended welfare states with overly generous rates of income replacement that have raised reservation wages and reduced the incentives to work.

The measure of success: employment ratios

However, I am not convinced that things are quite as simple as the conventional wisdom would have them. If the employment performance of different countries is to be evaluated and explained, there is, first, a need for valid criteria. For this, the usual reference to unemployment figures will not do. They do not include persons on disability pensions, in early retirement and other forms of paid non-work, and they are notoriously subject to political manipulation – the British Conservatives are said to have changed unemployment definitions more than thirty times during their period in office, each time reducing the number of the registered unemployed. Moreover, and even more importantly, the rate of unemployment is defined by reference to the size of the 'active population', which is, of course, strongly affected by factors on the supply side of the labour market. Thus, the willingness of married women to enter the labour market may be as much affected by the separate or joint taxation of spouses' incomes or the availability of day care as it is by the availability of jobs.

Compared to unemployment rates, employment figures and their changes over time seem to be a much better indicator of comparative performance – but they are also affected by changes on the supply side: larger populations imply more jobs. Even when employment figures are normalised by reference to the population of working age (15–64), comparability suffers from differences in working time and in the share of part-time employment (which happens to be unusually high in the Netherlands). With this caveat in mind, however, employment/population ratios still seem to be the most valid indicators of relative employment performance for which internationally comparative data are readily available in OECD (Organisation of Economic Co-operation and Development) publications (OECD 1996a). I will use these throughout.

Similarly, the causal relationship hypothesised by the conventional wisdom is not fully captured by the usual reference to the share of taxes and social security contributions in GDP, since a large (but variable) part of public expenditures is actually meant to increase the productivity and hence the international competitiveness of national economies. Instead, I will refer to the share of total social expenditures in GDP (OECD 1996b), which, better than any other internationally comparable indicator, should indeed reflect the 'dead weight' of the welfare state on the economy that is presumed to explain the poor European employment performance (see Fig. 12.1).

From the latest available OECD data on employment ratios for 1995, and on total social expenditures for 1993, it is certainly not obvious that the conventional wisdom has much explanatory power (OECD 1996a). It is true that the United States, at 73 per cent, and some other countries with very low shares of social spending had very high employment ratios, and it is also true that the German score, at 65.1 per cent, was significantly lower, closely followed by the Netherlands (with all those part-time jobs) at 64.3 per cent. France, at 59.5 per cent, was even further behind, and in Belgium only 55.7 per cent of the working age population were actually working. Ireland and the Southern European countries, with the notable exception of Portugal, scored even lower than the Belgian level. At the same time, however, the Scandinavian welfare states with extremely high shares of social spending were also highly successful in employment terms, reaching levels that were as high as or even slightly higher than the United States. Overall, it should be said, the statistical association between employment and social spending is practically zero. So much for the conventional wisdom?

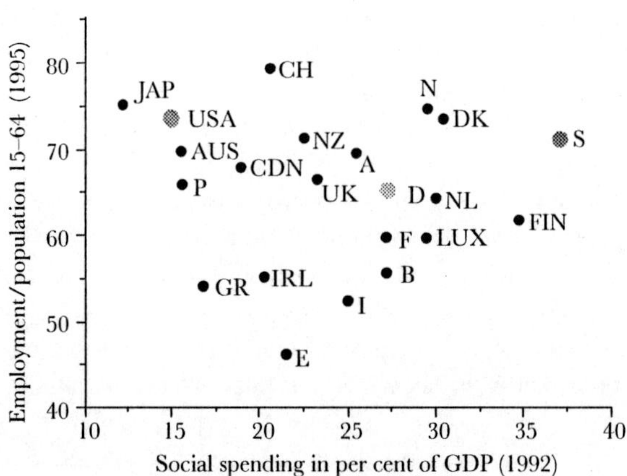

Figure 12.1 Total employment and social spending.

Exposed and sheltered sectors

How, then, might one account for the fact that the most expensive welfare states with the highest tax burden among OECD countries and with powerful unions should be doing just as well in employment terms as the United States, which has practically ceased to be a welfare state and has just about the lowest tax burden in the OECD, and where unions have lost all control over wage levels and structures? And why is it that Continental welfare states at similar levels of economic development and with intermediate levels of tax burdens should be doing so much less well?

In searching for an explanation, we should remember that the conventional wisdom, and practically all contributions to the current debate, tends to focus on international competitiveness. Thus, one might expect that the non-taxed, deregulated and de-unionised US economy should have comparative advantages in sectors exposed to international competition, while the Scandinavian welfare states would achieve high levels of employment in the sheltered sectors. Unfortunately, this theoretically interesting distinction is not directly represented in the employment data available in the OECD Labour Force Statistics (for example, see OECD 1996a). Also, the boundary is shifting as hitherto sheltered jobs – for instance in telecommunications, financial services or the construction industry – are becoming exposed to foreign competition with the completion of the European internal market and under the new WTO (World Trade Organisation) rules. Opting for the most comprehensive definition, I have included employment in all ISIC (International Standard Industrial Classification of all Economic Activities) major divisions whose products are, actually or potentially, exported or subject to import competition. This definition includes not only all agricultural and industrial employment, but also service employment in ISIC Divisions 7 ('Transport, storage, and communication') and 8 ('Financing, insurance, real estate, and business services'). If we take these branches together, and focus now more narrowly on the United States and two countries of the European Union, Sweden and Germany, the outcome is truly surprising (see Fig. 12.2).

Again, the overall statistical effect of the size of the welfare state is extremely weak (and in fact slightly positive). Even more remarkable, the United States is doing rather poorly in the exposed sectors, whereas some of the Scandinavian countries, and among Continental countries Germany, Austria and, remarkably, Portugal, are doing much better. In other words, the size of the welfare state as such does not seem to have any negative effect on employment in the internationally exposed sectors of the economy. The implications of these data for the present discussion are obviously ambivalent. On the one hand, countries with a high employment ratio in the exposed sectors will find a larger share of present jobs affected by the increasing pressures of international competition and by, perhaps temporary, downturns in the international demand for their products. This surely helps to explain the near-hysteria of the debate within Germany about the country's competitiveness (*Standortdebatte*) over the last few years.

There is an important message on the other hand, however, which is often overlooked: in the internationally exposed sectors of the economy, the 'Rhenish model' of stakeholder-oriented corporate governance and cooperative industrial relations has been, and is still, doing very well indeed in international comparison. That does not mean that there is no need for reforms – on the contrary. It does mean, however, that there is no reason at all to throw the model overboard, and to turn instead to American – or for that matter, British – models of market-driven corporate controls and industrial relations. In any case, the data demonstrate that the generally poor employment performance of, say, the German economy over the

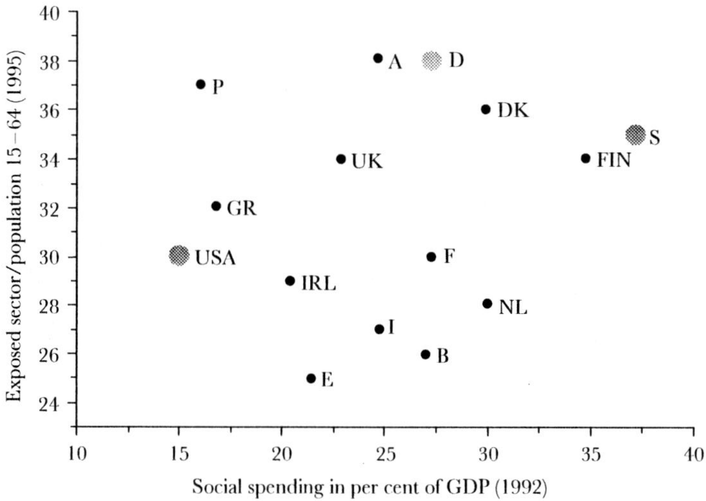

Figure 12.2 Employment in the exposed sectors (ISIC 1–5, 7, 8).

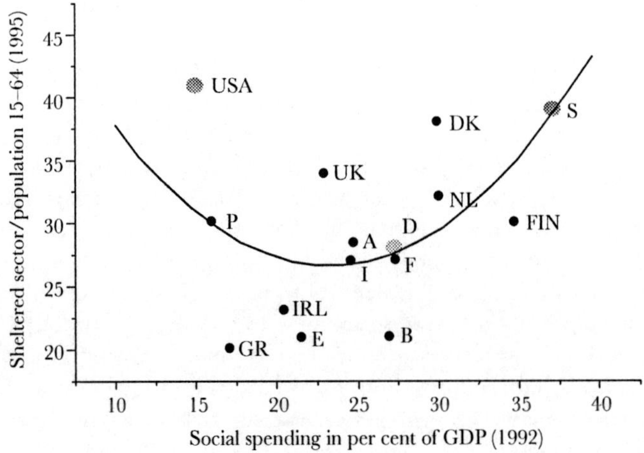

Figure 12.3 Employment in sheltered sectors (ISIC 6 and 9).

last decade cannot be ascribed to a general loss of international competitiveness. It must find its explanation in the sheltered sectors of the economy (see Fig. 12.3).

Within the definition used here, these sheltered sectors comprise the service branches in ISIC 6 ('Wholesale and retail trade, restaurants and hotels') and in ISIC 9 ('Community, social and personal services') – a heterogeneous collection which, however, shares the characteristic that local demand is served by locally supplied services, and that foreign competition plays practically no role. It is in these 'local services' that the data show a significant difference that could lead to an explanation of the poor employment performance of Continental welfare states.

Again, there is practically no linear relationship between employment and the size of the welfare state. Instead, the curvilinear relationship which exists ($R^2=0.30$) is U-shaped, with high employment at the upper and lower ends of the welfare-spending scale, and low employment in the Continental welfare states characterised by intermediate levels of welfare expenditures. Thus, in the United States, altogether 41 per cent of the working age population have jobs in the local services, and Sweden is not far behind at 39 per cent. In Austria, Germany, France and Italy, by contrast, the employment/population ratio of local services reaches only 28 per cent – thirteen percentage points less than in the United States (which would be equivalent to 6 million jobs in Germany). Figures in Denmark are almost as high as in Sweden, and Britain and the Netherlands are also faring better than Germany. In other EU member states, however, employment in the local services is even lower than it is in Germany. It is worthwhile, therefore, to further explore the underlying patterns.

Public and private services

In general, local services may be financed from either public or private sources, and they may also be produced by public agencies, by commercial firms or by non-profit organisations. As it turns out, it is this difference which finally points to an explanation. There is a weak ($R^2 = -0.10$) negative association between welfare spending and local services provided in the private sector[1] – with the United States and the Netherlands as the upper outliers, whereas France and Belgium have very few jobs in the private services (see Fig. 12.4).

At the same time there is a stronger ($R^2 = 0.36$) positive association between welfare spending and employment in the public sector – with Sweden and Denmark as the positive outliers. Not only the Netherlands, but also Italy and Germany are located well below the regression line here.

Germany, for instance, is not doing much better than Sweden with regard to local service employment in the private sector, whereas – in spite of much higher tax levels, and contrary to a near-consensus in public debate – the German public sector is not at all 'bloated'. In fact, it is exactly as 'lean' in employment terms as is true of the United States (see Fig. 12.5).

The curvilinear pattern of employment in the sheltered sector as a whole is thus a composite result of two separate effects: in the United States and other countries with a small welfare state, local service jobs are created in the private sector of the economy, whereas in Denmark and Sweden with large welfare states, the public sector is able to provide high levels of local service employment. Yet why should the Continental welfare states with intermediate-size social expenditures have the worst of both worlds, instead of combining intermediate levels of employment in the public and in the private sector to achieve equally high overall levels of service employment?

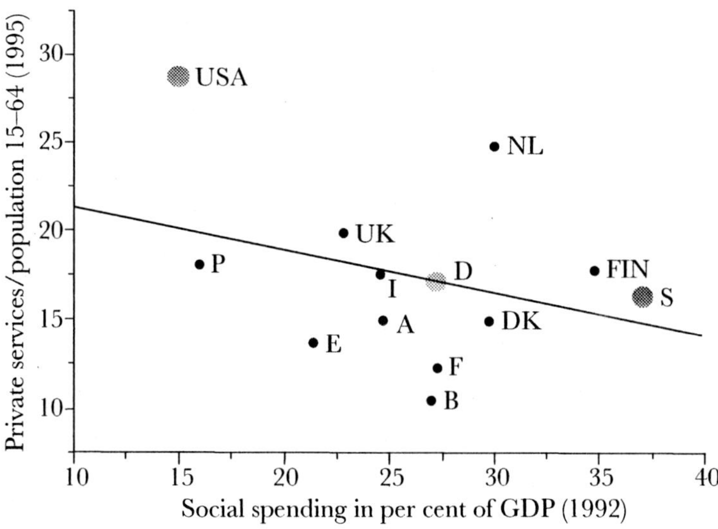

Figure 12.4 Sheltered employment in the private sector.

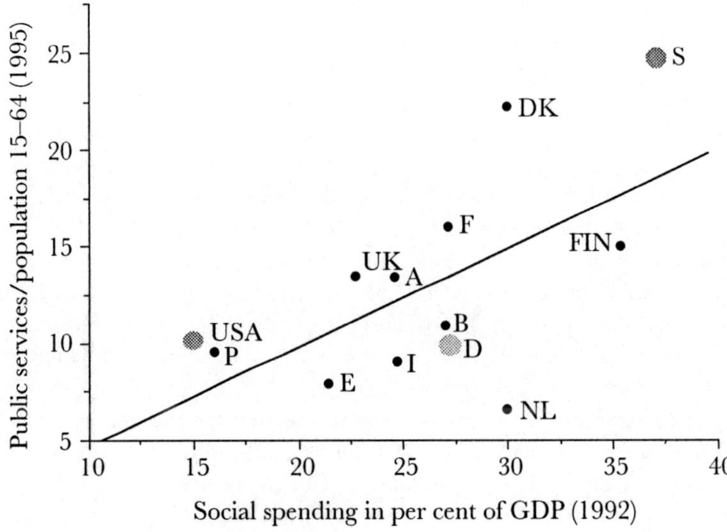

Figure 12.5 Public-sector employment.

Two roads to service employment

The explanation, I suggest, lies in differences in the levels and structures of national welfare state and industrial relations systems. In order to simplify the argument, I will now concentrate on three models only, the American, the Swedish and the German, even though I know that there are significant differences among the Scandinavian welfare states and even greater ones among the Continental systems that need to be brought out by much more careful analyses than I could present here. In the American and Swedish cases, the explanation for their exceptionally high levels of employment in the sheltered service sectors is fairly straightforward.

In the United States, generally low levels of taxation and the additional tax cuts of the 1980s have contributed to a highly unequal distribution of incomes, which has contributed in turn to a simultaneous expansion of service employment at both the upper and the lower end of the skill scale. Since education and health care are privately financed to a much greater extent than elsewhere, the growing demand of affluent consumers for high-quality educational and medical services increases the number of well-paid jobs at the professional level.

At the same time, however, weak or non-existent unions combined with the short duration of unemployment benefits and the virtual absence of social assistance for the long-term unemployed have facilitated the emergence of a low-wage labour market. This, in turn, has facilitated the creation, or maintenance, of service jobs in hotels, retail trade, restaurants, and a great variety of other household and personal services. In these jobs, labour productivity tends to be very low. But since wages are also very low, the American model allows large numbers of low-skilled workers to find employment in the private sector.

Thus, the upside of the American model is the dynamic expansion of service employment at all qualification levels. Its downside is the plight of the 'working poor' receiving incomes below the subsistence level even when employed full time.

In Sweden and Denmark, by contrast, very high taxes, strong unions and generous rates of income replacement in the event of unemployment have reduced income inequality and wage differentials to the lowest level among OECD countries. At the same time, education and health care are publicly financed and publicly provided. As a consequence, there is no low-wage labour market and little room for private services at the professional level. Instead, high levels of tax revenue are used to finance universal health services and education as well as a wide range of free social services for families with young children, for the elderly, the handicapped[2] and the sick, for drug addicts and immigrants. These services involve not only work for highly trained professionals but also provide a large number of decently paid jobs for persons with relatively low levels of formal training.

The downside of the Swedish model is, of course, its dependence on very high levels of taxation which, in the face of international tax competition for mobile capital and the growing tax resistance of mobile professionals, have become increasingly difficult to sustain. The results were, first, unsustainable budget deficits and, in the 1990s, a need for fiscal consolidation that forced governments to reduce not only the generosity of welfare payments, but also the level of public-sector employment – with the consequence that unemployment has risen to normal European levels, even though the level of employment continues to be very high by international standards.

The Continental dilemma

By contrast, the Continental failure to create high levels of employment in the local services cannot be simply explained by differences in the size of the welfare state. Total social spending amounts to only 15 per cent of GDP in the United States, and to more than 37 per cent in Sweden, whereas Continental welfare states tend to absorb between 25 and 30 per cent of GDP (OECD 1996b). If nevertheless public-sector employment is as low as it is in the United States, this appears as a path-dependent consequence of the Bismarckian model, which was originally meant to deal only with the social risks arising if the single (male) breadwinner was unable to support his family through full-time work (Esping-Andersen 1990). Hence, Continental welfare states are quite generous with regard to transfer payments in cases of retirement, disability and unemployment – but they have never developed a Scandinavian commitment to provide social services that would complement or compete with the functions performed in the family by mothers, wives and daughters. As a consequence, the Continental welfare state certainly does not help to increase employment in publicly financed social services.

There are, of course, well-paid professional jobs in public education and publicly financed health care provided in public hospitals or in private practice. Yet the mere fact that these services are publicly financed, from tax revenues or from social insurance funds, means that employment growth is held back or even reversed by efforts to reduce tax burdens and public-sector budget deficits, whereas in the United States employment will expand with the increasing demand of affluent consumers for high-quality services in education and health care.

At the low end of the labour market, however, the Continental welfare state is as effective as its Scandinavian counterpart in preventing the viability of low-wage service jobs in the private sector. Compared to the United States, at any rate, levels of taxation are high, unions are strong, income inequality and wage differentials are low, and reservation wages above the subsistence level are assured by relatively generous and continuous social assistance payments. The negative impact on service employment is particularly acute in those countries which, like France and Germany, rely to a large extent on payroll taxes for the financing of the welfare state. In Germany, for instance, 74 per cent of total social expenditures were financed through workers' and employers' contributions to social insurance systems in 1991, and in France that was true of 82 per cent. In Germany, by now, these contributions amount to about 42 per cent of the nominal wage paid by the employer.

In general, of course, there is no reason to think that stable rates of payroll taxes (as distinguished from rate increases) should have a particularly negative impact on employment. In the medium term, they will be taken into account, like all other factors affecting the total wage bill, when employers and unions are bargaining over wage increases. At the lower end of the pay scale, however, things are very different. Here, the availability of social assistance defines the reservation wage below which net wages cannot be reduced. Thus, certain types of 'bad jobs', which are economically viable in the United States, simply could not exist in Europe – which is, of course, a fully intended effect of the welfare state. What is not intended, however, is the impact of payroll taxes on jobs well above the subsistence level.

If the net wage of the worker cannot fall below a guaranteed minimum, the consequence is that any social insurance contributions, payroll taxes and wage taxes that are levied on jobs at the lower end of the pay scale cannot be absorbed by the employee but must be added to the total labour cost borne by the employer. Assuming that any other overhead costs are proportional to labour costs, the implication is that the minimum productivity that a job must reach in order to be viable in the market is raised by more than 50 per cent above the level of productivity required to pay the worker's net reservation wage. As a consequence, a wide range of perfectly decent jobs, which in the absence of payroll taxes would be commercially viable, are driven from the private service market.

In Germany, to give a numerical example, social assistance for a single person amounts to about DM 1,100 per month, in addition to which that person may earn up to DM 250 by part-time work (see Fig. 12.6). Any additional income from work, however, is fully set off against social assistance, i.e. is taxed at a

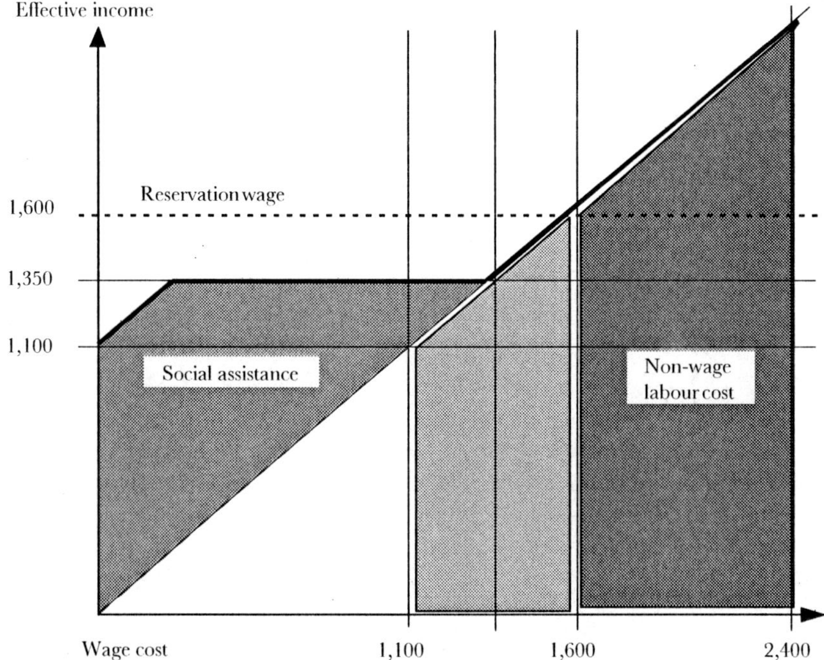

Figure 12.6 Social assistance in Germany (in DM).

marginal rate of 100 per cent. Assuming that an additional financial incentive is needed to make full-time work attractive, the minimum net reservation wage in Germany may presently amount to about DM 1,600 per month (i.e. about DM 10, or a bit less than US$ 6, per hour). In order to provide the worker with that net wage, however, the employer will have to pay a total wage bill of at least DM 2,400 per month which – if due allowance is made for other taxes and overhead – will allow only jobs with fairly high productivity to survive in the private sector.

In other words, financing the welfare state through social insurance contributions added to the wage bill prevents the creation of a considerable range of service jobs at the lower end of the present pay scale. In this sense, therefore, it is indeed fair to say that Continental welfare states are causing high levels of long-term unemployment for persons with low levels of marketable skills.

Options

The conclusion is that we have not two, but three distinct models of service employment and welfare-state arrangements – American, Scandinavian and Continental-European. Two of the former are able to provide high levels of employment in the domestic service sectors – the United States in the private sector and the Scandinavian states in the public sector. Both have also their characteristic weaknesses. The downside of the American model is the plight of the working poor, whereas the Scandinavian model has become highly vulnerable as the capacity to tax is eroding for economic and political reasons. The Continental welfare states, by contrast, are not able to expand domestic-service employment either in the public or in the private sector.

Moreover, while fairly straightforward solutions are available for the basic problems associated with either the American or the Scandinavian models, solutions for the weakness of Continental employment are less clear and, at any rate, much more difficult to implement. The easiest option is to be found in the United States, where large numbers of service jobs already exist in the private sector, and where an appropriate solution for the poverty of large segments of the working population is already available in the form of the Earned Income Tax Credit programme. There seems to be no reason why the goals of maintaining high levels of employment and of reducing mass poverty could not be realised in combination through an expansion and systematisation of income support for the working poor.

In the Scandinavian welfare states, by contrast, large numbers of service jobs already exist in the public sector. Their financial viability is in doubt, however, since the capacity of the state to tax mobile capital and the high incomes of mobile professionals has been greatly reduced. Nevertheless, if the commitment to high-quality public services for all is to be maintained, a straightforward solution does seem to be available which would shift a large part of the financial burden of these services to means-tested user charges. If high-income groups are no longer willing to pay very high taxes, they could at least be made to pay for the services of the state which they are in fact using. Social justice could, then, still be maintained by providing vouchers for low- and medium-income families – which would have the attractive side effect of introducing a strong element of consumer power into the governance of education and other service sectors. I am not suggesting that all this would be politically easy to achieve, but I do suggest that in this fashion the essential values of the Scandinavian welfare state could well be maintained even under the pressure of international economic competition.

The Continental situation is much more difficult because the domestic-service jobs that are needed to increase the overall level of employment do not yet exist either in the private or in the public sector – and they do not exist because the structures that could support them are still lacking.

In the abstract, Continental Europe might consider moving either in the American or in the Scandinavian direction. If both options were equally feasible, political preferences would widely diverge. Practically speaking, however, the Scandinavian option appears to be out of the question. The reasons are financial and political. Continental welfare states, even though less expensive than their Scandinavian counterparts, are already hard-pressed financially. Thus, a Scandinavian-type service expansion would either require substantial tax increases or further reductions of welfare transfers; at the same time, there is no large and well-organised political demand for additional public services, whereas the political opposition against either tax increases or further cutbacks in social transfers is already highly mobilised. Thus a Scandinavian solution is not even discussed on the Left, whereas the 'American way' is strongly advocated by neo-liberal demands to cut social assistance. It is equally strongly resisted by unions and political parties defending the 'Rhenish model'. As a consequence, change is blocked and mass unemployment continues to rise. To be effective and politically acceptable under Continental conditions, employment-increasing reforms would, at the same time, need to reduce the wage bill paid by the employer for low-productive private services and to assure that workers taking such jobs would nevertheless receive net incomes well above the subsistence level defined by present social assistance programmes. In principle, both conditions could be achieved by a negative income tax, which is presently discussed in Germany under the name of '*Bürgergeld*'.

Even if the reservation wages of workers at the low end of the labour market were to remain where they are presently assumed to lie, and even if all other rules remained unchanged, the proposal would reduce the total wage bill of the employer by more than one-third, from DM 2,400 to 1,500 (see Fig. 12.7). It would, thus, open up a wide range of economically viable employment opportunities at the lower end of the labour market.

That, however, is no reason for optimism. By its own logic, the negative income tax would require a far-reaching restructuring of the present systems of

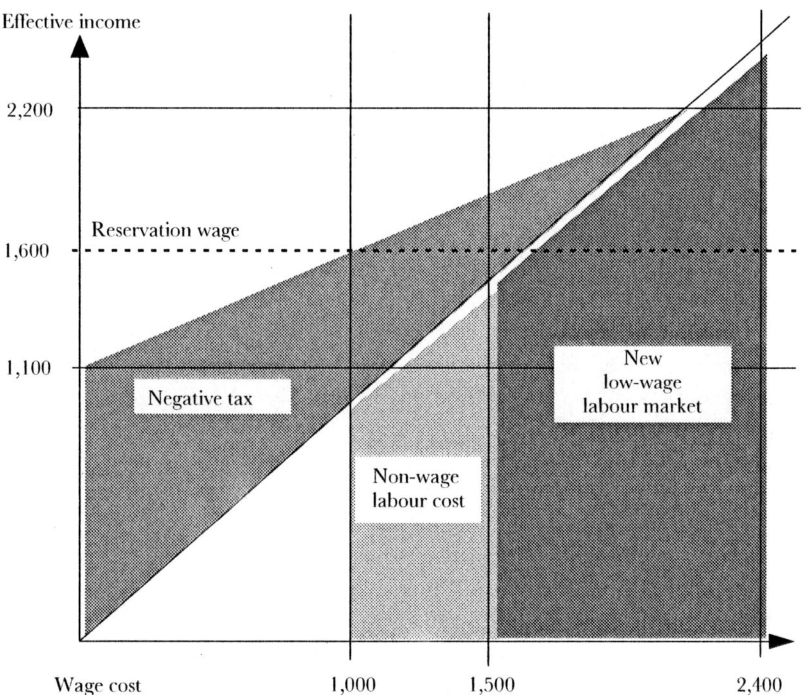

Figure 12.7 Negative income tax in Germany (in DM).

taxation, social assistance, social insurance and wage setting. Moreover, the available estimates of its overall financial consequences are still widely diverging. Thus, the chances are slim that German politics in its present shape could soon adopt this – theoretically optimal – solution to the Continental employment problem. Many of these difficulties could be avoided by a more modest and much simpler proposal that would not deal with the problems of income support for persons that are not working. It would simply provide income subsidies to workers in low-wage jobs below the present effective minimum, and leave all other present rules as they are.

In both versions, however, the employment effect of income subsidies would depend on the cooperation of unions that would have to agree to the creation of new wage scales below the present low-wage level. That is not an attractive function for unions that see their mission in raising, rather than lowering, minimum wages. Moreover, unions fear that wage reductions at the lower end could induce a general erosion of the present wage structure. Even though this objection may not be theoretically plausible, it has so far prevented political parties in Germany from responding to proposals of this nature.

Nevertheless, there is now slight hope that a functionally equivalent solution – which would not depend on the active cooperation of the unions – might find more political support. Its feasibility rests on precisely those features of the Continental welfare states that are so damaging to service employment, namely their dependence on social insurance contributions from employers and workers as a major source of welfare finance. In Germany, as I have said, these amount to about 42 per cent of the employer's wage bill, and they are shared equally between employers' and workers' contributions. Hence, if these contributions were (almost) completely waived at and below the present effective lower end of the pay scale of about 10 DM per hour, the wage bill of the employer would be reduced by 22 per cent, which would increase the profitability of service employment by the same percentage. At the same time, the take-home pay of the worker would also increase by the same percentage, which would increase the attractiveness of low-end jobs and, perhaps, would also make jobs below the present minimum wage more attractive.

Of course, these jobs would still need to be fully covered by the social insurance system. Hence, the contributions waived would have to be made up by insurance payments financed from general tax revenues. Like the negative income tax, the size of the subsidy would have to decrease at higher wage levels. Thus, one might eliminate contributions almost totally at and below the level of the present minimum wage, and the subsidy could be reduced to zero at twice that level. These are obviously matters for political judgement and compromise, which would also have to vary from one country to another. But in principle, I suggest, this avenue should be open to all countries that are financing very large shares of their social expenditure through non-wage labour costs.

In conclusion, I suggest, the Continental employment deficit does not seem to result from a loss of international competitiveness. It affects the sheltered sector only; it is caused not by the size of the welfare state, but by its characteristic structure and mode of financing; and these causes could be remedied by institutional reforms that would increase, rather than destroy, the level of social-policy support for disadvantaged groups in our societies.

In other words, the rigidities that matter seem to be the rigidities of political systems that are incapable of effective reforms, rather than rigidities of the labour market.

Notes

1 Again, these data are not directly available, but they can be obtained by deducting OECD figures on employment in the public sector from total employment in ISIC 6 plus ISIC 9. It should be noted, however, that the focus is on *provision*, rather than on finance. Thus services performed by private physicians or by charities would be included here even if they are financed by the state or by social insurance funds.

2 In 1993, Sweden spent 6.39 per cent of GDP on 'services for elderly and disabled people' and on 'family services'. In Denmark, the percentage was 4.36, and in Finland 3.01. The level is much lower in Luxembourg (1.23 per cent), in the Netherlands (1.16), in France (1.11) and in the UK (1.05), and it is lower still in West Germany (0.74) and Ireland (0.53). Expenditure on these services is minimal in Belgium (0.36 per cent), Italy (0.30), Spain (0.20) and Portugal (0.13) and practically non-existent in Greece (OECD 1996b).

References

Esping-Andersen, G. (1990). *The Three Worlds of Welfare Capitalism.* Cambridge: Polity Press.

OECD (Organisation of Economic Co-operation and Development) (1996a). *Labour Force Statistics.* Paris: OECD.

OECD (1996b). *Social Expenditure Statistics of OECD Members Countries. Preliminary Version.* Paris: OECD.

Part V

Conclusions

13 The politics of elective affinities

A commentary

Michael Shalev

This volume makes an invaluable contribution to comparative political economy by highlighting elective affinities between multiple institutional domains of the economy. The contributors have devoted most of their attention to the logic of 'institutional complementarities' between different domains, and their impact on economic coordination and performance. They are less interested in the political sources of these arrangements.

This choice of emphasis is not accidental. In the wake of the economic shocks of the 1970s, when political scientists and sociologists set about developing what Goldthorpe (1984) described as a 'new political economy', they were motivated to no small extent by a burning desire to demonstrate to both economists and sceptics in their own disciplines that 'politics matters'. With the zeal typical of this type of paradigmatic struggle, many of the protagonists lost sight of the fact that political economy is about the mutual interaction and embeddedness of politics and the economy. With the decline of Keynesian discourse and the rise of global capitalism, a new intellectual swing has occurred characterised by integration of economic models and methods, on the one hand, and on the other, greater attention to institutions – where economists and political scientists share potential common ground. I believe that it is time for a corrective, a reminder of the distinctive contribution that political sociologists and political scientists can and should make to the study of comparative political economy. Politics do matter, although there is an unsettled debate about what type of politics matter most. A second assumption guiding this commentary is that this debate has outlived its usefulness. Multiple political forces and mechanisms shape the formation and operation of the institutions which govern the economy.

My remarks are intended to clarify and somewhat extend the accounts that are offered or hinted at in the other chapters of this book concerning the politics of elective affinities. But before doing so, I offer some preliminary observations intended to frame and recapitulate the agenda pursued by the contributors and editors of the volume.

The analytical premises of this book may be succinctly summarised. Three different facets of economic activity – production, finance and labour – are closely interrelated. They co-develop historically, in an interactive process, and one of the results is their distinct clustering across countries in a limited number of underlying configurations. Among the key institutional formations that regulate the multiple spheres of economic activity are 'industrial relations' and 'the welfare state'. An integrated view of these regulatory arrangements is essential for identifying distinct varieties of capitalism, understanding how they came to be, and assessing their strengths, weaknesses and capacities for adaptation and change.

Integration is not easy for it requires breaking down disciplinary barriers, including those that separate labour studies, social policy and institutional economics. But the moment an encompassing view is contemplated, we are forced to notice the parallels (and the differences) between typologies of 'production regimes', 'welfare regimes' and 'industrial relations systems'. We also notice that essential structures of advanced capitalism take on a wide variety of concrete national forms.

Elective affinities between labour relations and welfare states are the central concern here. These linkages have been noticed by scholars in several different ways. Observers from Continental Europe including the editors of the present volume tend to perceive them as a natural part of their home landscape, which is characterised by labour participation in social policy administration, corporatist political bargaining over linkages between economic, welfare and labour policy, and traditions of state administration and academic inquiry alike that are premised on a comprehensive understanding of 'the social'. Given the absence of these conditions, it is the liberal, Anglo-Saxon world that has had to periodically remind itself that there exists a 'social division of welfare' (Titmuss 1958) which includes market-based arrangements as well as the welfare state proper – in other words, it is possible to achieve 'social protection by other means'. That phrase was coined by Castles (1989), who pointed in the Australian context to protectionism, immigration controls and statutory wage tribunals as mechanisms of labour de-commodification that historically substituted for social rights of citizenship.

While Castles employed this insight into the Australian case in order to expose a significant weakness of Gøsta Esping-Andersen's typology of welfare state regimes, it is sometimes forgotten that *The Three Worlds of Welfare Capitalism* was not only about classifying welfare states. One of the most important contributions of Esping-Andersen's approach to social policy, developed in association with Kolberg, Rein and others, has been his insistence that social insurance and social services have momentous consequences for labour markets (Esping-Andersen 1990; Kolberg and Esping-Andersen 1993). This is precisely the type of linkage between multiple institutional spheres which is the central concern of this volume. Specifically, Esping-Andersen was inspired to no small extent by the observation that the German welfare state precludes low-wage service work and keeps potential labour at home, while the Swedish welfare state has both supply- and demand-side effects on women that have drawn them into the social service labour force (Esping-Andersen 1996). Fritz Scharpf elegantly extends this perspective on the German case in his contribution to this collection, while a recently published paper by Huber and Stephens (2000) further develops the argument that arises from the Swedish experience.

The elective affinities

The mutual linkages between labour relations, welfare states and the economy have been especially transparent in research into what is variously known as employment-based social protection or 'the social policy of the firm' (Rein 1982; Rein and Wadensjö 1997; Shalev 1996). The case is especially clear for occupational pensions, which serve three different functions (von Nordheim Nielsen 1986): social protection (where they are a substitute or supplement to public income maintenance); personnel management (encouraging labour commitment and protecting firms' investments in training); and capital formation (pension accumulations often form the dominant pool of investment finance, operating variously through stock markets, financial intermediaries or state-controlled funds). The implications for labour relations are far-reaching. Highly developed systems of enterprise-based occupational pensions tend to emerge where unions are decentralised and weakly incorporated into the state; and they have the effect of further solidifying this institutional and political setting.

Many of the chapters of this book fruitfully extend this perspective. Bernhard Ebbinghaus uses it in Chapter 4 to offer a compelling explanation of cross-regime variation in the mix between early retirement and other job-shedding techniques. In the USA, as a result of Fordist production, an uncoordinated economy and 'impatient' finance capital, downturns in the business cycle have prompted major bouts of job shedding. Given its liberal welfare state regime and highly developed, decentralised and collectively bargained occupational pension system, the extension of this system to early retirement was a natural response. In Germany the opposite traits of diversified quality production, economic coordination and 'patient' capital created a need for job shedding as a tool of structural adjustment. Given the parameters of industrial relations and the welfare state and the role of 'social partnership' in both, the response was to expand the public pension system to accommodate early retirement. In other words, *institutional complementarities* 'structure the incentives under which actors make decisions'. (They are also 'formidable obstacles to reform'.)

The same notion of complementarity also informs the treatment of linkages between pension systems and varieties of capitalism in Part III. In similar fashion to Albert (1993), the authors of both chapters contrast the 'Rhine model' of capitalism (including Japan) to the liberal-market model epitomised by the US. The key contrasts proposed are the degree of short-termism of the financial system and the weight of shareholder interests in corporate governance. Interestingly, both Estevez-Abe and Jackson and Vitols go beyond the assertion of complementarity to posit a model with a distinct causal arrow that points to the role of pension arrangements in shaping the development of different modes of financing and governance of firms, different types of financial markets, and different potential roles for the state in supervising capital formation. As Estevez-Abe points out, this is a fruitful but neglected point of interface between the 'varieties of capitalism' and 'welfare state regime' literatures. Attention to the financial dimension not only makes it possible to demonstrate functional compatibilities between welfare institutions and multiple dimensions of the wider political economy, but it also elucidates why cases like Japan and the USA which are similar in some respects are different in others.

Empirically, Jackson and Vitols (Chapter 8) make a strong case for the reciprocal fit between pensions and the financial system, but because their analysis is comparative–static they cannot nail down the direction of causality.[1] Estevez-Abe's historical survey of the Japanese case (Chapter 9) is better suited to this purpose, although one need not necessarily accept her own interpretation of the findings. My own reading is that the institutional contours of old-age protection exerted little formative influence on the structuring of corporate finance in Japan. Rather, the design of the private savings and pension systems seems to have been explicitly intended to help concentrate scarce capital funds in the hands of a limited number of public and private financial institutions whose investment decisions were directly or indirectly shaped by the state.

Whether the key direction of influence is from finance to the welfare state or vice versa, in stressing the functional consequences of one institutional arena for another both of the chapters on pension finance downplay the role of purposive, self-interested collective action or 'politics'. Yet the Japanese story told by Estevez-Abe, as well as the better-known case of the Swedish ATP funds to which she briefly alludes, indicates that politicians and state managers engaged in struggle or collaboration with labour, capital, or sectoral alignments of labour and capital in forging what they saw as a desirable economic role for the state. Coalitions formed between the state and economic actors had the effect in both Sweden and Japan of privileging big business, but they generated quite different consequences for labour solidarity and the strength of the political left. Similarly, Jackson and Vitols point out that private pension systems offering yields via the capital market align the interests of the middle class with those of capital, whereas 'solidaristic' pension regimes financed by taxes or compulsory contributions promote shared interests with labour. As the literature on social democracy has long suggested, it is precisely because of these political consequences that the shaping of institutional arrangements for social protection and capital formation become objects of political struggle and have profound political consequences.[2]

Bringing in politics

The integrative view proposed in this volume offers two undeniable benefits: it fruitfully stretches our conceptual field of vision, and it suggests causal relationships that are highly policy-relevant. But it also poses a theoretical dilemma. While it is undoubtedly important to perceive the interconnectedness of spheres that by discursive or scholarly convention are seemingly unconnected, we must also beware of arguments that 'everything is related to everything' and that linkages between different institutional spheres come into being in the first instance as a result of complementarities and affinities. Even if the main purpose of jointly analysing welfare states and the economy is to shed light on the consequences for economic performance or social justice, we still need to address the perennial question of what it is that binds the diverse aspects of the political economy together.

Marxism and its latter-day echoes like the regulation approach (Jessop 1990) provides an answer which is not much different in principle from the economistic functionalism that sometimes tempts the 'varieties of capitalism' literature. On this sort of view the social policy of states and the rules generated by collective bargaining are there to serve economic interests. Whether these interests are defined benignly as 'the economy' or in more sinister fashion as 'the requirements of capital accumulation' is a secondary issue. Most political economists have insisted that there are 'political' or 'institutional' forces that at the very least mediate and may even moderate (buffer or alter) the impact of economic pressures and interests. This insistence has been especially loud and clear in the defensive response of most sociologists and political scientists to globalisation, much to the chagrin of those who believe in the imperative force of economic internationalism (Strange 1997).

A classic alternative to economistic approaches is the social-democratic or 'class politics' model (Shalev 1983). Inspired by the contrast between the relative organisational and political power of labour and capital in Sweden and the United States, this model suggested that both industrial relations and the welfare state are conditioned by the power of labour unions and parties. Strong unions played an important role in social democracies, both in propelling labour parties to power and subsequently engaging in corporatist political exchange with friendly governments. But the crucial factor was usually seen as long-term left party domination of the political executive (Korpi 1983; Stephens 1979; for a variation on the same theme, see Castles 1978).

Whereas the notion of 'elective affinities' permits a certain vagueness about the causal forces that link regimes of social protection and industrial relations, the class politics model is very explicit on this point. The persistent ascendancy of the left was seen as altering the strategic calculations of both capitalists and labour leaders, with the result that unions no longer had to struggle for survival against hostile employers and could instead cooperate with them in raising production while using their political leverage to achieve favourable outcomes in the sphere of distribution. Hence, industrial peace and generous welfare states were part and parcel of a labour-dominated political constellation (Korpi and Shalev 1980). Labour and social policy were not merely linked by serendipity, but on the other hand there was a clear rejection of the functionalist view of multiple institutional arenas as necessarily complementing one another for the greater systemic good.

First decline and then transformation of left parties, not to mention changes in union strength, collective bargaining and union-party relations in many countries, have caused the social-democratic model to fall out of favour in comparative political economy. But even disregarding what many see as a decline in the salience of class politics, from a historical perspective it is clear that dramatic shifts in the balance of political power between labour and capital are not the only contingency that has played midwife to major reconfigurations of social protection and industrial relations. Other circumstances have included popular uprisings (Piven and Cloward 1977) and total war (Klausen 1998). Analytically, the literature suggests at least four types of politics other than the social-democratic variety.

1 State-centred theory suggests that the initiatives of professional state managers and the institutional logic of varying state structures have decisive effects on economic and social policy (Heclo 1974; Weir and Skocpol 1985).
2 Retracing the origins of social-democratic class compromise, some scholars have argued that a labour-centred view neglects the interests of employers (Fulcher 1991) and fails to notice the role of collusive cross-class alliances in specific segments of the economy (Swenson 1991a).
3 The role of parties and government is only one possible dimension of labour participation in class politics. Extra-parliamentary modalities are diverse, they include both industrial and political contestation and institutionalised forms of cooperation between labour and capital (e.g. Works Councils and Social Security Commissions).[3]
4 Labour and social policy have been shaped by political forces from outside the class nexus. In some European countries conservative parties and state traditions, often linked to strong Catholic influence, cross-cut or even supersede left–right politics (Esping-Andersen and Korpi 1984; van Kersbergen 1995). Gender politics, evident for instance in the contrast between Southern Europe 'familialism' and Nordic 'de-familialisation' (Esping-Andersen 1999), also appear to operate independently of class politics (Korpi 2000).

The remainder of this chapter is devoted to drawing attention to echoes in this book of the original class politics perspective and these four additional perspectives. A convenient starting point is Chapter 11, in which Anne Wren returns to the core claim of the social-democratic model that left/right parties favour opposed policy preferences and that these preferences impact strongly on their performance when in power (Martin 1973; Tufte 1978). Following Iversen and Wren (1998) it is argued that the exhaustion of Fordism (de-industrialisation) and the constraints of globalised financial markets (which rule out traditional Keynesianism) pose stark choices for contemporary labour market policy. The price-tag on job creation is either rising inequality (the American model) or unbearable fiscal burdens (the Swedish model); the goals of employment, equality and fiscal probity can no longer be simultaneously achieved.

Wren's central claim is that while governments now face harsher policy choices than in the past, their choices continue to differ according to the political complexion of the decision makers. Partisanship matters in ways that are thoroughly reminiscent of the class politics literature of two decades ago, as well as contemporary practitioners like Garrett and Lange (1991) and Stephens *et al.* (1999). Drawing not only on earlier cross-national research but also her own case studies of Britain, France and the Netherlands, Wren finds that governments of the left have offered more generous unemployment benefits and more public sector jobs and have been more prone to intervene directly or indirectly in aid of the low-paid.[4]

Wren's study is an example of comparative analysis that is relatively wide in coverage. Variations in multiple outcomes across numerous countries are explained by appeal to a parsimonious theoretical model. Hemerijck and Manow's chapter follows a different approach, in-depth attention to only a few cases. In Chapter 10 they seek to explain contrasting outcomes in countries that share the same general production, welfare and labour relations systems. The Continental type of welfare state is dominated by insurance-based transfer payments financed out of wage and payroll taxes, which discourages an obvious source of job growth – female part-time work in the service sector. The authors ask why the Germans have failed and the Dutch succeeded in breaking the employment-depressing effects of 'tight coupling' between the spheres of production and protection. Their analysis shows that the broad brushstrokes that are so helpful in distinguishing between ideal-typical policy regimes are much less useful in accounting for intra-regime diversity which, as in the present instance, may be considerable. Both Dutch and German unions were driven to practise wage restraint by a combination of sectorally centralised wage bargaining and imposed monetary discipline. But only the Dutch unions were willing (beginning with the 1982 Wassenar Accord) to break their habit of trading wage restraint and consensual restructuring for costly schemes of social protection for their core membership.

As I read Hemerijck and Manow's account, the key difference between the two countries was the role of active and explicit state intervention. In the early eighties a determined Dutch government imposed deflationary policies that deepened ongoing trends towards rising unemployment and falling union membership. (Crouch adds in Chapter 5 that compared to Germany, the 'looming existential crisis' of Dutch union movement was also due to its lack of flagship organisations based in powerhouse manufacturing industries.) Combined with credible threats to institute state-imposed solutions, these debilitating conditions persuaded union leaders to deepen wage restraint in a negotiated pact with employers. Subsequent governments went on to impose radical welfare state reforms which overcame popular resistance by a combination of crisis construction, elite consensus and recourse to expert opinion. Under the cover of cost containment, crucial changes in the rules of the game were implemented which not only restored 'work incentives' but also privatised parts of the social security system and seem to have largely eliminated its autonomous management by the 'social partners'.

In other words, *strategic action by the state* led to fateful changes in institutional arrangements that to some extent redistributed power between the state, organised interests and the market. To put the point more generally, linked patterns of labour relations and welfare are not written in stone; they can sometimes be broken and then reconstructed in a new image. But why was the state able to stimulate change in the Netherlands but not in Germany? The capsule summary above suggests that the presence or absence of forceful leadership at the summit of the state may explain the difference. However, other political factors can also be inferred from Hemerijck and Manow's discussion, and from Wren's chapter as well.[5]

From Chapter 10 itself it appears that the structure of the political system may have played a role. Germany is a large, federally organised country whereas the Netherlands is a small unitary state. Ultimate responsibility for wage discipline in Germany lies with the conservative central bank, whereas in the Netherlands (as in Austria) the monetarist whip came to be exercised as the result of a conscious decision by the government to link the national currency to the Deutschmark. Is this not merely a superficial institutional difference masking functionally equivalent mechanisms? Apparently not, for it runs parallel to a difference in political structure which according to Hemerijck and Manow's account turned out to be extremely important to the politics of reform. Whereas in Germany governments of any colouration can apparently do little to challenge the autonomy of organised labour and capital in collective bargaining and social administration, the more 'hierarchical' Dutch state is disposed to playing a proactive role, especially when favourable economic and political conditions arise.

Complementing these structural predispositions are strong hints at the role played by political agency which go beyond 'determined leadership'. Wren's version of the Dutch story draws attention to the role of shifts in the partisan composition of government. She notes that the Wassenaar Accord was reached following a significant political shift: while the Christian-Democrats retained their cabinet majority, their partnership with the socialists was replaced by an enlarged role for the liberal VVD party (Volkspartij voor Vrijheid en Democratie). Another noteworthy policy shift, the restoration of wage linkage to social benefits, followed the return of the social-democrats as coalition partners late in 1989. Consistent once again with the 'parties matter' literature, Wren also points to the politics of non-decisions. Reminiscent of other countries (notably Austria) where the left has had to coexist with powerful confessional parties, the Dutch Labour Party was not in a position to deviate from areas of policy consensus shared by both right and centre parties – notably their opposition to expanding the public sector's role as employer.

Theoretically, the appropriate conclusion seems to be that the scope of strategic intervention by governments or state officials is a function of both state structure and the political conjuncture. But as shown by Isabela Mares' contribution in Chapter 3, this does not exhaust the range of possible explanations. The subject of her chapter is also a contrast between two relatively similar settings, but the puzzle is historical rather than contemporary: the introduction of divergent systems of national unemployment insurance in France and Germany. The two countries both broke with the poor relief tradition but by adopting quite different insurance systems, each one of which embodies a different type of linkage between industrial relations and social protection and a different form of labour/capital/state interaction. Early in the century the French opted for a Ghent system in which the government subsidises union-administered unemployment assistance. More than twenty years later the Germans chose to institute a universal contributory scheme financed and administered jointly by workers and employers.

Using game-theoretic analysis, Mares argues for an underlying theoretical unity between the two cases based on the expected interests of different actors. A different analytical interpretation is also possible. In my view, Mares' study shows that *the appropriate causal model of the politics of policy innovation depends on the setting.* In France 'reform-minded policy entrepreneurs' imposed the Ghent system on the representatives of both labour and capital. They were driven by fear of union demands for radical social protection, as well as by their own political interest in devolving responsibility for depriving ineligible workers onto the unions. In Germany, large employers came to desire an insurance-based system administered in partnership with labour since this was the only way to increase their control over eligibility criteria and the generosity of benefits. A 'strategic alliance among large firms and trade unions' was responsible for the final outcome.

In other words, whereas a state-centred explanation in the tradition of Heclo and Skocpol best fits the French case, the type of cross-class coalitions on which Swenson has focused are more suited to understanding the German case. The historical portrait sketched in Mares' chapter also seems to show that the political dynamic dominating each case depended on *historical contingencies* of a quite predictable type: cataclysmic events (for Germany, the First World War and the depression that followed it), temporal order (new policies were made in response to the assumptions and failings of older ones), and the specific political, economic and fiscal climate prevailing at a given time.[6] Temporal contingencies of the latter kind include, but are not limited to, the balance of class power in the political economy.

While Swenson's approach to welfare state politics plays a significant yet limited role in Mares' study, it clearly occupies centre-stage in Philip Manow's study of the origins of coordinated bargaining and expanded social protection in post-war Germany and Japan. Swenson (1991b, 1996) has argued that even on its home turf of Swedish social democracy, the traditional class politics model overstates labour's industrial solidarity and the importance of its political power for welfare state innovations. These innovations have rested more on the interests of employers in specific sectors in regulating labour markets than on the will of social-democratic governments, and the shared interests of labour and capital within sectors have meant that the trade unions' impact on social policy has typically been channelled through limited cross-class alliances rather than class-wide solidarity.

In Chapter 2 Manow offers a persuasive sectoral analysis of post-war innovations in German wage and social policy. Confronted with the generous Adenauer pension reform of 1957 at a time of tightening labour markets, the export-oriented metalworking industries learned to welcome welfare state expansion because of its synergy with wage restraint. As the literature on corporatist labour relations insisted nearly two decades ago (Goldthorpe 1984), such synergy rests on the mutually reinforcing motives of defending the competitiveness of export industries and compensating workers and unions for the exercise of moderation.

Germany's sheltered iron and steel industries were in a different position. They, too, accepted the welfare state as the price of coordinated wage bargaining, but in their case its function was to combat the spectre of unregulated internal competition raised by the elimination of the old cartel system after the war. In yielding to the temptation of centralised wage fixing, both sectors inevitably lost their earlier attachment to company-based welfare.

There is more to Manow's argument than its functionalist implication that calibrations of the systems of wage determination and social protection served the shared or paired interests of capital and organised labour in specific sectors of the economy. His historical analysis also reveals the importance in 1950s Germany and Japan of challenges to employer interests raised by waves of union militancy, on the one hand, and on the other, industrialists' fears of what they viewed as 'excessive competition'. In other words, cross-class coalitions were not born fully formed on the basis of self-evident mutual interests, but worked themselves out in conditions of experimentation and struggle. Moreover, capital did not purposively design systems of coordinated wage bargaining and social protection, but instead was obliged by externally imposed constraints to discover their beneficial implications. Manow's nuanced analysis in effect brings working class mobilisation and state activism back into policy analysis through the unguarded back door of Swenson's employer-centred model of class politics.

Still, labour commitment to sectoral interests shared with capital is a variety of class politics that clearly has little in common with 'politics' as narrowly understood by the 'politics matters' school. In this sense the Manow/Swenson view resembles other critiques of the social-democratic model which deny that party politics and control of the political executive are the front line of the 'democratic class struggle'. A long tradition of scholarship has focused on political action that takes place in the factories or on the streets, beyond the pale of formal politics. In keeping with the tenor of the current epoch, by and large these contentious politics are peripheral to the studies collected here. However, several of the contributors to this book usefully draw our attention to a different form of extra-parliamentary power, the integration of labour leaders into state or quasi-state fora responsible for the administration of social and labour policy. Anke Hassel in particular focuses attention on what she describes as the 'degree of institutional integration of organised labour into the political system'.

The puzzles which Hassel sets out to explain in Chapter 7 derive from her pairing of highly contrasting cases, Britain and Germany. The patterns of employment regulation and social protection that characterise the two countries and the nature of their employment–welfare linkages are distinctly different. This was true in the wake of the oil shocks, and it is equally true of their responses to the contemporary challenge of creating low-productivity service sector jobs. Hassel argues that these differences can best be explained by *governance*, not *government*. Hassel's analysis sidelines labour's political power in the parliamentary arena in favour of the role of labour associations in collective bargaining, workplace rule (co-determination), and delegated public authority in relation to social security and labour market policy.

In the 1970s the German pattern of labour inclusion coupled with sectorally centralised wage fixing and a high degree of income maintenance encouraged cooperative and efficient adjustment to price shocks. In the very different British setting, manufacturing became less competitive to the accompaniment of rising industrial warfare and inflation. But unintended consequences and feedback effects ultimately resulted in a reversal of fortunes. Egged on by militant protests against plant closures, the institutional features of the German system which generated such positive results for competitiveness also had the effect of 'externalising' the costs of restructuring onto the social security system. This, in turn, together with unification – a uniquely German shock – shrank the governance capacity of worker and employer organisations, making the old model of industrial adjustment progressively less viable.

According to Hassel the parallel evolution in Britain followed the same analytical logic despite different substantive outcomes in the two cases. Not only were the British unable to engage in smooth restructuring, but the veto power of militant albeit fragmented labour organisations blocked technical change and labour flexibility. However, this impasse eventually brought about a crisis in which the Thatcher government was able to exploit precisely the institutional features of trade unionism which had blocked labour restraint in the inflationary era – decentralisation, dependence on membership consent rather than legal guarantees, and lack of involvement in the running of either the social security system or the management of production. Militancy was curbed by unilaterally cutting unemployment benefits and job tenure protections at a time when unemployment was on the rise, and by using the law to weaken the organisational bases of union authority.

What Hassel does not point out – perhaps because it is so obvious – is that all of this happened only *after the political balance of power shifted radically* to labour's disadvantage. As is well known, this shift consisted not only in the Labour Party's ousting in the 1979 elections, but also the widespread promulgation after 1973, by the OECD and other authoritative sources, of the idea that full employment was no longer feasible (Korpi 1991); the failure of both the previous Tory government and the Labour government that followed it to reform industrial relations (Soskice 1984); and Mrs Thatcher's neo-liberal economic philosophy and undoubted leadership capacities.[7] Put in more general terms, shifts in parliamentary politics and the dialectics of policy failure in the face of a worldwide economic crisis caused the weak institutional linkages between labour and the state to be transformed from a source of labour militancy to a basis for labour repression. For a complete account, the politics (in multiple senses) of Thatcherism are thus indispensable partners to the institutional dialectics to which Hassel directed her attention.

Colin Crouch's contribution to this volume also supports a synthetic approach. In Chapter 5 he proposes a cross-national typology based on several different models of the constitutive foundations of labour-plus-welfare regimes. First, Crouch defines patterns of labour incorporation in relation to both the composition of the political executive and the extra-parliamentary institutional linkages to which Hassel drew attention. Thus, corporatist systems are subdivided into those in which labour inclusion rests on pronounced political and organisational power, as in Scandinavia, and those like Germany, where the organisation of employers is superior to that of the workers but both industrialists and the state nevertheless 'incorporate [labour organisations] within the general task of economic management'.

Crouch's second and more radical modification of the social-democratic model is his insistence that the politics of labour incorporation are only one of the sources of European socio-political diversity. *Pre-capitalist* institutions and cultural cleavages, which continued to impact on European societies long after the rise of class politics, also structure political – economic variation (cf. Rokkan 1968). In this respect there is a clear parallel between Crouch's (1993) comparative-historical analysis of industrial relations and Esping-Andersen's (1990, 1999) work on welfare states. Under the general heading of 'traditionalism', our attention is drawn to the varying political and institutional legacies of the church (especially the Catholic church), the pre-democratic *ancien regime*, the pre-industrial guild system and long-standing cultures of kinship.

Crouch's argument is that paying attention to traditionalism as well as class politics is not only important for building a cross-national typology that works. He also finds it essential to another scholarly project, the uncovering of traces of 'the obscure and forgotten by-ways of past repertoires' in contemporary developments. There is a further potential use for Crouch's emphasis on traditionalism which is hinted at in his chapter, namely its relevance to explaining gender inequalities. Attention to gender politics is however conspicuously absent from this volume, as it has been until recently from most mainstream research in comparative social policy and political economy (O'Connor 1996). This is true despite the fact that several chapters make clear that differences in the interests and power of men and women are reflected in both social protection (most obviously its bias in favour of male breadwinners) and labour markets (especially the impact of norms concerning married women's obligations on the growth of service sector employment).

There are many indications that gender roles vary across countries and over time, and that this variation structures policy choices. Cross-nationally, Fritz Scharpf shows convincingly in Chapter 12 that Germany's plight of undeveloped services in both the public and private sectors is closely linked to the traditional division of labour between the sexes that is privileged by the German welfare state. But Scharpf does not raise the question of why German social policy so heavily privileges male breadwinners[8] and conserves familism, and why it is that (in his own words) 'there is no large and well-organised political demand for additional public services'. Similarly, Ann Wren (Chapter 11) notes, from an overtime perspective, that by the time of the economic crises of the seventies, keeping women at home was no longer 'politically acceptable', which is why the Dutch relied so heavily on disability. But Wren does not take the further step of questioning what determines stability and change in the political acceptability of gender roles.

Unless comparativists are ready to fall back on exogenous cultural explanations, there is a need for greater analytical attention to the political institutions and processes through which gender is played out in social policy and industrial relations. The mechanisms by which men preserve their advantages and women challenge them are not well understood in macro-political research (Shalev 2000). Crouch points out that traditions which enjoy political articulation – such as Catholic-Conservatism on the one hand and French Republicanism on the other – have shaped quite different approaches to child benefits and social security. Esping-Andersen (1999) has made this point at length in his latest book. Given that gender is variously manifested in different welfare states and systems of labour relations, the recent appearance of a major integrated study of class and gender inequality by a founder of the social-democratic school may be an important harbinger of paradigmatic change (Korpi 2000). Also noteworthy is the recourse to both gender-political and class-political arguments in Huber and Stephens' (2000) recent work. But political economists will also need to learn from the extensive feminist literature on social policy.[9] Feminist studies have enlarged our understanding of gender roles not only as passive historical legacies, but also as consequential upon resistance and change. In particular, as Hobson (1999) has argued, the politics involved in gender role definition and redefinition are likely to be even less confined to the formal exercise of political power than class politics.

Conclusion

The principal achievement of this volume, of considerable importance in its own right, is in showing how and why scholars must link multiple institutional spheres of the economy (production, finance, labour) and their regulation by both 'public' and 'private' arrangements (labour/social policy and industrial relations). Some chapters have used this perspective fruitfully to understand puzzles from the distant or recent past, others have employed it to offer a fresh look at ongoing policy dilemmas. All have demonstrated the power of comparative analysis, typically the mode that peers intensively at a small number of partly or wholly dissimilar cases. The argument of this commentary has been that whether the concerns are historical or contemporary, whether the aim is to reinterpret familiar facts or to enlighten policy makers, a grasp of the underlying politics will add essential insights to analysis of institutional or economic logics. In focusing primarily on the need to get left politics right, this chapter is not arguing for a retreat to the safe havens of analytical or political debate. The practical stakes are also high. Indeed, in the most policy-oriented contribution to this volume Fritz Scharpf insists that the sources of mass unemployment – arguably the gravest socioeconomic ill of our times – do not lie in 'the usual suspects' but in political rigidities.

Despite its seeming anachronism, the social-democratic model, along with the limitations that were already evident twenty years ago, provides a way to think about the theoretical choices that face us. I have tried to show that there are choices to be made. But they need not be mutually exclusive and ought to be sensitive to both historical and social contingencies.

Notes

1 The Jackson–Vitols hypothesis invites a historical analysis that at the formative pole would uncover whether innovations in pension systems indeed preceded developments in the other arenas while seeking to demonstrate empirically, at the contemporary pole, that pension reforms have indeed been 'one of the driving forces changing patterns of corporate governance'.

2 These interrelationships were the subject of Esping-Andersen's dissertation (1980) and first major article (1978), and for more than two decades they have been a prominent theme in Walter Korpi's work (Korpi 1978; Korpi and Palme 1998).

3 There is a large but dispersed literature on extra-parliamentary labour politics, including waves of strikes and mass protest in countries like France and Italy (e.g. Franzosi 1995), labour's role in the governance of enterprises and social security in Germany (e.g. Janoski 1990), and the debate over whether the Japanese case is functionally equivalent to German-style corporatism (Shalev 1990).

4 Wren does qualify some of these generalisations. She notes that partisan effects on public employment weakened after the eighties, and that unlike other social-democratic contexts Sweden experienced dismantling of solidaristic collective bargaining.

5 As noted, Crouch's chapter also offers an interpretation of the 'Dutch miracle'. His brief but trenchant survey emphasises the economic vulnerability of its unions, compared to Germany's, alongside their continued institutional strength. Since my ambitions here are largely pedagogical, I prefer to leave the final substantive word on the Netherlands to the experts.

6 For example, Mares' account of the French case indicates that the ability of public officials to act autonomously *vis-à-vis* employers was enhanced by increases in left party strength that placed employers on the defensive.

7 This hardly exhausts the list of factors that contributed to the ability of the Thatcher government to implement its strategic programme. Other relevant assets were the unitary and centralised structure of the British state and the privileged role of the Treasury within it.

8 The issue of male-breadwinner bias has been extensively raised in the work of Jane Lewis (1992, 1997).

9 Diane Sainsbury (1994, 1996) provides useful overviews of this literature in a book and an edited collection. The journal *Social Politics* is the most prominent forum for publication of feminist studies of welfare state issues.

References

Albert, M. (1993). *Capitalism vs. Capitalism.* New York: Four Walls Eight Windows.

Castles, F. G. (1978). *The Social Democratic Image of Society.* London: Routledge.

Castles, F. G. (1989). 'Social protection by other means: Australia's strategy of coping with external vulnerability', in F. G. Castles (ed.), *The Comparative History of Public Policy.* Cambridge: Polity Press, 16–55.

Crouch, C. (1993). *Industrial Relations and European State Traditions.* Oxford: Clarendon Press.

Esping-Andersen, G. (1978). 'Social class, social democracy, and the state: Party policy and party decomposition in Denmark and Sweden', *Comparative Politics* 11(1), 42–58.

Esping-Andersen, G. (1980). *Social Class, Social Democracy and State Policy: Party Policy and Party Decomposition in Denmark and Sweden.* Copenhagen: New Social Science Monographs.

Esping-Andersen, G. (1990). *The Three Worlds of Welfare Capitalism.* Cambridge: Polity Press.

Esping-Andersen, G. (1996). 'Welfare states without work: The impasse of labour shedding and familialism in Continental European social policy', in G. Esping-Andersen (ed.), *Welfare States in Transition: National Adaptations in Global Economies.* London: Sage Publications, 66–87.

Esping-Andersen, G. (1999). *Social Foundations of Postindustrial Economies.* Oxford: Oxford University Press.

Esping-Andersen, G. and Korpi, W. (1984). 'Social policy as class politics in post-war capitalism: Scandinavia, Austria, and Germany', in J. H. Goldthorpe (ed.), *Order and Conflict in Contemporary Capitalism.* Oxford: Oxford University Press, 179–208.

Franzosi, R. (1995). *The Puzzle of Strikes: Class and State Strategies in Postwar Italy.* Cambridge: Cambridge University Press.

Fulcher, J. (1991). *Labour Movements, Employers, and the State: Conflict and Co-Operation in Britain and Sweden.* Oxford: Oxford University Press.

Garrett, G. and Lange, P. (1991). 'Political responses to interdependence: What's "left" for the left?', *International Organization* 45(4), 539–64.

Goldthorpe, J. H. (ed.) (1984). *Order and Conflict in Contemporary Capitalism.* Oxford: Oxford University Press.

Heclo, H. (1974). *Modern Social Politics in Britain and Sweden.* New Haven: Yale University Press.

Hobson, B. (1999). 'Women's collective agency, power resources, and citizenship rights', in M. P. Hanagan and C. Tilly (eds), *Extending Citizenship, Reconfiguring States.* Lanham, MD: Rowman & Littlefield Publishers, 149–78.

Huber, E. and Stephens, J. D. (2000). 'Partisan governance, women's employment, and the social democratic service state', *American Sociological Review* 65(3), 323–42.

Iversen, T. and Wren, A. (1998). 'Equality, employment, and budgetary restraint: The trilemma of the service economy', *World Politics* 50(4), 507–46.

Janoski, T. (1990). *The Political Economy of Unemployment: Active Labor Market Policy in West Germany and the United States.* Berkeley: University of California Press.

Jessop, B. (1990). 'Regulation theories in retrospect and prospect', *Economy and Society* 19(2), 153–216.

Klausen, J. (1998). *War and Welfare: Europe and the United States, 1945 to the Present.* New York: St. Martin's Press.

Kolberg, J. and Esping-Andersen, G. (1993). 'Welfare states and employment regimes', in J. Kolberg (ed.), *Between Work and Social Citizenship.* Armonk NY: M.E. Sharpe, 3–35.

Korpi, W. (1978). 'Social democracy in welfare capitalism – structural erosion, welfare backlash and incorporation?', *Acta Sociologica* 21(Suppl.), 97–111.

Korpi, W. (1983). *The Democratic Class Struggle.* London: Routledge and Kegan Paul.

Korpi, W. (1991). 'Political and economic explanations for unemployment: a cross-national and long-term analysis', *British Journal of Political Science* 21(3), 315–48.

Korpi, W. (2000). 'Faces of inequality: Gender, class, and patterns of inequalities in different types of welfare states', *Social Politics* 7(2), 127–91.

Korpi, W. and Palme, J. (1998). 'The paradox of redistribution and strategies of equality: Welfare state institutions, inequality, and poverty in the Western countries', *American Sociological Review* 63(5), 661–87.

Korpi, W. and Shalev, M. (1980). 'Strikes, power and politics in the Western nations, 1900–1976', *Political Power and Social Theory* 1, 301–34.

Lewis, J. (1992). 'Gender and the development of welfare regimes', *Journal of European Social Policy* 2(3), 159–73.

Lewis, J. (1997). 'Gender and welfare regimes: Further thoughts', *Social Politics* 4(2), 160–77.
Martin, A. (1973). *The Politics of Economic Policy in the United States: A Tentative View from a Comparative Perspective.* Beverly Hills, CA: Sage.
O'Connor, J. S. (1996). 'From women in the welfare state to gendering welfare state regimes', *Current Sociology/La Sociologie Contemporaine* 44(2), 1–124.
Piven, F. F. and Cloward, R. A. (1977). *Poor People's Movements: Why They Succeed, How They Fail.* New York: Pantheon.
Rein, M. (1982). 'The social policy of the firm', *Policy Sciences* 14(2), 117–35.
Rein, M. and Rainwater, L. (eds) (1986). *Public/Private Interplay in Social Protection: A Comparative Study*. Armonk, NY: M. E. Sharpe.
Rein, M. and Wadensjö, E. (eds) (1997). *Enterprise and the Welfare State.* Cheltenham: Edward Elgar.
Rokkan, S. (1968). 'The structuring of mass politics in the smaller European democracies: A developmental typology', *Contemporary Studies in Social History* 10(1), 173–210.
Sainsbury, D. (ed.) (1994). *Gendering Welfare States.* London: Sage.
Sainsbury, D. (1996). *Gender, Equality, and Welfare States.* Cambridge: Cambridge University Press.
Shalev, M. (1983). 'The social democratic model and beyond: Two 'generations' of comparative research on the welfare state', *Comparative Social Research* 6, 315–51.
Shalev, M. (1990). 'Class conflict, corporatism and comparison: The Japanese enigma', in S. N. Eisenstadt and E. Ben-Ari (eds), *Japanese Models of Conflict Resolution.* London: Kegan Paul International, 60–93.
Shalev, M. (ed.) (1996). *The Privatization of Social Policy? Occupational Welfare and the Welfare State in America, Scandinavia and Japan.* London: Macmillan.
Shalev, M. (2000). 'Class meets gender in comparative social policy', *Social Politics* 7(2), 220–28.
Soskice, D. (1984). 'Industrial relations and the British economy, 1979–1983', *Industrial Relations* 23(3), 306–22.
Stephens, J. D. (1979). *The Transition from Capitalism to Socialism.* London: Macmillan.
Stephens, J. D., Huber, E. and Ray, L. (1999). 'The welfare state in hard times', in H. Kitschelt, P. Lange, G. Marks and J. D. Stephens (eds), *Continuity and Change in Contemporary Capitalism.* Cambridge: Cambridge University Press, 164–93.
Strange, S. (1997). 'The future of global capitalism; or, will divergence persist forever?', in C. Crouch and W. Streeck (eds), *Political Economy of Modern Capitalism: Mapping Convergence and Diversity.* London: Sage, 182–91.
Swenson, P. (1991a). 'Bringing capital back in, or social democracy reconsidered – employer power, cross-class alliances, and centralization of industrial relations in Denmark and Sweden', *World Politics* 43(4), 513–44.
Swenson P. (1991b). 'Labour and the limits of the welfare state: the politics of intraclass conflict and cross-class alliances in Sweden and West Germany', *Comparative Politics* 23(4), 379–99.
Swenson P. (1996). 'Employers wanted the social democratic welfare state: the cross-class alliance for social and labour market policy in Sweden', Annual Meeting of the American Political Science Association, 29 August–1 September, San Francisco, CA.
Titmuss, R. M. (1958). 'The social division of welfare', in R. M. Titmuss (ed.), *Essays on 'the Welfare State'*. London: George Allen and Unwin, 34–55.
Tufte, E. R. (1978). *Political Control of the Economy*. Princeton: Princeton University Press.
van Kersbergen, K. (1995). *Social Capitalism: A Study of Christian Democracy and the Welfare State.* London: Routledge.

von Nordheim Nielsen, F. (1986). *Occupational Pensions in Northern Europe*, Working Paper No. 1. Copenhagen: Department of Sociology, University of Copenhagen.

Webb, S. and Webb, B. P. (1897). *Industrial Democracy*. London: Longmans Green and Co.

Weir, M. and Skocpol, T. (1985). 'State structures and the possibilities for "Keynesian" responses to the Great Depression in Sweden, Britain, and the United States', in P. B. Evans, D. Rueschemeyer and T. Skocpol (eds), *Bringing the State Back In*. Cambridge: Cambridge University Press, 107–63.

14 Varieties of welfare capitalism

An outlook on future directions of research

Bernhard Ebbinghaus and Philip Manow

In this epilogue, we will discuss some of the challenges that future research on the linkage between protection and production needs to take into account. We will delineate three directions of research that may prove worthwhile in further advancing the political economy perspective of the welfare state and that shaped the contributions to this volume.

First, we would like to address the role of politics in the 'making and maintenance' of the strategic complementarities between social protection and capitalist production. What is the role of parties in 'the politics of elective affinities' (see Shalev, Chapter 13)? To what degree have political forces shaped national welfare state regimes and social systems of production? What is the impact of shifts in the balance of power between capital and labour or between right and left parties on the protection–production nexus? The approach undertaken in this volume underlines the positive feedback of given protection and production systems on power relations in electoral politics and industrial relations. Instead of concentrating on the impact that party politics have on the political economy, this approach complements political accounts by looking also at the reverse causality: how welfare capitalism affects politics.

Second, gender issues have been rather neglected in political economist analysis of welfare states, as Michael Shalev (Chapter 13) sensibly observes. We concur with Esping-Andersen (1999) in his recent acknowledgement of the added value that lies in focusing on the family/household in studies on welfare state regimes and their political economy. In this respect, we are confronted with a terrain that is still largely uncharted. The study of political economy could indeed benefit a great deal from current research on gender, family and the life course. It is therefore important that the following questions be addressed: How much are existing production regimes embedded in social relations? To what extent do specific production regimes generate particular patterns of intra-family division of labour? Do varieties of capitalism correspond with differences in female and male labour participation and variations in skill profiles? How much will changes in family structure and life course patterns challenge the established models of covariance between labour markets and welfare systems?

Third, several contributions indicate different reform trajectories within similar regime constellations. Colin Crouch (Chapter 5) warns against crude theories of path dependency that assume institutional inertia and regularly underestimate the importance of institutional change. Several contributions emphasise the importance of social concertation as an avenue toward consensual adaptation, one that takes advantage of social learning, societal deliberation and corporatist implementation. Future research will need to focus more on the conditions of institutional change. The question for the future is whether these established 'institutional complementarities' that have been the focus of the comparative and historical analyses of this volume will remain advantageous or whether the national 'comparative institutional advantages' (Peter A. Hall) need to be and are capable of being adapted.

Politics of elective affinities

When it comes to the 'politics' of the elective affinities between production and protection, we fully concur with Michael Shalev's commentary (Chapter 13) about the importance of politics in the construction of coordinated political economies. The role of political parties in the formation and reproduction of national models of capitalism needs to be studied more systematically. In our view this can be undertaken very fruitfully within the analytic framework that has been presented and employed in this volume.

Some years ago, Paul Pierson argued that we have to account more seriously for the impact of a given welfare state on the processes of interest formation and political mobilisation in current social policy reform debates (Pierson 1994). He emphasised that existing welfare programmes often create their own political support and nurture their own clientele. We think that his insight applies to more than modern mature welfare states with their broad coverage, their enormous extractive and redistributive potential, and their formative impact on life-chances, life-courses and family patterns.

It is also true that welfare state programmes had an impact on the political forces shaping the early social policy programmes, which played an integral role in the nation-building efforts in Europe, the United States and Japan (Flora 1986). The emerging welfare state contributed to the national 'cleavage management' and 'cleavage stabilisation' and thus exerted a critical influence on the 'politics of welfare' as well. For instance, the outcome of religious conflicts in the denominationally mixed nation-states of continental Europe led in some conservative welfare states to a compromise between 'Church and State' in sharing welfare functions (e.g. the Netherlands), while in other nation-states, denominational groups remained opposed to state-provided social policy (e.g. Germany). These historically derived cleavages had important repercussions on the politics of welfare, and consequentially, on the equilibrium between protection and production that became established on the European continent. The political consequences are clearly visible even today. For example, the Continental welfare state regime provided strong support for Christian Democracy and political Catholicism (van Kersbergen 1995), and today these are the political forces that have contributed to the resilience of the Continental welfare state regime against all pressures to change.

The reverse impact of welfare states on politics seems also to be at work in the formation and growth of the labour movement itself. There is ample historical evidence that the institutional make-up of the early welfare state has critically influenced both the strength of the labour movement (Rothstein 1992) as well as its basic character. For example, the swift transition from craft unions to industrial unions in Germany between 1890 and 1910 was decisively eased by the advent of the Bismarckian welfare state, which assumed responsibility for the insurance of social risks, previously an important 'selective incentive' of craft unions (see Heidenheimer 1980; Steinmetz 1993; Manow 1997). By making social insurance mandatory and offering labour a role in the self-administration of the state schemes, the Bismarckian state tilted the balance of power in favour of the modern industrial unions in their fight against craft unions. In contrast, the British welfare state integrated the insurance funds of craft unions, though they retreated during the economic crises of the 1920s and 1930s. British unions remain divided along occupational lines and still mobilise the workforce to defend rigid job descriptions, pay differentials between different jobs and the closed shop. Japan offers another good illustration of how the welfare state affected the labour movement. Japan's bureaucratic state-elite fostered the expansion of company welfare schemes and thereby provided positive incentives for workers to organise along company lines, while political repression hindered unions from organising along class lines. Once Japanese unions had been established at the company level, worker mobilisation for universal and central welfare schemes was less powerful, since 'what was in the best organisational interests of the enterprise unions was not always compatible with national welfare programs' (Shinkawa and Pempel 1996: 161).

These examples of 'reverse causality', in which the welfare state affects the labour movement, contradict the 'power resource' theory (Korpi 1983; Shalev 1983), which assumes that political power of the left determines welfare politics. Similarly, Gøsta Esping-Andersen concedes today that 'the labour movement's role cannot have been decisive in the original institutional designs [of welfare states], but only in their subsequent evolution'. He now suggests that one has to 'rethink the historical role of labour movements in the development of social policy. (…) Welfare states may be influenced by labour, but labour-movement evolution is, itself, affected by the institutions of the welfare state' (Esping-Andersen 1994: 139). Hugh Heclo observed as early as 1974 that 'pensions helped advance the organization of the British labour movement as much as the reverse' (Heclo 1974: 165). Hence, the development of the labour movement and welfare state development should be studied – in the words of Esping-Andersen (1994: 139) – as a 'cybernetic phenomenon'. At the same time, we also need to study the feedback process over time, with particular regard to mutual interaction, between the welfare state and other political forces, such as Christian Democracy.

In this light, it becomes evident what distinguishes the approach taken in the contributions to this volume from the traditional 'left labour' thesis in comparative welfare state and political economy studies. The 'left politics' approach usually starts from the (often implicit) neo-Marxist assumption that, in all capitalist economies, the interests of capital and labour are thoroughly antagonistic. The apparent variance in capitalist market economies is then accounted for by differences in the power of Social Democracy and allied trade unions. Differences in the economic and political strength of the left explain the varying degree to which the struggle of 'politics against markets', advanced by left parties and labour unions, has been successful. These differences also explain the varying extent to which the market is politically and institutionally controlled, constrained, disciplined and refracted. The success of 'politics against markets' is measured primarily against one yardstick: how much is labour 'de-commodified'? We claim, however, that the basic dichotomy of interests between labour and capital is too general to explain the different institutional trajectories of modern welfare capitalism. The new political economy of the welfare state recognises that varieties of capitalism, which more or less deviate from the pure market model, have developed for various reasons, not only political ones. Starting from institutions that incorporate the interests of collective actors, this approach can account for a much wider variety of interest constellations. In particular, it points out the fact and explains why the interests of capital and labour have not always been antagonistic. As shown by Peter Baldwin (1990) and Peter Swenson (1991), one can find many historical instances in which inter-class alliances with other social groups or sectors of organised capital and labour were possible. Also, political and social legacies – such as state, church and guild traditions as Colin Crouch (Chapter 5) points out – mediate the labour–capital conflict. For instance, traditions of social partnership embedded in conservative welfare states and corporatist industrial relations had a crucial impact on interest formation and organisation. In fact, social concertation on wage and social policy may lead to very different results than unilateral welfare retrenchment and the decentralisation of industrial relations in Britain. Before discussing social concertation, we would like to discuss the importance of gender politics and other demographic changes that cannot be addressed by the perspective of labour–capital conflict.

Gender, family and life course perspective

Gender issues have thus far not gained much attention in political economists' accounts of welfare states. Studies analysing cross-national differences in female employment participation constitute an exception (Esping-Andersen 1990; Kolberg and Esping-Andersen 1991). Female employment rose earlier and more quickly in Nordic and Anglo-American societies than elsewhere, in particular through the expansion of public and private service employment. For their part, Continental European societies maintained the male-breadwinner model for a long time and did not facilitate female employment participation. Insofar as political economists took notice of these societal changes, they were seen as consequences of changes in the demand for labour, namely the new opportunities provided by the service economy – whether public or private – and by part-time work. Comparative studies of welfare regimes show the mediating impact of public policies (universal benefits, child care, educational policies) on labour supply.

These institutional differences reflect and are amplified by cultural and social traditions. All these historical and social factors seem to account for the significant variations in timing, scope and pattern of female employment participation across modern capitalist societies.

A gender perspective would certainly enhance our understanding of the production–protection nexus and could help answer several pertinent questions: Have women fewer labour market opportunities in economies that rely heavily on occupational skills than in those that rely on general education? More specifically, do women face labour market discrimination especially in those production regimes that rely on long-term stable employment relations with high skill requirements? Are more women gainfully employed in welfare states with public service provisions and professionalised welfare systems than in those with a stronger reliance on voluntary welfare agencies and largely unpaid family self-help? Are coordinated market economies based on the highly skilled, highly paid, highly protected male-breadwinner model (and on the unpaid work of housewives, mothers and female family caretakers) hampering female employment?

At least the last question has been dealt with in this volume. Fritz W. Scharpf (Chapter 12) attributes the low potential rate of women employed in the service sector to the labour-costs problem found throughout the Continent. Anne Wren (Chapter 11) explains the differences between the growth in Anglo-American private service sectors, the expansion in Scandinavian public sectors, and the failure in Continental Europe of both by highlighting the specific political choices at hand, given the problematic triad of employment growth, wage equality and public deficits. Seen from a gender perspective, the difference in the way Dutch and German labour markets have developed is striking: in the Netherlands, the transition to service and part-time work has helped improve the participation of women in the labour force and introduced a new division of labour within the home, while in Germany, the increased participation of women occurs despite the inflexibility in labour markets and welfare provisions. As Shalev points out, Colin Crouch's emphasis on 'traditionalism', for instance the legacy of the church or of kinship, is important in explaining gender inequality (see also Crouch 1999). Hugh Compston's findings on the importance of Christian Democracy for legislation regulating work hours (Chapter 6) point also to particular socio-political constellations that have maintained the male-breadwinner model by favouring of reducing the hours of a normal week. Since the opportunities to pursue gender politics vary considerably, we should also examine (Cook *et al.* 1992) how women are organised by trade unions and have gained a voice in union politics, and to what degree unions pursue their interests in collective bargaining and in social policy lobbying.

Bowing to the criticism levelled by gender theorists of his previous work, Gøsta Esping-Andersen has recently acknowledged that the 'family (…) tends to disappear within the perspective of comparative political economy. Political economy needs to become more sociological' (Esping-Andersen 1999: 35). He sees the 'family' as a major social institution that patterns individual behaviour. The household, in all of its different forms, is also a unit of service production and social self-help protection. The traditional, single breadwinner, family household is being replaced increasingly by 'post-modern' family forms. How important families are for the reproduction of social capital has been shown again and again by social mobility research (see Erikson and Goldthorpe 1993). Welfare state studies using household data show that household structures are a major determinant for income inequality and poverty (Daly 2000). As Esping-Andersen's acknowledgement of the significance of family indicates, the micro-level analysis of family/household structures is relatively new in the political economy analysis of welfare state regimes. This late acknowledgement of the family/household is rather surprising given the new emphasis on micro-level studies of the firm in comparative political economy. The flexible small-firm sectors of the Third Italy, the German artisan trades, or the Japanese small supplier firms are all cases illustrating the importance of kin-based, social relations and a family-based division of labour that provide very flexible forms of specialised quality production. In the Japanese case, these family businesses may also provide an additional source for social protection for those who have retired from the primary labour market (see Ebbinghaus, Chapter 4). Japanese women also tend to be employed in this secondary labour market. In fact, the unequal division of labour within families has contributed to the post-war Japanese model, which is constructed around the lifelong employment of male workers in the primary labour market (see Brinton 1994, 1998).

The Japanese example of older workers entering a 'second' employment after their mandatory retirement from a large enterprise also points out the importance of studying the link between work and welfare from a life course perspective. The household and extended family are, in fact, the major units for intergenerational 'risk sharing' (Esping-Andersen 1999: 41). Parents help their children, who will in turn later help their parents after retirement, both in terms of financial and instrumental transfers (Kohli 1999). Seen from a life course perspective, women tend today not only to interrupt work due to family responsibilities later than earlier generations but also to return more often to the labour market after child rearing. Also, more and more women tend to combine work and family. As for men, they tend not only to enter the labour market later due to longer periods and, ever more frequently, higher levels of education as well as to periods of unemployment in their youth, but they are also leaving work much earlier due to early retirement. Early exit from work has thus become a widespread strategy to cope with structural economic change and enhance productivity, and this labour shedding has particularly affected older male workers (see Chapters 4 and 10). At least in the view of many employers, older workers tend to be less productive while more expensive, and any investment into training them new skills is not profitable enough (Casey 1997). In general, occupational changes and skill renewal still occur less through lifelong learning than through intergenerational change: new cohorts tend to have more updated skills and enter new occupations. This perspective sheds new light on the problems created by de-industrialisation due to technological change and by downsizing due to international competition. Older industrial workers who have been laid off will not be helped much by a growing new service economy; the expansion of this sector will benefit younger, better educated men and women. This explains while both socioeconomic trends, early retirement and new service job growth may coincide.

Social partners and social concertation

Several contributions to this volume have dealt with the relationship between industrial relations and welfare regimes. Indeed, there seems to be a consensus that 'there is some evidence that types of welfare states and industrial relations systems go hand-in-hand' (Esping-Andersen 1999: 20). These 'elective affinities' may be partly attributable to power politics as Michael Shalev reminds us (Chapter 13). Certainly, especially in Scandinavia, the labour movement was politically strong: the Social Democratic party became dominant, their allied unions were well centralised and organised, and both pressed for universalist welfare state expansion. Yet there have been also voices that pointed out inter-class alliances between different social groups (Baldwin 1990) and between employers and unions (Swenson 1991). For Continental Europe, the influence of Christian Democracy has also been crucial for the development of a conservative welfare state and for social partnership in industrial relations, that is, for 'social' capitalism (van Kersbergen 1995).

With a new assessment of the interests of employers and workers in the welfare state, we also come to a new understanding of the role both employer associations and trade unions play in social policy making and implementation. In conservative, Bismarkian welfare states, the 'social partners' were given self-administrative functions and even consultative rights in social insurance schemes. As Colin Crouch (Chapter 5) notes, this 'sharing of public space' (Crouch 1986) goes back to pre-democratic authoritarian legacies, corporatist guild traditions and Christian social teaching. Despite the existence of friendly societies and occupational company pensions, neither British unions nor employers acquired such institutionalised roles in the rather voluntarist industrial relations tradition and the more centralised Beveridge type of welfare state. Moreover, the Thatcher government was successful in weakening British trade unions by unilateral interventions and with the help of employer attacks (see Hassel, Chapter 7). Given no institutionalised role in social policy and suffering from a weakened organisational capacity, British unions could not mobilise against increased privatisation of welfare state functions and services. Although regime configurations and their linkages are not permanently fixed, as Colin Crouch forcefully argues (Chapter 5), they remain nevertheless the context under which economic pressures and social changes might undermine or reinforce given institutional complementarities.

When studying the production–protection linkage, the scholars in this volume have indicated that industrial relations have remained very diverse, despite the pressures of globalisation and flexibilisation. That cross-national diversity seems to have revived more than declined is a standpoint that has been argued by previous studies on comparative political economy (Berger and Dore 1996; Crouch and Streeck 1997; Kitschelt *et al.* 1999). The current changes show some parallelism in the adaptation of industrial relations and welfare regimes: decentralisation of collective bargaining and welfare retrenchment in Anglo-Saxon countries, continuing coordinated sectoral bargaining and resilience of conservative welfare states in continental Europe, 'centralised decentralisation' of collective bargaining and recalibration of welfare states in Nordic countries (Iversen 2000 *et al.*). Although the globalisation debate was not a central concern in this volume, the political economy approach undertaken here provides some clues as to why we would not expect a convergence of industrial relations and welfare regimes. The existing institutional complementarities provide institutional advantages under international competition, and therefore employers too have an interest in adapting industrial relations and social protection in a way that does not undo the beneficial production regimes already in place (Manow 2001; Soskice 1991).

Our study of the varieties-of-production systems, welfare regimes and industrial relations documents the strong institutional complementarities that exit in Rhenish 'coordinated' market economies compared to Anglo-Saxon 'free' market economies. However, a more careful look at both types of production regimes reveals two puzzles that need to be dealt with in future research on the 'varieties of capitalism' (see Hall and Soskice 1999). First, there is more variation in welfare regimes and industrial relation systems than matches the two 'varieties of capitalism'. While the uncoordinated market economies go neatly together with liberal welfare states and decentralised collective bargaining systems, there are more pronounced differences among coordinated market economies. The group of coordinated market economies includes the corporatist welfare states of continental Europe, the Nordic universal welfare states, and Japan's peculiar mix of liberal-company-based and conservative-familist welfare regimes. Moreover, with respect to industrial relations, there are also significant differences between the more centralised bargaining systems of the Nordic countries, the coordinated sectoral bargaining in the Germanic countries, the more contentious labour relations of Latin countries, and the decentralised company unionism of Japan (Ebbinghaus 1999). Further research is needed to understand whether these variations reflect mere functional *equivalents* that serve similar institutional complementarities or whether they entail significant functional *alternatives* with distinct institutional advantages.

Second, countries with very similar regime types seem to diverge significantly with regard to their current reform trajectories, as exemplified by the Dutch sequential reforms and the German reform blockages described by Hemerijck and Manow (Chapter 10). One explanation for this is certainly the different opportunity structures for social concertation: the possibility of state intervention into collective bargaining in the Netherlands and the constitutional restrictions on state intervention into collective bargaining under the German *Tarifautonomy* (see also Ebbinghaus and Hassel 2000). Thus the *prima facie* tight coupling of the social security and industrial relations in the two countries might indeed conceal more subtle differences in the capacity to coordinate across both policy fields.

The emergence of social pacts in some countries that have only a weak or declining corporatist tradition has gained much attention in comparative political economy (Fajertag and Pochet 2000). Some observers interpret this as a renaissance of neo-corporatism (Schmitter and Grote 1997), a new 'competitive corporatism'

(Rhodes 1998), or a new form of 'supply-side corporatism' (Traxler 1997). Social concertation may be an alternative to unilateral deregulatory strategy *à l'anglaise,* achieving wage moderation, labour market flexibilisation and welfare reform by social consent (Regini 1999). Governments may find negotiated reforms advantageous in order to circumvent any blockage of reform by unions, to increase legitimacy (and diffuse blame) for unpopular measures, and to help coordinate adaptation across interdependent policy fields (Ebbinghaus and Hassel 2000). It seems surprising that some of the countries with relatively well-developed 'coordinated' market economies, including Germany, Sweden and Japan, have not been very successful in using social concertation for national reform processes. Social concertation might have proved crucial in smaller democracies (the Netherlands, Denmark) and in economies (Spain, Ireland) that were catching up with those of other European advanced capitalist economies, but among the larger economies, only Italy seems to be able to modernise its collective bargaining system and reform its pension system via negotiations with the trade unions. Moreover, given the relatively limited amount of experience thus far, we still lack studies that analyse how social concertation change the production regime, industrial relations and the welfare regime in the long run.

The past, present and future of institutional complementarities

Instead of speculating about future development, the contributions to this volume investigate past and present institutional complementarities between political economy and social protection. While most authors concentrate on contemporary linkages between production and protection, mapping out in their comparative analyses the differences found across regimes, several others conduct historical studies of the origins of today's institutional complementarities. Isabela Mares' historical case study of unemployment insurance (Chapter 3) applies rational choice theory to the reconstruction of German and French employer interests. In contrast to functionalist accounts that assume that institutions come about because they are functional, she shows that the beneficial outcome may have not initially been intended by any of the parties involved. By theoretically analysing and historically reconstructing the interaction between the strategic considerations of the government, employers and unions, she can account for the outcome, which indeed differed from the pre-strategic preference of employers but turned out to be their second best alternative. Similarly, Margarita Estevez-Abe (Chapter 9) studies the post-war Japanese economic development by unravelling a 'forgotten link' between occupational pensions and corporate finances.

Some studies apply a comparative design to highlight the variations across production systems. These studies focus on the institutional complementarities between specific social protection and industrial relations, production systems or financial governance. For instance, Anke Hassel's study of British and German cases (Chapter 7) shows how much the distinct forms of associational governance are embedded in uncoordinated and coordinated production regimes respectively, each with its own consequences for employment and welfare. Bernhard Ebbinghaus' comparison of early retirement (Chapter 4) shows that the labour shedding serves distinct functions, depending on the production system and the consensual industrial relations culture, that it is not merely a consequence of more or less generous welfare arrangements. Another example is Gregory Jackson and Sigurt Vitols' analysis of the consequences of different public–private pension arrangements on financial markets and corporate governance (Chapter 8): the German and Japanese pension systems – though with some variations in the importance of state versus private pensions – both foster patient capital, while the British and American pension systems reinforce the pressures of financial equity markets.

These comparative studies are less concerned with the origins of these institutions and their co-evolution than they are with the discovery of the consequences of these institutional complementarities. They highlight institutional advantages of these arrangements, for instance, by showing how generous social protection systems help maintain high-skill production systems, which in turn can contribute to increasing exports in a fiercely competitive international economy. But there may also be 'perverse' effects, as in the 'welfare-without-work' problem of Continental welfare states (see Hemerijck and Manow, Chapter 10). Anne Wren has argued (Chapter 11) that policies reflect political choices set by the triad of inequality, public deficit and employment growth. Fritz Scharpf's remedy for the Continental 'welfare-without-work' problem is to introduce institutional reforms that would alleviate the labour cost-employment problem in the service sector (Chapter 12). Social concertation may provide an avenue to create a political and social consensus on how to adapt policies, but this may well be a long-term, step-by-step process of social learning, as we have seen in the Dutch reform process (Hemerijck and Manow, Chapter 10).

Past research has often focused too much on institutional inertia, path dependence and historical contingency. In the future, it would be more worthwhile to study the conditions for institutional change. Even if we had all information on the origins and the positive feedback of institutional complementarities thus far it still remains an open question whether these will survive in the future. For instance, the increased importance of equity markets for stock companies in coordinated market economies may not only undermine the established financial and corporate governance structures, these gradual changes may also have long-term repercussions on industrial relations and the social security system. As governments foster capitalised pensions to complement the public pay-as-you-go system, as already enacted in Sweden and discussed in Germany, Anglo-style shareholder capitalism will gain in popularity even in 'stakeholder' capitalist societies. What the long-term effect of such changes are, whether they will completely undermine the institutional complementarities or whether adapted institutional mixtures of old and new forms will prevail can only be answered in the future. Given the comparative-historical studies of this volume that show how highly contingent change is, we would rather bet on renewed diversity than on radical convergence. Whether the different production–protection linkages will prove viable remains an open question.

References

Baldwin, P. (1990). *The Politics of Social Solidarity. Class Bases of the European Welfare States 1875–1975.* Cambridge: Cambridge University.

Berger, S. and Dore, R. (eds) (1996). *National Diversity and Global Capitalism.* Ithaca, NY: Cornell University.

Brinton, M. C. (1984). *Women and the Economic Miracle: Gender and Work in Postwar Japan.* Berkeley: University of California Press.

Brinton, M. C. (1998). 'Instiutional embeddedness in Japanese labor markets', in M. C. Brinton and V. Nee (eds), *The New Institutionalism in Sociology.* New York: Russell Sage Foundation, 181–207.

Casey, B. (1997). 'Incentives and disincentives to early and late retirement', ILO Conference, Geneva, September 1997.

Cook, A. H., Lorwin, V. R. and Daniels, A. K. (1992). *The Most Difficult Revolution. Women and Trade Unions.* Ithaca: Cornell University.

Crouch, C. (1986). 'Sharing public space: States and organized interests in Western Europe', in J. A. Hall (ed.), *States in History.* Oxford: B. Blackwell, 177–210.

Crouch, C. (1999). *Social Change in Western Europe.* Oxford: Oxford University Press.

Crouch, C. and Streeck, W. (eds) (1997). *Political Economy of Modern Capitalism. Mapping Convergence and Diversity.* London: Sage.

Daly, M. (2000). *The Gender Division of Welfare. The Impact of the British and German Welfare States.* Cambridge: Cambridge University Press.

Ebbinghaus, B. (1999). 'Does a European Social Model Exist and Can it Survive?', in G. Huemer, M. Mesch and F. Traxler (eds), *The Role of Employer Associations and Labour Unions in the EMU. Institutional Requirements for European Economic Policies.* Aldershot: Ashgate, 1–26.

Ebbinghaus, B. and Hassel, A. (2000). 'Striking deals: Concertation in the reform of Continental European welfare states', *Journal of European Public Policy* 7(1), 44–62.

Erikson, R. and Goldthorpe, J. H. (1993). *The Constant Flux. A Study of Class Mobility in Industrial Societies.* Oxford: Clarendon Press.

Esping-Andersen, G. (1990). *Three Worlds of Welfare Capitalism.* Princeton: Princeton University Press.

Esping-Andersen, G. (1994). 'The emerging realignment between labor movements and welfare states', in M. Regini (ed.), *The Future of Labour Movements.* London: Sage, 133–49.

Esping-Andersen, G. (1999). *Social Foundations of Postindustrial Economies.* Oxford: Oxford University Press.

Fajertag, G. and Pochet, P. (eds) (2000). *Social Pacts in Europe: New Dynamics.* Brussels: ETUI.

Flora, P. (1986). 'Introduction', in P. Flora (ed.), *Growth to Limits. The Western European Welfare States Since World War II. Sweden, Norway, Finland, Denmark.* Berlin: de Gruyter, xii–xxxvi.

Hall, P. A. and Soskice, D. (1999). *An Introduction to Varieties of Capitalism (ms.).* Harvard University, Cambridge, MA/Wissenschaftszentrum Berlin.

Heclo, H. (1974). *Modern Social Politics in Britain and Sweden: From Relief to Income Maintenance.* New Haven: Yale University Press.

Heidenheimer, A. J. (1980). 'Unions and welfare state development in Britain and Germany: An interpretation of metamorphoses in the period 1910–1950', Science Center Berlin, Discussion Paper IIVG 80-209, Berlin.

Iversen, T., Pontusson, J. and Soskice, D. (eds) (2000). *Unions, Employers, and Central Banks. Macroeconomic Co-ordination and Institutional Change in Social Market Economies.* New York: Cambridge University Press.

Kitschelt, H., Lange, P., Marks, G. and Stephens, J. (1999). 'Convergence and divergence in advanced capitalist democracies', in H. Kitschelt, P. Lange, G. Marks and J. Stephens (eds) *Continuity and Change in Contemporary Capitalism*. New York: Cambridge University Press, 427–60.

Kohli, M. (1999). 'Private and public transfer between generations. Linking the family and the state', *European Societies* 1(1), 81–104.

Kolberg, J. E. and Esping-Andersen, G. (1991). 'Welfare states and employment regimes', in J. E. Kolberg (ed.), *The Welfare State as Employer*. Armonk, NY: M.E. Sharpe, 3–35.

Korpi, W. (1983). *The Democratic Class Struggle*. London: Routledge & Kegan Paul.

Manow, P. (1997). *Social Insurance and the German Political Economy. MPIfG Disscussion Paper* 2.

Manow, P. (2001). 'Comparative institutional advantages of welfare state regimes and new coalitions in welfare state reforms', in P. Pierson (ed.), *The New Politics of the Welfare State*. New York: Oxford University Press, 146–64.

Pierson, P. (1994). *Dismantling the Welfare State? Reagan, Thatcher, and the Politics of Retrenchment*. New York: Cambridge University.

Regini, M. (1999). *Between De-regulation and Social Pacts: The Responses of European Economies to Globalization, Estudio/Working Paper 1999/133*. Madrid: Juan March Institute.

Rhodes, M. (1998). 'Globalization, labour markets and welfare states. A future of "Competitive corporatism"', in M. Rhodes and Y. Mény (eds), *The Future of European Welfare*. Houndsmills: Macmillan.

Rothstein, B. (1992). 'Labor-market institutions and working-class strength', in S. Steinmo, K. Thelen and F. Longstrength (eds), *Structuring Politics: Historical Institutionalism and Comparative Analysis*. Cambridge: Cambridge University Press, 33–46.

Schmitter, P.C. and Grote, J. (1997). 'Der korporatistische Sisyphus: Vergangenheit, Gegenwart und Zukunft', *Politische Vierteljahresschrift* 38(3), 530–54.

Shalev, M. (1983). 'The social democratic model and beyond: Two 'generations' of comparative research on the welfare state', in R. Tomasson (ed.), *The Welfare State, 1883–1983*, Greenwich, CT: JAI Press, 315–51.

Shinkawa, T. and Pempel, T. J. (1996). 'Occupational welfare and the Japanese experience', in M. Shalev (ed.), *The Privatization of Social Policy? Occupational Welfare and the Welfare State in America, Scandinavia and Japan*. Basingstoke: Macmillan, 280–326.

Soskice, D. (1991). 'The institutional infrastructure for international competitiveness: A comparative analysis of the UK and Germany', in A. B. Atkinson and R. Brunetta (eds), *Economics for the New Europe*. London: Macmillan.

Steinmetz, G. (1993). *Regulating the Social: The Welfare State and Local Politics in Imperial Germany*. Princeton: Princeton University Press.

Swenson, P. (1991). 'Bringing capital back in, or social democracy reconsidered', *World Politics* 43, 513–44.

Traxler, F. (1997). 'The logic of social pacts', in G. Fajertag and P. Pochet (eds), *Social Pacts in Europe*. Brussels: ETUI, 27–36.

van Kersbergen, K. (1995). *Social Capitalism. A Study of Christian Democracy and the Welfare State*. London: Routledge.

Index

Printed in the United Kingdom
by Lightning Source UK Ltd.
105869UKS00001B/52